MONETARY THEORY AND PRACTICE

ALSO BY C. A. E. GOODHART

Money, Information and Uncertainty

The New York Money Market and the Finance of Trade, 1900–1913

The Business of Banking, 1891–1914

MONETARY THEORY AND PRACTICE

The UK Experience

C. A. E. GOODHART

First published 1984 by
THE MACMILLAN PRESS LTD
London and Basingstoke
Companies and representatives
throughout the world

ISBN 0 333 36059 1 (hard cover)
ISBN 0 333 36060 5 (paper cover)

Typeset in Great Britain by Photo-Graphics, Honiton, Devon

Printed in Great Britain at The Pitman Press, Bath

Contents

Introduction

During the course of the last fifteen years (1968–83) I have had the privilege of acting as a specialist adviser in monetary economics at the Bank of England. All the papers now republished in this collection were written during this period. Although some of them could, in principle, have been written by a monetary economist without close contact with the monetary authorities, the contents of all of them have been informed and influenced by my work in the Bank; and several of the papers arose directly and immediately from that work. As I shall explain at some greater length later, however, the papers represent my own views, and are my own responsibility, and should not be treated as a reflection of the views, or position, of the Bank as a whole. Nevertheless I am extremely grateful to the Bank for having allowed me to prepare them initially, and to republish them now.

In order to provide a background to these collected papers, it may be useful to describe in some greater detail the scope of my work in the Bank. Section 1 of this Introduction therefore sets out a specification of my job there. Job specifications can be, perhaps, somewhat dull; some readers will find my role as specialist adviser on monetary economics (with regular access to the Governors and senior officials in the Bank) self-explanatory. They may prefer to skip directly to Section 2. Having presented this background in Section 1, in Section 2 I then try to put the collected papers into a temporal and conjunctural framework. I describe briefly the various developments – the interrelated play of theory, events and policy that lay behind the individual papers and how the various papers relate to one another.

1. The Bank's Monetary Specialist

The particular purpose here is to show how my role in the Bank occasioned the preparation of these papers, but there is also a more general intention to describe the various functions that I have undertaken as monetary specialist in the Bank. I carried out much the same functions throughout this period, but the importance attached to the job (and my seniority through the passage of time) increased through the years. So at the end of this period, I was one of the Chief Advisers at the Bank, one of the more senior officials.

There are, perhaps, four main components of my job, as follows:

1. Monitoring, assessing and forecasting the development of the monetary aggregates, i.e. monetary analysis.
2. Policy discussion and advice.
3. Monetary research.
4. Maintaining two-way communication with monetary analysts (both academic and other) outside the monetary authorities.

Monetary analysis

The core of my job in the Bank has been to interpret and to analyse monetary developments as they occur. By 'monetary developments' I mean primarily the quantitative movements in the monetary aggregates and their credit counterparts. Other officials have the responsibility for interpreting conditions in the various financial markets, e.g. the gilt market and the money market. This analytical function is inevitably and properly closely connected with a role as monetary forecaster, since an analysis of factors causing current monetary movements has obvious implications for prognosticating future trends.

Currently such assessment and forecasting take place over two separate horizons, in different formats and with somewhat different data bases. The short-run exercise of assessment and forecasting takes place on the basis of monthly data and developments, and occurs every month, shortly following the availability of the monthly money and banking data. In this case these monetary developments form the focus for the exercise, and other information, e.g. of incomes, expenditures and sectoral financial developments, is at best partial and usually not available to provide more than limited illumination. The main exception to this lies in the accounts of the central government itself – generally available at least as quickly as the monetary data. With the focus being on short-run developments, the forecast horizon extends for only a few months.

The longer-run exercise involves the monetary dimension of the more comprehensive longer-term quarterly national income forecast. In this case complete national accounts data are fully articulated. Monetary developments represent only one facet – though certainly an important one – of a forecast whose canvas covers developments in the economy more widely. The forecasting rounds obviously need to use the latest, and most accurate, information possible, but their timing is dependent more on the parliamentary calendar, notably the date of the Budget, than on the receipt of particular new data. As noted above, the data base is quarterly, and the horizon extends several years. Indeed, the forecasting models involved could churn out 'predicted' numbers to an indefinite horizon in a mechanical way, but most attention is normally and sensibly concentrated on the next year or two.

As noted above, the data bases for the main monetary and banking series for the monthly and quarterly forecasting exercises are, unfortunately, not strictly comparable. The main monthly banking data are observed on the third Wednesday of each month (except December) – in order to reduce erratic fluctuations, e.g. arising from day-of-the-week effects – whereas the end-quarterly data are affected by peculiar end-month, end-quarter and varying day-of-the-week effects. The latter, quarterly, series run at a constantly higher level (raised by end-month and end-quarter effects) than the monthly series. They are also not only perforce more occasional, but the lag in collection is greater, and they appear subject to considerably more erratic fluctuation. At times the pattern of growth rates over two or three quarters (but most rarely, if ever, for much longer) for a given monetary series appears to differ between the quarterly and monthly data. Because of its statistical advantages, mainly in frequency, the monthly data have formed the basis on which monetary targets have been set, and against which progress through the year has been monitored. This has, however, led at times to some technical complications in transforming the national income forecasts for the monetary series into a compatible monetary target based on monthly series.

Assessment and analysis of monetary developments is, of course, done both in the Bank and the Treasury, but we join forces to prepare the monetary forecasts, both monthly and quarterly. This has several advantages, not least that the Treasury has a comparative advantage in its knowledge of the public-sector accounts, while the Bank has a comparative advantage in its knowledge of financial markets and banking developments.

This work, of assessment, analysis and forecasting, forms the central function of a specialist monetary economist in the Bank, culminating each month in a series of regular meetings relating to the regular monthly round (whose purpose is to inform senior officials both in the Bank and the Treasury of current and prospective monetary developments), interspersed with the more occasional quarterly forecasts, in which, however, the specialist monetary economist is but one cog in a large group of forecasters, economists and advisers.

Policy advice

In terms of the time involved, policy advice normally represents a relatively small proportion of the work of a specialist adviser in monetary economics. It also generally follows directly and immediately from the functions of analysis, assessment and forecasting discussed earlier. If some development in the monetary field appears to be going 'wrong', e.g. the aggregates are diverging from their target value, senior officials in the Bank, and the monetary authorities more widely (defined as the Bank, the Treasury and Ministers responsible for economic policy), will want an assessment of why this is happening, what may be the wider implications for the economy, and how such a divergence might be mitigated or rectified. Again some policy option may be mooted elsewhere, e.g. in operations in financial markets, which could have an impact on monetary developments, and the adviser must give a view on what that impact might be.

The above might be described as tactical policy decisions, relating to possible adjustments within a given framework of targets and objectives on the one hand, and of institutions on the other. In addition, there are the more strategic policy decisions aimed at trying to achieve the best possible framework. Within this field lie such questions as the choice of targets/objectives for the monetary authorities, both the nature of the target itself, (e.g. £M_3, or several monetary targets, or a different form of target altogether, etc.), and when that is settled the selection of the precise form for the chosen target, e.g. a range or single point, the actual numbers, etc. Again, there are changes that the authorities may consider making in the institutional framework of the banking and financial systems, which may on occasions arise mainly out of macroeconomic concerns, e.g. a possible move to monetary base control, but are frequently posited for other reasons, e.g. prudential or microeconomic. Work on such strategic policy issues is the most important part of the job. When such an issue, e.g. a possible switch to monetary base control, is under consideration, such work has priority and may fill a large part of the time. Indeed, the specialist monetary adviser may, on some occasions, take a lead in advocating, or opposing, such changes, but in each case will be closely involved.

Although a specialist in monetary economics is chosen for supposed ability in this field, his views on the monetary implications of various possible future developments necessarily remain largely subjective, and open to doubt. Moreover, there are many considerations to be borne in mind on any issue, and the specifically monetary implications of any particular step bear a varying weight in coming to a decision. So the advice of a specialist monetary economist forms only a part in the process of reaching a common view within the Bank on matters with a domestic monetary relevance. Moreover, as earlier noted, the Bank itself forms only a part of the wider monetary authorities where the main monetary policy decisions are taken as part of the government's overall economic policy.

Research

Similarly, the research work undertaken by a monetary specialist will follow mainly from the core function of analysis and assessment – though, given the wider duties of the specialist adviser, he/she will generally be responsible for initiating and directing such research, and will often not have the time to undertake the detailed work personally. If, for example, some monetary development has been difficult to understand it could be useful to undertake a research exercise to explore it more thoroughly. A recent case is the paper based on the work of John Trundle, assisted by Paul Temperton, in the *Bank of England Quarterly Bulletin*, December 1982, exploring the reasons for the surprisingly slow growth of currency in the hands of the public. Even when the monetary series appear to be behaving just as expected, there is usually a need for a regular reconsideration and refurbishment of the explanatory and forecasting equations; an example is provided by the various papers on the demand for narrow money, M_1; some of the earliest of these to be estimated in the Bank are shown in the first paper in this collection, but such equations have since been re-estimated and reconsidered several times since, e.g. by Coghlan, in the *Bank of England Quarterly Bulletin,* March 1978, and by Trundle, Bank of England, mimeo, 1982.

As described earlier, forecasts of monetary developments form only one part of the wider, *quarterly* forecasting models. Accordingly equations explaining such monetary developments need to be prepared to fit into the wider quarterly forecasting models. In several cases the econometric work described above, either undertaken on an *ad hoc* basis to illuminate current conundrums or to extend earlier work, can be slotted into these models, but quite often additional work will be needed to keep the monetary parts of the model in reasonable working order.

There are, however, many different economic models of the economy. In some cases the models incorporate a broadly similar view of how the economic system works. Thus the main quarterly forecasting models of the Treasury, the Bank and the National Institute have often tended to have many common features, though forecasts constructed from a common model can still differ widely depending on differing judgmental assumptions. But there are nowadays widely differing views of how the economic system works, ranging, for example, from the school of rational expectations monetarists, exemplified in the UK by Professor Minford at Liverpool University, to those who evince pessimism about the ability of the price and market mechanisms to restore equilibrium, as exemplified by Professor Godley at Cambridge. In each case they have been able to construct a model to incorporate the main elements which, they contend, drive the economic system.

Over time I developed some doubts, in my role as monetary economist, whether the main model in use in the Bank necessarily fully represented the transmission mechanism or functioning of monetary forces within the economy. The genesis of these doubts is outlined in the final paper of this collection, which describes my reasons for thinking that monetary developments in the UK may be better described by disequilibrium models than by models in which money holdings are constantly maintained at their equilibrium level. If so, the working off of such disequilibrium holdings will have a subsequent impact on the economy, not currently modelled in any explicit fashion by the main current forecasting models. In consequence, with the help of others who thought that there might be merit in such an approach, a (limited) amount of research support was allocated to this study, and papers exploring the nature of such a small monetary model were undertaken by Richard Coghlan, Brian Hilliard, Jon Hoffman and Barry Johnston. This work, however, still remains at an exploratory stage.

As reported in this final paper, the ideas involved in this latter, disequilibrium, approach were developed by others outside the Bank, and, as several of the earlier papers in this collection reveal, I remained sceptical of this approach for a long time after I was first introduced to it. But the more general point here is that a considerable proportion of the monetary research done within the Bank does not derive from the central assessment and analysis role: it also derives from the final, communications, function. There is a continuous development of ideas and econometric research in the monetary field outside the Bank. Some of these outside econometric studies obviously have direct and major implications for the work of a central bank; among the many examples are the Andersen – Jordan reduced-form equations (in the *Federal Reserve Bank of St Louis Review*, November 1968), and the Sims test (from his paper on 'Money, income and causality' in the *American Economic Review*, September 1972) for the direction of causality between money and incomes. Much of this work originates in the USA, and is based on American data. Thus a second major impetus for research work is the desire to replicate and, perhaps, to extend research work done by others on other data sets, with the object of seeing how far such work might have practical implications for the Bank. One example of such work was the replication of Sims's paper in the note by Goodhart, Gowland and Williams in the *American Economic Review*, June 1976. A current example is the technical paper by T.C. Mills (Bank of England, Technical Paper, forthcoming, 1983) reviewing the work by Barnett and Spindt of the Federal Reserve Board on Divisia monetary indices, and applying it to the UK.

It may have been noticed by now that, in the description of the work of a specialist monetary economist in analysis and forecasting, no mention was made of support staff, while in discussion of the research role many other names have been mentioned. This does not represent a true picture. Even though a specialist monetary economist must reach an assessment and provide policy advice individually, he/she will rely, as I have done, greatly on assistants and the more senior members of the Monetary Policy Group in reaching those views. Moreover, there are many related exercises involved in writing up and presenting our assessments of monetary developments: internally; for discussion with other bodies, both domestic and international, e.g. Select Committees of Parliament, the IMF, the OECD, and so on; and for public consumption, e.g. in the *Bulletin*. Such work requires, and has been provided with, excellent support staff.

Furthermore, the forecasting function has expanded to require a team, albeit a small team, of specialist financial forecasters. In the forecasting role, as in the research role, I increasingly came to have a mainly supervisory role. Given the range of functions, there was simply not enough time to do basic empirical research myself. Thus in several of the papers in this collection there are associated empirical studies, often in appendices, where the actual work was done by others under my supervision. My supervisory role for monetary research in the Bank has, however, gone much wider than those papers where I am the sole, or joint, author. There has been hardly a research, or empirical, paper on monetary economics prepared within the Bank, since I joined it, with which I have not been intimately involved in a general supervisory and assisting role. Many, perhaps most, of them I initiated.

Apart from the specialist role of the financial forecasters, the support staff in the Monetary Group are concerned primarily with two tasks, first preparing and writing up (for a variety of audiences) assessments of monetary developments, and second, background research into such developments. The Bank showed its appreciation of the importance of this work, both in itself and as training for future senior officials, by allocating to the Monetary Group for these years many of the most able young economists to enter the Bank. It would, perhaps, be invidious to select particular names, but their imprint on my own work has been pervasive. I am deeply grateful to all the assistants and members of the Monetary Group who have worked with me during these last fifteen years.

Communications

One aspect of the communication function of a monetary specialist in the Bank has already been mentioned. There is a continuous development of ideas, analysis and research about monetary issues going on outside the Bank, often in other countries. It is, in my view, part of the job of a monetary specialist to consider the implications of such external work. One feature of this has already been noted, the impetus that outside research may give to seek to replicate within the Bank the exercise in a UK context. But the function is much more general than that. For example, I recently reviewed, in the *Journal of Economic Literature*, December 1982, the latest book by Friedman and Schwartz on *Monetary Trends in the United States and the United Kingdom*, and considered it part of my job to know what they had to say about UK monetary developments. Moreover, the development of new ideas about monetary issues does not always come from academics. There are groups of analysts in other central banks, and more general commentators, whose work needs to be read, analysed and filtered for more senior officials. Thus in the City in London there are a number of non-academic monetary experts whose work repays careful watching.

Besides trying to act as a conduit to transmit new ideas in monetary economics to senior officials (in digestible form), there is a communication function in the other direction, outwards from the Bank to the community of those interested in monetary developments. This task is, perhaps, more difficult. Not only is there a need for reticence on matters of confidentiality and secrecy, but, perhaps more important, no one in a specialist position is well placed to give a wholly rounded account of all the various considerations that went into decisions. A monetary specialist will, of course, have the opportunity for some input into those public pronouncements dealing with domestic monetary issues that are made with the full consideration and weight of the Bank, such as speeches by the Governors and (unsigned) papers in the *Quarterly Bulletin.* In these cases, however, one's personal contribution is partial, often very small – though occasionally considerable – difficult, even afterwards, to determine, and anonymous.

The position does change somewhat when the subject-matter of an article is particularly specialised. In such cases, even when the paper is published by the Bank, either in the *Quarterly Bulletin* or in the *Discussion* and *Technical Papers*, there are only a limited number of officials in the Bank with the expertise to comment. It would hardly be reasonable to regard such work as representing the considered view of the Bank as a whole; such papers are therefore published under the individual name of the author. Although such papers published by the Bank will have been read, and commented upon, by others involved in the Bank in that particular field of expertise, they remain the author's personal responsibility.

Besides papers published by the Bank itself in one of its publications – as noted above – some of the research work undertaken in the Bank may be of a kind suitable for submission to an academic journal. In addition, there are frequent requests from outside to present papers, generally at conferences; some of these conferences are limited to central bankers, or central bank economists; others are more regular academic conferences. If asked myself, I would discuss the invitation and show at least the outline of my intended paper to some of my colleagues for their comments. Certainly I have tried to reflect honestly and accurately in these papers the position as I saw it from my own personal vantage-point in the Bank. Nevertheless they cannot be guaranteed to give a fair view of the position of the Bank as a whole, and clearly represent only my own position and remain my personal responsibility.

Of the papers in this volume, two were formerly published in the *Quarterly Bulletin*. These are 'The Importance of Money' published in 1970, with the assistance of A.D. Crockett (Chapter I), and 'Monetary Base Control', prepared jointly with M.D.K.W. Foot and A.C. Hotson, published in 1979 (Chapter VII). Six of the other papers have been given at conferences. Of these four have already been published, one is in the process of publication, and one is first published here, though it was publicly delivered at a conference in 1979. Thus the second paper in this collection (Chapter II), 'Bank of England Studies of the Demand for Money Function', was presented at a conference of European central bank economists at Perugia in Italy in 1974 and republished by the Banca d'Italia as part of *Econometric Research in*

European Central Banks in 1975. The paper included here in Chapter III, 'Problems of Monetary Management: The UK Experience', was presented at a monetary conference organised by the Reserve Bank of Australia in Sydney in 1975, and reproduced by them along with the other papers presented at the conference in mimeo form. It has since been reproduced in *Inflation, Depression and Economic Policy in the West*, ed. A.S. Courakis, published 1981. The paper shown here in Chapter IV on 'Bank Lending and Monetary Control' was given at a Money Study Group Conference in Oxford, September 1979, but has not been previously published. The paper reproduced here in Chapter V, 'Structural Changes in the Banking System and the Determination of the Stock of Money', was given at the inaugural Conference of the Centre for European Policy Studies in Brussels, December 1982, and is in the process of publication of the proceedings of the Conference. The sixth paper (Chapter VI) on 'Analysis of the Determination of the Money Stock' was given at the Conference of the Association of University Teachers of Economics in Aberystwyth, 1972, and published in the proceedings, entitled *Essays in Modern Economics*, in 1973. The eighth paper, (Chapter VIII), 'Money in an Open Economy', was given at a conference on model-building held at the London Business School in July 1978, the proceedings of which were published under the title of *Economic Modelling*, ed. Paul Ormerod, in 1979. The penultimate, ninth, paper (Chapter IX) was a contribution, entitled 'The Measurement of Monetary Policy', to a series of seminars, organised by the Institute for Fiscal Studies in London, comprising academics and officials in the UK, to discuss some general issues on the interrelationship of fiscal and monetary policy. The resulting seminar papers, including my own contribution noted above, were reprinted in the book entitled *Essays in Fiscal and Monetary Policy*, ed. M. Artis and M. Miller, published in 1981. The final paper on 'Disequilibrium Money – A Note' was written in 1982 and has not been previously published.

2. The Contents of the Collected Papers

In my work in the Bank I have acted as an applied monetary economist. Few of my papers have been purely theoretical, and none of them have used mathematics as a major tool. Virtually all of them have empirical content, and many of them are supported by quantitative, econometric exercises, often the work of an associate. Some of the papers, of which I have been joint author, have been primarily econometric, without much practical, policy content. I have excluded these from this collection; among the excluded works are three papers written jointly with David Gowland, the first, already mentioned, being a replication of the Sims test on the direction of causality between money and incomes for the UK (also with David Williams); the other two reported a series of studies on the factors determining the shape of the yield curve (published in the *Bulletin of Economic Research* in 1977 and 1978). I have also excluded all my articles, reviews and other works which were not directly connected with the practical issues of current British domestic monetary affairs.

Instead, I have reproduced here the articles that illustrate some of my main concerns as a specialist monetary economist at the Bank, that concentrate on the assessment and analysis of current British monetary developments, with further implications for the conduct of monetary policy. The articles are divided into three main groups. The first five papers include those mainly concerned with current issues of monetary management; analytically, they share a common interest in the question of the stability, or otherwise, of the demand for money; as the years proceeded, and the movements in the main monetary target of that period (£M_3, a broad monetary definition) came to appear largely inexplicable in terms of a demand-for-money function, the main focus of attention shifted towards an attempt to comprehend what forces had caused the movements in £M_3, notably disturbances in credit markets and various structural changes (these two factors often being interrelated, *not* separate).

The next two papers are concerned primarily with the supply of money, and in particular with various controversies concerned with focusing on the monetary base, either analytically as a key element in the determination of the supply of money, or practically in the sense of considering whether the authorities should adopt monetary base control as their main *modus operandi*. These papers take a contrary view, that focusing on the monetary base is misleading analytically and likely to have untoward consequences if put into practice.

The final three papers are miscellaneous. One paper deals with the linkages between the balance of payments and domestic monetary developments in an open economy. In this paper it is argued that the suggested direction of causality often follows from a prior *assumption* of exogeneity, i.e. that domestic credit expansion is exogenously determined. The next paper deals with various problems about how to measure the thrust of monetary policy. Finally, because it became increasingly hard to relate shifts in £M_3 since 1971 to fluctuations in a stable demand function, this forced one to consider the possibility that various shocks were driving the actual quantity of £M_3 away from the 'underlying' level that would be demanded in equilibrium. The last paper therefore discusses the genesis of 'disequilibrium money', the empirical evidence for it in the UK, and the implications of its existence for the transmission of monetary shocks more widely in the economy.

I turn now to discuss in slightly greater detail the context of each paper.

I. The importance of money

My arrival in the Bank in 1968 occurred at a time of concern with the apparent failure of the 1967 devaluation to revive the current account of the balance of payments. Sterling remained weak. The IMF diagnosed this weakness as largely due to domestic monetary laxity, and the government adopted ceiling limits for DCE early in 1969. Indeed my first major task, under the supervision of W.M. Allen, was to take a part in preparing the *Bulletin* paper on DCE, published in 1969. Such a monetary approach to the balance of payments, pioneered in the IMF by Polak and Argy, depended crucially on an assumed stability in the demand for money. At the same time, a number of economists were demonstrating that, not only in the USA but also in the UK, the demand for money – defined narrowly or broadly – appeared a stable function of a few variables: prices, incomes and interest rates; moreover, the coefficient on the latter appeared significant, stable, and neither too high nor too low to prevent focusing on the monetary aggregates as a proximate, intermediate objective of policy appearing to be a practical proposition.

These findings appeared to refute the main analytical thrust of the 1959 Radcliffe Report, which emphasised that money was but one asset in the liquidity spectrum, and argued that its velocity would be unstable and that its control was incidental to interest-rate policy. Furthermore, the changing conjuncture, in particular with the onset of high and variable inflation – and the difficulty of observing inflationary expectations – and the progressive collapse of the pegged exchange-rate Bretton Woods international monetary system, was undermining the previous approach towards focusing directly on an 'appropriate' interest rate. Finally, the authorities in general, but the Bank in particular, were keen to escape the increasingly stifling constraint of controls over bank lending. The demand-for-money functions appeared to promise that credit and money could be controlled by price (interest rates), so that ceilings could be abandoned. Although some older and more experienced officials doubted all the econometrics (quite rightly as it happened), they wished to embrace this latter message.

This is the context in which 'The Importance of Money' was written. There is, however, a curious lacuna (the explanation of which, if any, I cannot now recollect) in that virtually nothing was said in this paper about the importance of the external regime, i.e. whether fixed or floating exchange rates, for the choice of target. Otherwise the form of the main paper largely consisted of an analytical discussion of the current state of monetary theory, the views of Keynesians and monetarists respectively, and areas of agreement; this was supported by appendices reporting econometric work in the Bank and elsewhere on the demand-for-money function.

Although the paper was theoretical in form, it had clear, practical conclusions. The Radcliffe Report had been wrong to deny the stability of the demand for money, and to attach no importance to monetary aggregates. In inflationary conditions, 'the rate of growth of the money stock may be a better indicator of the direction of policy than the level of interest rates'.

There were several qualifications: thus

> no single statistic can possibly provide an adequate and comprehensive indicator of policy... Moreover, as the statistical relationships derived from the past depended on the particular kind of policy aim pursued by the authorities over the period considered, there would be no guarantee of their exact continuation in the future, should that policy be altered.

I did not appreciate how quickly that general warning would come home to roost. In particular, the possibility of a massive surge in bank lending, funded through the new technique of liability management, was not sufficiently foreseen in 1970–1. Whereas a surge in bank lending, as reintermediation took place, had been expected, the effects of a combination of unfettered lending *plus* liability management had not been.

II. Bank of England studies of the demand-for-money function
III. Problems of monetary management: the UK experience

These two papers may, in a sense, be taken together. They overlap in that the purpose of both is to try to explain and to comprehend what happened in the 1971–3 period of massive expansion of broad money, M_3. However, the scope of the two papers differs. The paper on 'Problems of Monetary Management' concentrates on the practical story of what happened, and why. Moreover, having been written a year or so later, it has the advantage of a slightly longer perspective. It remains, I believe, the best published record of the 1971–3 monetary events, albeit from a Bank point of view; and it contains the initial source of 'Goodhart's Law'.

In re-reading these papers, it was, however, the other paper on 'Studies of the Demand-for-Money Function' that appeared to give the most vivid impression of what it was actually like to work as a monetary specialist in the Bank. 'The Importance of Money' is a general theoretical paper, though with clear practical implications. 'Problems of Monetary Management' is essentially a descriptive paper. But 'Studies' is an account, from my own viewpoint, of how research and theoretical developments interacted with conjunctural considerations to influence the course of policy. This paper shows monetary economics at work.

The massive monetary expansion of those years came to an end at the close of 1973, an end brought about by several factors, among them the imposition of the 'corset' in December 1973, the financial crisis in the 'fringe' banking system, and the swift economic downturn in 1974. All of these induced bankers to become more cautious, and the demand for credit subsided. Indeed, monetary growth remained well below the growth of nominal incomes over the next few years. Although the collapse of sterling in 1976 led to measures to tighten monetary policy, e.g. increased interest rates, the reimposition of the 'corset', the public announcement of monetary targets and the adoption of DCE ceilings – under the aegis of the IMF – that episode did not appear at the time primarily, or perhaps even largely, a consequence of domestic monetary policies.

Indeed, it was the aftermath of that external crisis, in 1977, that laid the seeds for the next period of major difficulty for domestic monetary policy. In the attempt to hold the exchange rate down to the competitive levels that were attained in 1976–7, against market pressures convinced that it was undervalued, interest rates were lowered very sharply in 1977 to levels far below the current, or expected, rate of inflation. Although that policy was abandoned in October 1977, with the exchange rate and interest rates both allowed to rise, the basis for a sharp revival in bank lending and monetary growth had already been set.

IV. Bank lending and monetary control

The above view that bank lending in 1978–9 was stimulated by the fall in interest rates in 1977 is subjective, since research work in the Bank has not been able to establish with any confidence the determinants of bank lending. Indeed, we have not generally been able either to forecast in advance, or even to explain in retrospect, the fluctuations in bank lending to the private sector, the explosion in 1971–3, the period of quiescence 1974–7, the extended surge 1978–82.

What can be established, and this is done in this paper, is that fluctuations in bank lending to the private sector have formed the main counterpart to fluctuations in the broad money stock over the last decade, and that errors in forecasting such bank lending have also represented the main source of errors in forecasting monetary growth.

What is, perhaps, more disturbing is the econometric finding that the rampaging course of bank lending could not be quickly, or easily, controlled by variations in interest rates. Many critics of the Bank contended that we were then continuing to vary interest rates too little and too late, and that our operations in the gilts market could be reformed in such a way as to provide much greater stabilisation to monetary growth. This paper provides empirical evidence that we did vary interest rates as quickly and as vigorously in response to divergences of the money stock from its intended target as any of the other major countries examined. It also provides evidence that gilt sales were consistently more stabilising (in respect of monetary growth) either than the original forecast for such sales, or than a constant rate of sales – i.e. that such sales were capable of being used to offset some part of previously unforeseen monetary shocks. The problem lay not mainly with the willingness of the authorities to vary interest rates, nor with the conduct of debt sales, but with the fact that we could neither clearly foresee, nor quickly and reliably control, bank lending.

This led at frequent intervals to internal reconsideration within the Bank of whether a broad money aggregate was the best target. Fluctuations in bank lending had their main impact on broad money, much less on a narrower definition, M_1. The demand for M_1 by the mid-1970s seemed much more stable than for £M_3, and M_1 seemed more controllable with a much higher, and better defined, interest elasticity. Initially the adoption of M_3 as the main focus of attention depended – since in the earlier work the stability of demand functions for M_1 and M_3 seemed about the same – in part on its better statistical properties (i.e. less erratic, less affected by estimates of 'float', etc.), but more on the ability to relate M_3 directly to the credit counterparts, in particular to relate M_3 to DCE, and its components.

In the event, the course of M_3 during the period 1971–3 was different from, and more explosive than, the course of M_1. Particularly when the surge, 1971–3, and relapse, 1974–5, of £M_3 neatly preceded the surge and relapse of inflation two years thereafter (much more closely than M_1), general opinion became fixed in the view that the broad monetary aggregate was the key one. Furthermore, some econometric support could be claimed for the argument that movements in £M_3 had more effect on *subsequent* variations in nominal incomes than did movements in M_1.

In any case, experience with the breakdown of the demand-for-money function for £M_3 in 1971–3 did not provide a confident basis for placing great faith in the future stability of the M_1 function. In addition, although the latter equation appeared stable, it did not forecast closely enough for practical policy purposes, i.e. it had a large standard error, of the order of $\pm$ 4 or 5 per cent. Finally, towards the end of this period, structural changes were apparent on the horizon which could alter the characteristics of narrow money holdings.

V. *Structural changes in the banking system and the determination of the stock of money*

Over the last fifteen years the monetary system has been buffeted by a series of structural changes. Some of these have already been mentioned, Competition and Credit Control in 1971, the adoption of liability management, the imposition of the 'corset' on several occasions in the 1970s – the postmortem on which appeared in the *Bulletin* in March 1982. Some of these structural changes were particular to the UK, but the more important structural changes have been reflected more generally in many countries, i.e. the adoption of liability management, the adjustment of the financial system to more inflationary conditions, e.g. in the trend towards variable, instead of fixed, rate lending, and now, foreseeable in the future, technological developments which may change the form of the payments system and the characteristics of transactions balances/retail deposits. This paper, discussing structural changes, was given at a European conference attended by representatives from many countries. So it was my aim to focus on these more general structural developments, common to a number of countries, rather than to concentrate on specifically UK experience.

The first main section, on liability management, describes those structural changes, and the problems which they brought for monetary control that occurred at the end of the 1960s and the first half of the 1970s. The second section describes the adjustment of banks to high and variable inflation during the 1970s, the increasing adoption of variable rate lending, and the growing importance of the 'spread', i.e. the margin between borrowing and lending rates, as a major determinant of banks' profitability and of the growth of banks' books.

The final section tries to look forward to the changes that developing technology, in conjunction – in some cases – with adjustments in the regulatory framework, may make to the characteristics of the payments system and of retail deposits. It is argued that the forthcoming changes could be fundamental – and thereby cause associated major shifts in demand-for-money functions – but that the speed of introduction of these changes is unforeseeable. Such structural changes would, in turn, have implications for the way in which a central bank should seek to direct its operations and activities.

VI. Analysis of the determination of the stock of money
VII. Monetary base control

These two papers should also be taken together, since they deal with different aspects of the same issue, the determination of the supply of money, and, in particular, the role of the monetary base, both analytically and operationally, in the money supply process. There is, perhaps, no wider gap in monetary economics between practitioners in central banks and the majority of academics than on this subject. The practitioners feel that, in reality, there is no alternative for a central bank but to provide the banking system with the cash base that it needs. The effective choice of central banks is limited to the terms on which such cash is made available. On this view, the process of money stock adjustment is one aspect of portfolio adjustment in which the authorities are influencing certain prices/interest rates rather than physically rationing the base itself.

The standard textbook analysis, applied by academics to money stock control, treats the monetary base as a quantity which either is, or could be, controlled by the authorities, and is therefore deemed (mistakenly) to be exogenous. Then the base is related to the money stock by a (relatively) simple multiplier, which is a function of a couple of ratios. Even though these ratios vary in response to economic conditions, their behavioural response can be reasonably well modelled and, in practice, they have generally remained quite stable. Not only does this approach allow a nicely simple analysis of money stock determination, and its decomposition into a few simple categories (i.e. the growth of the base, the shift in the ratios), but also it suggests that control of monetary growth should be a much simpler, and more straightforward, exercise than central bankers contend. The monetary base represents (mostly) the liabilities of the central bank. Academics enjoy taunting central bankers as to why they seem to find so much difficulty in controlling their own liabilities. Moreover, with control of the money stock and the achievement of monetary targets becoming a more important objective of policy towards the end of the period, failures by central banks, not only here but also in the USA, to achieve such control led to the question of the adoption of monetary base control methods becoming a major strategic issue of policy.

It would be wrong, however, to claim that all academics analysed money supply determination in terms of the monetary base/money multiplier. Tobin wrote a brilliant, innovative paper on the correct way to analyse the determination of the money supply, 'Commercial Banks as Creators of "Money" ', published in *Banking and Monetary Studies*, ed. D. Carson (Irwin, 1963) which convinced me that the base/multiplier approach was analytically unhelpful long before I joined the Bank.

Indeed, the earlier paper of these two, given in 1972, was almost entirely analytical in content, trying to show why the base/multiplier analysis, though in one sense obviously correct as a description – since it derives from an identity – was misleading, since it tended on the one hand to draw attention away from the crucial behavioural forces and the process of portfolio adjustment, and on the other to lead analysts to presume (incorrectly) the exogeneity of the base and a consequential direction of causality.

That said, the monetary base approach does imply the valid point that, if the authorities had been much more vigorous in their open-market operations, they might have had more success in achieving monetary control; also, a related, and correct, implication is that the authorities have no means of knowing what level of interest rates would be consistent with a desired monetary growth rate (or any other objective) – and that an interest-rate policy tended to lead the authorities to vary interest rates too little and too late, so that monetary fluctuations became pro-cyclical. The question then becomes one of deciding how vigorously the authorities *should* act to eliminate a divergence in monetary growth from its trend. This depends on many considerations, e.g. the relative stability of the demand-for-money function, the lag structures within the system, the perceived costs of monetary variability and interest-rate variability over differing time horizons, etc.

At a later date, the growing importance attached to monetary control, and the difficulties and failures that central banks found in carrying out this remit, led to the question of the adoption of (some form of) monetary base control becoming a pressing policy issue. The second of these two papers therefore addresses much more directly the practical consequences of the adoption of monetary base control.

It was hardly to be expected, however, that this contribution would do much to resolve the issue. Indeed, in the UK, the subject became even more heated, especially after the major jump in £M_3 in July–August 1980, following the abolition of the 'corset'. It had by then already become the subject of a Green Paper, *Monetary Control*, Cmnd 7858, 1980. This examined various forms of monetary base control, and concluded that, while the adoption of one, or another, form of monetary base control would be possible, the results of such a switch would be difficult to predict, and would not necessarily be advantageous. Thereafter, in the final years of this period, with the rate of growth of prices and incomes slowing rapidly, although monetary growth generally remained at, or above, its upper target limit, outside interest in this structural change seemed to diminish.

Meanwhile, in the USA, dissatisfaction with a policy of seeking to control monetary growth through interest-rate adjustments led to the adoption of a version of monetary base control in October 1979. Flexibility was maintained by applying the control to *unborrowed* bank reserves, thereby allowing the banking system to adjust, without exaggerated pressures on the system, by borrowing more, or less, reserves from the Fed's discount window. Even so, this experiment led to significantly more variability in interest rates, while still allowing considerable short-term fluctuations in monetary growth. Proponents of monetary base control claimed that such variability was caused by still allowing too much flexibility to the total reserve base (via borrowing at a non-penal rate and limits to the range of the Federal Funds rate). Opponents claimed that such variability was an integral feature of the control system, and would only worsen if the system was tightened further. But the more serious problem that occurred in 1982 followed a series of structural innovations, leading to shifts in the demand-for-money function, that threw into question the ability to choose a satisfactory target objective, at least for M_1, the previous main objective.

VIII. Money in an open economy

The subject of this paper is the relationship between the balance of payments and domestic monetary developments, and the associated issue of how to model external monetary flows and exchange-rate adjustments under differing exchange-rate regimes: fixed, floating and dirty. The first section sets out the relevant accounting identities; the main point of interest is to show that, even if the authorities do *not* intervene at all in the exchange market, there will generally still be external flows influencing the domestic monetary stock.

The accounting framework sets out the identities relating domestic credit expansion to the balance of payments. Such an identity provides no indication of the direction of causality. Instead, a view about causality follows from the selection of one, or other, of the elements in the identity as (mainly) exogenous, thereby causing the other endogenous elements to adjust. Keynesians tended to view current accounts and interest rates as the (comparatively) exogenous elements in this relationship, so that capital flows and domestic monetary growth responded endogenously. International monetarists saw domestic credit expansion (DCE) as (comparatively) exogenous, so that reserve flows (with fixed exchange rates), or the exchange rate (when floating), responded endogenously.

A major problem in forecasting external developments has been that the exchange-rate regime has been neither a pure float nor firmly pegged since 1972. Instead, external policy has varied at times from almost pegging, as in early 1977, to almost pure floating, as in 1980; external policy has been 'spasmodic' and indistinct to the outside observer. In general, forecasting has proceeded on the basis of treating the exchange rate 'as if' it were either pegged or freely floating, but this builds a mis-specification into the forecasting process.

Whether or not this mis-specification is much to blame, it has been the case that forecasts of the exchange rate, both in official circles and outside, have *not* been noted for their accuracy. Moreover, a careful study undertaken in the Bank by Townend and Hacche, published in *Oxford Economic Papers*, July 1981, failed to find *any* significant, stable determinants for the UK exchange rate.

IX. The measurement of monetary policy

The main structure of this paper is lifted from chapter 12 of my earlier book, *Money, Information and Uncertainty*, published in 1975, which had been written in 1973 during a sabbatical from the Bank. Nevertheless, this structure seemed suitable for responding to the question on the measurement of monetary policy which Sir Alec Cairncross had asked me to address at the Institute for Fiscal Studies seminar in 1977–8 on the interrelationship of fiscal and monetary policy. Moreover, I was also able to extend and to illustrate the main theoretical structure with some additional practical examples from current UK experience.

X. Disequilibrium money – a note

At the start of this period, 1968–82, there had been growing optimism that a stable demand function for money, whether M_1 or M_3, had been uncovered. For the reasons earlier indicated, the broad money definition (M_3 and later £M_3) became the main focus of policy.

From 1971 onwards, however, the stock of broad money fluctuated in a fashion that could not be explained by the demand-for-money functions then to hand. In some part, the fluctuations were probably due to structural changes, notably the competitive freedom and the adoption of liability management after 1971, but attempts to model these factors directly did not serve to re-establish a stable function, or one with satisfactory predictive qualities.

The choice effectively seemed to lie between returning to the much earlier view that the demand for (broad) money was inherently unstable, or accepting that shocks, emanating, for example, from disturbances in credit markets, could drive the actual supply of money away from the level that it would have reached in full equilibrium. The former alternative, an unstable demand function, although no doubt acceptable to more extreme Keynesians, seemed not only too nihilistic, but also to run contrary to too much accessory empirical evidence, for example of the kind presented by Friedman and Schwartz, of the longer-run stable relationships between the growth rates of money, prices and nominal incomes.

Accordingly, I became, initially unwillingly, driven to accept the other alternative, that shocks could force the actual (broad) money supply away from its desired level. Some of the conceptual and empirical reasons for this view are set out in this final paper, at the same time noting some of the objections to, and difficulties of, this concept.

One of the advantages of this conceptual approach is that it is neither Keynesian nor monetarist, but borrows analytical insights from both camps. This approach might just provide a bridge, a *rapprochement*, between the two schools of thought, as well as bringing some understanding of the monetary fluctuations of recent years in the UK. Alas, even then, we would not be out of the woods. The massive fluctuations in bank lending to the private sector in the last fifteen years may well have formed the shocks forcing similar (but lesser) fluctuations in broad money growth. But what caused the initial fluctuations in bank lending? How can we learn to explain, to foresee and to control them? Our comparative inability to do any of those has lain at the very heart of the difficulties with monetary management and monetary control in the UK over the last fifteen years.

July 1983 C.A.E. GOODHART

I

The Importance of Money

1. Definition and Function

The distinguishing characteristic of that set of assets which may be described as money is that they perform the function of a medium of exchange. This definition does not, however, allow for a clear-cut distinction in practice between those assets which should be regarded as money, and those which cannot be so treated. Cash and cheques drawn on banks are the means of payment for transactions which are generally acceptable in most developed economies, and this fact has led many to conclude that cash and demand deposits in banks are the only real monetary assets. There are, however, certain demand deposits, for example compensating balances held with banks in the USA, which cannot be freely used for transactions purposes. On the other hand, possession of a balance on time deposit, or access to overdraft facilities, may allow a purchaser to draw a cheque on his bank account even when he has insufficient demand deposits to meet that cheque. A more fundamental point is that the set of assets which is acceptable as payment for transactions is not immutable over time; it has changed in the past and could do so again in the future. If people should find it economically advantageous to accept, and to proffer, other financial claims in payment for transactions, then the set of assets which is to be described as money will alter.

This difficulty in distinguishing exactly which set of assets most nearly accords with the definition of money, as set out above, has led some to emphasise other characteristics which monetary assets possess, for example 'liquidity' or 'money as a temporary abode of purchasing power'. Such alternative definitions have, in general, proved too indistinct for practical, and more particularly analytical, purposes. Others have argued, on *a priori* grounds, that one or another definition of money, though admittedly imperfect, is the best approximation to the underlying concept of money. Others again have argued that the matter can be determined empirically. If people should regard time deposits with deposit banks, but not time deposits with accepting houses, as close substitutes for demand deposits, then the former asset should be included in the definition of money and the latter asset excluded. To seek a definition in this way implies the expectation of finding a clear division whereby assets to be defined as money are close substitutes for each other, but markedly less close substitutes for all other – non-monetary – financial assets. Whether such a clear division is found in reality is considered later.

The function of money as a medium of exchange makes it a convenient asset to hold, because it enables the holder to avoid the time and effort which would otherwise have to be involved in synchronising market exchanges (i.e. by barter). Convenience, particularly where it involves time saving, is something of a luxury. For this reason one might expect the demand for money, to provide such services, to rise by more than in proportion to the growth of real *per capita* incomes.[1] On the other hand, there are certain economies (of large scale) in cash management that can, in principle, be obtained as transactions get bigger and more frequent. This factor would result in the demand for money increasing by less than in proportion to the growth of real incomes.

The convenience to be enjoyed by holding money balances is only obtained at a cost – the cost, in effect, of not using the funds thereby tied up for puchases of more goods or alternative assets. As a broad principle, holders of money will adjust their holdings of money balances until the extra convenience from holding such balances just offsets the additional costs of having to make do with fewer other goods or assets. In order to bring about this adjustment, the money holder can, in principle, vary his purchases of anything else – financial assets, real capital goods, consumer goods – or of everything equally, in order to bring his money holdings into the desired balance with other possible uses of his funds.

In general, if the additional attraction (utility) of any good or asset does not match its cost, the main weight of the adjustment process falls, at least initially, upon changes in expenditures on close substitutes. If tomato soup seems to be getting rather expensive, the normal response is to buy less tomato soup and more oxtail soup, not less tomato soup and more company securities.

The transmission mechanism, whereby monetary influences affect decisions to spend generally, will be determined by the way in which people adjust their equilibrium portfolio of assets in response to a disturbance initiated, for example, by the intervention of the authorities in financial markets. These reactions, and therefore the transmission mechanism, will depend on which assets people view as particularly close substitutes for money balances.

---

[1] Holding additional money balances, as compared with bonds or equities whose capital value is subject to variation, tends to reduce the risk of unforeseen variation in the capital value of a portfolio of assets taken as a whole. In so far as risk avoidance is also something of a luxury, proportionately more money might be held in portfolios for this reason as people became more affluent. On the other hand, the development of the financial system has led to the introduction of a number of alternative capital-certain assets, in addition to money, which can be encashed at short notice. Therefore, one would not expect the demand for money to have been strongly affected, at least in recent years, by the desire to avoid risk, because this motive can be equally well satisfied by holding alternative capital-certain assets yielding a higher return.

The distinction between that theoretical approach to monetary analysis which may, perhaps unfairly, be termed 'Keynesian', and that approach which, equally unfairly, may be described as 'neo-quantity' or 'monetarist', turns mainly on divergent *a priori* expectations about the degree of substitution between money and other financial assets, and between financial assets and real assets. These differences are purposely exposed, and perhaps exaggerated, in the following sections, which provide a short résumé of the two approaches. As the points of contention between the two schools of thought can be reduced to issues that are, at least in principle, subject to empirical verification, it is not surprising that the results of the many statistical tests recently undertaken, mainly, however, using US data, have brought many proponents of both views to modify their initial positions.

2. The Transmission Mechanism

Keynesian analysis

It is the conviction of Keynesian theorists that financial assets, particularly of a short-term liquid nature, are close substitutes for money, whereas goods and real assets are viewed as not being such close subsitutes. In support of this position, Keynesians emphasise (i) the difficulty of defining which set of assets actually comprises the stock of money (which implies that such assets are similar in many respects), (ii) the ease and simplicity with which a cash position can be adjusted at any given time by arranging the portfolio of financial assets to this end, and (iii) the similarity of the character of financial assets adjoining each other in the liquidity spectrum ranging from cash at one end to, say, equities at the other.

If the authorities should bring about an increase in the money stock[1] by open-market operations,[2] for example, the extra convenience which such augmented money balances would provide would, other things being equal, not match the opportunity cost represented by the return available on other assets. Under such circumstances the adjustment back to a position of portfolio equilibrium would, according to Keynesian theory, take place mainly, if not necessarily entirely, by way of purchases of money substitutes, i.e. alternative liquid financial assets, rather than directly through purchases

[1] As the authorities can, in theory, control the level of the money stock, it is customary in textbooks to treat the money stock as determined exogenously, that is to say, independently of the rest of the economic system, by the authorities. At a later stage (pp. 38–9) this method of treating the authorities' policy actions will be questioned.

[2] Open-market operations are undertaken in financial markets. Actions by the authorities to alter the money stock do not therefore affect everyone in the economy equally, but have their initial impact upon people and institutions active in such markets. It is quite possible that those active in such markets could have a higher interest-elasticity of demand for money than the average for the economy as a whole. The possible distributional effects of the particular nature of the authorities' monetary actions have received surprisingly little attention in the literature.

of goods and physical assets. This would raise the price and lower the yield on such financial assets, and would cause in turn further purchases of somewhat less liquid assets, further along the liquidity spectrum. The effect of a change in the money supply is seen to be like a ripple passing along the range of financial assets, diminishing in amplitude and in predictability as it proceeds farther away from the initial disturbance. This 'ripple' eventually reaches to the long end of the financial market, causing a change in yields, which will bring about a divergence between the cost of capital and the return on capital.

The effect of changes in the money supply upon expenditure decisions is regarded, by Keynesians, as taking place almost entirely by way of the changes in interest rates on financial assets caused by the monetary disturbance. This analysis, if true, has an immediate and obvious implication for monetary policy. It implies that monetary policy could be undertaken with greater certainty by acting directly to influence and to control interest rates than by seeking to control the money stock.[1]

In addition to the familiar cost-of-capital effect, the impact of changes in interest rates upon expenditures should be understood to include 'availability' effects and 'wealth' effects. Availability effects, in general, result from the presence of rigidities in certain interest rates and the consequent divergence of these rates from the more freely determined market rates (a good example of 'sticky' rates is provided by the Building Societies Association's recommended rates). In such cases a divergence of free market rates from the pegged rate may cause such large changes in the channels through which funds may flow that certain forms of credit may be rationed or entirely cut off. In those markets, such as housing, where credit subject to such effects is of great importance, the impact of availability effects can be considerable. The wealth effect occurs, in the main, because changes in interest rates alter the present value of existing physical assets. For example, if interest rates fall, the present value of physical assets will rise.[2] The ultimate owners of such real assets, very largely the holders of the company securities, will feel better off, and no one will feel worse off.

Notwithstanding the theoretical argument, it for long seemed doubtful whether changes in interest rates had much effect on expenditure decisions, which appeared in general to be unresponsive to changes in interest rates.

[1] It is, however, the level of real interest rates that influences expenditure decisions, while the authorities can directly observe only nominal interest rates. In order to estimate the real cost of borrowing, the nominal rate of interest has to be adjusted by taking into consideration expectations of the prospective rates of inflation, the possible impact of tax arrangements and expectations of future levels of nominal interest rates themselves.

[2] In some cases there may also be a wealth effect following a fall in interest rates even when the financial asset held is not backed by real capital assets, as (for example) in the case of deadweight National Debt. In this instance a rise in the present value of these debt instruments – British government securities, etc. – to their holders should in theory be matched by a rise for the generality of taxpayers in the present value of their tax liabilities. In practice this is not likely to happen.

This implied, for Keynesians, that monetary policy could have little effect in influencing the level of expenditures; and this appreciation of the situation has been influential in conditioning the conduct of monetary policy in recent decades. In part this finding, of the lack of response to interest-rate changes, may have been owing to the coincidence of movements of interest rates and of expectations about the future rate of price inflation, so that variations of real interest rates – even if usually in the same direction, perhaps, as nominal yields – have been much dampened. Indeed, in those cases when the main cause of variations in the public's demand for marketable financial assets was changes in expectations of future price inflation, a policy of 'leaning into the wind'[1] by the authorities in, for example, the gilt-edged market would cause divergent but unobservable movements in real and nominal interest rates. If people became fearful of a faster rate of inflation and so began to sell gilts, support for the market by the authorities, who can in practice only observe nominal interest rates, would tend to prevent these rates rising sufficiently to reflect the more pessimistic view being taken of prospective inflation.

In recent years, however, more detailed empirical investigation has suggested the existence of some noticeable interest-rate effects – though most of the work has used US data, and the most significant effects have been found on State and local government expenditure, public utilities, and housing,[2] all of which are probably less sensitive to interest-rate changes in the UK. There is, however, need for additional work in the UK to examine how changes in financial conditions affect expenditure decisions. Making use of the improved information that has become available during the last decade or so, further research in this field is being planned in the Bank of England. One recurrent problem is how to estimate the level of real interest rates, when only nominal rates can be observed.

The less that alternative financial liquid assets were felt to be close substitutes for money balances, the greater would the variation in interest rates on such assets need to be to restore equilibrium between the demand for and supply of money, after an initial disturbance; the larger, therefore, would be the effect on expenditures, *via* changes in interest rates, of open-market operations undertaken by the authorities – given the climate of expectations in the economy. The greater the degree of substitution between money and other financial assets, the less would be the expected effect from any given change in the money supply. In conditions where other financial assets were

[1] That is, absorbing stock when the gilt-edged market is weak, and selling stock when prices are rising.

[2] One of the most carefully researched studies of monetary effects in recent years came as part of the Federal Reserve – MIT econometric model of the USA. The results of this study, reported by F. de Leeuw and E.M. Gramlich in the *Federal Reserve Bulletin*, June 1969, show a sizeable and fairly rapid wealth effect (*via* changes in stock exchange prices) on consumption, and a sizeable and fairly rapid cost-of-capital effect on residential construction. There is also a significant, but considerably lagged, cost-of-capital effect on business fixed investment. No evidence that inventory investment is sensitive to such monetary effects was found.

very close substitutes for money balances, it would be possible, in principle, to envisage adopting a policy of enforcing very large changes in the money supply in order to affect the level of interest rates and thus expenditure decisions. But there would still be severe practical difficulties – for example, in maintaining an efficient and flexible system of financial intermediation – and such a policy would require considerable faith in the stability of the relationship between changes in the volume of money available and in the rate of interest.

If there were a high degree of substitution between money and other financial assets, which could be estimated with confidence, then a change in the money supply would have a small, but predictable, effect on interest rates on substitute financial assets. If financial assets were not good substitutes for money balances, on average, but the relationship seemed subject to considerable variation, then changes in the money supply would have a powerful but erratic effect.

There is therefore a close relationship between the view taken of the degree of substitution between money and alternative financial assets, and the stability of that relationship, and the importance and reliance that should be attached to control over the quantity of money. At one pole there is the view expressed in a passage in the Radcliffe Report: 'In a highly developed financial system...there are many highly liquid assets which are close substitutes for money', so 'If there is less money to go round...rates of interest will rise. But they will not, unaided, rise by much' (para. 392). It is only logical that the Committee should then go on to conclude that control over the money supply was not 'a critical factor' (para. 397). At the opposite pole there is the monetarist view, of which Professor Friedman is the best-known proponent.

'Monetarist' analysis

In the monetarist view money is not regarded as a close substitute for a small range of paper financial assets. Instead money is regarded as an asset with certain unique characteristics, which cause it to be a substitute, not for any one small class of assets, but more generally for all assets alike, real or financial.

> The crucial issue that corresponds to the distinction between the 'credit' [Keynesian] and 'monetary' [monetarist] effects of monetary policy is not whether changes in the stock of money operate through interest rates but rather the range of interest rates considered. On the 'credit' view, monetary policy impinges on a narrow and well-defined range of capital assets and a correspondingly narrow range of associated expenditures... On the 'monetary' view, monetary policy impinges on a much broader

> range of capital assets and correspondingly broader range of associated expenditures.[1]

In simple terms this means that if someone feels himself to be short of money balances, he is just as likely to adjust to his equilibrium position by forgoing some planned expenditure on goods or services, as by selling some financial asset. In this case the interest-elasticity of demand for money with respect to any one asset, or particular group of assets, is likely to be low, because money is no more, nor less, a substitute for that asset – real or financial – than for any other. More formally, all goods and other assets which are not immediately consumed may be thought of as yielding future services. The relationship between the value of these future services and the present cost of the asset can be regarded as a yield, or rate of return, which is termed the 'own-rate of interest' on the asset concerned. Keynesians and monetarists agree that asset-holders will strive to reach an equilibrium where the services yielded by a stock of money (convenience, liquidity, etc.) are at the margin equal to the own-rate of interest on other assets. Keynesians by and large believe that the relevant own-rate is that on some financial asset, monetarists that it is the generality of own-rates on all other assets. Keynesians therefore expect people to buy financial assets when they feel that they have larger money balances than they strictly require (given the pattern, present or prospective, of interest rates), whereas monetarists expect the adjustment to take place through 'direct' purchases of a wider range of assets, including physical assets such as consumer durables.

According to a monetarist's view the impact of monetary policy will be to cause a small, but pervasive, change on all planned expenditures, whether on goods or financial assets. The impact of changes in the quantity of money will be widely spread, rather than working through changes in particular interest rates. A rise in interest rates, say on national savings or on local authority temporary money, would not cause a significant reduction in the demand for money – because these assets are not seen as especially close substitutes for money balances. Such changes in interest rates would, rather, affect the relative demand for other marketable assets, including real assets. Expenditure on assets, real and financial, is viewed as responding quite sensitively to variations in relative own-rates of interest; indeed, monetarists generally regard most expenditure decisions as responding more sensitively to variations in interest rates than Keynesians are prone to believe. The generalised effect of monetary policy in influencing all own-rates of interest will, however, tend to be outweighed in each individual case by factors special to

---

[1] M. Friedman and D. Meiselman, 'The relative stability of monetary velocity and the investment multiplier in the United States, 1897–1958', Research Study in *Stabilization Policies,* prepared by E. Cary Brown for the Commission on Money and Credit, Prentice-Hall, 1964, p. 217. This section provides an excellent statement of the theoretical basis of the monetarist viewpoint.

that asset (changes in taste, supply/demand factors particular to that market, etc.), so that no single interest rate can be taken as representing adequately, or indicating, the overall effect of monetary policy. As monetary changes have a pervasive effect, and as their effect is on relative 'real' rates, it is a fruitless quest to look for *the* rate of interest – particularly the rate on any financial asset – to represent the effect of monetary policy.

The crucial distinction between the monetarists and the Keynesians resides in their widely differing view of the degree to which certain alternative financial assets may be close substitutes for money balances; and in particular whether there is a significantly greater degree of substitution between money balances and such financial assets than between money balances and real assets. An example may help to illustrate the importance of this difference of view. Assume that the authorities undertake open-market sales of public-sector debt (effectively to the non-bank private sector). The extreme Keynesian would argue that interest rates would be forced upwards by the open-market sales (and by the resulting shortage of cash in relation to the volume of transactions to be financed). Interest rates would not rise by much, however, because an increase in rates on financial assets, such as finance house deposits, which were close substitutes for money, would make people prepared to organise their affairs with smaller money balances. The authorities would therefore have reduced the money supply without much effect on financial markets. Because expenditure decisions would be affected, not directly by the fall in the quantity of money, but only by the second-round effect of changes in conditions in financial markets, there would be little reason to expect much reduction in expenditures as a result – both because the interest-rate changes would be small and because of the apparent insensitivity of many forms of expenditure to such small changes in interest rates.

The extreme monetarist would agree that interest rates on financial assets would be forced upwards by the initial open-market sales. This increase in rates would not, however, tend to restore equilibrium by making people satisfied to maintain a lower ratio of money balances to total incomes, or to wealth. The initial sales of financial assets (as part of the open-market operation), resulting in higher interest rates, would only bring about a short-run partial equilibrium in financial markets. In other words, because of the fall in their price, people would wish to hold more of these financial assets, and this would be achieved through the open-market sales. But the counterpart to the desire to hold more of the cheaper financial assets would not, probably, be to hold smaller money balances, but rather to hold less of other goods. It therefore follows that open-market transactions enable people to make the desired changes in their portfolio of non-monetary financial assets, but leave them holding too little money. Full equilibrium, in the market for goods as well, would only be re-established when the desired ratio of money balances to incomes was restored. This would be achieved (and could only be achieved) by a reduction in real expenditures. Which expenditures would be cut back would depend on the response to the changing pattern, overall, of prices (yields) on the full range of assets, set in motion by the initial monetary disturbance. In sum, monetary policy, by causing a reduction in the quantity of money, would bring about a nearly proportionate fall in expenditures elsewhere in the economy. In the meantime interest rates, initially forced upwards by the authorities' activities in undertaking open-market sales, would have drifted back down, as the deflationary effect of the restrictive monetary policy spread over the economy, affecting both the demand for capital (borrowing) in the markets and the rate of price inflation.

Thus, if alternative financial assets were very close substitutes for money balances, monetary policy (in the restricted sense of operating on the quantity of money in order to alter rates of interest) would be feeble; if they were not, it could be powerful. The issue is almost as simple as that. Furthermore, as was pointed out earlier, if people appear to treat all liquid, capital-certain, assets as close substitutes for each other, it makes it extremely difficult to attach any useful meaning to that sub-set of such assets which may be arbitrarily defined as 'money'. Thus, the questions of the definition and of the importance of money both hang on the empirical issue of whether it is possible to identify a sub-set of liquid assets with a high degree of substitutability among themselves, but with a much lower degree of substitutability with other alternative liquid financial assets. Whatever the composition of this sub-set, it must include those assets commonly used for making payments, namely cash and demand deposits.

Testing the alternative views

The first stage in any exercise to establish the importance of control over the money stock must therefore be an attempt to discover whether money is a unique financial asset, without close substitutes, or is simply at one end of a continuous liquidity spectrum, with a number of very close substitutes. The empirical findings on this matter should help to settle the major difference between the theoretical position of the Keynesians on the one hand and the monetarists on the other. The usual method of estimating the extent of substitution between any two assets is to observe the change in the quantities of the two assets demanded as the relative price (rate of interest) on these assets varies, other things being equal. In the case of money balances, where there is no explicit interest paid on cash and current accounts, the normal procedure to test whether money is a close substitute for other financial assets is to examine how much the quantity of money demanded varies in response to changes in the price (rate of interest) of other financial assets which are thought to be potentially close substitutes. If the demand for money should be shown to vary considerably in response to small changes in the price (rate of interest) of alternative financial assets, this finding would be taken as strong evidence that money was a close substitute for such assets. This relationship is usually described, and measured, in terms of the interest-elasticity of the demand for money, which shows the percentage change in the money stock associated with a given percentage change in interest rates on alternative assets. A high interest-elasticity implies that a large percentage fall in money balances would normally accompany a small percentage rise in interest rates on alternative financial assets, and so suggests a high degree of substitution.

There have been in the last decade a large number of statistical investigations designed, *inter alia*, to provide evidence on the degree to which 'money' usually defined as currency and bank demand deposits – M_1 – or as currency plus bank demand and time deposits – M_2 – is a close substitute for other financial assets. A survey of this evidence is presented in Appendix 1 (pp. 44–55). Most of these empirical studies are concerned to discover the factors that influence and determine the demand for money. In these studies on the nature of the demand for money, the total of money balances is usually related to the level of money incomes and the rate of interest ruling on some alternative financial asset, for example on Treasury bills. Alternatively, the ratio of money balances to money incomes (the inverse of the income velocity of money) may be taken in place of the total of money balances, as the variable to be 'explained'. In most important respects, these two methods of approach are interchangeable. There are, however, a considerable number of optional variations in the precise manner in which these equations are specified, which form the subject of fierce debate for the *cognoscenti*.

In particular, there is dispute over the form of the income (or wealth) variable which should be related to the demand for money. This issue is, however, peripheral to the question of the extent of substitution between money balances and other financial assets. Evidence on this latter question is deduced from the statistical results of fitting these equations and examining the estimated coefficient measuring the apparent change in money balances associated with a change in interest rates, which is interpreted as the interest-elasticity of the demand for money.

Most of the statistical work of this kind has been done using data from the USA,[1] but the results of similar studies using UK data[2] give broadly confirmatory results, though there seems, perhaps, some tendency for the estimated stability of the relationships and the statistical significance of the coefficients to be slightly less. Considering, however, that these studies cover a number of differing periods and employ a range of alternative variables, the

---

[1] The source of the monetary data used in these studies is shown in each case in the selected survey of empirical results presented in Appendix 1.

[2] The results of work using UK data are also presented in Appendix 1, including some early results of studies in the Economic Section of the Bank of England.

main results of these exercises show a fair similarity and constancy in both the USA and the UK.

The conclusion seems to be, quite generally, that there is a significant negative relationship between movements in interest rates and money balances (i.e. that the higher the interest rate, the lower will be the quantity of money balances associated with any given level of money incomes), but that the interest-elasticity of demand appears to be quite low. The results, as shown in Table A of Appendix 1, generally lie within the range −0.1 to −1.0. This range is, however, rather wide. An interest-elasticity of −1 means that an upwards movement in interest rates of 10 per cent, for example from 4.0 per cent to 4.4 per cent (not from 4 per cent to 14 per cent), would be associated with a decline in money balances of 10 per cent. At 1970 levels, this amounts to £1,500 million, which implies a considerable response of money balances to changing interest rates. On the other hand, an interest-elasticity of −0.1 implies a much smaller response, of only £150 million. This range, however, exaggerates the diversity of the findings, because the intrinsic nature of the data causes the estimated interest-elasticities to vary depending on the particular form of the relationship tested. If M_2 (money supply defined to include time deposits) rather than M_1 is the dependent variable, the estimated interest-elasticity will be lower, because part of the effect of rising interest rates will be to cause a shift from current to time deposits. If short-term rates rather than long-term rates are used, the estimated elasticity will also be lower because the variations in short-term rates are greater. If the data are estimated quarterly rather than annually, there again appears to be a tendency for the estimated elasticity to fall, probably because full adjustment to the changed financial conditions will not be achieved in as short a period as one quarter. In fact statistical studies using annual data with M_1 as the dependent variable and a long-term rate of interest as an explanatory variable do tend to give an estimate for the interest-elasticity of demand for money nearer to the top end of the range of results, and those with M_2 and a short-term rate of interest will tend to give an estimate nearer the bottom end. Even so, there still remains quite a considerable range of difference in the results estimated on a similar basis, but with data for different periods or for different countries.

The findings, however, do seem sufficiently uniform to provide a conclusive contradiction to the more extreme forms of both the Keynesian and the monetarist theories. The strict monetarist theory incorporated the assumption of a zero interest-elasticity of demand for money, so that adjustment to a (full) equilibrium after a change in money balances would have to take place entirely and directly by way of a change in money incomes (rather than by way of a variation in interest rates). On the other hand the estimated values of the interest-elasticity are far too low to support the view that the result of even a substantial change in the money supply would be merely to cause a small and ineffectual variation in interest rates.

The area of agreement

The considerable efforts expended upon the statistical analysis of monetary data in recent years have produced empirical results that have limited the range of possible disagreement, and have thus brought about some movement towards consensus. It is no longer possible to aver, without flying in the face of much collected evidence, that the interest-elasticity of demand for money is, on the one hand, so large as to make monetary policy impotent, or, on the other hand, so small that it is sufficient to concentrate entirely on the direct relationship between movements in the money stock and in money incomes, while ignoring interrelationships in the financial system.

Any summary of the area of agreement must inevitably be subjective. Nevertheless the following propositions would, perhaps, be widely accepted:

1. The conduct of monetary policy by the authorities will normally take place by way of their actions in financial markets, or through their actions to influence financial intermediaries. To this extent it is really a truism, but nevertheless a useful truism, to state that the initial effects of monetary policy will normally occur in the form of changes in conditions in financial markets.
2. Monetary policy, defined narrowly to refer to operations to alter the money stock, will normally have quick and sizeable initial effects upon conditions in financial markets. It is not true that operations to alter the money stock would only cause a small change in interest rates without any further effect or that the velocity of money will vary without limit.
3. Open-market sales of debt by the authorities raise the return, at the margin, both on holdings of money balances and on holdings of financial assets. Any subsequent effect on expenditures, on the demand for real assets, results from the attempt to restore overall portfolio balance, so that rates of return on all possessions are equal at the margin. In this sense monetary policy is always transmitted by an interest-rate effect.
4. The initial effect of monetary policy upon nominal interest rates may tend to be reversed after a period. For example, any increased demand for physical assets, encouraged by the lower rates of return on financial assets (including money balances), will stimulate additional borrowing in financial markets, thus driving up interest rates again, and the extra money incomes generated by such expenditures will cause an additional demand for money balances. If the increased demand for physical goods leads to a faster expected rate of price inflation, the resulting rise in nominal returns from holding financial assets and money balances will be reduced in real terms, so that the subsequent increase in nominal interest rates will have to be all the greater to achieve equilibrium.
5. The strength of monetary policy depends mainly on the elasticity of response of economic decision-makers – entrepreneurs, consumers, etc. – to a divergence between the rates of return on financial assets, including

the return on money balances, and the rate of return on real assets. Some empirical studies of the elasticity of response of various kinds of expenditures – company fixed investment, stockbuilding, housebuilding, consumer spending on durable goods, etc. – have found evidence, particularly when working with US data, that demand does respond significantly to variations in nominal interest rates. But these estimated effects, although significant statistically, do not seem to be very large, and they appear to be subject to lengthy timelags in their operation.

6. Although these statistical findings, of the fairly slight effect of variations in nominal interest rates on expenditures, are widely accepted, the inference that monetary policy is relatively impotent is not generally accepted. It is argued, and is becoming widely agreed, that variations in nominal interest rates may be a poor indicator of changes in real rates. As was already suggested in proposition (4), an expansionary monetary policy is consistent with, and can lead directly to, rising nominal rates of interest, while real rates remain at low levels. If nominal rates of interest do provide a poor index of monetary conditions, many of the studies purporting to estimate the effect of changes in financial variables on expenditures become subject to serious error. This raises the problem of how to measure approximately variations in the real rates of interest facing borrowers and lenders, as these cannot be simply observed from available data.

A qualification

The evidence from the empirical studies shows that there is a statistically significant association between variations in the size of the money stock and in interest rates on alternative financial assets. This relationship is, however, neither particularly strong nor stable.[1] These results are often interpreted as evidence that money balances and such financial assets are not especially close substitutes, and that there may also be a significant degree of substitution between money balances and other assets, including real assets. This, taken together with the much closer statistical association between the money stock and economic activity, induces belief in the importance of controlling the money stock.

The observed loose association between changes in interest rates and in the money stock may, however, be due in part to another cause. It may well be that the relationship between interest rates and the demand for money is obscured by the volatile nature of expectations about the future movement of prices of marketable assets. Most of the statistical studies of the demand for money have related the total of money balances to the calculated yield to

[1] Although the ratio of the estimated value of the coefficient of the interest-elasticity of demand to the estimated standard error of that value (as measured by the *t*-statistic) is large enough in almost all cases to show that the coefficient is significantly different from zero, the confidence interval frequently covers rather a wide range.

redemption of marketable financial assets, e.g. Treasury bills or gilt-edged stocks. This procedure implictly assumes that the redemption yield is a good guide to the expected yield over the holders' relevant planning period; an assumption which will be generally invalid. People may, at certain times and in certain conditions, expect prices in the market to continue changing in the same direction as in the (recent) past for some (short) time (i.e. they hold extrapolative expectations). Or they may expect past price movements to be reversed over some future period, usually when this implies some return to a 'normal' level of prices (i.e. they hold regressive expectations).[1]

If people expect a fall in the price of an asset to continue even for a short time, and sell because of that expectation, then the calculated yield to redemption would be rising, while the real yield over the immediate short future could well be falling. This could mean that the effect of rising interest rates in causing some people to economise on money balances was being partly offset, or more than offset, by their effect in causing others to go liquid in anticipation of even higher rates. If market expectations were volatile, one might expect to observe quite large swings in interest rates associated with small changes in the level of money balances, or vice versa, sometimes even in a perverse direction (i.e. that rises in interest rates would be associated with increases in desired money balances). This result need not, however, imply that such financial assets were not good substitutes for money, but rather that the calculated yields did not always provide a good unbiased approximation to the true yields on which investors based their portfolio decisions.

There are therefore certain complications involved in the use of the yield (to maturity) on any marketable asset, with a varying capital value, as an index of the opportunity cost of holding money. It should, however, be feasible to observe more accurately the true relative return on holding assets with a fixed capital value – for example, building society shares and deposits, national savings, local authority temporary money[2] – rather than money, because there is no problem of estimating the expected change in capital values. It is still, however, difficult to refer to *the* opportunity cost of holding money because, when interest rates are generally increasing – and widely expected to continue increasing – the expected return (over the near future) on holding marketable assets may be falling, at the same time as the return on alternative capital-certain assets is rising.

---

[1] It is quite possible, indeed probably fairly common, to find that expectations of price changes in the near future are generally extrapolative, while expectations for price changes in the more distant future are regressive.

[2] If there are additional penalties imposed for encashment of an asset before some predetermined time period has elapsed, then the alternative yields on such assets cannot be properly estimated without further knowledge of the expected holding periods. Moreover, in some cases the rates offered, for example on building society shares and deposits, can be varied at short notice, while in other cases the rates may be fixed over the expected holding period. These are, however, probably lesser complications.

It might, perhaps, be thought otiose to distinguish between these alternative reasons (volatile expectations or a limited degree of substitution) for finding a low response of the demand for money balances to changes in interest rates. As long as open-market operations cause a significant change in interest rates in financial markets, where the initial effect must occur, it could be argued that the fundamental reason for this reaction, whether it be a low extent of substitution or volatile expectations, was of secondary importance: what mattered was that the change could be foreseen and was large. On the other hand, in so far as market expectations of a volatile nature are regarded as having an important influence on developments in the market, the emphasis of policy under actual working conditions of uncertainty and changing circumstances will be inevitably transferred to market management, away from simple rules of operation on monetary quantities. Furthermore, the importance, indeed the existence of any useful definition, of money depends largely on finding a break (of substitution) in the liquidity spectrum between money and other financial assets. If the finding of a fairly low interest-elasticity of demand is not taken as incontrovertible evidence of such a break in the spectrum, the issue of the central importance of the money stock as compared with some wider set of financial assets (even, perhaps, the much maligned concept of liquidity) remains open. It may indeed be questioned whether it is helpful to assign crucial importance to any one single financial variable. The need is to understand the complete adjustment process.

3. The Stability of the Income Velocity of Money

It is not possible to observe with any clarity either the real rates of return on asset holdings, which decision-makers in the economy believe that they face, or the precise process of portfolio adjustment. It is therefore difficult to chart and to measure the transmission of the effects of monetary policy. If, however, the sole aim of monetary policy is to affect the level of money incomes, it does not necessarily matter whether it is possible to observe and to understand the transmission mechanism in detail. It is enough to be able to relate the response of a change in money incomes to a prior change in the level of the money stock.

The statistical evidence

So the next stage in the analysis is usually to examine the direct statistical relationship between changes in the money stock and changes in money incomes. As was to be expected – for such a result would be predicted by almost all monetary theorists, irrespective of their particular viewpoint – movements in the money stock and movements in money incomes are closely associated over the long term. Over the last half century the demand for money appears to have grown at more or less the same rate as the growth of incomes. There have, however, been long spells within this period during which money balances have been growing faster or slower than money incomes. The American evidence suggests that money balances were growing at a faster rate than incomes before 1913, and the reverse has been the case for both the USA and the UK since about 1947.

The apparent fall in the velocity of circulation of money in the early part of this century in the USA may have been due to higher incomes enabling people to acquire proportionately more of the convenience (mainly in carrying out transactions) which the holding of larger money balances allows. The recent rise in velocity, in both the UK and the USA, may in turn have been brought about by people, especially company treasurers, seeking to obtain the benefit of economies in monetary management, spurred on by the rise in interest rates.

Alternatively these trends may have been associated with underlying structural changes, for example in the improvement of communications, in the change to a more urban society, in the growth and increasing stability of the banking system, in the emergence of non-bank financial intermediaries issuing alternative liquid assets and competitive services, and in technical developments in the mechanism for transmitting payments. In general it is not possible to ascribe the changing trends in the relative rates of growth of money balances and money incomes to any one, or any group, of these factors with any certainty; nor is it possible to predict when the trend of several years, or decades even, may alter direction. By definition, however, these trend-like movements are slow and quite steady. Only at or near a turning-point is the relationship between movements in money incomes and in the stock of money balances likely to be misjudged.

The existence of a significant statistical relationship between these two variables does not of itself provide any indication of the causal mechanism linking the two series. The monetarists, however, usually argue that the money stock has been determined exogenously, meaning that the money supply is determined without regard to the value of the other variables, such as money incomes and interest rates, within the economic system. As the money stock is thus assumed to be determined in such a fashion that changes in money incomes do not influence changes in the money stock, it follows that the existence of a statistical relationship between changes in the money stock and changes in money incomes must be assumed to reflect the influence of changes in the money stock on incomes.[1]

[1] In a slightly more sophisticated version of this approach the cash (reserve) base of the monetary system (the cash reserves of the banks, including their deposits with the central bank, together with currency held by the public outside the banking system – high-powered money in Professor Friedman's terminology) is taken as exogenously determined, while certain functional relationships (e.g. the public's desired cash-deposit ratio), which determine the total volume

For the moment this basic assumption that the money stock is determined exogenously will be accepted, so that the relationship between changes in the money stock and in money incomes can be treated as cause and effect, running from money to money incomes. On this assumption it is possible to measure both the extent of the effect of a change in the money supply upon money incomes and the extent of variation in this relationship[1] These results generally show that the residual variation in the relationship between changes in the money stock and in money incomes is large as a proportion of short-run changes in these variables – over one or two quarters – but much smaller as a proportion of longer-run changes, over two or more years.

The interpretation, which has been drawn by monetarists from similar work done in the USA, is that the statistical significance of the relationship between changes in the money stock and in money incomes provides evidence of the importance of monetary policy. But the considerable extent of residual variation in the relationship, especially in the short term, combined with the likely existence of long and possibly variable time lags in operation, prevents monetary policy – in the restricted sense of control over the money supply – being a suitable tool for 'fine-tuning' purposes. From this appreciation of the statistical results comes Professor Friedman's proposal for adopting a rule of maintaining a constant rate of growth in the money stock.

In Keynesian theory changes in the money supply initially affect interest rates on financial assets, and these interest-rate variations subsequently influence the demand for capital goods (investment). Once the level of autonomous expenditure is set,[2] the level of money incomes is determined through the multiplier process. As monetary policy is but one factor affecting the level of autonomous expenditures, in particular fixed investment, one should, perhaps, expect to see a closer relationship between autonomous expenditures and money incomes than between the money stock and money incomes. The monetarists instead believe that expenditures on all goods and assets are pervasively affected by monetary policy (though the transmission process can still be regarded as taking place through interest-rate changes in the process of restoring portfolio equilibrium). Thus, if the stock of money remains the same, an increase in demand at one point in the economy ('autonomous' or 'induced'; indeed, the monetarists are sceptical about the value of this distinction) will have to be broadly matched by a fall in demand elsewhere in order to maintain equilibrium. Therefore, they would expect changes in money incomes to vary more closely with exogenous changes in

---

of the money stock consistent with a given cash base, are treated as behavioural relationships influenced by other variables in the system (i.e. they are endogenous). This minor variation in the approach makes no fundamental difference to the analysis.

[1] The empirical results of such an exercise are reported in Appendix 2.

[2] 'Autonomous' is defined as meaning those expenditures, generally taken to be exports, government expenditures and fixed investment, that are not largely determined by the contemporaneous value of other variables within the economic system.

the money supply than with autonomous expenditures. The next step is usually to see which relationship appears to have a closer statistical fit. A commentary on, and critique of, such exercises is given in Appendix 1; it is suggested there that such exercises do not provide a satisfactory method of discriminating between the alternative theories.

The crux of this whole approach, of drawing conclusions from the statistical relationship between movements in the money stock and in money incomes, lies in the assumption that the money supply, or more precisely the monetary base,[1] is exogenously determined. This assumption allows a simple statistical association to be translated into a causal sequence. Is this crucial assumption justified? Clearly some of the factors which result in changes in the money supply/monetary base are endogenous (i.e. determined by the contemporaneous value of other variables within the economic system). Thus a large domestic borrowing requirement by the central government or a balance-of-payments surplus tends to enlarge the money supply. As a large borrowing requirement (fiscal deficit) and balance-of-payments surplus also result in expansionary pressures in the economy, there are reasons to expect increases in money incomes and in the money stock to be associated, without there being any necessary causal link running from money to money incomes.

But, in theory, a central bank can undertake such open-market operations that, whatever the extent of increase in the money supply/monetary base caused by endogenous, income-associated factors, the final level of the money supply is whatever the central bank wants it to be. In this sense the level of the money supply can be a policy instrument. A policy instrument is not, however, *ipso facto* an exogenous variable; it would only be so if policy were not influenced by the contemporaneous (or anticipated) value of other variables within the system, such as the level of incomes and interest rates. This clearly is not the case.

Obviously, if an increase in incomes causes the authorities to alter the money supply/monetary base, then the existence of a simple statistical association between movements in money incomes and in the money supply does not allow one to distinguish the strength of the intertwined causal mechanisms. In order to investigate whether this raises a serious problem, it is necessary to examine the factors which have apparently led the authorities to cause, or to accept, changes in the money supply/monetary base.

In the UK a general aim of policy has been to reduce the size of variations in interest rates, while at the same time moving towards a pattern of rates that would seem appropriate in the overall economic context. In so far as a policy of stabilisation of financial markets is pursued, the money supply must tend to vary with money incomes – without necessarily having any causal effect on

[1] The monetary base includes those assets that either are, or could be, used by the banks as cash reserves. It consists of the cash reserves of the banks, including their deposits with the central bank, together with currency held by the public outside the banking system.

incomes. An increase in incomes relative to money balances will cause some tightening of liquidity; people will be induced to sell financial assets to restore their liquidity, thus pushing interest rates up; the authorities, to a greater or lesser extent (depending on their view about the preferred pattern of interest rates), will 'lean into the wind' and take up these assets; the money supply increases. There may even be a tendency for changes in market conditions to precede changes in money incomes, in so far as people are able to predict changes in the rate of inflation and activity accurately, and to make their asset dispositions in the light of their expectations. If this were the case an increase in inflationary pressures would be preceded by weakness in financial markets and an increase in the money supply.

There is little doubt that changes in the levels of certain key variables within the system (income levels and interest rates, for example) have brought about changes in the money supply. Therefore, the money supply is not exogenous, and the statistical association between changes in the money supply and in money incomes cannot be advanced as evidence in itself of the importance of a quantitative monetary policy. Moreover, as the statistical relationships derived from the past depended on the particular kind of policy aim pursued by the authorities over the period considered, there would be no guarantee of their exact continuation in the future, should that policy be altered. In other words, although velocity has been fairly stable in the past, this would be no guarantee of its stability in the future if the authorities chose to alter the rules of the game.

Post hoc, ergo propter hoc?

There is therefore a two-way relationship between movements in the money stock and in money incomes, with causal influences running in both directions. It may, however, still be possible to isolate and to estimate the strength of the causal relationships separately. It will be easiest to do so if the interactions are not simultaneous, but consecutive. Thus, if the money supply responds to changes in money incomes only after a time lag, or if money incomes respond to changes in the money stock only after a time lag, it may be possible to distinguish the separate relationships.

In particular, if changes in the money stock cause changes in money incomes, then changes in the money stock would be expected to precede the resulting changes in money incomes with perhaps a rather long lead, depending on the duration of the transmission process. If, however, money stock variations result in part automatically from increases in autonomous expenditures – for example, in exports, fiscal expenditures or investment – and in part from the authorities' response to pressures in financial markets, then money incomes would be expected to rise more or less simultaneously with the stock of money. Thus investigation of the extent to which changes in the money stock lead, or lag, changes in money incomes could be of considerable importance in any attempt to distinguish the main direction of causality.

The preliminary results of research done in the Bank suggest that, in the UK, movements in the money stock have preceded movements in money incomes. The pattern of this lead/lag relationship is, however, intriguing, for the relationship between the two series appears to be bimodal, i.e. to have two peaks. There was a fairly strong correlation between the two series when the monetary series had a very short lead over money incomes, of about two or three months. There seemed to be a further peak in the correlations indicating a much longer time lag, with changes in the money stock leading changes in money incomes by some four to five quarters. The correlations were generally stronger when the monetary series used was narrowly defined (M_1 rather than M_2).

There have been a fairly large number of other statistical studies attempting to determine whether changes in the money stock do have a significant lead over changes in money incomes. The tests have used different series, from different countries, over different time periods, and the lag relationships have been estimated in different ways. Practically without exception they show that changes in the money stock appear to lead changes in money incomes, but the calculated length of lead has varied quite widely between the various studies, though to some extent this may have been due to the different forms in which the relationship was estimated. Professor Friedman, for example, has claimed that there is evidence of a long and variable time lag in movements of incomes after variations in the money stock. Other statistical work on this subject, both in the UK and in the USA, has tended, rather, to suggest that the interval by which the change in the money stock precedes the change in money incomes is quite short, a matter of months rather than of quarters.

A statistically significant lead therefore seems to exist even if it is quite short. Does this, then, make it possible to disentangle the causal effects of changes in money supply on money incomes from those running in the opposite direction? It does not follow that the series which appears to lead always causes the change in the following series. There is a close association between visits to travel agents and tourist bureaux and trips abroad. The visit to the agent precedes the trip abroad, but does not cause it – though it facilitates it. Rather, the desire for travel abroad causes the initial visit to the travel agent. Analogously, desires for increased expenditure may be preceded by an accumulation of cash necessary to finance that expenditure. The demand for such additional money balances will cause pressure on financial markets, and so the authorities, seeking to maintain interest rates within some broad range, may in part accommodate the demand.

It is, however, unlikely that such accumulation of cash would take place far in advance of planned expenditures, for if the balances to be spent were at all sizeable it would be generally economic to lend them at interest on higher-yielding assets in the meantime. From this source, a lead of money stock over money incomes of only a few weeks might, perhaps, be expected – though rather longer in the USA, where the custom of making loans (together with compensating balances), rather than overdrafts, could distort the observed timing between changes in money incomes and money balances.

There are, indeed, a number of other hypotheses which are consistent with a situation in which changes in the money stock precede, but do not cause, subsequent changes in money incomes. However, in the absence of evidence to the contrary, a consistent lead is a *prima facie* indication of causation.

Most detailed investigations, however, of the effects on expenditures resulting from interest-rate changes (including wealth effects) show quite long average time lags of the order of one or two years between changes in the monetary base and changes in expenditure.[1] Furthermore, Professor Friedman suggested that changes in monetary conditions affect expenditures only after a long and variable lag. If the duration of the transmission process, whereby changes in monetary conditions affect money incomes, is as long as these studies suggest, it would seem implausible to attribute the finding of a fairly strong relationship between the money stock and money incomes with a very short lead mainly to the impact of monetary changes on money incomes.

The preliminary results of studies made in the Bank which indicated that the lag pattern in the relationship between the money stock and money incomes was a dual one – a very short lead of two to three months and a much longer lead of four to five quarters – further suggested that the relationship between these series might result from the existence of separate causal relationships, each with its own lag pattern, whereby the levels of the money stock and money incomes approached a joint equilibrium.[2]

These findings do not make possible any confident measurement of the relative contributions of the adjustment of the money stock to changes in money incomes, or of the adjustment of money incomes to changes in the money stock, towards the simple overall statistical association between the two series. Even so, some of these results, particularly the observed relationship between bank advances and investment, seem to suggest that

---

[1] See, for example, the FRB-MIT model as reported by F. de Leeuw and E.M. Gramlich in 'The channels of monetary policy', *Federal Reserve Bulletin*, June 1969, tables 1 and 2, pp. 487–8.

[2] In order to examine this proposition further, the series were disaggregated into their main components to discover whether the estimated relationships between the component series were significantly different from those of the aggregate series. The results of this exercise suggested that this was indeed the case. The relationship between the money stock and consumption appeared to be strongest when the two series were synchronous. The relationship between the money stock and investment suggested that changes in the money stock preceded investment with a long lead of some four to five quarters. When the monetary series was disaggregated into two components – advances to the private sector and other assets (mainly holdings of public-sector debt) – movements in bank advances appeared to have a long lead over movements in money incomes, while the relationship between holdings of public-sector debt and money incomes was strongest when the two series were synchronous. Indeed, the relationship between the two series when bank holdings of public-sector debt led money incomes was, perversely, negative. Finally, an examination of the relationship between bank advances and investment suggested the presence of a long (four to five quarters) lead over investment.

changes in monetary conditions do have a significant effect upon expenditures. Equally, other results do not remove scepticism of the view that the simple relationship between movements in the money stock and in money incomes could be interpreted entirely, or even mainly, in terms of the direct impact of monetary conditions upon money incomes.

It follows that these studies of the simple statistical relationship between movements in the money stock and in money incomes can by themselves provide very little information about the strength of monetary policy. The statistical relationship is quite close, but this may reflect to a very large extent the accommodation of movements in the money supply to autonomous changes in money incomes (given the authorities' policy aims and operational techniques). If the authorities should make an abrupt change in their operations (altering the 'rules of the game') the old-established regularities might cease to apply.

4. Conclusions

The monetary authorities are in a position to alter financial conditions decisively by their operations in certain key financial markets. These market operations can have a considerable influence upon interest rates and also upon the climate of expectations. The existence of financial intermediaries other than banks, which are not so closely controlled, does not, in practice, prevent the authorities from bringing about sharp and considerable changes in financial conditions. Rather, the danger is the other way around – namely, that aggressive actions by the authorities in markets subject to volatile reactions could cause exaggerated and excessive fluctuations in financial conditions.

The effect of these operations in financial markets is to cause disequilibria in portfolios. Expansionary monetary policy (narrowly defined to refer to operations to increase the money stock) will cause rates of return on a very wide range of assets, including stocks of all real goods, to be higher, at the margin, than the return available on money balances and other financial assets. In this general sense, monetary policy is transmitted to expenditure decisions via interest rates.

Attempts to measure the effect on expenditures of changes in interest rates on financial assets have on occasions shown these effects to be significant, though relatively small and often subject to long time lags. There are, however, reasons for believing that these studies may underestimate the strength of monetary policy. In particular, most of these studies use calculated nominal rates of return as an indicator of the impact of monetary policy. Expenditure decisions, however, are affected by relative real interest rates, and these cannot be directly observed. A strongly expansionary monetary policy, which would maintain low real rates of interest, might well be associated, after an initial decline, with rising nominal interest rates.

On the other hand, attempts to measure the effects of monetary policy by correlating changes in the money stock with changes in money incomes probably greatly overestimate the strength of monetary policy. There is a two-way relationship between these variables. It is not correct to regard changes in the money stock as having been determined independently of changes in money incomes; for example, the actions of the authorities in financial markets, which will directly affect the money supply, will usually be strongly influenced by current and expected future developments in the economy. Attempts to disentangle this two-way interaction by considering, for example, the lead/lag relationship reinforce the view that monetary policy has some causal impact on money incomes, but do not allow this to be clearly isolated and quantified.

Monetary policy is not an easy policy to use. The possibility of exaggerated reactions and discontinuities in application must condition its use. We are not able to estimate the effects of such policy, even in normal circumstances, with any precision. Such effects may well be stronger than some studies undertaken from a Keynesian approach, relating expenditures to changes in nominal interest rates, would suggest, but weaker than some of the monetarist exercises may be interpreted as implying. Furthermore, there are probably quite long time lags in the operation of monetary policy before it affects most kinds of expenditure. These considerations underline the difficulties of using monetary policy for short-run demand management.

A particular problem, perhaps, is to distinguish what the thrust of monetary policy at any time is. Indeed, it may be harder to decipher what effect monetary policy is having at any moment than to decide what effect should be aimed at. The level of nominal interest rates is not a good indicator of the stance of monetary policy. Rising nominal interest rates are quite consistent with falling real rates of interest. Professor Friedman has argued that the rate of change of the money supply would be a better indicator of the thrust of monetary policy than variations in the level of nominal rates. To the extent that price stability ceases to be an accepted norm, and expectations of inflation, or even accelerating inflation, become widespread, this claim that the rate of growth of the money stock may be a better indicator of the direction of policy than the level of interest rates takes on a certain merit. As, however, there will always be multiple objectives – for example, the balance of payments, the level of employment, the distribution of expenditure, etc. – no single statistic can possibly provide an adequate and comprehensive indicator of policy. And basing policy, quasi-automatically, upon the variations in one simple indicator would lead to a hardening of the arteries of judgement.

Appendix 1: The Evidence of Empirical Investigations

References in [square brackets] are listed on page 000

Professor Friedman [**15**] has redefined the Quantity Theory as a theory of the demand for money. Many economists have therefore turned to the estimation of the money demand function (and its analogue, the velocity function) to test the theories advanced by monetarists. These tests have been designed to throw light on a number of issues, some of which – for example, the appropriate definition of money, whether income or wealth is the main determinant of desired money balances, and whether money is a luxury good – are not the really critical issues in the current debate between 'Keynesians' and 'monetarists'.[1] Other questions are, however, vitally important to this debate, and in this review the following are isolated:

(a) the basic predictability of the demand for money
(b) the role of interest rates in the demand-for-money function
(c) the relative importance of short-term and long-term interest rates in explaining the demand for money.

Empirical tests have been successful in partially confirming some, at least, of the monetarists' theories. This has encouraged further work designed to compare the stability of Keynesian and monetary relationships. Commentary on, and criticism of, such tests is provided in the final section of this appendix.

The predictability of the demand for money

Although there is nothing in Keynes's work to suggest that the demand for money should be unpredictable (except at very low interest rates), a widespread feeling grew up among Keynesians in the post-war period that the availability of money substitutes would render the money – income relationship too volatile to be of much practical use for economic management or forecasting. This was the view that was challenged by the monetarists. Friedman and Schwartz, in their monetary history of the USA[**19**], demonstrated that real income and real money balances were connected in a reasonably predictable way over the period 1867–1959. Since then, the work of Meltzer[**31**], Chow[**9**], Laidler[**25**] and Courchene and Shapiro[**11**], among others, have borne out the contention that the demand-for-money function for the USA is fairly well determined over the long period, with coefficients of determination[2] in the range 0.9–0.99. The pioneering long-range study for the UK carried out by Kavanagh and Walters[**24**], for the period 1877–1981, established a coefficient of determination of 0.98 in the demand-for-money function.

It is, however, relatively easy to establish an apparently close-fitting relationship when there are strong trends in both dependent and independent (explanatory) variables. A possibly more searching test of the strength of the basic relationship is its predictability when estimated using changes in, rather than levels of, the data. Using changes reduces dramatically the coefficient of determination. For example, in Laidler's very comprehensive study based on US data, the coefficient of determination in a typical equation was lowered from 0.99 to 0.51 when the data were transformed

---

[1] As in the main section, the terms 'Keynesian' and 'monetarist' are used to characterise views that would not necessarily be held by all, or even most, members of each school of thought.

[2] The coefficient of determination, or R^2 statistic, is the proportion of the variance of the dependent variable in an equation which can be associated with, or 'explained' by, changes in the independent variables.

into first differences (i.e. changes). For UK data, the coefficient of 0.98 by Kavanagh and Walters, noted above, was reduced to 0.49 by first differencing.

The use of lagged dependent variables[1] is another way by which the danger of inferring false relationships from trend-dominated variables can be reduced, though similar dangers are raised in interpreting the lagged term. Most tests using lagged dependent variables (including the models reported in Appendix 2) have shown the estimated coefficient of the lagged variable to be highly significant, while the explanatory power of other variables has been correspondingly lower. One explanation of these findings is the presence of time lags in the process by which a dependent variable adjusts to an equilibrium; but an equally plausible one is the existence of first-order serial correlation in the residuals;[2] both influences are probably present to some extent.

The empirical evidence suggests that the demand for money is more predictable than, say, the Radcliffe Committee would have imagined, but probably not predictable enough to be used as an instrument of short-term policy. Furthermore, the predictability of the relationship in a period when control of the money supply was not a major feature of policy will not necessarily be a good guide to its predictability under conditions when it is more actively used.

The role of interest rates in the demand-for-money function

The next important point of dispute is the relationship between the level of interest rates and the quantity of money. Many Keynesians have supposed that the interest-elasticity of the demand for money would be relatively high,[3] while monetarists have believed the elasticity would be low, because money was seen by them as a general substitute for all assets, rather than a specific substitute for interest-bearing financial assets.

In his early writings, Friedman[**16**] conceded that interest rates might feature in the demand-for-money function but, on the basis of empirical work, contended that in practice they did not. Thus it was argued that the observed relationship between money and incomes must be a 'direct' one. It has since been shown, however, that interest rates do play a significant role in the demand for money. Of all the studies of this subject published since Friedman's, and which are noted in Table A (pp.52–3), only those by Heller[**22**] for the USA, and by Fisher[**13**] for the UK indicate an inability to find a significant role for interest rates.[4] The volume of evidence is now quite widely accepted, at least among Keynesians and some monetarists, as contradicting the view that 'only money matters'. However, the fact that interest rates are significant in the demand-for-money function undermines only the extreme version of the quantity theory, namely that there is a fixed short-term link between the stock of money and money incomes. It leaves open the question of the *relative* importance of income and interest rates in determining desired money holdings.

---

[1] Where one of the factors explaining the level of the dependent variable is its level in the previous time period.

[2] The residuals associated with any estimated relationship are defined as:

$$u_t = y_t - \hat{y}_t$$

where y_t = the observed value of the dependent variable at time t
$\hat{y}_t$ = the value of the dependent variable at time t calculated from the estimated relationship

First-order serial correlation in the residuals is the correlation between u_t and u_{t-1}.

[3] See, for example, the Radcliffe Report [**33**].

[4] See footnote 3 on page 47 for a possible explanation of Heller's finding.

Nearly all the work that has been done on *levels* of data has shown income to be much more important than interest rates in determining the demand for money. Partial coefficients of correlation[1] are not generally given, but it may reasonably be inferred that incomes are more important from the fact that the margins of error in the estimates of coefficients are relatively much lower for income variables than for interest rates.[2]

That this should be so in the long term is not surpising, because there are long-term trends in both incomes and money. It is in this context more revealing to look at models which are estimated in first difference form (using changes, rather than levels, of data), or with the use of a lagged dependent variable. The study of US data by Laidler[**25**] showed that the significance of an income variable was much reduced when the data were transformed into first differences, though it was still somewhat greater than that of the interest-rate variable. Hamburger[**21**], in a study using logarithmic first-differences, found that the coefficient on incomes became insignificant.

Once a role has been conceded to interest rates the question becomes one of how large an interest-elasticity is consistent with according primary importance to money. There is no unambiguous answer to this question, since it hinges on the meaning that is given to words such as 'large', 'primary', etc. This is an example of how the two theories have, partly as a result of empirical testing, drawn together.

The numerical value of the interest-elasticity[3] that has been observed has generally been found to lie in the range -0.1 to -1.0. This is quite a wide band, but part at least of the variation is due to the different forms in which the demand-for-money function has been tested. Some economists, following the letter of Keynes, have used the bond rate in their equations as the opportunity cost of holding money. Others, recognising that Keynes was using a restrictive theoretical model, have suggested that in practice short-term financial assets are more likely to be thought of as substitutes for money, and so have used a short-term rate of interest. Short-term and long-term rates are closely linked as to the direction of movements; but fluctuations in short-term rates are perhaps two to three times larger. Thus it is to be expected that a higher interest-elasticity will have been observed for long-term rates than for short-term rates.

Another difference lies in the definition of money which has been used. The usual definition in the USA restricts money to currency and demand deposits; but certain monetarists, particularly Friedman, have argued that the definition should be widened to include time deposits, on the grounds that these too are a 'temporary abode of purchasing power'. It is to be expected that the narrower definition would probably have the greater interest-elasticity, because the wider definition includes assets bearing a yield which moves broadly in line with other market rates.

---

[1] The partial coefficient of correlation measures the degree of association between two variables, after allowing for the impact of other variables in the equation. Another means of measuring the relative strength of two separate effects is by beta coefficients (see Goldberger [**20**]).

[2] It is convenient to compare margins of error by the use of '*t*'-statistics (the ratio of an estimated coefficient to its estimated standard error). In general, the smaller the *t*-statistic, the more subject is the estimated coefficient to sampling fluctuations (random errors), and conversely the higher the *t*-statistic. It is because of sampling fluctuations that a non-zero coefficient may be recorded even though the true value of the coefficient may be zero.

[3] The most commonly used measure of interest-elasticity measures approximately the percentage change in money balances resulting from a 1 per cent change in interest rates, a 1 per cent change being a change from, say, 4 to 4.04 per cent. To produce equations with constant interest-elasticities, interest rates are usually put directly into logarithmic form. This implies that a change in interest rates from, say, ½ to 1 per cent would have the same effect as a change from 4 to 8 per cent.

For these reasons it is, perhaps, to be expected that models using a narrow definition of money and a long-term rate of interest would yield the highest interest-elasticities, and that those with a wide definition and a short-term rate of interest would yield the lowest elasticities. This is broadly the picture which emerges from the empirical results presented in Table A, certainly for those based on annual data. The highest[1] estimates of interest-elasticity are those of Meltzer[**31**], Brunner and Meltzer[**7**], Chow[**9**] and Courchene and Shapiro[**11**]; all are derived on the basis of the narrow definition of money and a long-term interest rate, and none is below −0.7. Laidler[**25**] specifically set out to test the relative elasticities using different specifications; and Tobin[**35**] did much the same thing using a velocity function. Using annual US data from 1892 to 1960,[2] Laidler produced elasticity estimates ranging from −0.16 using a wide definition of money and short-term interest rates as an argument, to −0.72 using a narrow definition of money and long-term interest rates, Tobin's estimates were much the same, ranging from −0.12 to −0.55.

For the UK, the only study of note using annual levels of the money stock is that of Kavanagh and Walters[**24**]. They used a wide definition of money, and a long-term interest rate, and obtained an elasticity of −0.30 for the period 1877–1961; and of −0.50 for the period 1926–61. The relationships between interest-elasticities estimated using US data suggest, perhaps, that had a short-term interest rate been used, the estimated elasticity for the shorter period would have been closer to −0.2.

Thus, despite the superficial appearance of diversity, most of the work done with long runs of annual data produces a fairly consistent picture. The elasticity of currency and demand deposits with respect to long-term interest rates is probably about −0.7, and with respect to short-term interest rates about −0.25. For a wider definition of money, the relevant figures are slightly lower, and seem to depend more on the particular specification of the model.

Those studies which have used quarterly data have tended to produce lower estimates for the interest-elasticity of the demand for money. Heller[**22**] was unable to detect any significant influence of long-term interest rates[3] on the demand for money and, when he used short-term rates, the estimated long-run elasticity fell between −0.1 and −0.2. Hamburger[**21**] used two interest rates (the equity yield and the long-term bond yield) in his study of the demand for money of the household sector, and the sum of their coefficients was about −0.3. Teigen's work[**34**], undertaken in the framework of a simultaneous equations model, produced long-run elasticities of less than −0.1; though when a similar equation for annual data was estimated, an elasticity of nearly −0.2 was recorded.

The use of quarterly data has presented a number of problems. Chief among these is the existence of time lags in the adjustment process, the correct specification of which becomes of greater importance when quarterly rather than annual data are used. These time lags are presumably not due primarily to imperfections in financial markets, because it is relatively easy to move into and out of money balances. It seems more likely that money holders take time to adjust their behaviour after changes in their incomes and in relevant interest rates.

Fisher[**13**], and Laidler and Parkin[**26**] found that the results of their quarterly models using UK data were much improved by the inclusion of lagged terms.[4]

---

[1] In the sense of being furthest from zero.

[2] The data for money on a narrow definition are available only from 1919.

[3] These results, however, are partly due to the fact that the estimation period chosen includes the years prior to 1951 when interest rates were pegged. If these years are excluded, both long and short rates become highly significant.

[4] It should be noted, however, that this improvement may owe something to serial correlation in the basic equation, as well as to the existence of time lags.

Furthermore, the coefficient of the lagged terms was generally large and significant, indicating quite long adjustment lags. A study using quarterly data for the period 1955–68, which is reported in more detail in Appendix 2, bears out these conclusions. On average, around two-fifths of the adjustment of money balances towards a new equilibrium seems to take place within the first year.

The existence of time lags in the demand-for-money function implies that the restoration of equilibrium after an increase in the money supply would require a much greater change in the other variables (income and interest rates) in the short term than in the long term. This is because, at a point in time, the demand for money depends primarily on past values of incomes and interest rates (which by definition cannot be changed) and only to a relatively small extent on current values of these variables. It is therefore changes in current values of either income or interest rates which must in the first instance take the strain of adjustment to an exogenous monetary change. If the role of interest rates in the demand for money is considered to be of secondary importance, the response of incomes to a monetary change should be larger in the short run than in the long run, as Friedman[**17**] acknowledges; however, other evidence which he has produced[**19**] suggests that in practice changes in the money stock do not appear to affect income until after quite a long and variable time lag. This inconsistency disappears if a transmission mechanism working via interest rates is postulated. If the demand for money responds slowly to changes in income and interest rates, a change in the stock of money could have a rapid and powerful effect on interest rates, which in turn could have a lagged effect on expenditure, causing income changes to follow an initial change in the money supply. Under these conditions, Burstein[**8**] has argued that rigid pursuit of a money supply target might lead to unnecessarily wide fluctuations in interest rates and hence in incomes.

The relative importance of long-term and short-term interest rates in the demand-for-money function

If money is simply the most liquid in a spectrum of assets, one would expect the demand for it to be most closely related to the yield on near substitutes, that is to say, on other short-term assets. If, on the other hand, money is an asset that is fundamentally different from other assets, there is no reason to expect the demand for it to be any more closely related to the yield on short-term than on long-term assets. These two hypotheses may perhaps be empirically distinguished by testing whether a short-term or a long-term interest rate gives rise to the highest coefficient of determination in a demand-for-money function. Laidler[**25**] suggests a further test: if the demand function for money is stable, the 'right' interest rate would be expected to show the same relationship to the demand for money in different time periods while the 'wrong' one need not.

Many of the studies noted in this appendix do not provide any direct evidence on this issue. Those that do, however, tend to support the view that in the USA money has been a closer substitute for short-term than for longer-term assets. Laidler finds that using the wide definition of money, the coefficient of determination is much greater for short-term rates than for long-term rates, though in first differences, the superiority of short-term rates is less marked. He also found that when his data were divided into sub-periods, the estimates of interest-elasticity were much more stable with respect to short-term rates than to longer-term rates. Confirmation is provided by the work of Heller[**22**], who, using quarterly data for the post-war period, detects a significant elasticity for short-term interest rates but not for long-term rates.[1] Lee[**29**],

[1] Though see footnote 3 on page 47.

using differential rather than absolute rates, finds that the yield on savings and loan shares (an asset which may be thought of as being very close to money on the liquidity spectrum) explains the demand for money, under either a narrow or broad definition, better than the yield on longer-term assets.

The results of the study set out in Appendix 2, which reports the estimation of demand-for-money equations from data for the UK, left almost nothing to choose between long-term and short-term rates. Long-term rates were marginally more significant when the definition of money was restricted to currency plus clearing bank deposits; but the short-term (local authority) rate appeared slightly better at explaining changes in money as defined in the Central Statistical Office's *Financial Statistics*. This may result from the deposits of the 'other' banks being more directly competitive with rates in the local authority market. When first differences were used, however, the short rate performed markedly better than the long rate. The estimated values of the coefficients corresponded much better with values recorded using levels, and the significance of the estimates was considerably greater.

Tobin's results[**35**] (based on Friedman's data) also suggest that there is little to choose between long-term and short-term rates, with long-term rates being marginally more successful in explaining the demand for 'narrow' money, and short rates slightly better for 'wide' money.

The relative stability of Keynesian and monetary multipliers

As noted earlier, a further means of testing the relative importance of Keynesian and monetarist hypotheses of income determination is provided by estimates of the direct relationship between incomes and money on the one hand and between incomes and autonomous expenditures on the other. This approach is open to the objection that it tests only a very simple representation of the underlying models, ignoring the improvements and refinements suggested by theoretical developments. As Johnson[**23**] has noted, this may be defended on the grounds that the 'test of a good theory is its ability to predict something large from something small, by means of a simple and stable theoretical relationship'; but it is nevertheless quite possible that the relative explanatory power of simple equations may be a poor guide to the explanatory power of more complex equations derived as reduced forms from a set of interacting relationships.

More specifically, such an approach requires that the explanatory variables introduced should be the main exogenous variables influencing the economy, and that they should not themselves be functionally related to the dependent variables, or else erroneous conclusions may be reached. In general, a single-equation model, which is not derived as a reduced form from a full set of structural equations, may be open to question as to whether the explanatory variables included are, indeed, truly exogenous. In particular, these tests of the monetarists' hypothesis hang crucially on the assumption that the money supply is exogenously determined, a question which is treated more fully in the main section.

Quite apart from these problems with the specification of single equations, such equations can only provide information on the behaviour of one variable – albeit a variable of great significance to the economy. No government can possibly be content to rely on a model which only provides a forecast of, say, money income. It is essential to be able to make an informed and consistent judgement on a whole range of other variables, for example, productivity, inflation, unemployment, the balance of payments, the allocation of resources between various kinds of expenditure, etc. Furthermore, the authorities need to have some understanding of the route whereby they affect money incomes by changing their policy instruments. For example, it makes a difference whether monetary policy has its effect overwhelmingly on, say, private housebuilding, or more widely over all forms of expenditure. For this reason a proper test of the adequacy of the alternative models must be whether they can provide information on the behaviour of all the variables which are of concern to the authorities and to economists.

The pioneering comparison of Keynesian and monetary models was that of Friedman and Meiselman[**18**] in their research study for the Commission on Money and Credit. Using US data for a 62-year period (1897–1958), which was divided into a number of sub-periods, thay found that consumers' expenditure was more closely linked with the money stock than with autonomous expenditure in every period except the depression years. For the post-war period, when quarterly data were available, the picture was much the same, though neither hypothesis was at all successful in explaining quarterly *changes* in gross national product (GNP). However, in the long run, velocity appeared to be more stable than at least one definition of the autonomous expenditure multiplier.

But Ando and Modigliani[**2**], using a definition of autonomous expenditure that was more in line with modern theory, obtained an explanation of consumers' expenditure which was better[1] than the one Friedman and Meiselman had detected using monetary variables. Their main argument, however, was methodological – namely, that to say the average value of the monetary multiplier had been more stable than the autonomous expenditure multiplier over a long run of years did not necessarily make it a particularly useful policy tool. Stabilisation policy would need to take into account a much wider body of knowledge about how economic variables interacted; there was no reason to treat Keynesian and monetary measures as alternatives, nor any justification for picking a single independent variable – which was anyway not always truly independent – to represent each type of policy.

The same criticisms could be applied to a similar study based on UK data undertaken by Barrett and Walters[**5**] which, however, did not produce any very conclusive results. When levels of data were used, there was little to choose between the alternative hypotheses – though both achieved quite high correlation coefficients because of strong trends in all series. When first differences of data were used, the estimated explanatory power (as measured by the coefficient of determination) of both hypotheses was low, though the autonomous expenditure 'explanation' of consumers' expenditure was somewhat better than the monetary explanation for the interwar years; and the monetary explanation was better before 1914 (when, however, the data are not entirely reliable). Barrett and Walters also showed that when money and autonomous expenditures were jointly considered as predictors of consumers' expenditure, the coefficient of determination was significantly increased, suggesting that, whether or not it is the major determinant, money does play some significant role.

A slightly different approach, followed by Andersen and Jordan[**1**], compared the impact on GNP of fiscal and of monetary measures respectively. Given the limitations of single-equation models, the tests used were subtle ones. Changes in GNP were separately related to changes in the full-employment budget balance, to changes in the money supply, and also to changes in the money base, which was assumed to be more nearly exogenous than the money supply.

The results obtained by Andersen and Jordan on US data indicated that monetary changes had an impact on GNP which was greater, more certain and more immediate than that of fiscal changes. De Leeuw and Kalchbrenner[**30**] challenged these conclusions on the grounds that the independent variables had been mis-specified; but although the alternative definitions proposed appeared to re-establish a role for fiscal

[1] As judged by the higher coefficient of determination.

policy, the case made by Andersen and Jordan for the importance of monetary factors was not refuted. Davis[**12**], however, showed that if the period to which the tests related was split into two equal sub-periods, the earlier part of the period (1952–60) showed very little relationship between money and incomes; the relationship discovered in the latter period (1960–8) might well have been due to common trends among the variables during these years.

For the UK, Artis and Nobay[**3**] have carried out tests very similar to those of Andersen and Jordan. In their study, fiscal policy was found to be more effective than monetary policy; but again little confidence can be attached to the results, because, as the authors themselves point out, these are critically dependent on the assumption that the authorities' fiscal and monetary policy actions are not functionally related to the level of money incomes. As much of the purpose of government action is to reduce deviations of actual incomes from some desired level, these assumptions must be suspect. Thus, if policy is used to offset a change in GNP deriving from another source, it appears as though the policy measure has no effect. Perfect anti-cyclical fiscal policy would produce the *statistical* conclusion that fiscal policy was impotent.

TABLE A

For reasons of space, this selection of empirical work has had to be extremely compressed. As far as possible, representative equations have been chosen from the work of each author, though often other equations have produced somewhat different coefficients. No reference is made to the other variables, besides interest rates, included in the equations.

Where the equations contain lags, the implied long-run elasticity is given; these equations are marked† and no t statistic is given as its meaning would be ambiguous.

Author	Data used	Definition of money[a]	Interest rate used	Interest-elasticity[b]	*t*-statistic[c]
Demand-for-money equations					
Bronfenbrenner and Mayer [**6**]	Annual: US 1919–56	Narrow	Short	−0.33	†
Chow [**9**]	Annual: US 1897–1958	Narrow	Long	−0.73	17
Meltzer [**31**]	Annual: US 1900–58	Narrow	Long	−0.92	22
		Broad	Long	−0.48	10
	Annual: US 1930–58	Narrow	Long	−1.15	12
		Broad	Long	−0.70	7
Brunner and Meltzer [**7**]	Annual: US 1930–59	Narrow	Long	−1.09	19
		Broad	Long	−0.73	15
Laidler [**25**]	Annual: US 1919–60	Narrow	Short	−0.21	12
				(−0.11)	(3)
		Narrow	Long	−0.72	12
				(−0.33)	(3)
	Annual: US 1892–1960	Broad	Short	−0.16	16
				(−0.10)	(5)
		Broad	Long	−0.25	4
				(−0.26)	(3)
Lee [**29**]	Annual: US 1951–65	Narrow	Short	−0.41	4
		Broad	Short	−0.67	3
Motley [**32**]	Annual: US 1920–65 (households only)	Broad	Short	−0.16	5
Courchene and Shapiro [**11**]	Annual: US 1900–58	Narrow	Long	−1.00	16
		Broad	Long	−0.58	10
Teigen [**34**]	Quarterly: US 1946–59	Narrow	Long	−0.07	†
	Annual: US 1924–41	Narrow	Long	−0.20	†
Heller [**22**]	Quarterly: US 1947–58	Narrow	Short	−0.12	4
		Broad	Short	−0.18	4
		Narrow	Long	*	..
		Broad	Long	*	

Hamburger [**21**]	Quarterly: US 1952–60 (households only)	Narrow	Long	−0.16	2
		Narrow	Equity yield	−0.13	3
Kavanagh and Walters [**24**]	Annual: UK 1880–1961	Broad	Long	−0.31	3
				(−0.22)	(3)
	Annual: UK 1926–61	Broad	Long	−0.50	6
				(−0.25)	(3)
Fisher [**13**]	Quarterly: UK 1955–67	Narrow	Short	−0.11	†
		Broad	Short	*	†
		Narrow	Long	−0.3	†
		Broad	Long	*	†
Laidler and Parkin [**6**]	Quarterly: UK 1953–67	Broad	Short	−0.26	†
Bank of England [**4**]	Quarterly: UK 1955–69	Narrow	Short	−1.05	†
		Narrow	Long	−0.80	†
		Broad	Short	−0.09	†
		Broad	Long	−0.35	†
Velocity equations					
Latané [**27**]	Annual: US 1919–52	Narrow	Long	−0.80	..
Latané [**28**]	Annual: US 1909–58	Narrow	Long	−0.77	..
Christ [**10**]	Annual: US 1892–1959	Narrow	Long	−0.72	..
Meltzer [**31**]	Annual: US 1950–8	Narrow	Long	−1.8	30
		Broad	Long	−1.3	20
Tobin [**35**]	Annual: US 1915–59	Broad	Short	−0.12	7
		Narrow	Short	−0.24	9
		Broad	Long	−0.24	6
		Narrow	Long	−0.55	10
Frazer [**14**]	Quarterly: US 1948–65	Narrow	Long	−0.8	27
		Broad	Long	−0.37	12
Kavanagh and Walters [**24**]	Annual: UK 1877–1961	Broad	Long	−0.20	2
				(−0.44)	(6)
	Annual: UK 1923–61	Broad	Long	−0.55	9

* not significant or wrong sign.
.. not available.
[a] The 'narrow' definition of money is usually currency plus demand deposits; 'broad' money includes time deposits.
[b] Values shown in brackets are obtained using first differences.
[c] The t-statistic is the ratio of the estimated coefficient to its estimated standard error.

References for Appendix 1

1 Andersen, L.C. and Jordan, J.L., 'Monetary and fiscal actions: a test of their relative importance in economic stabilisation', *Federal Reserve Bank of St Louis Monthly Review,* November 1968.

2 Ando, Albert and Modigliani, Franco, 'The relative stability of monetary velocity and the investment multiplier', *American Economic Review*, September 1965, pp. 693–728. See also other papers on the subject in the same issue.

3 Artis, M. J. and Nobay, A. R., 'Two aspects of the monetary debate', *National Institute Economic Review,* August 1969, pp. 33–51.

4 Bank of England, Appendix 2 (pp. 55–63 of this volume).

5 Barrett, C. R. and Walters, A. A., 'The stability of Keynesian and monetary multipliers in the United Kingdom', *Review of Economics and Statistics,* November 1966, pp. 395–405.

6 Bronfenbrenner, Martin and Mayer, Thomas, 'Liquidity functions in the American economy', *Econometrica*, October 1980, pp. 810–34.

7 Brunner, Karl and Meltzer, A. H., 'Some further investigations of demand and supply functions for money', *Journal of Finance*, May 1964, pp. 240–83.

8 Burstein, M. L., *Economic Theory: Equilibrium and Change*, Wiley, London, 1968, esp. pp. 289–326.

9 Chow, G. C., 'On the long-run and short-run demand for money', *Journal of Political Economy*, April 1966, pp. 111–31.

10 Christ, C. F., 'Interest rates and "portfolio selection" among liquid assets in the US', *Studies in Memory of Yehuda Grunfeld*, Stanford University Press, 1963.

11 Courchene, T. J. and Shapiro, H. T., 'The demand for money: a note from the time series', *Journal of Political Economy*, October 1964, pp. 498–503.

12 Davis, R. G., 'How much does money matter?', *Federal Reserve Bank of New York Monthly Review*, June 1969.

13 Fisher, Douglas, 'The demand for money in Britain: quarterly results 1951–67', *Manchester School of Economic and Social Studies*, December 1968, pp. 329–44.

14 Frazer, W. J., 'The demand for money, statistical results and monetary policy', *Schweizerische Zeitschrift für Volkswirtschaft und Statistik*, March 1967.

15 Friedman, Milton, 'The quantity theory of money: a restatement', *Studies in the Quantity Theory of Money*, ed. M. Friedman, University of Chicago Press; 1956, pp. 3–21.

16 Friedman, Milton, 'The demand for money: some theoretical and empirical results', *Journal of Political Economy*, August 1959, pp. 327–51.

17 Friedman, Milton, 'The demand for money: some theoretical and empirical results', *Journal of Political Economy*, August 1959, p. 347.

18 Friedman, Milton and Meiselman, David, 'The relative stability of monetary velocity and the investment multiplier in the United States, 1897–1958', in *Stabilization Policies*, CMC Research Papers, Prentice-Hall, 1964, pp. 165–268.

19 Friedman, Milton and Schwartz, A. J., *A Monetary History of the United States 1867–1960*, Princeton University Press, 1963.

20 Goldberger, A. S., *Econometric Theory*, Wiley, New York, 1966, pp. 197–200.

21 Hamburger, M. J., 'The demand for money by households, money substitutes, and monetary policy', *Journal of Political Economy*, December 1966, pp. 600–23.

22 Heller, H. R., 'The demand for money: the evidence from the short-run data', *Quarterly Journal of Economics*, May 1965, pp. 291–303.

23 Johnson, H. G., 'Recent developments in monetary theory: a commentary', in *Money in Britain*, eds. D. R. Croome and H. G. Johnson, Oxford University Press, 1970, pp. 83–114.

24 Kavanagh, N. J. and Walters, A. A., 'Demand for money in the UK 1877–1961: some preliminary findings', *Bulletin of the Oxford University Institute of Economics and Statistics*, May 1966, pp. 93–116.
25 Laidler, David, 'The rate of interest and the demand for money–some empirical evidence', *Journal of Political Economy*, December 1966, pp. 543–55.
26 Laidler, David and Parkin, Michael, 'The demand for money in the United Kingdom 1956–67: preliminary estimates', University of Essex Discussion Paper, unpublished.
27 Latané, H. A., 'Cash balances and the interest rate: a pragmatic approach', *Review of Economics and Statistics*, November 1954.
28 Latané, H. A., 'Income velocity and interest rates: a pragmatic approach', *Review of Economics and Statistics*, November 1960.
29 Lee, T. H., 'Alternative interest rates and the demand for money: the empirical evidence', *American Economic Review*, December 1967, pp. 1168–81.
30 Leeuw, Frank de and Kalchbrenner, John, 'Monetary and fiscal actions: a test of their relative importance in economic stabilisation–comment', *Federal Reserve Bank of St Louis Monthly Review*, April 1969.
31 Meltzer, A. H., 'The demand for money: the evidence from time series', *Journal of Political Economy*, June 1963, pp. 219–46.
32 Motley, Brian, 'A demand-for-money function for the household sector–some preliminary findings', *Journal of Finance*, December 1967, pp. 405–18.
33 Radcliffe Report, *Report of the Committee on the Working of the Monetary System*, Cmnd 827, August 1959, para. 392.
34 Teigen, R. L., 'Demand and supply functions for money in the United States: some structural estimates', *Econometrica*, October 1964, pp. 476–509.
35 Tobin, James, 'The monetary interpretation of history', *American Economic Review*, June 1965, pp. 464–85.

Appendix 2: The Demand for Money and Money Multipliers

The demand for money

Both in the main section and in Appendix 1 a number of issues were raised about the nature of the demand function for money[1] which are crucially important in assessing the role of money in the economy, and which are subject to empirical testing. These were:

(a) the basic predictability of the function
(b) the role of interest rates in the function
(c) the relative importance of long-term and short-term interest rates.

This appendix reports a number of statistical tests of the demand function for money, using quarterly UK data over the period from 1955 to 1969. It begins by considering a very simple model, and examines the empirical implications of modifying it to take account of theoretical refinements.

Perhaps the simplest model of the demand for money is

$$M = a_0 + a_1Y + a_2r + u \tag{1}$$

[1] It is largely optional whether the function is cast in demand-for-money or in velocity form. In fact, if income is included as a determinant of velocity, the two functions would be equivalent when cast in logarithmic form.

where

M = money stock
Y = income
r = some interest rate
u = an error term demonstrating the relationship to be a behavioural one

This single-equation model was estimated using the technique of ordinary least squares. Three definitions of the money stock, and two kinds of interest rate were considered. The results are given in Table B. The precise variables used are:

M_1 Currency and net current account deposits of the London clearing banks[1] (quarterly average of monthly observations), seasonally adjusted, £ million.
M_2 Currency and net deposits of London clearing banks (quarterly average of monthly observations), seasonally adjusted, £ million.
M_3 Currency and net deposits of UK residents with the UK banking sector (end-quarter figures), seasonally adjusted, £ million.[2]
Y Average of the three official estimates of gross domestic product at factor cost, separately derived from output data, expenditure data and income data, seasonally adjusted, £ million. (Before 1958 it was only possible to take the average of income and expenditure-based estimates.)
r_s The ratio of 100 plus the interest rate on three-monthly local authority debt[3] to 100.
r^L The ratio of 100 plus the yield of 2½% Consolidated Stock to 100.

Functions for M_1 and M_2 are estimated for the period including the third quarter of 1955 to the third quarter of 1969; and M_3 for the period including the second quarter of 1963 to the third quarter of 1969.

All the variables have been expressed in logarithmic form. The only departure from usual practice is that the interest-rate variable has been taken as the ratio of future to present value so that an interest rate of 4 per cent is expressed as 104/100 = 1.04.[4] This means that a percentage point change in interest rates is assumed to have much the same effect on the demand for money whether the level of rates is high or low; and so

[1] London clearing bank data were chosen primarily because of limitations in other series. However, it can also be argued that the liabilities of the 'other' banks are significantly less liquid than those of the LCBs, so that their omission would be justified on theoretical grounds. In 1955, almost 90 per cent of UK residents' deposits with the UK banking sector were with the LCBs; in 1969, some 65 per cent.

[2] Data for M_3 were also adjusted for day-of-the-week variations. M_3 is only available on an end-quarter basis, so that observations of this variable are not properly in phase with those of the independent variables in the equation. A half-quarter lag is thus built into the adjustment process. (It was not thought appropriate to average adjacent observations, since this would introduce serial dependence.)

[3] The yield on three-month local authority deposits was chosen in preference to the Treasury bill rate, on the grounds that in recent years the local authority market has attracted a wider range of active participants and has been less dominated by the direct influence of the authorities than has the Treasury bill market. The local authority rate is also somewhat suspect, however, because of the 'thinness' of the market in the early part of the estimation period. (Indeed, the first two observations in the series are not directly available, and have been estimated from changes in other short-term rates.)

[4] The logic of this approach may be seen more easily by considering interest as a measure of the future value of present assets. If the interest rate is 4 per cent, today's £1 will be worth £1.04 a year hence. If the interest rate rises to 5 per cent, the future value of today's £1 has increased by 1/104 (or very nearly 1 per cent) not by 25 per cent.

TABLE B

Estimated forms of equation (1)

Dependent variable	Constant	Nominal income	Interest rate Short	Interest rate Long	Coefficient of determination[a]	Standard error of estimate[b]	Durbin–Watson statistic[c]
M_1 (nominal)	4.57	0.47 (0.02)	0.28 (0.32)		0.959	0.0244	0.30
	4.40	0.50 (0.03)		−0.36 (0.79)	0.959	0.0245	0.28
M_2 (nominal)	3.34	0.66 (0.01)	0.78 (0.26)		0.987	0.0196	0.35
	3.50	0.64 (0.03)		1.31 (0.66)	0.986	0.0204	0.26
M_3 (nominal)	−1.50	1.22 (0.06)	−0.45 (0.46)		0.983	0.0168	0.93
	−0.75	1.13 (0.08)		0.58 (0.95)	0.982	0.0170	0.84

Note: Standard errors of the estimated coefficients are shown in parentheses.

[a] $\bar{R}^2$, the coefficient of determination adjusted for degrees of freedom.
[b] The standard error of the observed value of the dependent variable from its estimated value.
[c] This is a measure of serial correlation in the residuals (see footnote 2 on page 45). In general, the closer the statistic is to a value of 2, the greater the confidence with which the hypothesis of serial correlation can be rejected.

differs from the more conventional formulation, where the logarithm of the interest rate itself is used. A disadvantage of this latter approach is that it implicitly regards the conceptual floor to interest rates as being zero, and so cannot admit negative rates of return. However, to simplify comparison with other published work, elasticities have also been calculated on the conventional basis.[1]

Clearly the estimates shown in Table B suggest that the simplest formulation of the demand-for-money function is inadequate. It is true that the coefficients of determination are high and the income-elasticity of demand for money–though a little low for M_1 and M_2 in comparison with other studies–is not altogether implausible[2] but these results can be accounted for by common trends in the variables. More disturbing are the perverse signs on the interest-rate variables, and the strong evidence of first-order serial correlation in the residuals as indicated by the very low values of the Durbin–Watson statistic. It therefore seems likely that this simple model mis-specifies the demand-for-money function in one or more important ways.

[1] The equations reported in this appendix were also estimated using logarithms of the interest rates, i.e. log r rather than log $(1+r)$. The elasticities computed on this basis were very similar to those reported in Table D, and there was little change in the fit of the equations or in the significance of the estimated interest-rate coefficients.

[2] Most studies using US data have found the income-elasticity of demand for money to be in the range 1.0–1.5.

Lagged adjustment

One possible source of specification error is the implicit assumption in this simple model that adjustment to equilibrium is achieved within a single time period (in this case, one quarter). This seems unduly restrictive, for it may take time for money holders to become aware of changed external circumstances, and accordingly to rearrange their asset portfolios. A lagged process of adjustment to equilibrium suggests a two-equation model, defining not only the equilibrium relationship, but also the adjustment mechanism. One such model is:

$$M_t^* = a_0 + a_1 Y_t + a_2 r_t + u_t \quad (2)$$

$$M_t = M_{t-1} + b(M_t^* - M_{t-1}) + v_t \quad (3)$$

where M^* = desired (or equilibrium) money balances–all the other variables being defined as before–and b is a constant representing the average proportion of the discrepancy between actual and equilibrium money balances eliminated during a quarter. Combining equations (2) and (3) the following reduced form is obtained:

$$M_t = ba_0 + \mathrm{b}a_1 Y_t + \mathrm{b}a_2 r_t + (1 - b)\, M_{t-1} + w_t \quad (4)$$

where $w_t = bu_t + v_t$, a composite error term.

This equation was estimated using the earlier definitions of money stock and interest rates, and the results are presented in Table C.

The properties of these estimated equations are considerably better than those shown in Table B. The coefficients on interest rates have the right sign, the fit of the

TABLE C

Estimated forms of equation (4)

Dependent variable	Estimated coefficients of: Constant	Nominal income	Interest rate Short	Interest rate Long	Lagged dependent variable	Coefficient of determination	Standard error of estimate	Durbin–Watson statistic
M_1 (nominal)	−0.05	0.05 (0.02)	−0.77 (0.14)		0.96 (0.05)	0.994	0.0093	1.75
	0.03	0.12 (0.03)		−1.61 (0.32)	0.89 (0.05)	0.994	0.0097	1.76
M_2 (nominal)	0.29	0.10 (0.03)	−0.20 (0.10)		0.87 (0.04)	0.998	0.0067	1.31
	0.11	0.12 (0.02)		−0.73 (0.22)	0.89 (0.04)	0.999	0.0063	1.60
M_3 (nominal)	−0.54	0.24 (0.14)	−0.58 (0.25)		0.83 (0.11)	0.995	0.0092	2.03
	−0.47	0.17 (0.14)		−0.91 (0.58)	0.89 (0.13)	0.994	0.0097	2.13

Note: Standard errors of the estimated coefficients are shown in parentheses.

TABLE D

Interest-elasticities

	r_s		r_L	
	Short-run	Long-run	Short-run	Long-run
M_1	−0.04	−1.05	−0.09	−0.80
M_2	−0.01	−0.09	−0.04	−0.35
M_3[a]	−0.03	−0.21	−0.06	−0.51

Note: Since the interest-elasticity, under this definition, is not constant in equation (4), its value has been calculated at the mean value of the interest rate.

[a] As data for M_3 are end-quarter, the 'short' run refers to a slightly different period than for M_1 and M_2.

function is better, and the standard error is reduced. Although the Durbin–Watson statistic has a different distribution where an equation contains a lagged dependent variable, it is possible to adjust for this. When this is done, it is clear that in all cases serial correlation has been markedly reduced (though it is still present).[1]

The implied long and short-run interest-elasticities using the conventional definition of elasticity[2] are given in Table D. These elasticities are well within the range of values reported in the survey of empirical evidence in Appendix 1, and they suggest that the experience of the UK has not been markedly different from that of the USA in this respect.

Standard errors of estimate (expressed as percentages) are lowest for the broader definition of money, M_2, though the absolute size of the error is not much different because, of course, M_2 is larger than M_1. There is little to choose between the explanatory power of short and long rates; but whichever is used, its statistical significance is usually much the same as that of the income variable.

Although the equations in Table C gave quite satisfactory results,[3] the lagged adjustment model embodies a number of theoretical assumptions which can be questioned. Changes in income are implicitly assumed to have the same effect on the demand for money whether they result from changes in real output or in prices. As mentioned in the main section,[4] there are plausible reasons for expecting real money

[1] See J. Durbin, 'Testing for serial correlation in least squares regressions when some of the regressors are lagged dependent variables', *Econometrica*, May 1970. The Durbin two-stage test was also applied, and produced results very favourable to the hypothesis of partial adjustment rather than serial correlation.

[2] See page 57.

[3] As noted in Appendix 1, a more searching test of the strength of a relationship where trends are present is its explanatory power when the variables are transformed into first differences. The equations presented in Tables B and C were therefore estimated in first-difference form. None of the results of these tests could be taken as contradicting the results obtained using levels of the data, but neither do they provide strong confirmation. Coefficients of determination were uniformly low, with a maximum of $\bar{R}^2=0.22$. The short-term interest rate was always more significant than the long-term rate, giving some support to the hypothesis that money is more substitutable for short-term than for other assets.

[4] Page 22.

balances to increase either faster than real incomes, if money is considered a 'luxury good', or slower than incomes, if there are economies of scale in cash management; but there is no sound reason for expecting a change in the price level or a change in population size to have an effect on the equilibrium money/income ratio. This line of reasoning suggests that the appropriate formulation of the demand-for-money equation is one which explains real *per capita* money balances in terms of real *per capita* incomes. It is quite a simple matter to adapt the variables in equation (4) to take account of this. Thus money and incomes are each divided by np, where n is the adult population of the UK (obtained by interpolation of annual population estimates[1] and p is the price level (the GDP deflator).[2] The results of the equations run in real *per capita* terms are given in Table E.

TABLE E

Estimated forms of equation (4) in real *per capita* terms

Dependent variable	Estimated coefficients of: Constant	Real *per capita* income	Interest rate: Short	Interest rate: Long	Lagged dependent variable	Coefficient of determination	Standard error of estimate	Durbin–Watson statistic
$\frac{M_1}{np}$	0.30	0.06 (0.03)	−0.80 (0.16)		0.89 (0.04)	0.940	0.0116	1.78
	0.27	0.14 (0.04)		−1.82 (0.35)	0.83 (0.04)	0.941	0.0115	1.73
$\frac{M_2}{np}$	0.65	0.09 (0.02)	−0.21 (0.14)		0.80 (0.05)	0.908	0.0096	1.60
	0.45	0.14 (0.03)		−0.76 (0.28)	0.79 (0.04)	0.915	0.0092	1.69
$\frac{M_3}{np}$	−0.83	0.29 (0.23)	−0.59 (0.32)		0.89 (0.14)	0.966	0.0110	2.16
	−0.46	0.18 (0.23)		−0.63 (0.71)	0.92 (0.16)	0.962	0.0116	2.06

Note: Standard errors of the estimated coefficients are shown in parentheses.

[1] The population over 15 years of age was chosen as the series which most closely approximated the number of potential independent money-holding units. Total population includes children, who will in general not hold money, and working population excludes pensioners, who probably are significant money holders. A more appropriate series might have been the numbers of households, but data are not available.

[2] The choice of this deflator follows immediately from the fact that we have been working with GDP as our income estimate. As there is no separate deflator for income-based GDP, nor a quarterly deflator for output-based GDP, it follows that p is derived from the GDP estimates made from the expenditure side.

Somewhat surprisingly, these estimates are rather worse[1] than those presented in Table C, but the reason is not far to seek. Deflating both money and income by prices implies not only that the demand for money is homogeneous in prices in the long run but also in the short run. In other words, this last set of estimated equations implies that the demand for money will adjust almost immediately to an increase in aggregate money incomes due to a rise in population or in the price level, but only after a long time lag will it adjust to a rise in real *per capita* incomes. The fact that the estimated equations in Table E have higher standard errors of estimate than those of Table C suggests that this assumption is unjustified.

TABLE F

Estimated forms of equation (5)

	Estimated coefficients of:								
				Interest rate					
Dependent variable	Constant	Real *per capita* income	Price	Short	Long	Lagged dependant variable	Coefficient of determination	Standard error of estimate	Durbin-Watson statistic
$\frac{M_1}{n}$	0.11	−0.02	0.07	−0.82		1.02	0.990	0.0096	1.78
		(0.09)	(0.04)	(0.16)		(0.07)			
	0.11	0.07	0.14		−1.74	0.93	0.990	0.0099	1.82
		(0.09)	(0.05)		(0.36)	(0.07)			
$\frac{M_2}{n}$	0.26	0.07	0.10	−0.21		0.90	0.998	0.0070	1.26
		(0.05)	(0.04)	(0.11)		(0.05)			
	0.22	0.06	0.13		−0.87	0.92	0.998	0.0064	1.62
		(0.05)	(0.04)		(0.24)	(0.04)			
$\frac{M_3}{n}$	0.62	0.09	0.37	−0.49		0.81	0.995	0.0091	1.96
		(0.23)	(0.19)	(0.27)		(0.11)			
	1.08	−0.04	0.38		−0.83	0.86	0.994	0.0093	2.11
		(0.22)	(0.20)		(0.57)	(0.12)			

Note: Standard errors of the estimated coefficients are shown in parentheses.

It therefore seems appropriate to allow for a gradual adjustment to price changes. Since it was argued earlier that the effect of a change in real incomes may be different from the effect of a change in prices, the price level was included as a separate explanatory variable. The estimated equations when this is done are set out in Table F. In principle, population might also be included as an additional independent variable, but there is little theoretical justification for expecting lagged adjustment in the case of the population variable.[2] Thus in Table F, money and income are expressed in *per capita* terms, namely:

$$\left(\frac{M}{n}\right)_t = \mathrm{b}a_0 + ba_1\left(\frac{Y}{np}\right)_t + ba_2r_t + ba_3p_t + (1-\mathrm{b})\left(\frac{m}{n}\right)_{t-1} + w_t \qquad (5)$$

[1] Not only are the coefficients of determination lower (this could be explained by the lower initial variance in the dependent variable), but the standard errors of estimate are larger.

[2] Additions to the population will not affect the behaviour of existing money holders; nor are they likely to 'adjust gradually to their own existence'.

For the first two definitions of the money stock, Table F shows rather less satisfactory results than Table C; standard errors of estimate are greater. This is a little surprising, for the only changes introduced that would have any effect on the standad errors are the separate specification of price and real income as explanatory variables and the specification of income and money holdings in *per capita* terms. The first change would if anything tend to reduce the standard errors if the effects of prices and real incomes differ; indeed, it is evident from new estimates of equation (5) with money and real incomes no longer expressed in *per capita* terms that it is the latter adjustment which has caused most of the deterioration. This result casts doubt on the assumption that the demand for money is homogeneous in population, but it is also possible that the population series used is inappropriate.[1] Failing a more appropriate series, it seems preferable to use totals of money and of incomes, at least with regard to the relatively short time-series we are using.

The estimated coefficient of the real income variable in equation (5) is never statistically significant,[2] though for the price variable it is significant, or nearly so, and has the expected positive sign. But there is some degree of collinearity between the price and real income variables (the simple correlation coefficient is 0.972) so that not much can be read into these results. Furthermore, the implied long-run price elasticity is in some cases implausibly high, suggesting that the estimates are attributing to the price variable some of the effect on money holdings that should properly be accounted for by real incomes.

Models which included interest-rate differentials and the annual rates of change in prices of goods and services as explanatory variables were also tested. The interest-rate differential employed was the interest rate on three months' local authority deposits minus Bank Rate.[3] The estimated coefficient of this variable was statistically significant and of the expected negative sign when it was the only interest-rate variable appearing in the equation; but when included with the level of the local authority rate, multicollinearity was encountered, and implausible results were obtained. The rate of change of prices was included as a measure of the relative return on real as against financial assets.[4] The estimated coefficients attaching to this variable were rarely significant and the results obtained are not presented here.

All the results presented so far have indicated the importance of time lags, but little attention has been paid to the precise nature of the lag. An exponential adjustment mechanism has been used, but, while computationally easy, it is not necessarily the correct specification. It implies that a constant proportion of any disequilibrium will be eliminated in a given time period, irrespective of:

(a) the source of the disequilibrium
(b) the size of the disequilibrium.

If the reason for time lags is the existence of transactions costs associated with compositional changes in a portfolio, there is no reason to expect the speed of adjustment to be influenced by the *source* of the initial disequilibrium. But the speed

[1] The sharp post-war rise in births led to a rapid increase in the adult population in the early 1960s – a period not included in the data used to estimate the equations for M_3. It seems plausible to suppose that this rapidly increasing younger proportion of the population held less money than the average for the adult population as a whole.

[2] As throughout this work, 'statistically significant' is intended to imply that the estimated coefficient is significantly different from zero at the 5 per cent probability level. In other words, the estimated value is not attributable to sampling fluctuations.

[3] Bank Rate was used as a proxy for the interest rate paid on deposit accounts.

[4] Inflation would tend to make real assets more attractive than financial, and thus cause a switch out of money, though it could also be argued that rising prices would generate expectations of rising interest rates and thus cause a switch into money.

of adjustment might well be influenced by the *size* of the disequilibrium.

It is not necessary, however, to attribute the presence of time lags wholly to transactions costs. Indeed, it would seem more likely that transactions costs were relatively low in financial markets. A more plausible explanation might be that people take time to become aware that changes in incomes and interest rates made revisions in their money holding habits appropriate.[1] If these 'awareness' or 'inertia' lags are important, then it is not clear that the speed of adjustment can be regarded as invariant to the source of the disequilibrium. In other words, people may become aware of changes in their real income faster, or slower, than they become aware of changes in the price level or in interest rates.

All this implies a much more complex model incorporating a separate pattern of adjustment for each independent variable; but the estimation of such a model raises a number of problems. Unlike a common exponential adjustment lag, which can be simply estimated by taking into account lagged values of the dependent variables, a variety of lags would make the equation over-identified unless restrictions were placed on the values of the coefficients of the variables. Using exponential lags, different speeds of adjustment could be assumed to apply to different explanatory variables in the hope of finding some unique combination of lags which gave the best results. Alternatively, the Almon technique[2] could be employed, and a finite lag structure estimated for each variable.

Money multipliers

Although it is clearly of considerable importance to understand the factors governing the demand for money, the estimation of a demand-for-money equation does not immediately provide any indication of the response of an economy to changes in the money stock.

In this connection, it is more relevant to consider relationships where income is the dependent variable, and money the explanatory variable. Despite the many shortcomings of such a highly simplified approach, which are discussed in more detail in the main section and in Appendix 1,[3] it may be of interest to see whether such an approach provides any general indications about the strength and predictability of the relationship between the money stock and income levels.

Using the same data and definitions as in the earlier part of this appendix, two separate models were tested:

$$Y_t = a_0 + a_1 M_t + a_2 Y_{t-1} + u_t \quad (6)$$
$$Y_t = a_0 + a_1 M_t + a_2 M_{t-1} + \ldots + a_8 M_{t-7} + v_t \quad (7)$$

Both these equations were subject to very severe multicollinearity problems when estimated in levels, and little confidence could be attached to the results obtained. Using first differences of the data, no role for money could be detected in the estimated form of equation (6), which embodies an exponential adjustment lag. As a result attention was concentrated on equation (7).

---

[1] It should be remembered that three-quarters of clearing bank deposits are held by the personal sector, and 'persons' may well be slow to adapt to changes in interest rates.

[2] Shirley Almon, 'The distributed lag between capital appropriations and expenditures', *Econometrica*, January 1965.

[3] See pages 39, 49.

TABLE G

Estimated first-difference forms of equation (7)

Money series	Constant	Estimated coefficients of: ΔM_0	ΔM_{-1}	ΔM_{-2}	ΔM_{-3}	ΔM_{-4}	ΔM_{-5}	ΔM_{-6}	ΔM_{-7}	Estimated money multiplier[a]	Coefficient of determination	Standard error of estimate	Durbin–Watson statistic
Dependent variable–GDP													
M_1 (1957 II–1969 III)	77.1		0.42 (0.15)	−0.38 (0.16)	0.40 (0.15)		0.33 (0.15)	−0.27 (0.15)		0.50	0.216	70.6	2.69
	suppressed	0.35 (0.17)	0.28 (0.18)		0.49 (0.15)		0.63 (0.17)	−0.39 (0.20)	0.45 (0.18)	1.81	0.565	83.7	2.17
M_2 (1957 II–1969 III)	64.6	0.25 (0.14)					(0.37) (0.17)	−0.29 (0.16)		0.33	0.086	76.1	2.72
	suppressed	0.34 (0.12)			0.27 (0.15)		0.49 (0.16)	−0.45 (0.19)	0.27 (0.16)	0.92	0.629	77.3	2.47
M_3 (1964 III–1969 III)	91.7			0.19 (0.13)	−0.36 (0.13)	0.27 (0.13)		[b]	[b]	0.10	0.343	73.9	2.79
	suppressed			0.28 (0.11)	−0.31 (0.12)	0.32 (0.12)	0.20 (0.11)	[b]	[b]	0.49	0.742	74.4	2.54

Dependent variable–industrial output													
M_1 (1953 II–1969 III)	21.9	0.11 (0.05)	0.17 (0.05)	0.15 (0.06)		0.12 (0.06)				0.55	0.276	37.0	1.82
	suppressed	0.14 (0.06)	0.22 (0.06)	0.18 (0.06)	0.12 (0.06)	0.15 (0.06)	0.09 (0.06)			0.90	0.588	39.0	1.64
M_2 (1953 II–1969 III)	14.9		0.22 (0.06)		0.10 (0.07)					0.32	0.212	38.6	1.53
	suppressed	0.09 (0.07)	0.22 (0.07)		0.14 (0.06)					0.45	0.585	39.1	1.49
M_3 (1964 III–1969 IV)	−57.0	0.08 (0.06)	0.09 (0.05)	0.23 (0.06)		0.12 (0.06)		[b]	[b]	0.53	0.516	34.2	1.46
	suppressed		0.07 (0.05)	0.20 (0.05)				[b]	[b]	0.27	0.772	36.3	1.51

Note: Standard errors of the estimated coefficients are shown in parentheses.

[a] The sum of the estimated coefficients of ΔM_0 to ΔM_{-7}, measuring the expected effect of a change in the money stock during the first eight quarters from its occurrence.

[b] Theses variables were not included in the estimation.

This was estimated in two forms: with and without a constant term.[1] All variables whose estimated coefficients were not significantly different from zero at the 20 per cent probability level were excluded. In addition to the series for GDP used in the estimation of the demand-for-money functions reported earlier in this appendix, a variable attempting to measure the output of the industrial sector of the economy was used–consisting of the index of industrial production converted to current prices by the wholesale price index.[2] The estimates of all these equations are given in Table G. Both in terms of the coefficients of determination and of the shape of the lag-profiles, the industrial output variable performs much better than the GDP measure. This suggests that money may have a closer association with industrial activity than with other sectors of the economy–private and government services and agriculture.

The 'official' definition of the money stock, M_3, appears to give the best explanation of changes in output whichever output measure is used, but this may be due to the fact that the data for M_3 cover a rather shorter time period, during which there may have been a chance stability in the relationship. It will be recalled that M_3 performed no better than M_1 and M_2 in the estimates of the demand-for-money functions reported earlier.

In those equations in Table G where the constant term is suppressed, the estimated coefficients of the independent variables are generally increased, because some of the influence of the (normally positive) constant term is being attributed to them, and so the estimates of the long-run money multiplier tend to be larger.[3] Without a convincing explanation of what determines the size of the constant term, it is impossible to say which of the two estimates of the long-run multiplier is the more accurate. Indeed, the possibility cannot be dismissed that the apparent connection between changes in money and changes in output is merely a reflection of cyclical influences acting on both variables, with no direct causal connection.

[1] The transformation of equation (7) into first-difference form does not yield a constant term. The existence of a non-zero constant term would imply that income would rise (or fall) at a steady rate if the money stock were unchanged.

[2] The resulting series was expressed in £ million.

[3] The coefficients of determination of equations estimated with and without the constant term should not be compared directly.

II

Bank of England Studies of the Demand-for-Money Function

1. Introduction

Much of the econometric work undertaken in the Bank of England during the years 1969–74 has concentrated on the demand-for-money function. There have been three papers in the *Bank of England Quarterly Bulletin* specifically on this subject, by Goodhart and Crockett[**14**] by Price [**26**] and by Hacche[**17**].[1] Several other research papers have been on cognate topics. For example, there have been two papers on the timing (lead/lag) relationships between monetary aggregates and various expenditure series, the first by Crockett[**10**] and the second by Goodhart, Gowland and Williams[**15**]. Also there was a study on the substitutability among various capital-certain assets, examined within a portfolio adjustment model, which was started by Latter and Price, who reported on this work at the 1971 meeting of the Association of University Teachers of Economics, and carried to completion by Townend in a paper presented to the Econometric Society meeting at Budapest in 1972 and summarised in [**28**]. Although the econometric research work undertaken in the Bank has been by no means limited exclusively to studies on the demand-for-money function (or very closely related issues) – there have, to take an example, been a number of papers on the determinants of the shape of the yield curve by Burman[**7**], Burman and White[**8/9**] and Hamburger[**19**] – nevertheless it has formed a continuing focus for research work.

Although the main subject of this paper concerns these econometric studies, it is not the intention here to repeat, to criticise, or to extend the econometrics involved. Rather, it is the purpose of this paper to try to show how this research fitted into the wider context of the work of the Bank, to suggest why it was undertaken, how the results were incorporated and used both in forecasting and policy-making, and how the relationships apparently revealed in the econometric studies have met the tests of experience in the changing conditions beyond the initial estimation period.

The build-up of research on monetary relationships, in particular into demand-for-money functions, began in the Bank in 1969, soon after the Economic Section had been established. The background and circumstances that led to this development of research activity, a relatively novel undertaking for the Bank, are broadly outlined in section 2 of this Chapter. The main

[1] References are to be found on pages 89–90.

intellectual stimulus came from the previous work done in this field, much of it under the guidance of Professor Friedman, in the USA. The main practical incentive came from our experience with the adoption of domestic credit expansion (DCE) targets in 1969 in the effort to bring the balance of payments back into surplus after the 1967 devaluation.

The early research studies on demand-for-money functions (Goodhart/Crockett and Price), which appeared to show a fairly stable relationship between money holdings and current and previous incomes and interest rates, helped to dissipate the previous pessimism that financial markets were so fickle, and susceptible in the short term to the wayward play of extrapolative expectations, that control of the monetary aggregates through normal market mechanisms would be impracticable. Moreover, such stable functions might, it was hoped, provide a somewhat firmer guide for policy than had been available when credit ceilings were the main policy instrument. So this research provided an intellectual framework, a supporting rationale, for the major change of policy in 1971, with the adoption of Competition and Credit Control.[1] Admittedly, with the practical disadvantages of ceilings for the efficient working of the banking system becoming increasingly burdensome, there would have been strong pressures in any case to lift ceilings, at least for a period, at this point of time. But the reforms involved in Competition and Credit Control went much further than that, representing a strategic shift from concern with bank lending to the private sector and with the use of direct controls to limit and channel its flow to the various parts of the private sector towards more emphasis on the movements of the aggregate money stock and on market operations, undertaken within a freely competitive system, to influence the rate of monetary expansion. These reforms therefore incorporated an intellectual revision about the appropriate direction of monetary policy; the research undertaken in the Bank played some part in bringing about that revision.

Subsequent experience with the attempt to use demand-for-money functions as a guide for policy is described and assessed in section 3 of this chapter. This attempt was largely vitiated by the failure to find significant and robust relationships between financial factors and expenditures, with the private housing sector proving the main exception. It has not been possible to discern clearly in the UK the effect on the economy of altering the rate of expansion of the monetary aggregates. Nor has it been possible to pinpoint very accurately the effect of interest-rate variations on international capital flows. Yet despite the uncertainty about the strength of monetary effects, there are reasons to believe that they might, if pushed at all far, prove quite powerful. Given a potentially powerful but unpredictable instrument the tendency is to play for safety, so that supposedly more reliable instruments, e.g. fiscal policy, have been mainly used for macroeconomic demand-

[1] The change of policy takes its name from the discussion paper on *Competition and Credit Control*, issued by the Bank in May 1971.

management adjustments, leaving monetary policy to be generally accommodating.

As well as a guide for policy, the demand-for-money functions might in theory be used as an indicator, between policy reviews, of current economic developments. In practice, however, the relative infrequency[1] and erratic nature of the monetary observations prevent this. But, in any case, several of the monetary series, the broader series containing interest-bearing deposits and certificates of deposit (CDs), began to depart significantly from their predicted paths, given the developments of incomes and interest rates, shortly after the change to Competition and Credit Control. The reasons for this, not entirely unexpected, divergence from the previous pattern are explored in section 4.

The clearing bank cartel had pegged their rates on bank deposits and on lending in relation to Bank Rate up till 1971, and this had held *relative* interest rates roughly constant. After 1971, however, the clearing banks were free and encouraged to compete. As a result, interest rates on bank deposits were raised *relative* to rates on other instruments, and also relative to rates on bank advances. This had a powerful effect in stimulating a rapid expansion in both interest-bearing deposits and bank advances.

An alternative explanation, which has been advocated by some commentators, for the break-down of the demand-for-(broad) money functions after 1971 is that this was due to an excessive supply of money forcing money holders into a disequilibrium position. The question of how to ascertain the direction of causation between movements in the money stock and in money incomes is considered in section 5. There are *prima facie* reasons for believing that the direction of causation could have altered after 1971, with monetary changes having a greater effect on money incomes than formerly. Reasons are advanced for preferring the explanation of the change of behaviour in terms of relative interest rates, as described in section 4, but the two explanations are not mutually exclusive, and the increase in bank advances after 1971, especially the surge in lending for property development, could well have been responsible for certain disequilibria in the economy.

Finally, there is a short section (section 6) which attempts to provide a summary of the role of research in the guidance of policy.

2. Background to the Research

Undoubtedly the main stimulus to research into the demand-for-money function in the UK was the example of American work in this field. Friedman[**11**] redefined the quantity theory as a theory of the demand for

[1] In the UK banking statistics are reported on the third Wednesday of each month, the 'make-up' day, and at end-quarters. In comparison in the USA the authorities work mainly on the basis of weekly figures, which are themselves constructed from averages of daily figures.

money. If the demand for money was a predictable function of a few key variables, then variations in the money stock should have a determinate effect upon the economy. Furthermore, the work of Friedman and Schwartz[**13**], Friedman and Meiselman[**12**] and Andersen and Jordan[**1**] suggested that monetary disturbances had a more pervasive and stronger impact on the economy than fiscal policies or variations in other autonomous expenditures. This latter view, that monetary policy was more potent than fiscal policy, was vigorously challenged by other economists in the USA, but virtually no one disputed that monetary conditions did seem, in the USA at least, to have a major impact on the general level of demand. Moreover, the experience in the USA of the credit crunch in 1966–7 and the failure of the tax surcharge in 1968 to dampen the economy as much as expected gave further support to the propositions of the monetarists.

In the face of this example there was a strong incentive to see whether the American results could be replicated with UK data. This exercise produced a rather mixed outcome. As reported in Goodhart and Crockett[**14,** p. 167]:

> Most of the statistical work of this kind [on the demand-for-money function] has been done using data from the United States, but the results of similar studies using UK data give broadly confirmatory results, though there seems, perhaps, some tendency for the estimated stability of the relationships and the statistical significance of the coefficients to be slightly less. Considering, however, that these studies cover a number of differing periods and employ a range of alternative variables, the main results of these exercises show a fair similarity and constancy in both the United States and the United Kingdom.

Thus the demand-for-money function, in the UK as in the USA, seemed to exhibit a reasonable degree of stability, which held out a promise that controlling the monetary aggregate might have a significant and determinate effect upon the economy. Yet in another respect the empirical evidence available in the UK gave results which were at variance with those obtained in the USA. In the USA money multiplier equations, e.g. those run by Andersen and Jordan[**1**] and by Laffer and Ranson[**22**], showed that current movements in money incomes could be explained quite well by current and past changes in the money stock – together with a few additional variables which had a significant but quantitatively less important effect. Despite the simplicity of these single equations, they fitted sufficiently well to be used for forecasting, in competition with the forecasts produced by the much more comprehensive Keynesian models and also with the computer-assisted judgemental forecasts.

This was not the case in the UK. The statistical relationship between movements in GDP and current and previous changes in the money stock has been quite weak. The relationship became somewhat stronger when the dependent variable was changed from GDP to a variable attempting to measure the output of the industrial sector of the economy – consisting of the index of industrial production converted to current prices by the wholesale price index (see [**14**, pp. 197–8]). Nevertheless, the correlation remained quite low, and given as well the shortness of the estimation period, the difficulties of clearly establishing the appropriate lag profile, etc., this technique did not seem to offer much promise as a forecasting technique or as a simple policy guide. Furthermore, a direct replication of the Andersen/ Jordan experiment by Artis and Nobay[**2**] came up with the opposite conclusion, that in the UK fiscal policies seemed to have a more potent effect on the economy than monetary policies, though none of the relationships seemed robust.

The most obvious explanation of these somewhat conflicting results was that they arose from the differing circumstances of the two economies, with the USA being virtually a closed economy while the UK is an open economy, then maintaining a fixed exchange rate. Thus in the USA a monetary disturbance would have to work its way fully through the domestic economy, while in the UK the effects of a monetary disturbance could largely spill over into the balance of payments. Yet in a way this external, balance-of-payments, dimension to monetary policy introduced yet another strand among the interwoven factors leading us to pay more attention to the monetary aggregates.

In the aftermath of the 1967 devaluation the authorities followed, albeit only after some delay, the standard Keynesian policy recipes for making a devaluation effective: two consecutive, severely restrictive budgets in 1968 and 1969 and relatively attractive (at least on an uncovered basis) interest rates. Yet for an unconscionable lapse of time the devaluation did not appear to be effective in improving the current account.[1] It was argued, notably by the monetary theorists at the International Monetary Fund, in particular by Polak, that a contributory factor, at least, in the relative failure of the British devaluation to work as intended was the continued rapid domestic credit expansion (DCE) in the UK in 1967–8 and 1968–9. In this view excessive credit expansion at home led, initially, to surplus monetary balances, which would then be adjusted in some part by purchases of foreign goods and assets.

In a sense the argument for adopting a DCE target rather than trying to select an 'appropriate' interest rate in order to maintain external balance is analogous to the argument for preferring some quantitative monetary target to choosing an 'appropriate' interest rate for the pursuit of internal, domestic objectives. In the face of varying, and unobservable, expectations of future inflation, etc., and of unpredictable fluctuations in the pressure of demand, it is not possible to select an 'appropriate' interest rate, either for external or

[1] The delay in the improvement of the visible trade statistics was partly due to a bureaucratic lacuna, for a sizeable volume of exports in 1968 and 1969 was later found to have been leaving the country unrecorded.

internal purposes. So long as one can be reasonably confident that there will not be major fluctuations in liquidity preference, or that the authorities will be in a position to forestall those that do occur, then the adoption of a quantitative target should allow greater accuracy and stability in the pursuit of the authorities' macroeconomic objectives than fixing interest rates.

In any case the pressure of events, resulting from continued external weakness, forced the authorities, willy-nilly, to adopt a DCE target in 1969–70. Although the improvement in the balance of trade in the summer and autumn of 1969 cannot plausibly be ascribed to the concurrent slower growth of DCE, the tight domestic monetary conditions did contribute to the sizeable capital inflow that then resulted as soon as confidence in the UK's trade position perked up. In that limited sense the adoption of the DCE target was a success.

A DCE target is specifically tailored to the achievement of a balance-of-payments objective. When external problems eased in late 1969 and 1970, there was a tendency to turn towards other monetary indicators as a guide to the appropriate policy for achieving domestic internal objectives. Given the relative success of using DCE as a policy target, the natural switch was to turn to other monetary aggregates as a guide for domestic monetary policy, in particular to turn to the various money stock definitions, as set out in [**6**].

The alternative to a quantitative target is usually taken to be an interest-rate target. Yet it would be a gross simplification to state that before 1969 the authorities had an interest-rate target, or that since that date they have had a pure quantitative target. Certainly the Bank's short-term market tactics have reflected a concern with the efficient working operations of the gilt-edged market. As the Chief Cashier, J.B. Page, noted in the Sykes Memorial Lecture, November 1971[**25**]:

> The Bank first entered the gilt-edged market in order to improve the efficiency and smoothness with which they discharge this function [of financing the needs of the government] selling one or two new securities and buying in those approaching maturity. Gradually the Bank became willing to deal in a wider range of securities because by so doing it appeared possible to improve the effectiveness of their operations. At the same time, in the late 1950s and early 1960s, smoothing out the fluctuations in interest rates which market forces tended to bring about had come to seem an appropriate objective... Some time before the reappraisal of monetary policy which led up to *Competition and Credit Control* had been completed, the conclusion had been reached that the Bank's operations in the gilt-edged market should pay more regard to their quantitative effects on the monetary aggregates and less regard to the behaviour of interest rates. In application of this conclusion, the Bank's tactics in the gilt-edged market became much more flexible in respect of both the techniques they employed and the prices at which they were prepared to deal.

Towards the end of the 1960s the authorities' by then increasing concern to operate more effectively to control DCE was, however, still restrained by their fears about the possible impact of aggressive operations on the working of the gilt market. As stated in a paper on the operation of monetary policy presented by the Bank in 1969[**5**]:

> Because the market response to a moderate price change for gilt-edged has been found to be unstable and often perverse in the short term, the movement of interest rates required to achieve adequate liquidity absorption through debt operations may be so large that a rapid or seemingly arbitrary adjustment could permanently damage the willingness of investors to hold gilt-edged, compounding the difficulties of monetary management in the future... In short, official operations in gilt-edged continue to be constrained both by the underlying market situation and by long-term concern for the maintenance of a broad market. For much of the ten-year period [1959–69] the circumstances required more severe restraint on credit than could be achieved by acting on liquidity and ratios. It was therefore necessary to have recourse to direct forms of control – the imposition of lending ceilings.

It was not, therefore, that the authorites were unconcerned about the rate of growth of the monetary aggregates, or held some firmly preconceived idea about the appropriate level of interest rates. It was rather that they were pessimistic about their ability to control the aggregates by open-market operations, and expected that the likely consequence of any such attempt would be large movements in interest rates with little predictable effect on credit expansion. They therefore felt driven to rely more and more on physical controls to restrain credit expansion.

The research on demand-for-money functions within the Bank played some role in dissipating this state of interest-rate pessimism. In so far as the demand for money has a stable and predictable inverse relationship with interest rates, it would seem to imply that an increase in rates by the authorities would have a determinate effect on the money stock, whether the counterpart on the asset side of the banks' balance sheets was a (relative) reduction in advances or in holdings of public-sector debt. Furthermore, by concentrating on the relationship between the aggregate money stock, incomes and interest rates, the thrust of this research pointed towards a policy of controlling the monetary aggregates through market mechanisms and away from the previous policy of controlling a component of domestic credit, i.e. bank lending to the private sector, by physical rationing.

This, somewhat intellectual, impetus towards the structural changes involved in the adoption of Competition and Credit Control coincided with an ever-growing practical awareness and dislike of the severe disadvantages of quasi-permanent ceilings, for temporary ceilings always seem to become quasi-permanent fixtures. The impediment to efficiency and innovation of such ceilings, their tendency to increasing erosion over time as substitute channels are developed, their administrative complications, these disadvantages are all well known. One feature of ceilings control that is, perhaps, less well appreciated is the difficulty of choosing the ceiling number. Since the authorities had little enough ability to estimate what the uncontrolled demand for advances would have been, they had at best an exceedingly imprecise idea of the volume of unsatisfied borrowing cut off by the ceilings. Furthermore, they had virtually no information on the proportion of such unsatisfied borrowing that was being met through other channels. So they could not have any clear view of the quantitative effect of such controls on demand. In such circumstances the choice of ceiling number was, to say the least, somewhat arbitrary. The demand-for-money functions might, it was hoped, give a somewhat firmer guide for monetary policy than that.

Indeed, in the context of these years (1970–1) bank-lending ceilings had become so widely disliked that the authorities would surely have in any case chosen a period of slack in the domestic economy, as occurred in 1971, to relinquish ceiling controls and to prod the banking system towards more competition, even without the current trends in monetary research. Nevertheless the reforms involved wider aspirations and a larger canvas being introduced as a fundamental change of approach. These aspects of Competition and Credit Control, e.g. the greater emphasis on the rate of growth of the monetary aggregates, the reliance on general market mechanisms for credit control, placing more weight on the price mechanism in allocating credit[**24**] especially, were influenced by the general climate of thought on such matters, but in particular by the research work under way in the Bank.

3. Using Demand-for-Money Relationships as a Policy Guide

A DCE target is adopted in order to achieve a desired balance-of-payments objective. Setting the target is fairly straightforward. Given the estimated parameters of the economy, the authorities may reckon that their preferred attainable combination of domestic and external outcomes which can be obtained by manipulation of their policy instruments (e.g. fiscal policy and interest rates) will lead to an increase in incomes of X, and an accretion of reserves of Y, with interest rates of Z per cent. Then the money stock consistent with these estimated income and interest-rate levels can be calculated from the demand-for-money relationship. Subtracting the desired currency inflow from the money supply, for an external surplus requires the authorities to provide sterling in exchange for the foreign exchange tendered to them, then discloses the extent of domestic credit expansion that is consistent with the authorities' objectives.[1] This figure is then taken as the limit below which domestic credit expansion should be restrained. So, if it should transpire that the external balance-of-payments objective is not being met, the ceiling on DCE will force the money stock below the level consistent with the intended income and interest-rate levels, placing upwards pressure on interest rates and downwards pressure on incomes. The subsequent adjustments will then lead to an improvement in the balance of payments via both the capital and current accounts.

Clearly the adoption of a DCE target provides a form of insurance against failure to obtain a desired external surplus. It does this by forcing a deflationary adjustment – via a restriction on the money supply – on the domestic economy, whenever the external objective is not being achieved. This implies placing a larger weight on the achievement of external than of internal objectives.[2] In certain circumstances, as in 1969–70, this relative weighting may be appropriate, but during more normal periods the authorities are likely to place more weight on domestic objectives. Accordingly, once the UK balance of payments had recovered in 1969–70, the emphasis switched from a DCE target towards using movements in the money stock as a guide for policy. This, however, turned out to be much less straightforward. The demand for money is functionally related to income levels (positively) and to interest rates (negatively). So a given level of the money stock can be consistent with a whole set of combinations of incomes and interest rates. One cannot ascertain from the demand-for-money relationship by itself how changes in the money stock will affect money incomes unless one has some idea how monetary disturbances are transmitted through the system, especially since the initial impact of the authorities' open-market operations, influencing the rate of monetary expansion, will fall largely on interest rates.

Money multiplier equations may be tried as a short-cut to trace out the subsequent effect of a monetary change on aggregate incomes but, as already noted, they have not worked with any great success in the UK. In any case the authorities are bound to need a more comprehensive macroeconomic model, in order (for example) to try to assess the composition of expenditures, directional and allocational developments, etc. If the results of the quasi-

[1] 'Put briefly, DCE may be viewed as the total arrived at after adjusting the increase in the money supply to take account of any change in money balances directly caused by an external surplus or deficit. DCE is thus approximately equal to the increase in the money supply plus those sterling funds accruing to the authorities by their provision of foreign exchange, from one source or another, for the accommodation of an external deficit (or, conversely, minus the sterling finance required to accommodate an external surplus)' [**4**, pp. 363–4]. In practice, the relationship between DCE, the money stock and external flow is complicated by the need to take into account the banks' net external position, etc., but such details should not be allowed to obscure the general principles of the approach.

[2] For example, the adoption of a DCE target by a country with an undesirably or unexpectedly high external surplus would force that country to inflate its money stock, *pari passu*. It may, perhaps, be the case that a return to more stable parities might require a general adoption of, and international surveillance over, national DCE targets. But for the time being, with floating exchange rates and with considerations of national autonomy often taking precedence over international co-operation, the usual tendency will be to select more inward-looking monetary objectives.

reduced-form money multiplier do not accord reasonably well with those of the macroeconomic model, there will be doubt about which results (if either) to prefer. In the UK, however, we do not even have the luxury of such a choice. Not only does the money multiplier approach fail to show any very strong relationship, but the traditional extended Keynesian models in use at the Treasury, at the National Institute and at the London Business School [in the versions existing at the time in 1975] incorporate virtually no financial variables.

The private housing sector does provide an exception, but the marked directional bias of monetary policy on private housing represents something of a constraint on the positive use of monetary policy. If the housing market could be made less sensitive, while other forms of expenditure appeared more sensitive to monetary conditions, monetary management would become easier. Apart from housing, consumer-durable purchases can be significantly influenced by changes in hire-purchase (instalment credit) regulations on minimum downpayments and maximum repayment periods, though the effect of such changes wears off over time. For the rest it has proved remarkably difficult to find in econometric work done in the UK significant and robust effects of financial factors on expenditures – most of the tests have examined interest-rate effects, in both nominal and real forms. Certainly several of the routes whereby monetary forces were shown to affect expenditures in the USA in the FRB–MIT model – see, for example, [**23**] – have not been found to have the same force in this country. The impact in the USA of monetary forces on consumption via changes in stock market values fails in the UK at both links. There seems to be no consistent short- or medium-term relationship in the UK between the rate of monetary expansion and stock market indexes [**16**], and the wealth effect on consumption seems more muted in the UK, though the data on personal wealth are so unreliable that it is hard to be confident of the results of such studies. Again the main role of central government policies in determining local authority expenditure in the UK has rendered such expenditures, including the relatively large public-sector housing programmes, almost totally insensitive to interest-rate variations, whereas state and local government expenditures in the USA exhibit some such sensitivity.

It is not now possible in the UK to give a confident answer to the question of what would be the quantitative effect on the economy of altering the rate of expansion of the monetary aggregates. On the one hand, the evidence from the econometric studies of expenditure functions suggests that, apart from the private housing sector (which is furthermore subject to very long lags), monetary effects are weak and unreliable. On the other hand, the demand-for-money functions, having shown a stable relationship with current and past incomes and interest rates, would suggest that positive action to manage the rates of growth of the monetary aggregates would cause some extremely noticeable results, if only on interest rates. Whether the effects on the economy of altering the rate of growth of the monetary aggregates are weak or strong, they are anyhow not now predictable in the UK. This inability to estimate the effects of a monetary policy step contrasts with the relative confidence with which the results of fiscal policy measures are traced through the economy in the extended Keynesian models in use in the UK. In particular, it is not possible to calculate trade-offs between fiscal and monetary measures from these models: the authorities have not been able to calculate combinations of fiscal and monetary policies having the same effect on total expenditures but with differing allocation impacts, because they cannot quantify the effects of monetary measures in the same way that they feel able to calculate the quantitative effect of fiscal measures.

This, naturally, has shaped the conduct of monetary policy in the UK. Given two instruments, one of which is regarded as predictable and reliable, while the other is potentially powerful but unpredictable, the probable consequence will be that the supposedly reliable instrument will be preferred for making the adjustments, holding the other policy instrument in neutral. This is, indeed, basically the course which has been followed in most recent years. Fiscal policy is adjusted in the budget so as to achieve the preferred macroeconomic objectives and then the rate of growth of the monetary aggregates is intended to be consistent with that – an accommodating or passive policy.[1]

It is distinctly unsatisfactory for all those concerned with economic policy, particularly monetary policy, that this lack of confidence in the probable outcome of monetary measures persists. For example, Treasury ministers have often claimed in public how important they believe monetary policy to be, and indeed they are very likely correct in this assessment, *but* the forecasting models actually used in advising them show virtually no role for monetary variables. This condition is not, however, for want of trying to find such a role in econometric research on the expenditure functions. Perhaps we in the Bank could, and should, have done more work ourselves in this field, but it is an area which has been tilled many times by others and our comparative advantage, given the relatively few resources of skilled manpower which could be applied to full-time research, has so far seemed to lie more in delving into relationships within the financial system.

A possible reason for the relative failure to find well-defined monetary effects on domestic expenditures is that in an open economy major segments of the private sector, e.g. large companies and banks, can generally avoid domestic monetary pressures by adjusting their financial position by interna-

[1] On the other hand, fiscal policy is a relatively inflexible instrument. So shocks, especially external shocks, are likely to prompt the authorities to respond by adjusting monetary policy. With the fiscal position determined, this must involve placing the whole weight of adjustment either on direct control of lending, or on debt operations. Whereas the role of monetary policy in general, and of conditions in financial markets in particular, are allotted little attention during the regular policy reviews, nevertheless they may be called on to bear a considerable weight during crises.

tional transfers and transactions. If so, the main effects of monetary policy, even when the authorities are basically concerned with domestic objectives, will fall on the balance of payments. Under a regime of fixed exchange rates the consequential financial flows across the exchanges will result in changes in official reserves, while during a regime of flexible exchange rates such flows will alter these rates, and thereby in turn affect the pattern and total of expenditures. Indeed, in an open economy the main effect of monetary policy on domestic expenditures may be indirect via such exchange-rate movements rather than direct.

Considerable research effort has been applied, notably [**20**], by economists working in the Treasury and the Bank, to studying the determinants of capital flows between the UK and other countries in response to interest-rate differentials, confidence factors, etc. The study of capital flows is, however, complicated, especially in the case of the UK, by changes in institutional conditions, i.e. the numerous changes in exchange-control regulations, by the uncertain vagaries of confidence in sterling, and by structural changes in the international scene, for example the accruing vast surpluses of the oil producers. How, one may well ask, is one to forecast the pattern of international capital flows in view of all these serious disturbances?

We are, nevertheless, a good deal more confident about the considerable significance of domestic monetary conditions for capital flows and the UK's external position than we are about their direct effect on domestic expenditures. Even so, the precise effect of domestic monetary conditions, whether expressed in terms of interest rates or of monetary expansion, on capital flows (and on flexible exchange rates) cannot be accurately assessed.

In such conditions, therefore, the usual (forecasting) procedure has been to try to predict the path of US and international interest rates, and to aim to maintain UK rates roughly at a differential from these rates that, given such influences on confidence as the forecast balance of trade, relative rates of inflation, etc., would seem likely[1] to maintain desired external conditions. With the proposed path of interest rates then given largely by balance-of-payments considerations and the intended path of incomes manipulated by fiscal policy measures, the rate of growth of the monetary aggregates consistent with these objectives can, in principle at least, be obtained from the demand-for-money functions.

So monetary policy has not really been used to guide the course of the economy; rather, it has been held consistent with a course guided by other instruments. To have been more ambitious would either have required more knowledge (of the effects of monetary disturbances) or would have meant consciously endangering certain of the authorities' (short-term) macroecono-

[1] In rapidly changing conditions, and with little confidence anyhow in the stability of econometrically estimated previous relationships, it is not easy to judge what the required differential for this purpose might need to be. For example, during the summer months of 1974 there were capital inflows into the UK despite negative covered, and often uncovered, differentials over all short maturities ranging up to one year.

mic policy objectives. In this manner the demand-for-money functions have been used, but in a somewhat passive manner, as an approximate guide to the appropriate rates of growth of the monetary aggregates on the occasions of general policy reviews.

Besides helping to chart the general course of monetary policy on such occasions, the demand-for-money functions may, in theory, be used as an indicator of developments in the interim periods between policy reviews. Thus Price[**26**, p. 46] wrote:

> In practice, the authorities do not know the current level of incomes in the economy as a whole; a reasonably comprehensive and reliable picture emerges only some months after the event. Meanwhile, they must grasp at straws in the wind. As interest rates are known from day to day and monthly data on the money stock are received quite quickly, the demand-for-money equations can be applied to discover what level of income would be consistent with the observed interest rates and money stock; this provides an early, if approximate, indicator of movements in income besides those already available.

One might, indeed, go further by adding that, by taking steps to counteract the divergences of the monetary aggregates from their expected path – when such divergences were not held to be due to money market disturbances – one could hope to use such information to stabilise the path of incomes.

In practice, however, it has not been possible to use the relationships in this manner. To begin with, our demand-for-money functions are estimated on a quarterly basis, partly because the national income and expenditure data are all quarterly. It is not possible to translate the quarterly model directly into a monthly form since the basic data series would differ. The complete monthly monetary series have only been running for the relatively short period since June 1971. We did try some time ago to fit a monthly demand-for-money function, but the results were not sufficiently good to warrant then persisting with that exercise. Furthermore, the movements in the quarterly series for the monetary aggregate are often not very closely related to the movements in the monetary aggregates over the adjacent three banking months (a banking month ends on the third Wednesday of the month.)[1]

---

[1] When the quarterly rate of increase of M_1 was regressed on the rate of increase per adjacent three banking months over the period 1971II–1974II, the line of best fit was found to be close to that which passed through the origin at an angle of 45°. That is to say that, given the rate of increase in one series in any particular quarter, one's best estimate of the rate of increase in the other series would be about the same. However, the standard error of the equation was very high – just below 2 percentage points, only slightly below the average rate of increase over the period. That is, if in any particular three-monthly period M_1 was found to have risen by 2 per cent, the 95 per cent confidence interval for growth in the calendar quarter would be almost as wide as to include 6 per cent and −2 per cent. In the case of M_3 the standard error was lower – slightly more than 1 percentage point, compared with an average increase of more than 5 per cent. Thus, with a 5 per cent growth in M_3 over any three-monthly period, one could say with 95 per cent confidence that the quarterly increase would be between (approximately) 3 per cent and 7 per cent.

This is mainly a reflection of one of the chief features of the monetary aggregate series in the UK, which is that the individual observations of the money stock, whether monthly or quarterly, contain a great deal of stochastic variation. The extent of this random noise is small in relation to the level of the series, but looms large as a proportion of the monthly movements in the series. This can be shown very simply by just looking at the movements of the main monetary aggregates over 1973–4 (see Figure A). The ratio of noise to

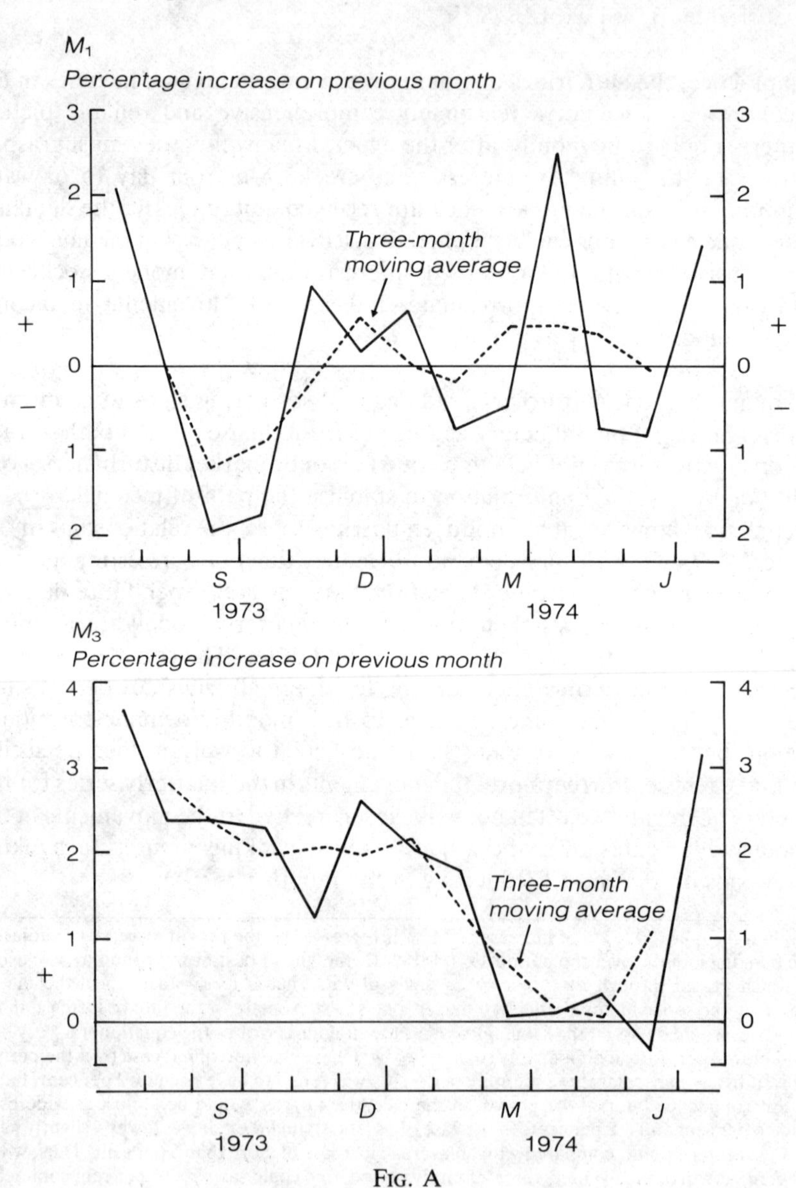

FIG. A

signal in these series of first differences is so large that some kind of averaging is necessary to try to discern the signal more clearly. In our case we tend to concentrate on the three-monthly average; possibly there may be technically superior ways of treating the data to dampen the noise in the system, but our present method has the advantage of simplicity.

What this does mean, however, is that the monetary data do *not* in the UK serve to provide an early, if approximate, indicator of movements in incomes and expenditures. By the time that we have sufficient monetary observations to feel confident that the monetary movements are systematic rather than random, a fairly full collection of direct indicators of the state of the economy are also available, e.g. industrial output, the balance of trade, retail sales, car sales, retail and wholesale prices, housing starts, etc. Given the extent of noise in the monetary data, and their comparatively infrequent collection, the monetary series do not, and cannot, now act as a useful indicator of the immediate, short-term movements in the economy as a whole.

4. Controlling the Monetary Aggregates

The reason given at the end of the previous section why the demand-for-money equations could not be successfully used as an early indicator of developments in the economy was that there was too much noise in the individual monetary observations. This would have been the case even if the demand-for-money equations had proved unbiased and relatively successful predictors of the systematic trends in the money stock, given the movements in incomes and interest rates. As it happened, however, certain of the broader monetary aggregates (e.g. M_3, the broad definition containing all bank deposits, including CDs and time deposits, held by UK residents; and also company sector money balances again including CDs and time deposits) began to depart significantly from their predicted paths, given the development of incomes and interest rates, immediately after the adoption of the new approach to Competition and Credit Control in the autumn of 1971.

As already noted in section 2, the finding of a stable inverse relationship between the money stock and interest rates had held out some hope that the authorities' operations in financial markets could serve to influence the rate of growth of the monetary aggregates in a reasonably predictable fashion. Given the level of incomes, the relationship implied that a rise in interest rates would, though with a lag, dampen the rate of growth of the money stock. With bank liabilities being restrained, the balance-sheet constraint requires that bank asset growth must also be restrained. Since financial forecasting in the UK is done within a flow-of-funds framework which enforces market and balance-sheet constraints, the need to understand the mechanism whereby bank liabilities and assets balanced became a matter of concern to the forecasters, if not to a wider audience.

Formerly with bank advances (largely) fixed by ceilings and with clearing bank interest rates determined by the cartel arrangements, the volume of bank lending to the public sector and the increase in the money balances of the private sector largely depended on how the private sector chose to divide its resources between taking up public-sector debt and adding to money balances. The forecasters had never felt able to predict with any accuracy what the private sector take-up of gilts would be. Now they had to forecast bank advances as well, and, given the previous history of direct controls over bank advances, though interspersed with occasional periods free of control, as in 1958–60, there was no reliable past experience to serve as a guide to probable developments in the novel circumstances occasioned by the structural reforms of 1971.

Furthermore, having attempted the difficult task of forecasting the likely volume of gilt purchases by the private sector and the likely extension of bank advances to the private sector, how could the 'independently' obtained forecast of bank asset growth be squared with the forecast of bank liabilities obtained (mainly) from the demand-for-money functions? Purely mechanically, it is possible to satisfy portfolio identities by making some flow(s), e.g. the private-sector take-up of gilts, a residual. But unless there is reason to believe that a sector does have to treat a flow as a residual source (use) of funds, this is an unsatisfactory approach, generally implying non-profit-maximising behaviour by the members of that sector.

Once the clearing banks abandoned their cartel arrangements, whereby their deposit and advances rates were fixed in relation to Bank Rate, there was no reason why the banks should not adjust their borrowing and lending rates in order to achieve their desired portfolio equilibrium. If the demand for advances was outstripping the demand for bank deposits at the going rates of interest, then the banks' reserves (liquidity) would be being exhausted. This would mean that the marginal yield on bank reserves would be rising. In order to maintain asset equilibrium, with the yield (adjusted for risk) on all assets equal at the margin, the banks would sell gilts and raise advances rates. With gilt and advances rates rising, it would be profitable for the banks to raise deposit rates to attract a larger volume of funds. So when the demand for bank advances, and the growth of bank assets, was tending to exceed (to fall behind) the demand for money, one would in a free competitive system expect to see an increase (a decline) in bank lending and deposit rates *relative* to interest rates elsewhere in the system. Although both bank lending and deposit rates would therefore be expected to rise relative to *other* rates at a time of strong demand for bank advances and pressures on banks' reserves, there was nothing in this analysis to suggest that the margin between bank lending rates and bank deposit rates should alter greatly under such circumstances.

The solution, therefore, to the forecasters' problem of how to reconcile the growth of bank liabilities with the expansion of bank assets is mainly by way of an adjustment in *relative* interest rates. But with bank deposit and lending rates having been pegged through the cartel to Bank Rate, there had been up till 1971 no real experience of the effect of significant changes in the relative differential between bank lending and deposit rates and other rates in the system. So it is not surprising that the problem of reconciling the expansion of bank assets with that of bank liabilities continued to trouble the forecasters for some time.

This was symptomatic of several of the analytical difficulties involved in understanding and interpreting monetary developments in the period after the structural reform in 1971. For in this free, competitive system the mechanism of bank portfolio adjustment depends on the response to relative interest-rate adjustments. Yet in the demand-for-money functions, in which a broad money stock series, including interest-bearing time deposits, was taken as the dependent variable, it had not been possible to find a significant own-rate of interest over the estimation period from 1963 to 1971, no doubt in some large part because of the previous restrictions on the clearing banks' ability to compete.[1] The likelihood of the previously estimated demand-for-money function underpredicting the rate of growth of interest-bearing deposits,[2] at least for a time, as the banks were freed to bid aggressively for additional business – a process of re-intermediation – was recognised in the Bank; no one, however, could forecast how extensive this process would be.

The failure of the demand-for-money functions fitted with broad monetary aggregates, including interest-bearing deposits, as the dependent variable, which had been estimated over the 1963–71 period, to predict well thereafter is documented in the research article by Hacche[**17**]. He argues that this failure was due to the absence of an own-rate in the relationship in the period since 1971, when after the introduction of Competition and Credit Control and the abolition of the cartel the clearing banks were able to vary their deposit rates, especially those offered for large size deposits, in order to compete for funds.

When the new system was introduced, and ceilings were removed from bank lending, it was known that there was little past experience to suggest how responsive the demand for bank advances would be to rising interest rates. It was always realised that it was uncertain whether the private-sector demand for advances would be sufficiently responsive to control bank lending and deposits without encountering unacceptable fluctuations in interest rates. But I do not recollect anyone at the time of the change to the new system

[1] Sterling CDs only began to be issued in 1968. They were not issued by the clearing banks before 1971. Although the sterling CD market grew rapidly from 1968 to 1971, it only really became of quantitative importance in 1972–3.

[2] The absence of an own-rate of interest from the equations, naturally enough, proved less serious in the case of the narrow monetary aggregate, M_1, containing currency and zero-yielding demand deposits. The M_1 demand-for-money equation predicted much better than any of the broader series containing interest-bearing deposits. Yet even in this case the period 1971–3 was characterised by competitive cuts in bank charges so that the implicit yield on demand deposits may have been rising.

pointing to the possibility of perverse movements in the *differential* between deposit and advances rates as a possible added complication. Presumably the implicit expectation was that, at a time of pressure on banks' liquidity and rising interest rates, profitability considerations would lead banks to maintain or even to increase the differential between their borrowing and lending rates. Certainly we believed that the effect of putting pressure on banks' reserves and thereby forcing up lending rates would act to reduce bank advances, even if the response was not very sensitive. In this we were mistaken.

The demand for bank loans responds not only to the differential between bank lending rates and the rates charged on other forms of borrowing but also to the differential between the banks' own lending and deposit rates. A payment to a third party can be made either by withdrawing funds already held on deposit with a bank or by borrowing more from the bank on loan or overdraft. The choice, whether to reduce deposit levels or to increase borrowing, will depend largely on the interest differential between the two sources of funds. Indeed, if the interest differential between them goes to zero, the demand for 'precautionary' advances, and also for 'precautionary' deposits, in theory becomes infinite.[1] In the UK for periods of months at a time in 1972 and 1973 yields on CDs stood above lending rates, so that companies could make an arbitrage turn by borrowing from the banking system merely to relend to it.

In theory the placing of pressure on banks' reserve (liquidity) ratios, say by open-market operations or by calls for special deposits, should lead to upwards pressure on gilt yields, advances rates, etc., while deposit rates should move upwards only in the wake of the general increase in asset yields. In practice it did not work like that. For a number of reasons, among them the public and political visibility of bank lending rates and bank profits – at a time when generally high nominal interest rates were providing large endowment profits to banks with sizeable curent account (zero-yielding) liabilities – the main banks preferred to respond to pressure on their reserve ratios by bidding more aggressively for (large) deposits on money markets, rather than by actively seeking to discourage loan demand, by rate increases, etc. The more pressure the authorities exerted on the reserve base, the more interest rates on large deposits moved upwards relative to bank lending rates, so the greater became the demand for loans, and the faster the growth of deposits, so the greater became the pressure on reserve ratios. It formed a vicious spiral. The standard technique of placing pressure on banks' reserve positions thus seemed to lead to a general increase in interest rates, in bank advances and in the broadly defined money supply. As can be seen from [**17**, chart B], from 1971 to 1973 the broadly defined monetary aggregate became positively related to interest rates, because of this relationship between movements in

[1] As Professor C. Sprenkle has often pointed out [and later analysed in his paper with M. Miller, on 'The precautionary demand for narrow and broad money', *Economica*, vol. 47, November 1980].

interest rates generally and in the differential between deposit and advances rates.

The structural reform of Competition and Credit Control released the genie of rate competition from its previous entrapment in the cartel. The genie has proven to be powerful and unpredictable. By the changes in their competitive behaviour, the banks, together with large companies, overturned previous, apparently stable, relationships.

In the immediate aftermath of the introduction of the reform much of the expansion in advances and interest-bearing deposits was attributed to re-intermediation, as the banks, freed from ceiling controls, bid for funds to take over intermediation that they had been previously prevented from undertaking. Then through 1971 and 1972 monetary expansion was in accord with the authorities' objectives of stimulating the economy and obtaining a higher rate of growth. It was not till 1973 that the apparent failure of the standard techniques to exert a restraining pressure on the banking system became seriously worrying.

It is possible that the standard techniques could have worked, in a sense, if they had been pressed hard enough,[1] and/or if we had been able or prepared to wait long enough. There is presumably some limit to the tendency of banks to raise deposit rates relative to lending rates. But during the course of 1973 rates rose sharply, with the bank blue-chip lending rate going from 8½ per cent in January to 14 per cent in November–December, while the rate of growth of bank lending steadily accelerated. There was no guarantee that even a further jump in rates would suffice to restrain aggregate bank lending, and meanwhile the financial system was becoming increasingly subject to strains in a number of ways, as the subsequent problem of certain fringe financial institutions revealed.

It is against this background that the introduction of the supplementary special deposits scheme needs to be seen. This scheme is intended to ensure that the rate of growth of advances and of interest-bearing deposits is not artificially exaggerated by an erosion of the margin between bank lending and borrowing rates.

5. The Direction of Causation

In the previous section and in Hacche's paper [**17**] the main reason for the breakdown of the demand-for-(broadly defined) money functions is held to

[1] The purpose of this passage in the main text is to describe certain technical problems which arose in trying to control the system through normal methods. This should not be taken as implying that all the problems of Competition and Credit Control could be ascribed to such technicalities. In particular, the combination of accelerating inflation and large sector deficits would have required large and prompt increases in nominal interest rates in 1973 in any case, in order to restrain monetary growth, and this was unwelcome to many. [*Author's note*: This footnote represents a guarded reference to the political pressures placed on the Bank of England during 1973 to limit the upwards movement in interest rates.]

be the more aggressive rate competition of the banks in the post-1971 period. There is an alternative explanation, advocated for example by Artis and Lewis[**3**]. This is that there was such a large autonomous expansion of the monetary aggregates after 1971 that it forced money holders off their preferred positions, leaving them holding excess money balances. When money holders find themselves in such a disequilibrium state they will subsequently adjust by purchasing goods and assets, thereby altering incomes and interest rates (and, during a period of flexible rates, the foreign exchange rates) until equilibrium is restored.

Under such circumstances when the disturbances come from autonomous supply-side shocks, incomes must adjust to current and past changes in the money stock rather than vice versa. In this case it would be more appropriate to fit a money multiplier relationship, which incorporates the former pattern of adjustment, rather than a demand-for-money function. It is possible to examine statistically what the pattern of adjustment has been. Sims[**27**] has done this for the USA and claims that his results demonstrate that the true relationship there has been of a money multiplier form.

There are a number of possible ways to examine this intriguing question of the direction of causation; here we shall consider two sorts of evidence, institutional and statistical. The chief institutional reason for believing that the correct relationship to fit over the period 1963–71 in the UK, the estimation period for many of our research exercises, was a demand-for-money function rather than a money multiplier was that the authorities appear to have attached more weight to maintaining their influence over interest rates than over the rates of growth of the monetary aggregates during much of this period. If the authorities are seeking to control interest rates, they cannot independently be controlling the money stock. Instead, given the choice of interest-rate policy, the private sector will adjust their portfolio in order to obtain their desired level of money balances, in the light of current and past movements in incomes. Indeed, an interesting implication of Sims's statistical findings is that they would seem to belie the charge of certain monetarists in the USA that the Federal Reserve has attached undue importance to interest-rate objectives.

A second institutional reason for believing that money balances were adjusted to incomes, rather than vice versa, during the 1960s is that the UK is an open economy with, during these years, a fixed exchange rate. Under such conditions, as already noted, the private sector can within certain limits (e.g. imposed by exchange controls) adjust its money balances by international transfers of funds.

At the beginning of the 1970s the authorities began to attach more weight to the rate of growth of the monetary aggregates, and from June 1972 the UK has been on a flexible exchange rate. There are therefore *prima facie* grounds for believing that the direction of causation could now have changed. The reasons for preferring the explanation in terms of more aggressive rate competition, rather than of supply-side disturbances, lie mainly in observation of the particular patterns of the monetary movements. The concentration of the 'excess' money balances in interest-bearing form, especially among companies; the simultaneous rapid expansion in both company sector deposits and advances, at a time when company expenditures remained relatively slow-moving; all these factors seemed to point to an explanation in terms of relative interest rates rather than in terms of a supply-side disturbance.

The statistical studies of the direction of causation examine the historical lead/lag relationship using techniques of differing degrees of subtlety and complexity. They are seeking to identify whether there is evidence of movements in incomes following movements in the money stock, without there being evidence of movements in the money stock following movements in incomes, in which case a money multiplier relationship would seem more appropriate; or whether there is an opposite lead/lag relationship, in which case a demand-for-money function would seem more appropriate; or whether the relationships seem to run in both directions.

The work of Sims[**27**] and Hamburger[**18**], using US data, suggests that in that country the lead/lag relationship is consistent with the direction of causation running from the money stock to incomes, and not vice versa. In the UK the statistical picture is much more mixed. A research study by Crockett[**10**] showed a somewhat stronger cross-correlation with money leading incomes than vice versa. However, a replication of Sims's procedures using UK data by Goodhart, Gowland and Williams[**15**] found that, if anything, the direction of causation ran slightly more strongly from incomes to the money stock than vice versa, so that a demand-for-money function was on this test the more appropriate. And a third study by Wall[**29**] suggested that the direction of causation had run in both directions.

In a sense this statistical argument in the UK is academic, since most observers concede on the institutional grounds already mentioned that the stock of money in the UK was demand-determined before 1971. Instead, the claim is that institutional changes since 1971 may have shifted the direction of causation. It is certainly possible that 'autonomous' supply-side factors have become more important in recent years, so that the analysis of the determination of the stock of money should be reconstituted during these later years.

6. The Relationship between Research and Policy: A Summary

Research can guide policy in a number of ways. First, research may help to quantify relationships (coefficients) within a system whose causal form and structural, institutional base is accepted and treated as given. This enables policy-makers to forecast and to simulate the results of their own actions on the economy. Second, research may suggest that the causal form of the real world is different from that in existing models, i.e. that our models of the system need revision and/or that welfare would generally be served by changing the structure of the system.

The research so far undertaken on monetary relationships within the Bank has not been conspicuously successful on either count. The earlier studies on the demand-for-money functions, showing apparently stable relationships, seemed to provide a piece of the wider jigsaw puzzle, but our failure to trace the further links between monetary forces and expenditures drastically reduced the usefulness of those findings for forecasting and simulation (section 3). Moreover, since that work was done, several of these relationships seem to have broken down (section 4).

Turning next to the second role for research, there have, perhaps, been three major structural changes in the direction of policy from 1969–74. First there was a change of emphasis from concern with stabilising interest rates towards giving more attention to the monetary aggregates. The initial impetus for this came from the need to correct our balance-of-payments position in 1968–9, when we adopted DCE targets. Much of the work on the use of DCE targets had been carried out in the IMF, but the mainspring behind this policy measure, as indeed for all approaches involving concern with the growth of the monetary aggregates, lies in the assumption of a reasonably stable demand-for-money function. The initial research work on such functions was previously done mostly in the USA. The main role of our own research in this respect was to assess and to examine the validity of this work in a UK context and to play an educational role in interpreting such work both within the Bank and more widely. This has been of some value. While several of the main results of the US work could be replicated, there *are* important differences, pre-eminently the much weaker links running from monetary changes to subsequent movements in money incomes in the UK.

The second main, but related, structural change was the adoption of Competition and Credit Control in 1971. As already noted (section 2), the research in the Bank played a considerable role in the discussion leading up to that structural reform. There would, no doubt, have been a (temporary) relaxation of ceilings on bank credit in any case, but the wider aspects of the reform, involving major changes in the conceptual approach to monetary management, owed quite a lot to the research work undertaken in the Bank. A third major – though somewhat less important – development has been the adoption of the supplementary special deposits scheme in 1973 as a reinforcement for Competition and Credit Control. Research had little direct role in this, for the need for this measure arose largely because the banking system in this new context behaved rather differently than had been expected (section 4); by definition, since it was a new context, there was no previous experience to consult and examine. Nevertheless the need to interpret how and why the monetary aggregates were diverging from their previous pattern, which the econometric exercise had revealed, provided part of the analytical background to the adoption of this last measure.

But in a way it is claiming both too much and too little for research to try to ascribe it to a specific share of the responsibility for particular policy measures, or the general direction of policy. It is asking too much of it, because pragmatic and political considerations, current received wisdom (judgement), and the random shocks of chance events will always tend to dominate any particular decision. It is claiming too little for research, on the other hand, because it tends to ignore the longer-term effect of research in changing current received wisdom (judgement) and even the tone of pragmatic and political considerations.

References

1 Andersen, L. and Jordan, J., 'Monetary and fiscal actions: a test of their relative importance in economic stabilization', *Federal Reserve Bank of St Louis Review*, vol. 50, no. 11, November 1968.
2 Artis, M. and Nobay, A. R., 'Two aspects of the monetary debate', *National Institute Economic Review*, no. 49, August 1969.
3 Artis, M. and Lewis, M., 'The demand for money: stable or unstable?', *The Banker*, vol. 124, no. 577, March 1974.
4 Bank of England, 'Domestic Credit Expansion', *Bank of England Quarterly Bulletin*, vol. 9, no. 3, September 1969, supplement.
5 Bank of England, 'The operation of monetary policy since the Radcliffe Report', *Bank of England Quarterly Bulletin*, vol. 9, no. 4, December 1969.
6 Bank of England, 'The stock of money', *Bank of England Quarterly Bulletin*, vol. 10, no. 3, September 1970.
7 Burman, J. P., 'Yield curves for gilt-edged stock: further investigation', *Bank of England Quarterly Bulletin*, vol. 13, no. 3, September 1973.
8 Burman, J. P. and White, W. R., 'Yield curves for gilt-edged stocks', *Bank of England Quarterly Bulletin*, vol. 12, no. 4, December 1972.
9 Burman, J. P. and White, W. R., 'The term structure of interest rates – a cross-section test of a mean-variance model', *Issues in Monetary Economics,* ed H. G. Johnson and A. R. Nobay, Oxford University Press, 1974.
10 Crockett, A. D., 'Timing relationships between movements of monetary and national income variables', *Bank of England Quarterly Bulletin*, vol. 10, no. 4, December 1970.
11 Friedman, M., 'The quantity theory of money – a restatement', in *Studies in the Quantity Theory of Money*, ed. M. Friedman, University of Chicago Press, 1956.
12 Friedman, M. and Meiselman, D., 'The relative stability of monetary velocity and the investment multiplier in the United States, 1897–1958', Research Study No. 2 in *Stabilization Policies*, prepared by E. Cary Brown and others for the Commission on Money and Credit, Prentice-Hall, Englewood Cliffs, N.J., 1964.
13 Friedman, M. and Schwartz, A. J., *A Monetary History of the United States 1867–1960*, National Bureau of Economic Research, Princeton University Press, 1963.
14 Goodhart, C. and Crockett, A. D., 'The importance of money', *Bank of England Quarterly Bulletin*, vol. 10, no. 2, June 1970.
15 Goodhart, C., Gowland, D. and Williams, D., 'Money, income and causality: the UK experience', mimeo, Bank of England, 1974.
16 Gowland, D., 'The money supply and stock market prices', mimeo, Bank of England, 1973, read at the 1974 AUTE meeting.

17 Hacche, G., 'The demand for money in the United Kingdom: experience since 1971', *Bank of England Quarterly Bulletin*, vol. 14, no. 3, September 1974.
18 Hamburger, M. J., 'Indicators of monetary policy: the arguments and the evidence', *American Economic Review*, vol. 60, May 1970, papers and proceedings.
19 Hamburger, M. J., 'Expectations, long-term interest rates and monetary policy in the United Kingdom', *Bank of England Quarterly Bulletin*, vol. 11, no. 3, September 1971.
20 Hutton, J., 'A model of short-term capital movements, foreign exchange markets and official intervention in the UK, 1963–1971', mimeo, University of York, 1974.
21 Keran, M. W., 'Monetary and fiscal influences on economic activity: the foreign experience', *Federal Reserve Bank of St Louis Review*, vol. 52, no. 2, February 1970.
22 Laffer, A. B. and Ranson, R. D., 'Formal model of the economy', *Journal of Business*, vol. 44, July 1971.
23 de Leeuw, F. and Gramlich, E., 'The channels of monetary policy', Staff Economic Study, *Federal Reserve Bulletin*, vol. 55, no. 6, June 1969.
24 O'Brien, Sir Leslie, 'Key issues in monetary and credit policy', *Bank of England Quarterly Bulletin*, vol. 11, no. 2, June 1971.
25 Page, J. B., 'Competition and Credit Control', the text of part of the Sykes Memorial Lecture, November 1971, reprinted in *Competition and Credit Control*, Bank of England, 1973.
26 Price, L. D., 'The demand for money in the United Kingdom: a further investigation', *Bank of England Quarterly Bulletin*, vol. 12, no. 1, March 1972.
27 Sims, C. A., 'Money, income and causality', *American Economic Review*, vol. 62, no. 4, September 1972.
28 Townend, J. C., 'Substitution among capital – certain assets in the personal sector of the UK economy 1963–71: a summary', *Bank of England Quarterly Bulletin*, vol. 12, no. 4, December 1972.
29 Wall, K. D., 'An application of simultaneous estimation to the determination of causality between money and income', mimeo, Programme of Research into Econometric Methods, Queen Mary College, London, 1974.

III

Problems of Monetary Management: The UK Experience

1. Introduction

In 1971 the monetary authorities[1] in the UK adopted a new approach to monetary management, a change of policy announced and described in several papers on competition and credit control. The subsequent experience of trying to operate this revised system has, however, been troublesome and at times unhappy. The purpose here is to examine certain aspects of recent monetary developments in order to illustrate a number of more general analytical themes which may have relevance among several countries.

The outline is as follows. In the remainder of this section the pre-1971 *modus operandi* of monetary management is sketched in, and reasons given why the authorities found it increasingly unsatisfactory. In the next section on the money supply and bank behaviour, the intended new method of credit control is described; the intention is then compared and contrasted with actual results. Part of the intellectual and theoretical basis for the changeover to a new *system* of monetary management depended on the belief that it was possible to identify in the UK, as in other countries, a stable demand-for-money function.[2] What became of that belief thereafter is recorded in the third section on the demand for money. The developments reported in the second and third sections posed some difficult problems for the conduct – even for the interpretation and assessment – of monetary policy. In order to deal with some of these problems a new instrument, the supplementary special deposit, was introduced (in December 1973) in conjunction with guidelines for the growth of interest-bearing bank deposits, familiarly known as 'the corset'. Experience with this, in some ways novel, instrument is assessed in the final section on the operation of monetary policy.

---

[1] A term encompassing the Bank of England and the Treasury, the responsible Minister being the Chancellor of the Exchequer.

[2] It is probable that the opportunity – provided by a period of recession during 1970–71 and the accession to office of a new government dedicated to competition – to remove bank lending ceilings, at least temporarily, would have been taken in any case. It was not this step, but rather the attempt to construct a completely alternative *system* of monetary management – alternative to a continuation of long periods of ceilings interspersed with (shorter) periods of relaxation – in which the work on the demand-for-money function played a role.

Turning to the *modus operandi* of monetary policy prior to 1971, interest-rate adjustments were mainly conditioned by the state of the balance of payments, with short rates being pushed up whenever sterling weakened, and allowed to fall – in order to encourage the housing market and company investment – when sterling strengthened. No attempt was made to peg long rates or to offset market trends in the gilt market entirely, but the Bank usually 'leant into the wind' to reduce the rate of change in market prices, in the interest of maintaining a broad, orderly market for government debt. The Bank was continually keen to sell marketable government (gilt-edged) debt, i.e. to fund the debt, in order to finance over time a 'reasonable proportion' of the government's current needs, and to refinance the steady stream of maturities. Such funding was done when market opportunities arose (i.e. when the market expected rates to fall); little or no attempt was ever made to press sales on an unreceptive market, even if the government's borrowing requirement was very large and/or if domestic credit and the money stock was growing unusually fast. This was partly because, until perhaps the last few years before 1971, the behaviour of the monetary aggregates played no part in deciding the authorities' actions, but even more because it was felt that there was no predictable relationship in the short term between gilt-edged sales and the level of interest rates.

With interest rates thus determined, the authorities turned increasingly in the years up till 1971 to direct control (by quantitative ceilings) of bank lending to the private sector. The purpose was to reduce private-sector demand, mainly in the interests of the balance of payments. This was certainly the case in the series of requests (for the ceilings had no statutory backing) which began in December 1964 and continued in ever more precise form until 1971. These requests were occasionally supported by calls for special deposits which had to a large extent a symbolic character, and were intended to underline the Bank's intentions. In the final few years of this period, from 1969 onwards, such ceilings were also seen as playing a supporting role in restraining the broader monetary aggregates, i.e. the money stock as variously defined or domestic credit expansion (DCE), to which attention was increasingly turning.[1]

Direct controls over bank lending had many disadvantages. Even leaving on one side the problems of administering them, their effect was naturally to reduce competition and efficiency within the banking system. These base-dated controls were in operation, fairly continuously from 1964 till 1971, so that for a prolonged period the main job of bank managers became to refuse new business (or to direct such business to subsidiaries with more leeway for lending), not to encourage it. In so far as such controls did not serve to freeze proportionate shares of banking business at its base-date position, it encouraged the growth of certain 'fringe' institutions outside the banking sector, and

[1] This is set out in more detail in 'The operation of monetary policy since the Radcliffe Report', *Bank of England Quarterly Bulletin*, vol. 9, December 1969.

also the development of secondary money markets (e.g. an inter-company market was emerging at the end of the period) which allowed money and credit to flow around such quantitative credit barriers.

Not only was the amount of lending restrained by such direct controls, but also the rates charged on such loans were largely conditioned by the London clearing banks' cartel arrangements (effectively in force since 1917 with the support of the authorities), which tied the deposit and lending rates of these banks (eleven in number in 1964, reduced through mergers to six in 1971) to Bank Rate. Other banks were free to set their rates at more competitive levels, and also did not have to observe the 8 per cent cash and 28 per cent liquid-asset ratios which the clearers maintained, which restricted the clearers from operating in the new parallel money markets, i.e. the Euro-dollar market and the sterling markets in inter-bank and local authority money, which operate on very small margins. In some part the clearers were able to respond to this situation by forming subsidiaries. Nevertheless, they would have been in an even more disadvantageous position after the abolition of ceilings controls – which in some ways had fallen less severely on them – unless such competitive disadvantages had been removed.

For such micro-level and structural reasons there would, in any case, have been an urge to seize the opportunity of a period of slack in the economy to get away, even if only temporarily, from the base-dated ceilings, and perhaps also to encourage the abandonment of the interest-rate cartel. In the meantime, however, the rationale for this whole strategy was being queried at the macro level. It was doubtful whether such direct controls on this one component of domestic credit creation were having a significant effect in restraining the money stock, or on real domestic expenditures. No evidence of any such effect could be observed from the studies made of the demand-for-money function. These studies showed that the demand for money, both narrowly and broadly defined, over the period 1963–70 (an observation period limited by the availability of data) could be well explained by current and previous movements in income and interest-rates. In some part, potential borrowers refused loans from banks raised the money instead by selling public-sector debt themselves, or by borrowing from other financial intermediaries who sold public-sector debt in their turn, or by bringing in funds from abroad, a response which was at times most welcome. With interest rates determined along the lines already noted, this just led to a reshuffling of bank assets, with lending to the public sector replacing lending to the private sector with little effect on the money stock.

In any case, outside of the limitation of bank lending to persons which did appear to bite (see Figure A), the severity of the control was possibly exaggerated. At the time it was quite difficult to discern whether the ceilings were having any marked effect in restricting bank advances to companies (see Figure B). The Bank, in general, resisted the predictable pressures to exempt 'desirable' kinds of lending (e.g. exports, agriculture, housebuilding) from

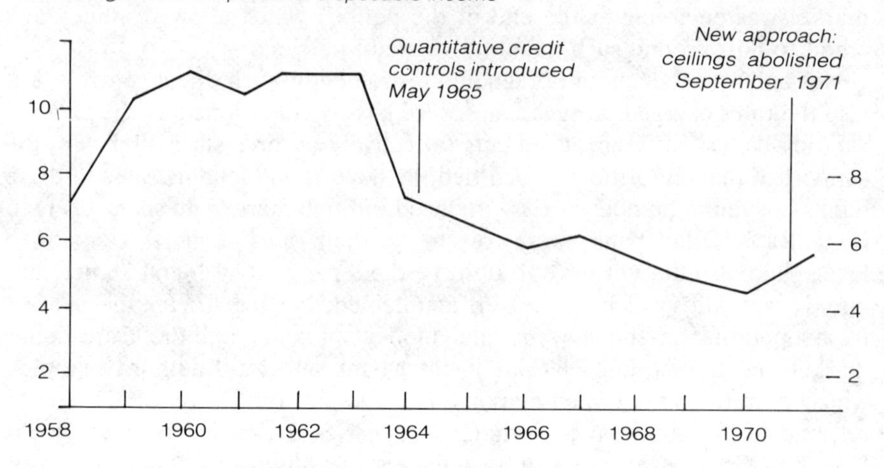

FIG. A *Bank lending (outstanding) to the personal sector*

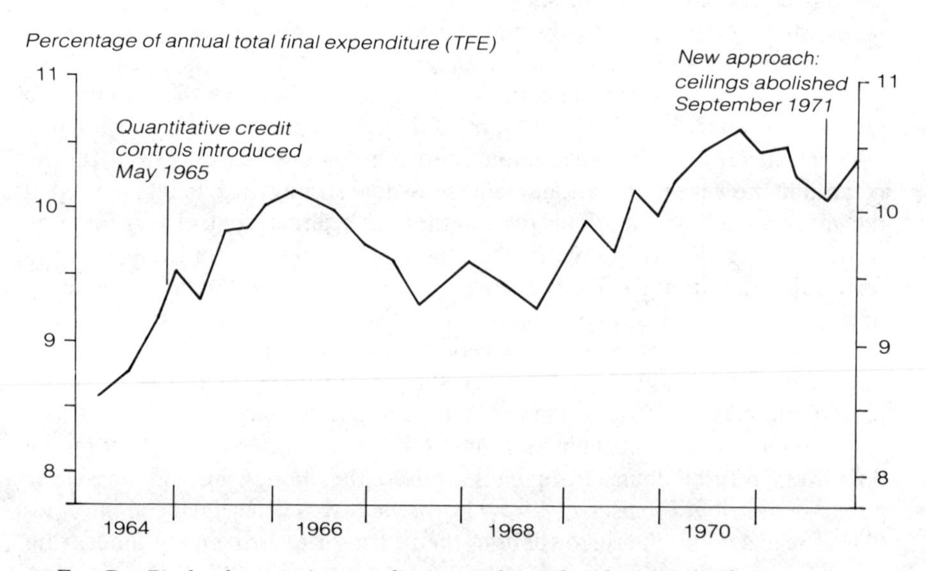

FIG. B *Bank advances (outstanding) to industrial and commercial companies*

such ceilings. This was partly so that room should have to be made for expansion in these areas by restricting less desirable borrowers more severely, and partly because any such exemption is liable to provide a bigger loophole than intended. Definitional difficulties arise; moreover, the exempted activities tend to be financed to the hilt by bank loans releasing funds for other uses, including on-lending. Even so, one important exemption was made in the interests of preserving the medium-term fixed-rate schemes for finance for exports and shipbuilding. In all the circumstances, measurement of the

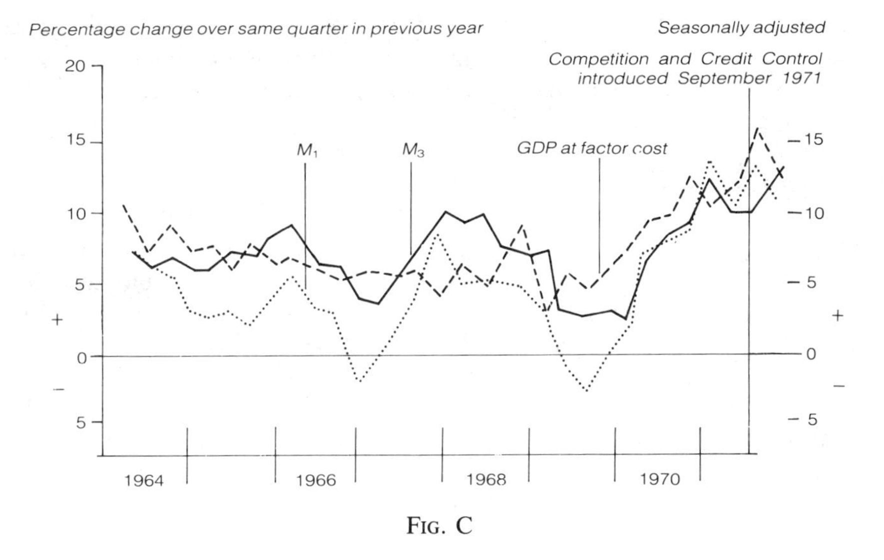

FIG. C

economic effect of such direct controls was hardly possible, and the selection of numbers for the ceilings was somewhat arbitrary.

In the meantime a number of academic econometric studies on the demand-for-money function in the UK had been completed both in the universities,[1] and within the Bank itself,[2] following mainly the example and methodologies of prior US work. These all seemed to show that the development of the monetary aggregates during previous years could, after appropriate adjustment for the lagged relationships involved, be reasonably well explained by the movements in incomes and interest rates. As shown in Figure C, both M_1 and M_2 over the period 1964–71 varied fairly closely together and in line with money incomes, and after separation of incomes into real and price elements, the inclusion of an interest-rate variable and adjustment for lags, the fit could be much improved.

If these past relationships could be expected to hold in the future also, such findings seemed to carry a number of implications. First, velocity itself did not appear to be, as the Radcliffe Report had implied, unstable or unpredictable, so a change in the money stock would have a substantial effect either on money incomes or on interest rates; the question, however, of the transmission mechanism whereby either changes in interest rates or monetary

[1] See, for example, D. Fisher, 'The demand for money in Britain: quarterly results 1951 to 1967', *Manchester School*, vol. 36, December 1968; and D. Laidler and J. M. Parkin, 'The demand for money in the United Kingdom, 1955–1967: preliminary estimates', *Manchester School*, vol. 38, September 1970.

[2] C. Goodhart and A. D. Crockett, 'The importance of money', *Bank of England Quarterly Bulletin*, vol. 10, June 1970; and L. D. Price, 'The demand for money in the United Kingdom: a further investigation', *Bank of England Quarterly Bulletin*, vol. 12, March 1972.

aggregates then fed through on to income and expenditure decisions remained then, and since, wrapped in mystery in the UK. But at least monetary management would seem likely to have some effect. Moreover, if the level of interest rates was largely determined by external considerations, e.g. in a fixed exchange-rate system, the equation(s) would seem to allow one to read off what rate of monetary growth would be consistent with (or more restrictive or expansionary than) the government's domestic income objectives. Alternatively, if exchange rates were floating or the external position did not represent a constraint (as in 1971–2), the equation could be used – though the relationships involved were more complex – to explore the effect of differing rates of domestic credit expansion on domestic incomes, interest rates, international capital flows and exchange rates. Finally, the finding that interest rates appeared to have a significant and predictable effect on the demand for money tended to dissipate the previous pessimism that markets were too unpredictable to rely on variations in interest rates to control the monetary aggregates. The econometric evidence seemed to suggest that, one way or another, whether by restraining bank borrowing or by encouraging non-bank debt sales, higher interest rates did lead to lower monetary growth. In one fell swoop, therefore, these demand-for-money equations appeared to promise:

(a) that monetary policy would be effective
(b) that an 'appropriate' policy could be chosen and monitored
(c) that the 'appropriate' levels of the monetary aggregates could be achieved by market operations to vary the level of interest rates.

Ignoring Goodhart's law, that any observed statistical regularity will tend to collapse once pressure is placed upon it for control purposes, these findings, which accorded well with the temper of the times, helped to lead us beyond a mere temporary suspension of bank ceilings towards a more general reassessment of monetary policy. The main conclusions of this were that the chief intermediate objectives of monetary policy should be the rates of growth of the monetary aggregates, i.e. the money stock, in one or other of its various definitions, or DCE (and not particular components of these, such as bank lending to the private sector), and that the main control instrument for achieving these objectives should be the general price mechanism (i.e. movements in interest rates) within a freely competitive financial system.

2. Bank Behaviour and the Money Supply

Under this new approach the method of control was expected to be roughly as follows. When the authorities wished to act restrictively they would aim to push up interest rates either by raising the rate at which they relieved the normal cash shortages arising in the market (since the Treasury bill tender is usually set somewhat larger than necessary, in order to hold money markets under slight tension) or by a call for special deposits, etc. One of the previous limitations on the authorities' freedom of action was that Bank Rate had been, and had been seen to be, an administered rate, subject to all the constraints that tend to restrain the flexibility of administered rates. In so far as Bank Rate was sticky, this in turn had limited the flexibility of other money market rates, e.g. Treasury bill rate. It was the intention in 1971 to allow all rates, including Bank Rate, to vary more flexibly. However, several of the (political) constraints preventing administered rates from varying flexibly remained. In the hopes of enabling the market mechanism to work more nearly as planned, a subsequent change, made in 1972, was to link the (penal) rate for lending from the Bank, the Minimum[1] Lending Rate (MLR), to Treasury bill rate, so that MLR would vary with changes in market rates;[2] the authorities, however, retained the option to make administered, fiat, changes in MLR at their own discretion.

The effect of operations which raise money market rates and place pressure on banks' reserve positions is to induce an upwards pressure on interest rates more generally. In practice banks do not respond to pressure on their cash positions by some large-scale, multiple cutback in their asset portfolio, by calling in advances, etc. Instead their immediate response will be to bid for funds, by raising rates offered on deposits, or by selling liquid assets from their second line of reserves. With the cost of marginal funds rising, banks would, we believed, raise the rates charged on advances to maintain their profitability. Meanwhile with interest rates on public-sector debt pushed higher, e.g. when banks had sold such assets to maintain their liquidity, persons might shift out of banks deposits into public-sector debt.[3]

The transmission mechanism whereby restrictive pressure on banks' liquidity positions became translated into a more general reduction in the rate of growth of their advances and deposits was seen to run via portfolio adjustments in response to changing relative prices (interest rates) by banks, persons, etc. Pressure on the banks' cash position was a means to this end. The adoption of a cash reserve (or high-powered money, or reserve-base) target seemed to us to confuse ends and means. Apart from the fact that the provision of monetary data is too infrequent in the UK to make such a system possible (a feature which could, perhaps, have been changed at some

[1] 'Minimum' in the sense that this was the lowest rate at which the Bank would provide support to the market in this way. The Bank reserved, and has at times made use of, the right to exact a greater penalty for last-resort lending.

[2] MLR was then set ½ per cent higher than the average rate of discount for Treasury bills established at the weekly tender, rounded to the nearest ¼ per cent above.

[3] In so far as people have extrapolative expectations, at least in the short run (a condition which many of those close to the market believe to be the case), then a period of *rising* interest rates, while the banks sell gilts, would discourage, and *not* encourage, larger debt sales to the non-bank public. If at some, unforeseeable, point, however, the market subsequently reaches a plateau, where prices are no longer expected to slide down, *then* the higher yield level may encourage an increased demand.

considerable cost), such an approach would lead to much greater variance in short-term interest rates and subsequent structural changes. These would probably have had the effect of reducing the efficiency of the short-term money market since banks would tend to hold extra money balances rather than putting them into money market instruments. And if the authorities can control average short-term rate levels, there seems little to be gained by deliberately increasing the variance of such rates.

It was, indeed, partly for this reason that the new required reserve ratio, applied in common to all banks, covered a wider range of short-term assets, including Treasury bills, call money held with discount houses, gilts of under one-year maturity. Given, however, the previous picture of the supposed control mechanism working through interest rates, the question arises, as to exactly what was the function or purpose of this ratio. Partly, I think, the desire to maintain some required ratio was due to uncertainty about bank behaviour in a more competitive, unconstrained system, a fear that perhaps bank behaviour would be unstable, or unpredictable. What if banks should come to feel able to work on much lower liquidity ratios for their own purposes? The existence of a required ratio held out a promise of a stable fulcrum against which the authorities might be able to press. Nevertheless the coherence of the interrelationship between the cash-base/interest-rate mechanism spelt out earlier and the reserve-assets ratio has proved confusing to many. As Sir Leslie O'Brien stated in his speech to the international bankers at Munich,[1] the main method of control over the banking system was to be through the price mechanism, i.e. via interest-rate adjustments. In this respect ratio control, through the required reserve assets ratio, was to play only a supporting role.

When we embarked on this course in 1971–2, it was foreseen that the new control system would face certain initial, teething problems. In particular, there had been quantitative ceilings on bank lending since 1964, and within these ceilings there had been further qualitative guidance to banks to discriminate severely against certain types of borrower, e.g. persons. Once before when there had been 'a dash for freedom' in 1958–60, there had been a very sharp surge in lending to previously constrained groups. It was expected that this would occur again, but its magnitude was unpredictable. In the event it was very large, as shown in Figure D. With profitable lending business, which had been previously prevented, or diverted, by ceilings, returning to the banks, the banks would be in a position to raise the rates which they offered for funds to more attractive levels. Moreover, the margin between the rates charged for advances and offered on deposits had been pegged for years by the clearing bank cartel. With the cartel abolished and competition encouraged, this margin could be expected to shrink, leading to reintermediation by the banks, with a faster increase in both assets and deposits.

[1] Sir Leslie O'Brien, 'Key issues in monetary and credit policy', *Bank of England Quarterly Bulletin*, vol. 1, June 1971.

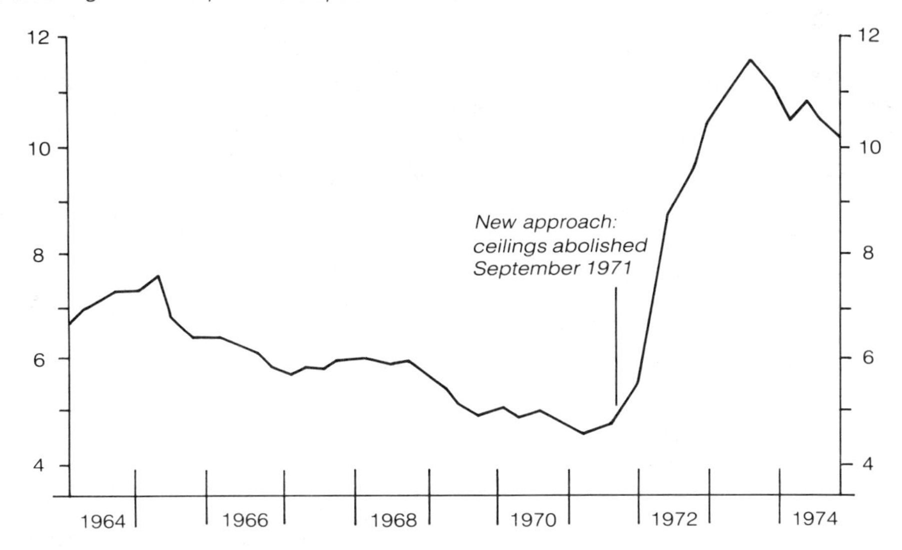

Fig. D *Bank lending (outstanding) to the personal sector*

Moreover, there was little or no previous experience to indicate how sensitively or rapidly the demand for bank borrowing might respond to increases in interest rates, since such borrowing had been mainly affected by the alternate imposition and relaxation of ceilings in previous years. If the elasticity of demand for such loans was low, interest rates might have to be pushed to levels which would have serious adverse effects on the politically sensitive mortgage and housing markets. This was the more likely since the combination of tax arrangements[1] and accelerating inflation brought about an increasing divorce between 'real' and nominal bank borrowing costs. The authorities would have to pass presentational and psychological hurdles like going into double figures with nominal rates without bringing about any comparable rise in real rates. This problem was, of course, intensified, at least at the presentational level, by the adoption of prices and incomes policies from 1972 onwards.

Even so, it was, perhaps, the unforeseen problems that caused the greatest difficulties. At much the same time as the authorities were abolishing direct ceilings on bank lending, the government was also relaxing certain controls on commercial rents and property development. The combination of generally falling interest rates in 1971–2 with a suddenly unconstrained banking and

[1] Interest payments have always been tax-deductible for companies. Shortly after their return to office in 1970, the new Conservative government also made interest payments tax-deductible for persons. Moreover, there was for a time a tax loop hole that could be exploited by borrowing to reinvest in CDs.

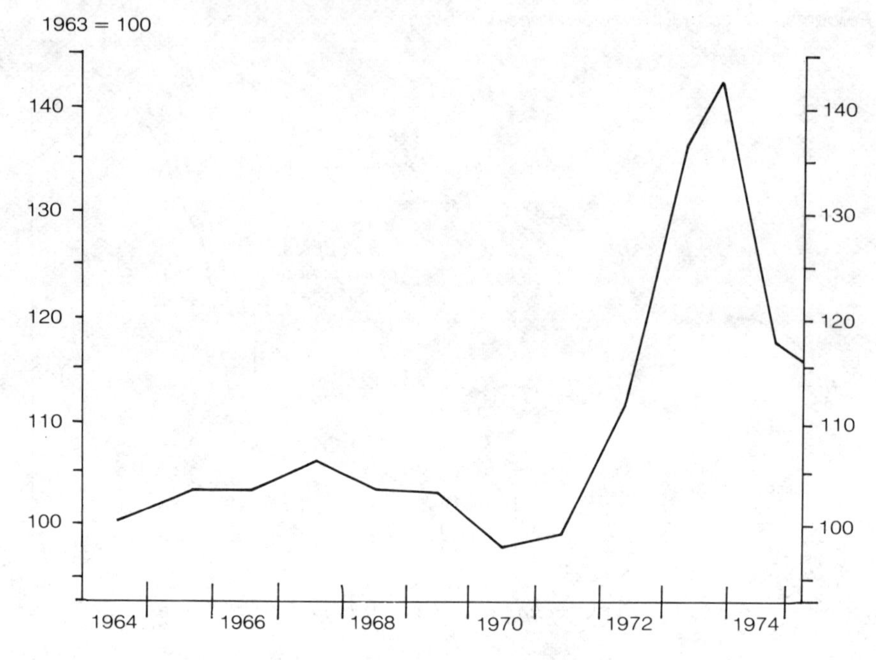

FIG. E *New house prices relative to average earnings*

property market led to a boom in housing and property prices (Figure E). By 1973, although interest rates began to rise, after June quite sharply, the rise in housing and property prices had become self-sustaining, in a quasi-speculative mania, which reached its bitter end at the turn of the year. The banking and financial community had not been immune from the lure of quick profits from participation in the property boom, though the involvement of the larger clearing banks was much less than that of several smaller 'fringe' financial institutions.

It was bad enough that the competitive process had been associated with instability in the housing and property markets. What was worse was that when the control mechanism was put to the test, especially in 1973, it appeared, at least in relation to the indicator by which its performance was commonly judged, which was M_3, the broad definition of the money stock, to have failed; indeed, the results seemed actually perverse. In 1971 and 1972 the government was trying to bring about a faster rate of economic growth. An accompanying acceleration in monetary growth, especially when much of it could be ascribed to reintermediation, seemed quite appropriate. But anxiety mounted as early as September 1972, and grew during the winter, by mid-1973 signs of overheating were apparent and the external position of sterling was becoming subject to stress. Accordingly interest rates were

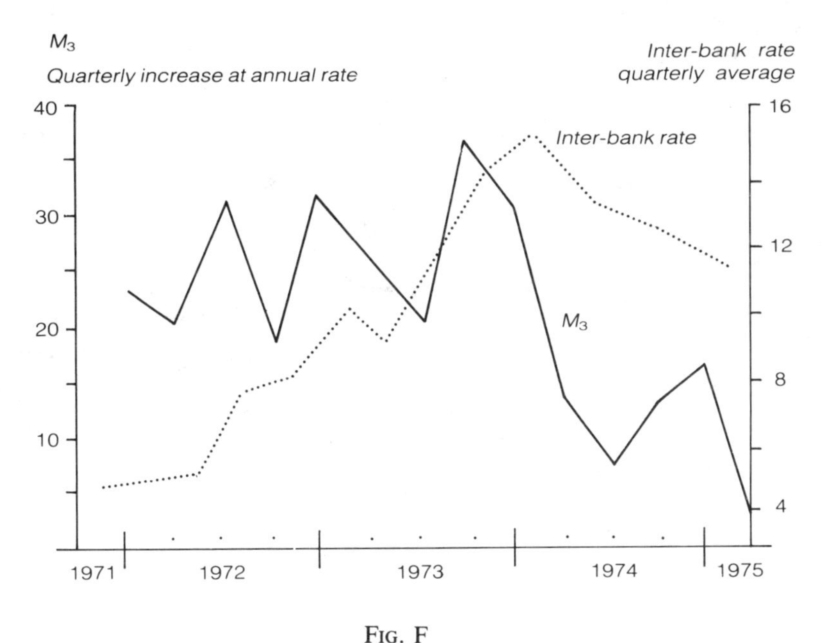

FIG. F

increased sharply, and the authorities wished to brake the rate of growth of the monetary aggregates. As interest rates rose in the latter half of 1973, the rate of growth of M_1, narrow money, slowed sharply, as was intended and expected. On the other hand, the rate of growth of M_3, the broad money aggregate,[1] accelerated still further (see Figure F), and bank lending in sterling to the private sector surged ahead. Indeed, in the period 1972–4 the relationship between the velocity of M_3 and the level of interest rates was perverse (Figure G), though the normal form of relationship continued to hold for M_1 (Figure H). Since 1972, therefore, the trends in the rates of growth of M_1 and M_3 have frequently been moving in markedly different directions.

It so happened, however, that M_3 was the monetary series to which most commentators in the UK paid closest attention. As an indicator it has several advantages over M_1. With M_3 comprising most domestic bank liabilities, it is possible to use bank balance-sheet and flow-of-funds data to relate M_3 to counterpart bank assets, domestic credit expansion and external balance-of-payments developments. Since policy measures tend to act more directly on

[1] There had been a further definition, M_2, but this had depended on an assumed broad difference in character between the smaller, retail-type, time deposits in clearing banks, which were in practice transferable to current accounts on demand, and larger, money-market, wholesale time deposits in other banks. After 1971 when the clearing banks entered the market for CDs and wholesale time deposits under their own names, the grounds for making such a distinction disappeared, and the M_2 series was dropped.

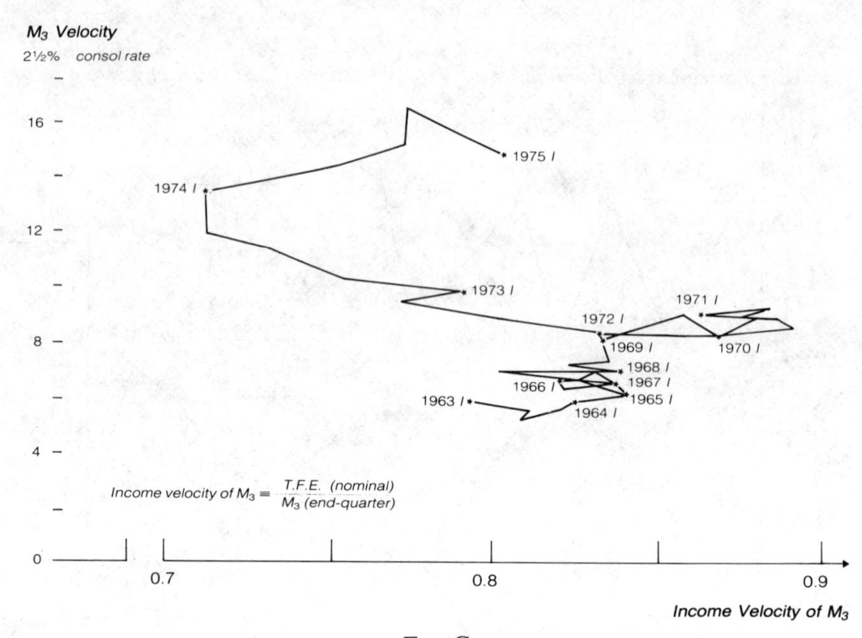
M_3 Velocity
2½% consol rate
16
12
8
4
0
1975 I
1974 I
1973 I
1971 I
1972 I
1969 I
1970 I
1968 I
1967 I
1966 I
1965 I
1963 I
1964 I
0.7
0.8
0.9
Income Velocity of M_3

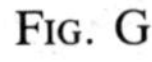
Income velocity of M_3 = T.F.E. (nominal) / M_3 (end-quarter)

Fig. G

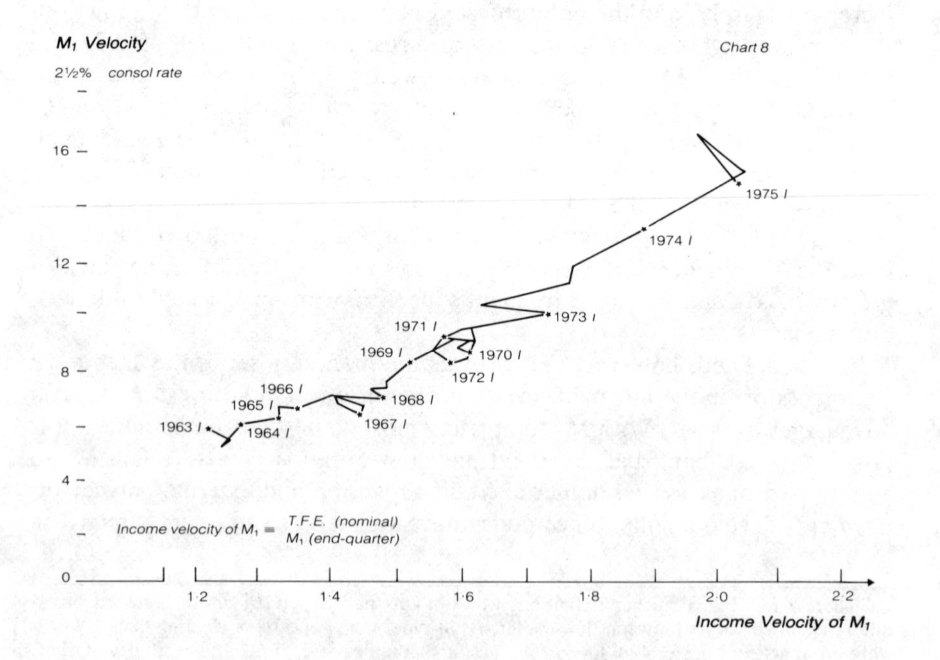
M_1 Velocity
Chart 8
2½% consol rate
16
12
8
4
0
1975 I
1974 I
1973 I
1971 I
1969 I
1970 I
1972 I
1966 I
1965 I
1968 I
1963 I
1964 I
1967 I
Income velocity of M_1 = T.F.E. (nominal) / M_1 (end-quarter)
1·2
1·4
1·6
1·8
2·0
2·2
Income Velocity of M_1

Fig. H

the public-sector borrowing requirement, on debt sales, and on bank lending to the private sector, than on the liabilities side of the balance-sheet, it is easier to attach reasons for the change in the money stock, to ascribe praise or blame to this or that policy, if the indicator is M_3 rather than M_1.

Therefore, whether or not it was true in fact, a large number of commentators claimed that the rapid rise of M_3 in 1973 (while M_1 was falling away and interest rates were rising ferociously) was a sign of an irresponsibly expansionary, and inflationary, monetary policy. Even doubting the validity of such claims, the rapid monetary expansion – in bank lending and M_3 – was having at the least an adverse presentational effect on expectations.

Clearly the standard control mechanism had not worked; the first need was to discover why this was. An important factor, in my view, was that we had failed to foresee the likely course of bank behaviour in an unconstrained system (a failure which may be more easily understood since British banks had not had the chance of operating in such a *milieu* in living memory). In particular, in an oligopolistic banking system, with a large element of 'endowment' profits accruing on assets held against zero-yielding current accounts, the extent to which the banks might take the expansionary and competitive bit between their teeth and gallop off was unexpected. The practical point is that the cash-base/interest-rate mechanism only works as the textbooks claim if the margin between the rates which the banks offer for (additional) funds in wholesale money markets and charge on (additional) advances remains constant (or increases) as interest rates rise. If this holds, the interest *differential* between advances (and public-sector debt) and deposit rates will at least remain constant, while the margin between rates on public-sector debt (and advances) and on other assets should widen, thus causing the standard portfolio readjustment.

In the UK this did not happen. As shown in Figure I, over the period 1972–4, whenever rates were rising, money market rates, represented by inter-bank rate, rose relative to bank lending rates (and to five-year bond yields). This, of course, made bank borrowing a relatively cheaper way of paying debts than running down liquid assets, as interest rates rose. Indeed, as Professor Sprenkle has noted,[1] when the rates on overdrafts and deposits are equal, the precautionary demand for overdrafts will be infinite; for many months in 1972 and 1973 money market rates were in excess of bank lending rates to prime customers. During 1973 this pattern of rates encouraged a massive increase in bank lending, and a corresponding accumulation of time deposits, largely within the company sector (sometimes within a single company), where firms had command over large enough sums to take advantage of arbitrage opportunities.

[1] C. Sprenkle, 'Effects of large firms and bank behavior on the demand for money of large firms', mimeo, American Bankers' Association, 1971, especially appendix C; also, with M. H. Miller, 'The precautionary demand for narrow and broad money', *Economica*, vol. 47, November 1980.

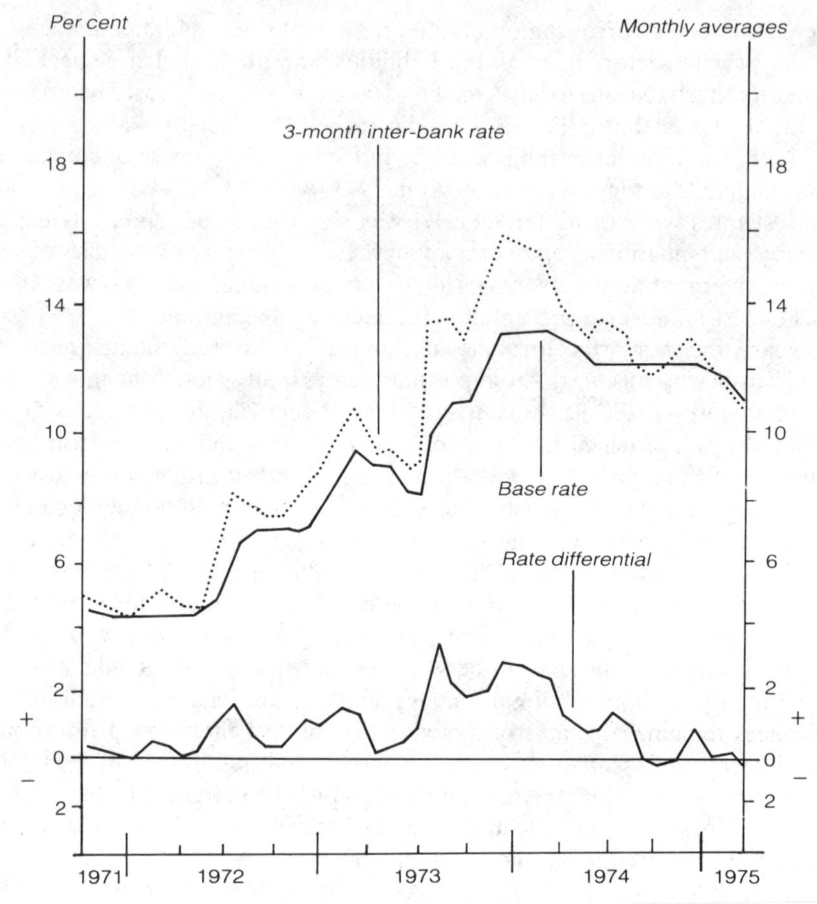

FIG. I *Base rate and three-month inter-bank rate*

Why did this happen? In the first place banks' base rates are administered rates, not market-determined, and, for a number of well-known reasons, administered rates tend to move more slowly than market rates, especially in an oligopolistic situation. In addition there was a technical problem. To prevent the discount houses creating reserve assets for the banking system on too large a scale, they were required to hold 50 per cent of their own assets in specified public-sector reserve assets – quite largely Treasury bills – which would be especially attractive to the discount houses when longer-dated gilts were expected to fall in price. But this meant that in circumstances when bank liabilities and interest rates were rising, Treasury bill rates would be relatively held down by strong bidding from the discount houses; but MLR was tied to Treasury bill rates, and bank lending rates could not be raised far from MLR without incurring public odium.

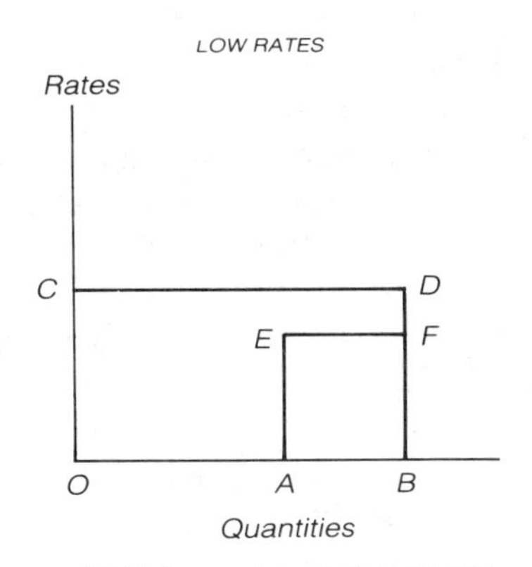

OA Volume of current accounts
AB Volume of time deposits
OC Rate on earning assets
AE Rate of interest on time deposits
OAEFDC Net interest-rate earnings

FIG. J

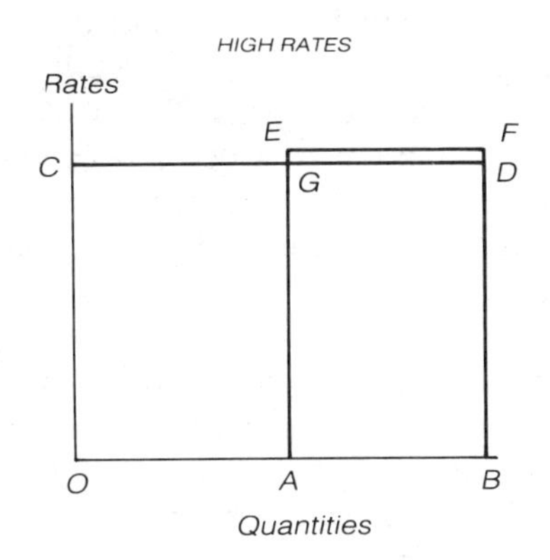

OA Volume of current accounts
AB Volume of time deposits
OC Rate on earning assets
AE Rate of interest on time deposits
OCGA – GEFD Net interest-rate earnings

FIG. K

This situation was put right in July 1973; in any case it probably only had minor influence. A much more important factor was that banks were not primarily concerned with short-term profit maximisation. They had been encouraged to compete aggressively, and this was often taken to mean competition for business, market shares, etc. The extension of new lending facilities in 1972–3 was enormous, and undertaken with little or no concern for capital adequacy. Second, a rise in interest rates of itself tended to lead to an increase in bank profits because of the greater endowment effect on higher-earning assets supported on an (albeit proportionately shrinking) base of zero-yielding current accounts. Thus, as rates rose, banks could undertake additional business at a small loss and still turn in higher profits, as illustrated in Figures J and K. Certainly banking profits rose very sharply over the period 1970–3, despite the shrinking margins between deposit rates and advance rates.[1] Indeed, this was so marked that it aroused at times some public hostility. So it was difficult for the banks to raise their base rates at a time when prices and incomes policies were in force and their profits had risen so fast. And once they had extended larger facilities, they could not, under the overdraft system, help lending more to customers taking advantage of

[1] Cf. the following figures taken from clearing banks' annual published statements.

Clearing bank pre-tax profits (£m.)

1970	*1971*	*1972*	*1973*	*1974*
255.1	299.3	413.0	618.7	471.3

relatively cheap borrowing rates. In any case, behaviour which increased banking growth, even if profitless, may then have seemed desirable.

Of course, the details of this story are particular to the UK, but the economic moral is of wider application. This is that the determination of the money stock in any country depends crucially on banking behaviour and objectives. These can differ from country to country, and over time (as is discussed later, banking objectives in the UK in 1974 were very different from those in 1973). Professor Tobin was among the first to remind us that banking behaviour and objectives matter.[1] The UK experience is a lesson of the truth of this view. In particular a 'free-market' system of control requires market-oriented and motivated participants – in their absence only a non-market control system can be effective. One can argue that the period, since 1971, marks a difficult stage of returning to a market system, or something approximating to it, and that this has required changes in institutional behaviour and structure that proved more difficult and prolonged than was initially expected.

3. The Demand for Money

The enormous increases both in bank lending and in interest-bearing time deposits in 1972–3 were largely due to the pattern of relative interest rates which the banks had allowed to develop. This was a new phenomenon. Prior to 1971 relative (bank) rates had been largely pegged by the cartel agreement: somewhat surprisingly it had not been possible to find in the econometric exercises any significant effect of such pegged own-rates in attracting deposits. After 1971, when, *inter alia*, the banks were able to compete for deposits more aggressively, the previous forecasting equations for M_3, and for the broad money holdings of persons (MP) and companies (MC) completely broke down, especially the latter (see Figures L, M and N). In each case the extent of the monetary expansion was far in excess of that predicted by the equation in most of the quarters of 1972 and 1973. Everyone now agrees that the demand-for-money equations, using the broader definition of the money stock, have proved unstable.

The situation is not so clear cut in the case of the demand function for narrow money, M_1. The quarterly forecasts, using our 1971 equation, have *not* been notably accurate (see Figure O), but taking the period 1972–4 as a whole it is not clear that they have been biased. Moreover, re-running the equation as these new observations have arrived has not altered the form of the equation significantly. On these grounds we would argue that the relationship has remained fairly stable, but is subject to such considerable

[1] J. Tobin, 'Commercial banks as creators of "money"', in *Banking and Monetary Studies*, ed. D. Carson, Irwin, 1963.

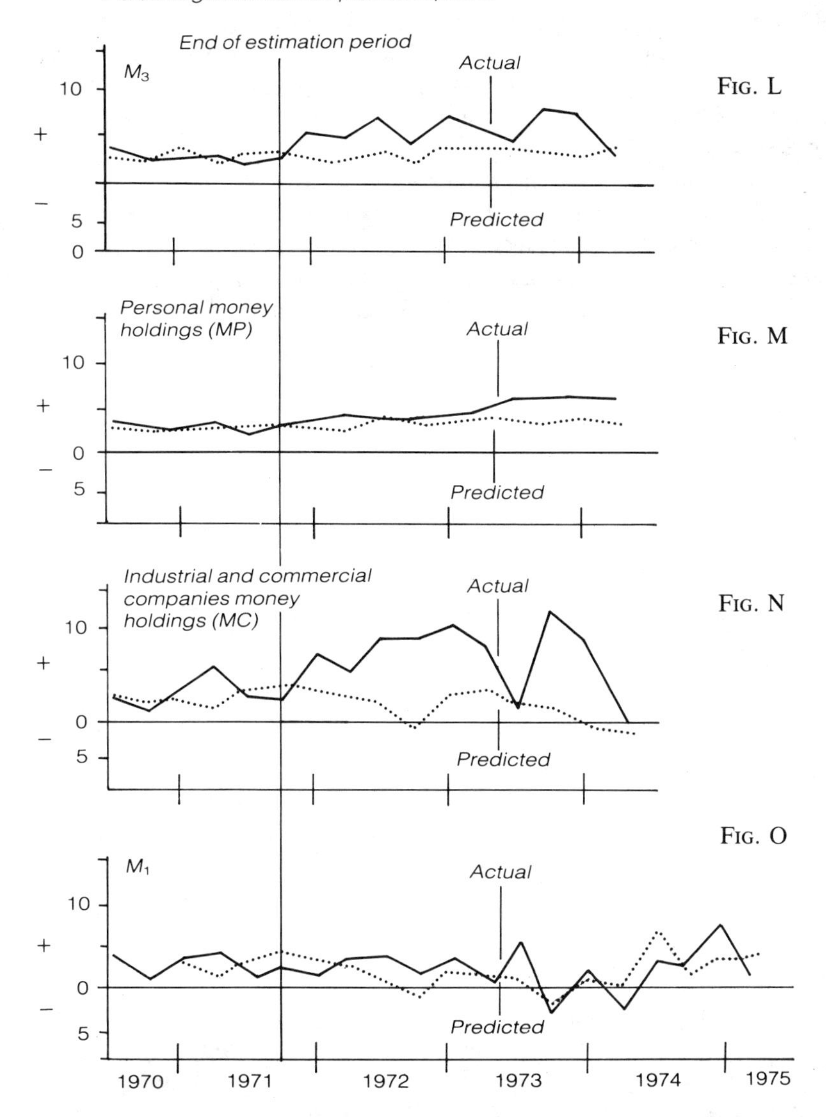

noise that it is only of limited help in monitoring quarterly, let alone, monthly developments. It is, however, only fair to add that this view that the demand for narrow money has remained a stable function (of current and past real incomes, prices and interest rates) has been disputed.

The interesting question, then, is not whether (most) demand-for-money functions in the UK ceased to be stable after 1971, but why this happened. The strict 'monetarist' analysis is, as I understand it, that the growth in the nominal money stock is exogenous to the private sector. The public has a demand for 'real' money balances, and as the nominal stock of money increases the public will then adjust its spending on real goods (thereby affecting both prices and real incomes) and financial assets (thereby affecting interest rates) until incomes, prices and interest rates have adjusted to a level consistent both with exogenous nominal balances and the demand function for real money balances.

Somewhat in this vein it has been argued, for example by Artis and Lewis,[1] that the extension of advances by the banking system in 1972–3 was so large that the above adjustment mechanism just could not work (see Figure P), The system moved into disequilibrium. The underlying demand function may not have changed, but the public could not reach their desired position.

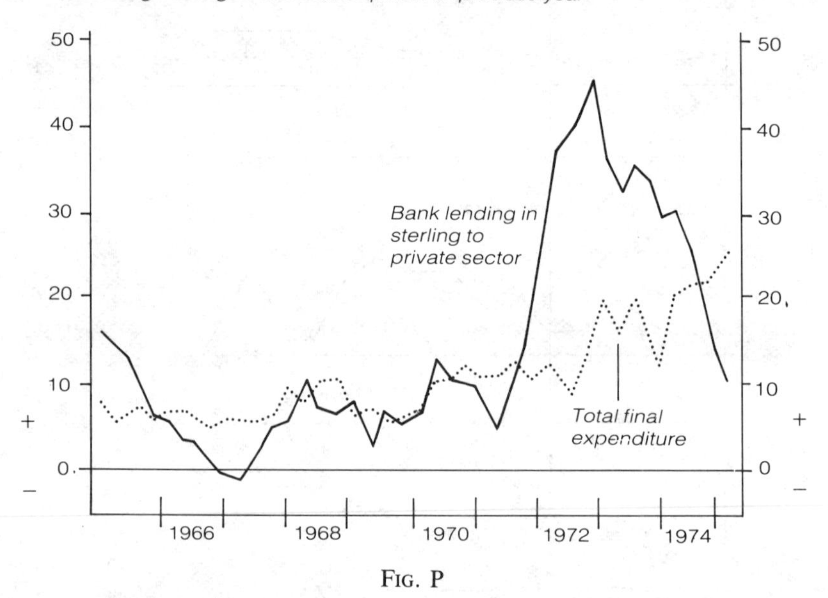

FIG. P

One can make a number of remarks about such a line of approach. First, if movements in the nominal money stock are indeed the exogenous, causal force, the appropriate relationship to fit is a money multiplier, not a demand-for-money function. Second, if an exogenous monetary shock causes people to adjust until *real* balances are some function of current *and past* real incomes and interest rates, one should observe considerable overshooting and instability in the economy in response to variations in monetary growth rates. Finally, if the lags between injections of nominal money balances and their effect on real incomes and prices are long and variable, it is difficult to see

[1] M. J. Artis and M. Lewis, 'The demand for money: stable or unstable?', *The Banker*, vol. 124, March 1974: and 'The demand for money in the United Kingdom: 1963–1973', *Manchester School*, vol. 44, June 1976.

how people can ever normally be close to their underlying demand function for real money balances.

For practical purposes, however, these can be treated largely as debating points. The question essentially at issue in assessing monetary developments at this time was whether the volume of interest-bearing time deposits that had been accumulated so hugely in 1973 by the private sector, especially by companies, was voluntarily held at existing levels of incomes and interest rates, or whether at those existing levels money holders were preparing to move into other assets. Whether or not such deposits were willingly held is perhaps to some extent a semantic issue. What is held at any point of time must in a sense have been chosen, otherwise something else would have happened. Moreover, even those of us who believed that this unprecedented build-up of time deposits was an explicable function of relative interest-rate movements recognised that under changed circumstances this did represent a disturbing overhang of purchasing power.

Nevertheless I did not, and do not, accept the Artis–Lewis explanation that the huge rise in interest-bearing deposits in 1973 was largely a disequilibrium phenomenon. Instead, I would explain it largely in terms of a rational response to movements in interest-rate differentials. In particular, I would refer again to the theoretical case that when the return on bank deposits rises to equal the cost of bank borrowing, the demand for both bank loans *and bank interest-bearing deposits* will be infinite, since one can obtain additional precautionary balances at zero cost. They become a free good. It was, moreover, noteworthy that throughout 1973 the increase in company-sector bank deposits kept quite largely in step with the increase in company-sector borrowing (while there was little growth in company sector real expenditures) (see Figure Q).

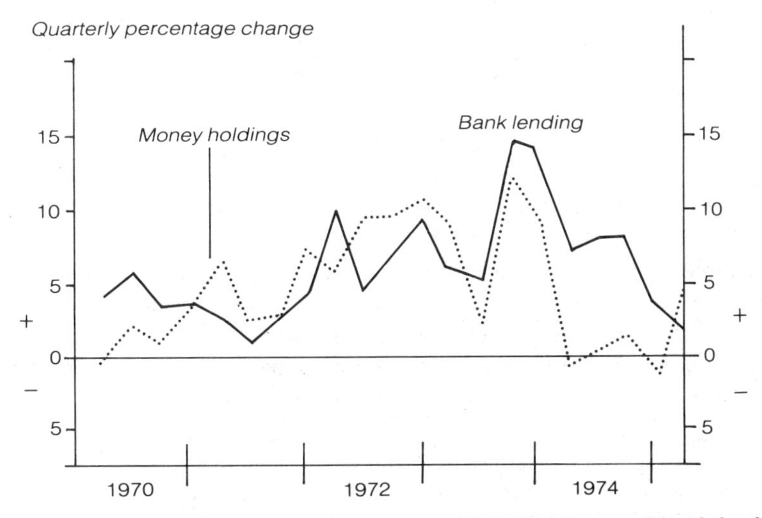

FIG. Q *Industrial and commercial companies: money holdings and bank lending*

One conclusion which we have reached is that our equations purporting to explain the movements in the holding of broad money balances (M_3) prior to 1971 were badly mis-specified. They were mis-specified because they did not contain an own-rate, and also left out some of the more important interest differentials, especially the margin between bank lending rates and deposit rates.[1] We have run a number of revised equations in this vein, and indeed get quite good fits over the period 1971–73 (see the Appendix). However, as Artis and Lewis very rightly point out,[2] it has not generally been possible to find the same kind of result within the earlier period 1963–71.[3] With only a few observations in the later period it is perfectly possible that the interest differential variables introduced then, and only then, were in fact acting as proxies for other factors. So for the time being I remain agnostic whether the experiences of 1971–4 reveal that the demand for money suffered a major structural change (after the introduction of the new system in 1971), or was not in equilibrium in these years, or was simply unstable. Either way reliance on the stability of the demand for money has been severely shaken. For our own internal forecasting purposes we have, at least for the time being, ceased to place *any* reliance on these equations except in the case of M_1, and to a lesser extent as a check on the judgemental forecast of persons' money holdings.

In the monetarist prescriptions for the appropriate conduct of monetary policy, a great weight depends on the stability of the demand-for-money function(s). Except, perhaps, in the case of M_1 we have not found these to be stable in use. It is not true that it does not matter which aggregate one looks at. The trend rates of growth of M_1 and M_3 have been moving in markedly differing directions for quite a lot of the period since 1972 (see Figure R). Moreover, in trying to understand and to interpret the movements in interest-bearing bank deposits we have come to the conclusion that holdings of these respond sensitively to interest-rate differentials. In so far as this is so, the grounds for drawing a sharp distinction between such 'monetary' liabilities and all other substitute sources of liquidity, including overdraft and trade credit facilities, as well as alternative liquid assets, seem weaker. This naturally raises the question of the appropriate monetary indicators. It may well be that a broad monetary indicator, M_3, is by its nature particularly unreliable. In the EEC committees concerned with monetary developments, for example, attention is concentrated on a primary liquidity total, nearly the same as M_1, and a much broader secondary liquidity total, which includes deposits with building societies, savings deposits, etc. It may not be sensible to pay much attention to anything between the narrow concept of money and

[1] In most demand-for-money functions only own-rates and yields on other alternative *assets* are included. Our experience suggests that yields on alternative liabilities, advances or trade credit should enter as well; indeed, portfolio theory suggests that this should be so.

[2] See the Artis and Lewis references in note 1 on p. 108.

[3] When own-rates and yields on other relevant assets and liabilities are included in such an equation over the period 1963–71, they do not appear very significant.

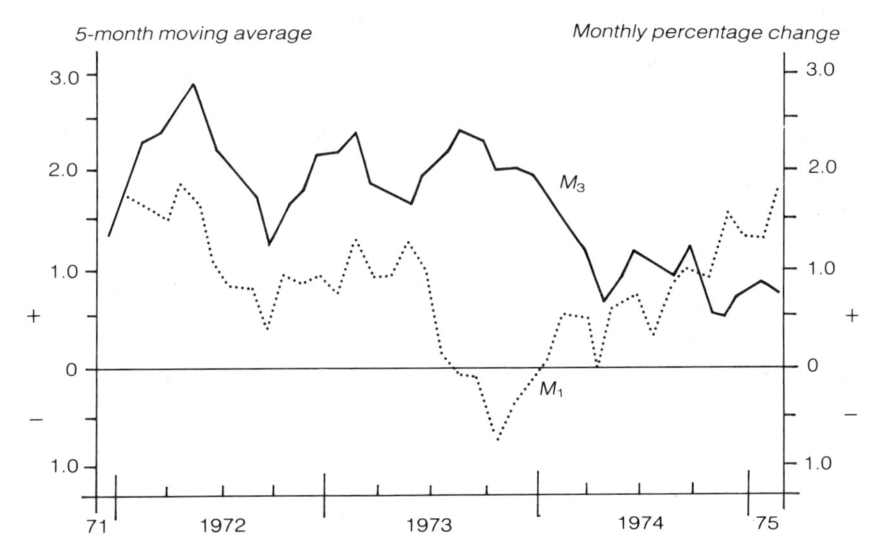

* *These were calculated by computing the 5-month moving average of seasonally adjusted levels, and then taking the percentage change over adjacent months.*

Fig. R *M_1 and M_3 trend rates of growth*

a broad, Radcliffe-type, liquidity measure. If so, the concentration on M_3 figures in the UK has been a bad mistake. In any case the unreliability of most of the demand-for-money functions and the disparate readings provided by the movements of the monetary aggregates have forced us, in some cases none too unwillingly, back to a more pragmatic approach to monetary analysis and policy.

Only with respect to M_1 can it still be argued that a fairly stable demand for money may exist. As already noted, with M_1 being only a component of total bank liabilities, its movements cannot be related to the various elements of domestic credit expansion. And in view of the ease of shifting between time and current accounts, the ability of the authorities to control M_1 at all tightly under any regime would seem limited. But the main disadvantage of the M_1 series in the UK is its extremely erratic nature. We only obtain once monthly (and end-quarter) data, so we have sixteen observations a year. The monthly changes of the seasonally adjusted data from July 1971 till March 1975 are shown in Table A together with the residuals from a five-monthly moving average. The standard deviation from the moving average is large in relation to the calculated values of that moving average. We receive the data several weeks after the monthly make-up date. The noise in the series is so loud that it takes us several months to discern a systematic trend with any confidence. In any case the demand for M_1 is a function of current *and past* incomes and interest rates. So the movements in the series, when the systematic trends can

TABLE A

M_1 monthly changes

		Change over previous month	Five-month moving average	Seasonally adjusted deviation
1971	July	+ 42	—	—
	August	+176	—	—
	September	+119	+106.2	+ 12.8
	October	+ 38	+144.2	−106.2
	November	+156	+107.4	+ 48.6
	December	+232	+ 89.0	+143.0
1972	January	− 8	+136.2	+144.2
	February	+ 27	+151.0	−124.0
	March	+274	+131.4	+142.6
	April	+230	+175.2	+ 54.8
	May	+134	+162.4	− 28.4
	June	+211	+118.4	+ 92.6
	July	− 37	+ 89.8	−126.8
	August	+ 54	+ 98.8	− 44.8
	September	+ 87	+ 52.4	+ 34.6
	October	+179	+105.8	+ 73.2
	November	− 21	+ 91.0	−112.0
	December	+230	+ 86.0	+144.0
1973	January	− 20	+ 68.4	− 88.4
	February	+ 62	+145.0	− 83.0
	March	+ 91	+101.8	− 10.8
	April	+362	+120.4	+241.6
	May	+ 14	+158.6	+144.6
	June	+ 73	+142.8	+ 69.8
	July	+253	+ 21.6	+231.4
	August	+ 12	− 24.4	+ 36.4
	September	−244	− 15.8	+228.2
	October	−216	− 61.8	+154.2
	November	+116	− 47.4	+163.4
	December	+ 23	− 17.0	+ 40.0
1974	January	+ 84	+ 14.6	+ 69.4
	February	− 92	+ 53.4	−145.4
	March	− 58	+ 31.4	− 89.4
	April	+310	− 5.8	+315.8
	May	− 87	+ 46.2	−133.2
	June	−102	+ 86.8	+188.8
	July	−168	+ 29.2	+138.8
	August	+145	+ 82.6	+ 62.4
	September	+ 22	+123.8	−101.8
	October	+180	+133.4	+ 46.6
	November	+104	+206.2	−102.2
	December	+216	+172.0	+ 44.0
1975	January	+509	+190.2	+318.8
	February	−149	—	—
	March	+271	—	—

The standard deviation: 135.775.

be interpreted, tell you where you have been, not necessarily where you are going. That at least is something. For example, it would suggest that monetary policy was becoming excessively tight at end-1973, easing thereafter in the latter half of 1974; and most British commentators believe the reverse.

The monetarist edifice rests largely on the stability, and predictability, of the demand-for-money function. Econometric study of the data in the 1960s had suggested that in the UK we, too, could build parts of our monetary policy on this basis. Subsequent experience has revealed weaknesses in this foundation.

4. Policy Response

We had intended, in the new approach to Competition and Credit Control, to control the monetary aggregates through the price mechanism by lowering or raising interest rates. This worked reasonably well in the case of M_1, since, with rates on most current accounts held at zero, an increase in rates engineered by the authorities represented, *ipso facto*, an increase in the interest differential between current accounts and other assets. This was not the case with M_3. Patently, the control mechanism in 1973 was failing. This occurred, we believed, because a rise in market rates does not, under certain circumstances, lead to a revision of interest *differentials* in a manner which would cause a fall in advances and deposits. Indeed, differentials were moving perversely as rates were being pushed up.

Since the problem was caused in large part by banks' aggressive bidding for interest-sensitive funds, the appropriate solution seemed to be to make such behaviour increasingly costly. That was the purpose of the supplementary special deposits scheme. Under this scheme a limit to the rate of growth of interest-bearing liabilities was fixed, admittedly rather arbitrarily. If banks bid so strongly for funds that they grew faster than this allowable rate (on a three-monthly average calculation to smooth out unpredictable variations), they paid an increasing penalty, in the form of having to place zero-yielding deposits with the Bank of England, the further over the limit they went – a progressive penalty.

There are a number of good features about this scheme. A major problem of running a more competitive banking system had been that the banks had been so keen on expansion, extending facilities on a large scale, bidding aggressively for funds to support expansion, that credit control had been gravely weakened. The existence of this new instrument, even when it is not actually in use, should serve to restrain bank behaviour in a manner that market disciplines failed to achieve. This instrument should prevent any future recurrence of the arbitrage 'bubble' that blew up in the autumn of 1973.

There are a number of features about the scheme that may be considered good or bad. The imposition of a tight 'corset' can go beyond forcing interest-rate differentials back to normal relativities. It could be used to make deposit interest rates unusually low in relation to rates on lending and on other assets, thereby bringing about artificial disintermediation. According to the monetarists, the resulting fall in bank lending and in time deposits, and the faster growth in personal-sector holdings of short-term public-sector debt, has little or no economic effect, only a presentational one. Similarly, the use of the corset could be so severe, especially if the banking system has only small reserves of public-sector debt to run off, that it could force banks to ration advances themselves in order to avoid penalties.

There are some clear disadvantages in this mechanism. It has the inherent defects of a base-dated mechanism, tending during its periods of imposition to fix the banking system into a rigid mould. It shares with other ceiling controls the problems of choosing arbitrary ceiling, guideline, limit numbers, and the many problems of administration.

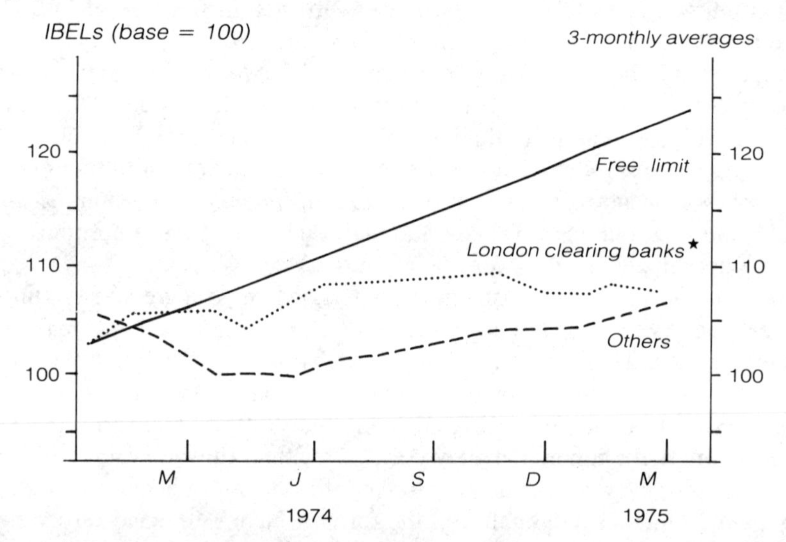

FIG. S

Figure S shows (for the clearing banks and other banks separately) the path of interest-bearing eligible liabilities (IBELs) relative to the free limit. The scheme did have an effect, more or less as intended, during the early months of 1974. Banks became considerably more conservative in extending facilities, and the competition for funds among themselves abated. Interest differentials reverted to a more normal level, and the arbitrage bubble was largely run off.

By the autumn of 1974, however, the effect of the 'corset' had been overtaken by other independent forces within the system. One of the factors bringing an end to the speculative boom in property development and housing towards the end of 1973 was the sharp rise in interest rates (changes in tax regulations were another). Some of the newer, 'fringe' financial institutions had over-extended themselves, especially in their involvement in the property business. An interrelated property development/secondary banking crisis developed at the turn of the year; a number of property companies and some financial institutions became insolvent; and the loss of confidence in a larger group of smaller banks (with or without justification) caused widespread withdrawals of funds and liquidity problems, which the Bank in concert with the clearing banks took steps to counteract.

This crisis led banks throughout the system to reassess their objectives, and to attach much greater weight to prudential considerations and safety, and less to growth for its own sake. This tendency was reinforced by further developments throughout 1975, e.g. bank failures in other countries, losses in international exchange markets, etc. Moreover, the growth of both sterling and foreign currency deposits was making banks' equity – deposit ratios (in several countries) look exposed. A general concern about banks' capital adequacy developed, for the first time for many years. In 1974, however, equity markets were so depressed that new issues were effectively ruled out. Anyhow a good profit record would be a desirable basis for a new issue. With interest rates falling during 1974–5, and with running costs, especially the wages and salary bill, rising at an inflated rate, profits were becoming harder to earn. So, during 1974–5, banks' objectives shifted markedly from growth to profit maximisation and retrenchment.

Meanwhile, during 1973–4, companies' cash-flow positions had been severely weakened by a combination of rampant inflation, price controls, additional taxation, the three-day week in early 1974 and, for many industries, stagnant output. Owing to the usual long lags before investment expenditures react to economic developments, companies moved into increasing and enormous deficit. With capital markets severely depressed, there was virtually no alternative source of external finance during 1973–4 except recourse to the banks. Figure T shows the growing indebtedness of the company sector to the banks. By the middle of 1974, however, the gearing of company-sector balance-sheets was becoming adverse; indeed, interest payments were taking a much larger share of company profits (see Figure U). By then companies were becoming increasingly hesitant about borrowing more from the banks, and began to trim back their stockbuilding (and fixed investment plans) quite severely. Towards the end of 1974 the price controls were relaxed and tax relief–on stock appreciation–was given, so their cash flow began to recover. In any case from mid-1974 the pressure of demand by companies for advances slackened off.

In this context with the banks more concerned with profit maximisation, slack demand for advances and a plentiful supply of reserve assets from the ever-growing budget deficit, banks sharply reduced the rates bid for deposits.

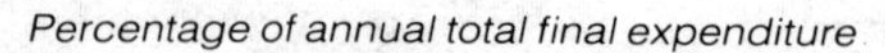

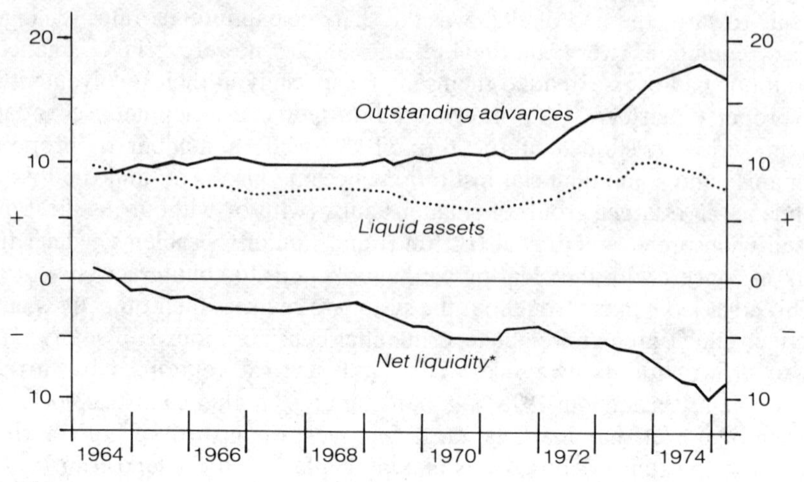

*Equals liquid assets ratio minus outstanding advances ratio

Fig. T *Industrial and commercial companies' outstanding advances, liquid assets and net liquidity relative to total final expenditure*

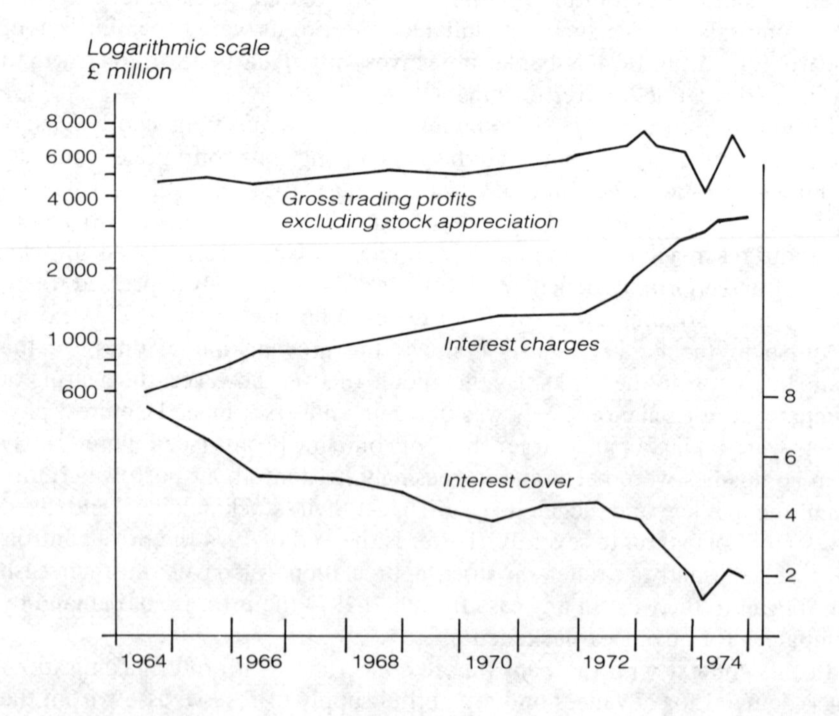

Fig. U *Interest charges and gross trading profits*

The margin between bank deposit rates and lending rates widened. Under such conditions it was much cheaper to pay bills by running down deposits than by increasing overdrafts, and more profitable to hold public-sector debt, or building society deposits, than bank deposits.

To some extent owing to these factors the 'corset' ceased to become binding for most banks after the autumn, and by the winter appeared otiose. Accordingly in February 1975 the opportunity was taken to suspend it.

This again illustrates the main theme here, which is the sensitivity of the financial system to interest differentials. In seeking to manage this system it is not sufficient to have a regard to *the* interest rate. One has to go further and keep an eye on the pattern of relative rates. The supplementary special deposits scheme was in a sense an instrument aimed at influencing this pattern.

For the rest, the experience of the last few years has gone a long way, at least in the UK, to undermine confidence in the stability of the demand for money and the applicability at least of the stricter monetarist prescriptions. In these conditions of uncertainty, there has been some return to a more eclectic, agnostic approach.

Appendix: Demand-for-Money Equations since 1971

The failure of the demand-for-money equations (with the possible exception of the M_1 equation) estimated up to 1971[1] to predict money stock growth subsequently stimulated, within the Bank, further research into the nature of the relationships.

Attempts to reinstate the equations have essentially taken the form of introducing new variables into existing equations[2] with a view to modelling more satisfactorily the structural changes in the demand for money which followed the introduction of Competition and Credit Control in September 1971. (See the descriptive account of post-1971 developments in the text.)

Research has been directed towards both the broad (M_3) and narrow (M_1) definitions of money and towards its sectoral allocation between the personal sector (MP) and the industrial and commercial company sector (MC). Equations have been re-estimated over the period 1963IV–1973IV.

Two developments following the structural change in 1971 may have affected the growth of M_3 and MC in 1972 and 1973. These were:

1. The growth in the banks' issues of negotiable certificates of deposit (CDs) and the subsequent expansion in the market for these instruments.
2. The distortions created by the inflexibility of banks' base rates (which determine lending rates) relative to borrowing rates (which are market determined). At times during 1972 and 1973 volatile market rates rose to levels above lending rates and made profitable arbitraging possible. As a result, both M_3 and MC aggregates were sometimes severely distorted by the response to the pattern of rates.

---

[1] Estimation period 1963I–1971IV.

[2] A stock-adjustment model is used throughout estimated in first differences with a Cochrane–Orcutt transformation.

Equations were estimated (1963IV–1973IV) for both M_3 and MC which included a CD rate as an own-rate alongside the competing rates which featured alone in the earlier equations–this was an attempt to capture the increasing attractiveness of such interest-bearing deposits in M_3 and MC. Indeed, there is strong theoretical support for including an own-rate in a demand-for-money specification. Furthermore, attempts were made to incorporate a variable representing the return to interest arbitrage.[1] Table B compares the results of estimations over the period 1963–73 with those of the earlier period 1963–71. The CD and arbitrage variables, it should be noted, were included in the estimations for the final observations only. Both variables proved statistically significant and improved the fit of the equations over the longer observation periods for both equations. However, experience in the use of these equations for forecasting purposes up to 1975I suggests that they may still be mis-specified. Both equations have consistently failed to predict accurately the subsequent growth of MC and M_3. Attempts to introduce further explanatory variables–such as the net acquisition of financial assets in the MC equation–have been fruitless.

Further research on the MP equations has been undertaken. The inclusion of the four quarters of 1973 in the estimation period yields real income elasticities well outside the plausible range,[2] though a better fit overall is produced (see Table C). It is clear that the exceptional growth of MP in 1973 has not, and perhaps cannot, be explained properly–at least with reference to past experience. Attempts to improve the MP equation by the addition of a net acquisition of financial assets variable has also been investigated–its inclusion has been found to add to the explanatory power of the equation. However, like the M_3 and MC equations, the MP equation (all specifications) has been markedly unsuccessful in explaining post-1973 developments.

Little further research has been done on the M_1 equations which have remained fairly stable over differing estimation periods (see Table D). Although the M_1 quarterly series moved erratically during 1974, the M_1 equation performed tolerably well–at least to the extent of not exhibiting any noticeable predictive bias.

The reasons for the poor performance of the re-estimated equations since the end of 1973 are difficult to pinpoint. It might be thought, however, that the introduction of the supplementary deposit scheme (and distortions thereby created) coupled with the rapidly accelerating rate of inflation (which could have significantly altered the behaviour of money holders) may have contributed to the equation failures.

If any conclusions can be drawn at this stage on the Bank's continuing research in this area, it is the rather negative one that with all but the M_1 equations exhibiting considerable instability and little predictive ability, the equations cannot be used with any confidence in an operational forecasting context.

---

[1] An adjusted differential between the three-month CD rate and banks' 'prime' lending rate.

[2] Similar equations estimated over the period up to the end-1972, however, had real income elasticities of unity.

TABLE B

M_3 and MC equations

Dependent variable	Estimation period	Coefficients										Long-run elasticities		
		TFE	P_t	$1+LA_t$	$1+CD_t$	D_t	M_{t-1}	$\bar{R}^2$	*SE* (%)	*DW*	ρ[b]	Real income	*LA*[c] rate	*CD*[d] rate
M_3	1963 IV–1971 III	0.175 (1.46)[a]	0.391	−0.491 (2.47)			0.609 (4.50)	0.51	0.911	2.20	−0.5	0.449	−0.08	
M_3	1963 IV–1973 IV	0.149 (1.42)	0.225	−0.665 (3.59)	1.139 (4.44)		0.775 (8.53)	0.88	1.032	2.36	−0.6	0.661	−0.19	0.47
M_3	1963 IV–1973 IV	0.197 (1.98)	0.272	−0.661 (3.70)	1.287 (4.59)	1.196 (2.97)	0.728 (8.51)	0.89	0.945	2.37	−0.5	0.724	−0.16	0.38
MC	1963 IV–1971 III	0.199 (0.81)	0.841	−1.306 (2.50)			0.159 (1.09)	0.16	1.873	2.13	0	0.236	−0.10	
MC	1963 IV–1973 IV	0.296 (1.31)	0.595	−1.122 (2.74)	3.465 (5.30)		0.405 (3.71)	0.72	2.112	2.09	−0.3	0.497	−0.14	0.47
MC	1963 IV–1973 IV	0.325 (1.52)	0.574	−1.244 (2.79)	3.145 (4.90)	2.215 (2.34)	0.426 (4.05)	0.72	2.005	2.05	−0.2	0.567	−0.14	0.44

Notes for this and following tables

All variables are in natural logarithms.
SE: standard error
TFE: total final expenditure at 1970 prices, £m, s.a.
PDI: personal disposable income at 1970 prices, £m, s.a.
P_t: the TFE deflator or PDI deflator where appropriate.
LA_t: the interest rate on three-month deposits with local authorities (quarterly averages of working days).
CD_t: the interest rate on three-month sterling certificates of deposit (quarterly averages of working days).
CON_t: the yield on 2½ per cent consolidated stock (quarterly averages of working days).
D_t: a variable representing the return to interest arbitrage–an adjusted differential between the three-month CD rate and bankers' 'prime' lending rate.
M_{t-1}: The appropriate money stock series lagged one quarter.

[a] *t* values are shown in brackets beneath the coefficients.
[b] For an explanation of ρ transformation see appendix to G. Hacche, 'The demand for money in the United Kingdom: experience since 1971', *Bank of England Quarterly Bulletin*, vol. 14, September 1974.
[c] Calculated at the mean values of the estimation period.
[d] Calculated at the rate for 1972: IV.

TABLE C

MP equations

Dependent variable	Estimation period	Coefficients										Long-run elasticites	
		Constant	*PDI*	P_t	$1+CON_{t-1}$	M_{t-1}	*NAFA*[a]	$\bar{R}^2$	*SE* (%)	*DW*	ρ	Real income	Consol Rate
MP	1963 IV– 1971 III		0.344 (4.13)	0.343	−0.433 (1.15)	0.657 (5.62)		0.75	0.754	2.47	−0.6	1.002	−0.08
MP	1963 IV– 1973 IV		0.269 (3.26)	0.093	−0.223 (0.63)	0.907 (9.81)		0.85	0.854	2.23	−0.6	2.900	−0.17
MP[b]	1963 IV– 1973 IV	0.00225	0.250 (2.67)	0.104	−0.303 (0.76)	0.896 (9.27)		0.76	0.864	2.17	−0.6	2.411	−0.02
MP[b]	1963 IV– 1973 IV	0.00325	0.236 (2.54)	0.171	−0.442 (1.08)	0.829 (7.70)	0.00001 (1.35)	0.77	0.854	2.18	−0.6	1.385	−0.03
MP[b]	1963 IV– 1973 IV	0.00217		0.147	−0.92 (2.12)	0.853 (7.25)	0.00002 (1.64)	0.68	0.899	2.07	−0.4		−0.06

[a] Net acquisition of financial assets by the personal sector.
[b] The three equations cannot be compared directly with previous ones as they are estimated with a constant term.

See also notes to Table B.

TABLE D

M_1 equations

Dependent variable	Estimation period	Coefficients									Long-run elasticites		
		TFE	P_t	$1+LA_t$	$1+CON_{t-1}$	M_{t-1}	R^2	SE (%)	DW	ρ	Real income	LA rate	Consol Rate
M_1	1963 IV–1971 III	0.205 (1.16)	0.749	−0.868 (2.35)	−1.227 (1.34)	0.252 (1.67)	0.37	1.385	2.09	−0.4	0.274	−0.07	−0.11
M_1	1963 IV–1973 IV	0.237 (1.64)	0.562	−0.709 (2.48)	−0.986 (1.12)	0.438 (3.05)	0.50	1.635	2.09	−0.7	0.422	−0.08	−0.12

See also notes to Table B.

IV

Bank Lending and Monetary Control

1. Introduction

During the course of the 1970s the monetary authorities in the UK, as in other countries, moved towards the adoption of publicly announced quantitative targets for monetary growth. Such a publicly stated target was first promulgated in the UK during 1976, but for some few years before then the authorities were setting (private, internal and undisclosed) monetary objectives for themselves.

The adoption of such a monetary target would seem to require the authorities to take corrective action to restore monetary growth to the chosen path when there is a (persistent and significant) deviation from it. The standard market mechanism that would be expected to return a deviating monetary out-turn to the targeted path works through variations in interest rates, which variations can be induced either through the discretion of the authorities or in consequence of the authorities seeking to follow some 'rule' for monetary base control.

Critics of the UK authorities' attempts to hold monetary growth smoothly and steadily to the monetary growth path have on several occasions compared performance in the UK disparagingly with that in more successful economies abroad, such as the USA and West Germany. In the face of such criticism, an applied quantitative test that seemed worth trying was to examine the authorities' reaction function to deviations in monetary growth (relative to target); the purpose of the exercise was to find out whether the monetary authorities in other countries (which also primarily used market mechanisms, rather than direct controls, to influence the growth of the monetary aggregates), reacted to variations in monetary growth by varying interest rates more quickly or more forcefully than in the UK.

The results of this exercise are shown in Appendix 1. They suggest that the authorities in the UK, over the data period used, behaved in a way that appears, at least at first sight, more consistent with determination to achieve monetary targets than did the authorities (on this test basis at least) in West Germany, the USA and Canada. Thus in the UK market interest rates during these years have been raised (lowered) at least as quickly and much more forcefully in response to accelerations (decelerations) in monetary growth in the UK than in these other countries.

Far from appearing as 'unbelieving monetarists', these results would suggest that the authorities in the UK acted relatively more forcefully and vigorously to attain their targets. Yet, despite the relatively prompt and comparatively forceful policy response to deviations in monetary growth, the actual outcome for monetary developments year by year has continued to give frequent cause for concern; it has not, for example, proceeded noticeably more smoothly than in these countries examined.

One possible reason to explain why monetary developments have remained so variable, despite the authorities' attempts to smooth and control, is simply that the UK economy in general has been rather more disturbed in a variety of ways than other economies, e.g. industrial disturbances, changes in political and fiscal conditions, etc. Critics, on the other hand, have tended to concentrate on supposed weaknesses in the techniques of debt management in the UK. Some partial and limited evidence in the next section is presented which would suggest that the authorities' techniques have been more successful than is perhaps commonly realised. In any case the arguments on debt management have by now been well aired, and it is hoped and intended here to avoid that quagmire of debate.

Instead, the purpose of this paper is to draw attention more closely to a reason, on this view the main reason, that complicates, and makes exceedingly difficult, shorter-term monetary control. This is the difficulty of either forecasting, or controlling, the pace of bank lending to the private sector. Such bank lending to the private sector is, of course, a large and volatile component of broad money, £M_3, which has been adopted as the target variable; the difficulty of predicting or controlling its fluctuations naturally results in serious problems in the attempt to predict and control the monetary aggregate of which it represents such a sizeable counterpart.

2. Volatility and the Lack of Offsets

Bank lending to the private sector is certainly volatile. It shares that characteristic, however, with all the other counterparts to monetary growth, e.g. PSBR, debt sales, external flows, as shown below in Table A. Indeed, as measured by the coefficient of variation it is, not perhaps surprisingly, external flows which exhibit most volatility, with the movements in £M_3 and in the domestic counterparts all having a roughly similar degree of variance.

However, the volatility of a component (of the money stock) matters only for the total if there are no major offsets among other components – if, in other words, a sharp change in the component is largely reflected in the total. It is here that bank lending to the private sector appears distinctive. As column 1 of Table B indicates, £M_3 and bank lending are more highly correlated than is £M_3 with any other major component (indeed, at the 99 per cent level this is the only significant correlation). This relatively close

TABLE A

The variance and coefficient of variation of £M_3 and its components (seasonally adjusted flows)

	Estimation period: 1968 IV-1979 I calendar quarters	
	1 Variance	2 Coefficient of variation[a]
1 £M_3	30×10^4	72
2 PSBR	102×10^4	85
3 Purchases of public-sector debt by non-banks	75×10^4	− 95
4 £ lending to the private sector	44×10^4	90
5 External and foreign currency finance	33×10^4	−715

[a] Equals $\left(\frac{\text{standard deviation}}{\text{mean}}\right) \times 100$.

relationship between movements in bank lending to the private sector and in £M_3, and the weaker relationship between the latter and the other counterparts, is also shown visually in Figure A. Inspection of the rest of Table B suggests that this is because changes in lending are not significantly offset by compensating changes in other components of £M_3 – with the possible exception of debt sales.

The interpretation of Table B is not, perhaps, straightforward and it may be helpful to rehearse it. *Ceteris paribus*, a rise in the PSBR (row 2), or in bank lending (row 4), or in the contribution, often in the form of a rise in the reserves, of external and foreign currency finance (row 5) expands £M_3. Therefore, one would expect positive partial correlation coefficients between £M_3 and these components. In contrast, *ceteris paribus*, a rise in debt sales (row 3) decreases £M_3 and one would here expect a negative partial correlation coefficient. In practice, of course, there may be natural or policy-induced offsets between components – i.e., the *ceteris paribus* assumption is unrealistic. (An example of such offsets is discussed further later.)

The figures reported in Table B are, however, simple correlations (not partial correlations) and the usual caveats about the use of such correlations must be kept in mind. Thus Table B reveals nothing about directions of causation, if any; nor is it possible to distinguish directly between offsets that occur 'naturally' as a result of the normal functioning of the financial and economic system as contrasted with those of a policy-induced nature.

Nevertheless, there is a contrast between the extent to which variations in bank lending become transmitted to (are correlated with) variations in £M_3,

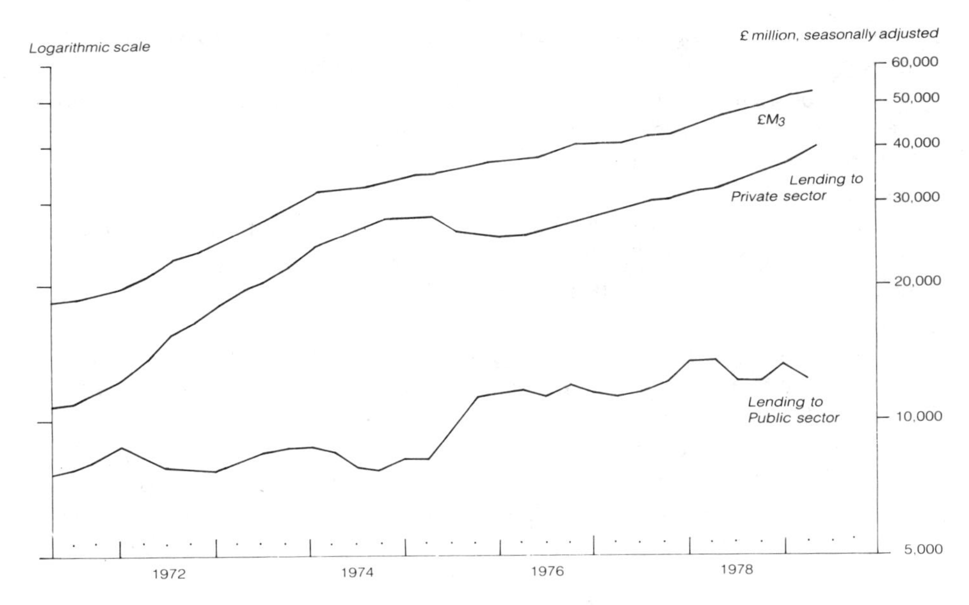

Fig. A *£M_3 and bank lending to the public and private sectors*

TABLE B

The correlation between £M_3 and its components (seasonally adjusted flow)

	Estimation period: 1968 IV–1979 I calendar quarters				
	1 **£M_3**	**2** **PSBR**	**3** **Debt sales**	**4** **£ lending**	**5** **Externals**
1 £M_3	1				
2 Public sector borrowing requirement	0.366*	1			
3 Purchases of public-sector debt by non-banks	−0.097	−0.709**	1		
4 £ lending to the private sector	0.583**	0.142	−0.311*	1	
5 External and foreign currency finance	−0.113	−0.418**	−0.096	−0.219	1

Number of observations = 42.

95% confidence interval = 0.3024 (* significant at this level).
99% confidence interval = 0.3975 (** significant at this level).

and the lesser extent whereby variations in the other counterparts, perhaps notably variations in the PSBR, are similarly transmitted to £M_3. Thus the PSBR is positively correlated with £M_3, as might be expected, but the size of the correlation has been greatly reduced, over the period examined, by the fact that the PSBR and debt sales to non-banks have a high, significant negative correlation and that the PSBR and external outflows also have a significant, if somewhat lower, negative correlation. Admittedly the correlation between bank lending and both debt sales and external flows is also negative (i.e. offsetting), but the extent and significance of these latter offsets are much less.

Such 'offsets' within the financial system may be either natural or policy-induced. Consider, for example, the correlation (−0.31) between the rise in bank lending (raising £M_3) and the increase in debt sales (reducing £M_3). This could have a 'natural' cause – e.g. the private sector borrowing to buy debt – or a policy-induced cause, with the authorities seeking to offset a known high level of bank lending. However, the most significant and sizeable offset is that between the PSBR and public-sector debt sales. As already noted, one possible interpretation of this is that the authorities have been moderately successful in offsetting high PSBRs through their debt-management policies (perhaps because they can forecast the future level of the PSBR reasonably well), though less successful at offsetting variations in bank lending (perhaps in part because these are less predictable). But another interpretation is more simply that the structure and normal workings of the financial system naturally encourages such a pattern of offsets.

In any case, although it is a digression from my main theme, it seemed of interest to examine somewhat further the interrelationship between the movements in monetary growth and in debt sales. First, the post-budget forecasts for each of the financial years 1972/3 to 1978/9 were examined to see what the rate of growth of £M_3 would have been had the actual sales to the non-bank private sector of

(a) gilts
(b) all central government debt

been as forecast. The answers were that, against an actual growth rate of £M_3 of 13.8 per cent per annum in this period, growth would have been 17.5 per cent under variant (a) and 17.1 per cent under variant (b). The exercise is simplistic – it assumes, for example, no offsets between a change in the level of debt sales and any other component of £M_3 – but the direction of the results supports the view that official reactions in the gilts markets to developments in the monetary aggregates (that were unforeseen at the time of the budget) have been relatively successful in offsetting such unforeseen variations. On this test 'discretionary' debt management would seem to have led to a more successful outcome than would have been obtained by merely achieving exactly the initial forecast, as then consistent with the 'intended' post-budget outcome.

The volatility of debt sales *within* each year, a subject that has caused considerable discussion, was then examined. Here, too, the authorities' tactics come out with colours unlowered. The coefficient of variation of £M_3 on a monthly basis over the period April 1972 to April 1979 was 91.0. Had gilt sales to the non-bank public in each separate year been smoothed over that period (i.e., had the total sales in each financial year been achieved at the rate of 1/12 per month, for example by the use of tenders), then the coefficient of variation would have been *higher* at 99.0. Only if one smooths total central government debt sales to non-banks does the coefficient fall and then only to 90.0. Put at its simplest, the so-called 'feasts and famines' in the gilt market in recent years are not such an easy target for criticism as is sometimes assumed. The feasts more often than not have taken place when there was a need for them to offset other expansionary factors, as (for example) in the first half of 1979.

On the second possible interpretation of the source of 'offsets' offered above, a number of possible 'natural offsets' within £M_3 come to mind. First, an increase in the PSBR, except to the extent that it is matched by a current-account deficit,[1] leads to an increase in nominal financial wealth, part of which might ordinarily be reinvested in gilts. Furthermore, to the extent that such increase in 'wealth' is regarded by the private sector as matched by contingent future tax liabilities, and/or largely represents higher nominal interest payments in (partial) recompense for the erosion of the real value of existing fixed interest debt, then the proportion 'naturally' being reinvested in gilts might reasonably be expected to be the higher.[2] On the other hand, an increase in bank borrowing does not, of course, raise net wealth, so one might on that account expect there to be a lesser 'automatic' offset. Part of the increased 'wealth' arising from a higher PSBR and/or current-account surplus should, perhaps, also go towards a reduction in bank lending. This effect does not, however, show up at all clearly in the correlations in Table B, perhaps because it is partly submerged by the positive indirect effect on bank lending of a higher PSBR that stimulates higher expenditures and nominal incomes.

Additionally, offsets might be expected between debt sales and external factors.[3] An external inflow often reflects an actual or prospective current-account surplus, which also raises net UK financial wealth – part of which would be invested in UK public-sector debt. Moreover, conditions propitious

---

[1] Table B suggests that there is indeed a negative correlation between the PSBR and the external factors in £M3.

[2] On the first of these propositions, see the literature on whether bonds are net wealth, which followed and was largely stimulated by R. J. Barro's article, 'Are government bonds net wealth', *Journal of Political Economy*, vol. 82, December 1974. On the second, see the papers on 'The trend of the National Debt in relation to National Income', by Miss C. V. Downton, *Bank of England Quarterly Bulletin*, vol. 17, September 1977, and *Real National Saving and its Sectoral Composition* by C. T. Taylor and A. R. Threadgold, Bank of England Discussion Paper No. 6, October 1979.

[3] This two-way interrelationship has been explored econometrically by B. C. Hilliard in *Exchange Flows and the Gilt-edged Security Market: A Causality Study,* Bank of England Discussion Paper No. 2, February 1979.

for gilt sales to domestic investors are likely to be such as to encourage capital inflows, and vice versa. Similarly, it might be expected that a tightening of monetary policy in the UK, making bank borrowing more difficult or more expensive to obtain, would encourage inflows over the exchanges, and indeed that such inflows – by raising liquidity – would reduce the need for UK residents to borrow. No strong evidence of either effect is visible in the results of Table B.

3. The Difficulty of Forecasting Bank Lending

The next step in the analysis is to offer some, necessarily limited, evidence on the difficulties of *forecasting* bank lending in sterling to the private sector. The material prepared by a colleague, Tony Hotson (in Appendix 2), is relevant here, for the second part of it surveys the forecasting 'ability', outside the relevant estimation period, for a number of bank lending equations for the UK published in recent years. On the whole, the results are poor; the average root mean square percentage error for the four models for which we have been able to run out-of-period 'forecasts' comes out at over 10 per cent over a projection period of one year, though the 'best' result does give a (probably highly flattering) RMS%E of under 1.

The aim of Appendix 2 is not to cast stones, however; rather, it is to serve as a reminder that the problems – to which I now turn – faced by official forecasters in recent years do not stem purely from their own inadequacies. (By way of registering a special interest, I should note here that I have been myself one of the longest-standing of these.)

The approach adopted for this exercise was to examine *ex post* the forecasting capacities of the authorities, as exemplified first by the accuracy of their post-budget forecast. With the budget representing the main occasion for adjusting macroeconomic policy instruments during the fiscal year, it may be argued that the post-budget financial forecast should represent for the policy-makers a satisfactory, or at least tolerable, projected outcome for the coming financial year.

Table B was thus replicated for these *forecasts* – though this time only for financial years rather than for calendar quarters, partly because the quarterly paths in the official forecasts, which are generally derived from, and considerably more uncertain than, the annual forecasts, have not always commanded as much attention as the figures for the year. It should be borne in mind that there are consequently far fewer observations than for Table B (ten against forty-two), but the idea is really just to make a very broad comparison between the statistical offsets as the forecasters have seen them (Table C) and those of 'real life' (Table B).

Two points may be made about these results. First, the correlation between movements in the PSBR and in £M_3 tends to dominate the forecast, whereas

TABLE C

The correlation between forecast £M_3 and its components (seasonally adjusted flow)

	Estimation period: financial years 1969/70 to 1978/79				
	1 £M_3	2 PSBR	3 Debt sales	4 £ lending	5 Externals
1 £M_3	1				
2 Public sector borrowing requirement	0.653*	1			
3 Purchases of public-sector debt by non-banks	−0.385	−0.802*	1		
4 £ lending to the private sector	0.578	0.290	−0.264	1	
5 External and foreign currency finance	−0.134	−0.443	0.039	−0.359	1

Number of observations = 10.

95% confidence interval = +/− 0.620 (* significant at this level).
99% confidence interval = +/− 0.815 (** significant at this level).

TABLE D

Errors[a] in post-budget forecasts

	Mean absolute error %	Estimation period: financial years 1969/70 to 1978/79				
		1	2	3	4	5
1 £M_3	4.7	1				
2 Public sector borrowing requirement	4.3	0.062	1			
3 Purchases of public-sector debt by non-banks	4.9	−0.008	−0.43	1		
4 £ lending to the private sector	5.7	0.83**	−0.24	0.08	1	
5 External and foreign currency finance	5.5	−0.175	−0.097	0.59	−0.35	1

[a] From actual forecast, expressed as a percentage of the money stock at the end of the preceding period.

Number of observations, significance levels, etc., as for Table C.

the correlation between movements in bank lending, and £M_3 dominates the outcome. This is very largely because the PSBR is, to some extent, a control variable and its developments are, within quite wide limits, both determinate by policy and predictable. Against this, bank lending is not a control variable in the same sense and, as already indicated, is not easy to control. Accordingly, forecasters have tended to extrapolate bank lending forward at its recent average, trend, rate, while projecting that the variations in £M_3 would follow the course of the PSBR.

The second notable point is that, apart from the higher correlation of the PSBR and £M_3, described above, the correlations are quite closely similar to, though the degree of significance is less than those reported in Table B. As will be subsequently shown, the forecasters made sizeable errors in their actual forecasts of both £M_3 and its counterparts. But Table C suggests that the forecasters captured reasonably closely the pattern of interrelationships between the counterparts and £M_3.

The next step was to calculate the errors between forecasts and outturns. Table D shows the mean absolute forecast error for each main counterpart and for £M_3 as a whole, together with the correlations[1] between the component errors and £M_3.

The first column indicates that the forecasts were not notably accurate, with an average yearly error for £M_3 of 4.7 per cent. The forecasts for all the major components are likewise rather bad, but top of the list, by a short head, comes bank lending to the private sector, with an average mean absolute error of 5.7 per cent.

The result of this exercise that stands out is, however, the high correlation between errors in the forecasts of bank lending and errors in the forecasts of £M_3. This relationship appears even more dominating in this study of errors in the forecasts than in the study of the interrelationships between the actuals in Table B; in this case it represents the only significant relationship. One inference from this finding would seem to be, particularly in so far as the forecasts for £M_3 were built up from forecasts of the separate main counterparts, that improved forecasts of the future path of bank lending would have been especially helpful in improving the forecasts for £M_3

We also looked at forecasts and outcomes over shorter (three-month) periods. Over these shorter periods the above finding of a close relationship

[1] Most correlation coefficients are presented after mean correction. In this case, when comparing actuals and forecasts, there seemed little value in so doing, and the above correlations are *not* so corrected. The differences between the set of mean corrected correlations and those shown above are not large, except in one case, that of the correlation between bank lending and debt sales, which after mean correction rises from +0.08 to +0.75. The statistical interpretation of this is that the mean error of bank lending forecasts is offset by the mean error of forecasts of debt sales (both being on balance under-predicted during this period), but in those years when the error in the bank lending forecast resulted in a larger than average under-prediction the offset in debt sales, also being under-predicted, was less sizeable than usual. In view of the small number of observations I am inclined to doubt whether this latter is more than a statistical curiosum, though it is possible that it is a cyclical effect.

between errors in the forecasts of bank lending and errors in the forecasts of £M_3 was less marked. In the case of these short-run forecasts, however, as contrasted with the post-budget forecast, the forecast is used itself as a guide to subsequent policy changes, so the interpretation of 'errors' in the forecast is perhaps somewhat more complicated. Moreover, over these shorter time horizons there does appear to be a somewhat greater degree of trend inertia in the path of the bank lending than in the course of the PSBR, which fluctuates very sharply month by month, week by week and even day by day. Thus the shorter the time period, the more 'errors' in the forecast of £M_3 become affected by the short-term volatility of the PSBR, as compared with the rather longer-term difficulties in forecasting the trend movements in bank lending.

The conclusion of these exercises is that it has been a very difficult task to forecast bank lending; in particular, the authorities have often not been able to predict in advance the main changes in trend of such lending. Events in early 1979, when what now appears as a clear upwards shift in the trend of bank lending was then ascribed to temporary factors and expected to subside, have rubbed this conclusion home.

4. Controlling Bank Lending

It would not matter greatly that one could not forecast a major component of monetary expansion, if unexpected deviations from its intended path could be quickly and easily reversed. The more action that is required to control a component, and the longer it takes to achieve that control, the more important it becomes to have accurate forecasts of its developments, so as to be able to make the other adjustments necessary, e.g., perhaps including fiscal policy, in order to maintain control over aggregate monetary growth.

The UK authorities have, in the past, tried to control the level of bank lending to the private sector by:

(a) pressure on short-term interest rates (and thus on the cost of bank credit)
(b) the use of direct controls (in the late 1960s and again periodically since 1973).

A major apparent difficulty during this period has been that the former has not worked well enough, or quickly enough, to avoid use of the latter.

In part, evidence of the difficulty of relying on interest-rate adjustments for the control of bank lending comes from a review of the applied econometric work of other academics in this field; this review occupies the first half of Appendix 2. The results of this survey are fairly fully written up there, so only the main points are summarised here:

1. A number of studies of bank lending to the private sector in the UK have been unable to find *any* negative influence of bank lending rates (or some

supposed proxy for them) on the demand for bank credit. Even after due allowance for data problems, multicollinearity between various 'own' and competing rates of interest, and the existence of long periods of direct controls, these findings are sufficiently numerous to be worrying.

2. Even where a significant effect is found (and I believe that there must be such an effect given time), the lag before the response is felt appears uncomfortably long (see Table H of Appendix 2) for policy-makers faced with uneasy financial markets and, in recent years, with annual monetary targets to be met. This slow reaction, together with the difficulties (already described) of accurate forecasting, constitutes a major control problem.

In consequence, direct controls have come to look more attractive than they might otherwise have been, because they have appeared at times to be the least uncertain limiting weapon in an uncertain world. This is particularly so, of course, when one remembers the political and social constraints that governments have at times felt about raising interest rates as far as was, perhaps, necessary. My purpose here is not, however, to argue the pros and cons of direct controls. The point is simply that the authorities have felt what the range of academic results also suggests: namely, that bank lending to the private sector is difficult to control over the operationally relevant time period.

5. Conclusions

Any attempt to influence £M_3 requires its counterparts to be influenced. Of these counterparts, two – the PSBR and external flows – are affected perversely, if at all, by fluctuations in interest rates.[1] With the demand for bank credit as insensitive as it appears to be now to changes in interest rates, the weight of adjustment of actual to desired £M_3 growth via interest rates in any short term – say over even a six- to nine-month period – must fall largely on debt sales. This would be true whether the system of monetary control remained roughly as now or whether some form of monetary base control were introduced.

Moreover, it may well be the case for the foreseeable future that bank lending will tend to remain unpredictable and hard to control. What consequences would flow from that appreciation? First, it would give some grounds for suggesting that direct controls, perhaps of an 'improved' and more permanent version, would have to be imposed. However, this would, in effect, represent equally permanent discrimination against the banking

---

[1] With the public sector normally being in deficit, an increase in interest rates raises net interest payments and raises the PSBR. An increase in interest rates, *ceteris paribus*, will induce capital inflows and thereby increase the likelihood of the private sector being in surplus on external account.

system, and would only result in driving the problem underground by forcing disintermediation from the controlled intermediaries to uncontrolled channels, perhaps with a growing proportion of domestic sterling banking being done abroad, as has occurred with the USA and West Germany. Second, it would give some grounds for redefining the chief target variable to be a narrower aggregate, e.g., M_1, as in Canada and the USA. In this case, the fluctuations in the demand for bank credit, and bank calls on the wholesale deposit market to finance such demands, do not disturb the pursuit and achievement of the narrower target. But in so far as the fluctuations in bank credit demands, and in £M_3, are thought to be important, this would represent, in a sense, simply abandoning the present ground, with control of £M_3 at its centre, an admission of inability to achieve current intermediate monetary objectives.

Third, one might search for structural ways to make bank lending more responsive to interest-rate variations; whatever the form of control, reliance on the market mechanism (rather than on some form of direct control) would be much more attractive if bank lending to the private sector were more easily and quickly controllable by such mechanisms. Unfortunately, it is hard to think of any structural changes that would not represent a retrogressive interference with the efficiency of bank intermediation. This problem, and that of forecasting lending, would benefit from a greater degree of academic interest than has been shown hitherto.

Appendix 1: An Examination of Interest-rate Responsiveness in the UK and Some Overseas Countries

Introduction

The purpose of this exercise was to examine the statistical evidence available for both the UK and those major overseas countries which have also been operating to declared targets for the growth of monetary aggregates[1] over a similar period to see whether the difficulties encountered by the UK authorities could be shown to arise from a relative unwillingness to accept interest-rate variability. The exercise was undertaken in two stages. At the first stage we sought to examine the simple correlations between a representative market interest rate and monthly changes in the relevant monetary aggregates. This does not, of itself, imply causality, but in so far as an active policy was being followed one might expect faster growth in the monetary aggregates to be subsequently associated with higher interest rates, and vice versa. As our results show, by this measure the responsiveness of interest rates to such changes over the relevant period was most marked in the UK.

The problems associated with the interpretation of these results are extensive. In particular, it may be argued that both the interest rate and the rate of growth of the money supply are simultaneously determined in a system to which the exogenous variables are to be found elsewhere. Consequently the second part of our exercise was to attempt to formulate a reaction function in a rather more explicit manner. This

[1] The USA, West Germany and Canada.

involved the calculation of deviations of the relevant monetary aggregates from their declared target paths in each country and then regressing changes in interest rates on these deviations. In so far as we can accept that the monetary authorities are able to engineer discretionary changes in market rates, the result from this exercise may be seen as some measure of their willingness to manipulate such rates in response to variations in the rate of growth of the targeted aggregates around their declared path. Once again it will be seen from the results that the interaction between interest-rate changes and (prior) monetary developments seems to be largest in the case of the UK.

Limitations of the exercise

Any exercise of this sort can at best be illustrative, and there are many reasons for caution in the presentation of these results. In so far as policy is in fact effective and changes in interest rates do result in reductions in the rate of growth of the monetary aggregates, there is clearly a problem of simultaneity which may result in perverse parameter estimates. Second, there is some question whether the authorities actually can impose a path for interest rates on to the financial markets. It may well be that we have a measure of market rather than official responsiveness to monetary developments. This may be a problem particularly when financial markets are both small and open to international influences, and this may explain the seemingly smaller responsiveness of Canadian interest rates indicated by this exercise. Third, the choice of different target aggregates in different countries may have a bearing on the relationships investigated here. Thus the interest-rate response to a deviation from an M_3 target may need to be greater than from an M_1 target because of differences in the relevant interest elasticities. Furthermore, the actual role and powers of the regulatory authority may be quite different – the operations of the Federal Reserve System's Open Market Committee (FOMC) in the USA, for example, differ markedly from those of the Bank of England both in their scope and their influence. Nevertheless, given all these caveats, such results as we have obtained seem sufficiently interesting to present here.

The data

Many of the major industrial countries have moved in recent years to a policy which formulates targets for one or more of their monetary aggregates.[1] This exercise is restricted to those countries where targetry has been in operation longest (the USA, West Germany and Canada), and throughout the period when the UK has operated to a declared target. In none of these countries, however, has the same aggregate as that chosen by the UK been targeted as a prime objective over the relevant period. Hence the preferred aggregate in both the USA and Canada has been M_1, while in West Germany the target is defined in terms of 'central bank money' (defined as notes and coin in circulation plus residents' sight, time and savings deposits weighted by the banks' minimum reserve requirement ratios in January 1974). By contrast, the target for the UK has been for the growth in sterling M_3.

In examining the relevant target for each country for this exercise, we did encounter two problems. First, the US authorities, unlike the other countries, had a procedure of rolling targets, whereby an annual target was declared at three-monthly intervals. This

[1] For a more detailed discussion, see M. Foot, 'Monetary targets: their nature and record in the major economies', in B. Griffiths and G. E. Wood (eds), *Monetary Targets* (Macmillan, 1981).

TABLE E

UK fiscal year	USA	Canada	West Germany	UK
1975/76	5–7½	10–15	8	15½
1976/77	4½–7	8–12†	8	12*
1977/78	4½–6½	7–11	8	9–13
1978/79	4–6½	6–10	8	8–12

* Target for July 1976–March 1977 at annual rate.
Target for March 1976–June 1976 imputed at 12½%.
† Target for March 1976–June 1977.
Targets are June–May thereafter.

allowed a degree of flexibility to the US authorities not available to the other countries, which over most of the period declared their targets only annually. To allow comparison, namely with respect to the problems encountered in attaining an annual target, the April – March target for the USA was treated as if in force for the whole year. This may render measurement of the discretionary element of US policy slightly biased, but does retain uniformity across the study.

The second problem related to the UK, which has only had formal targets for monetary growth since July 1976. Use of data from then onwards gives only two and a half years' observations, and to allow a rather longer period for comparison a target was imputed for the fiscal year 1975/76 and for the first three months of 1976/77. The target imputed was the rate of growth of M_3 as forecast in the budget statement. The targets used are shown in Table E.

The calculation of a series of the deviations of actual from target rates of growth of the monetary aggregates was undertaken by calculating an implied monthly rate of growth for the target aggregate (taking the mid-point for those targets which were actually expressed as ranges). This was subtracted from the actual monthly rate of growth in each case to give a series of percentage point deviations from the target.

Throughout the exercise the interest rate chosen was a representative market rate on three-month Treasury bills. This was preferred to an official rate, in that what was sought was a measure of the responsiveness of market rates rather than of administered rates (which can, at times, be well out of line with market conditions). At the same time, a three-month rate was felt to be less prone to erratic fluctuations than day-to-day rates.

Results

1 *Interest-rate responsiveness.* The first set of regressions undertaken seeks solely to indicate the extent to which the level of interest rates moved in line with the growth of the targeted monetary aggregate in the four countries. This was designed as a purely mechanistic measure, taking the level of interest rates as the dependent variable and regressing it against the current and five preceding monthly changes in the monetary aggregate, together with the two *subsequent* monthly changes and the previous level of the interest rate. The inclusion of the subsequent monthly changes is to provide some test of the hypothesis of perfect expectations (by both the authorities and the market) and acknowledges that the present rate of interest may adjust to forecast as well as to

past changes in the aggregates. The results of this exercise, which was run from 1974 to 1979 are summarised in Table F.

No attempt was made to specify an equation with stable, long-run properties. The sole purpose was to estimate the relationship of changes in the Treasury bill rate with changes in the monetary aggregates. These figures suggest that the rate of interest in the UK has been considerably more responsive to changes in the target aggregate than in the other three countries, and moreover, there is, with the exception of t_{-5}, a uniform positive sign on the coefficients throughout. In the USA there is also a positive effect from all lagged values with a particularly significant value at t_{-1}, but negative coefficients at $t+1$ and $t+2$, which could be the result of simultaneity rather than imply poor forecasting. In Canada the overall effect of a change in monetary growth on the Treasury bill rate is positive, too, but less marked than in the USA (possibly reflecting the dominating influence of US interest rates on the Canadian market). In West Germany, by contrast, it appears that interest rates broadly moved inversely rather than responded positively to changes in the growth of central bank money (CBM), possibly because over part of the period external considerations played a large part in German policy priorities.

Given the problems of multicollinearity, little confidence can be placed in any of the individual coefficient estimates. Nor should this be seen in any way as implying causality. What we attempted here was to measure, as simply as possible, the direction and extent of variability in interest rates associated with changes in the rate of growth of the relevant monetary aggregates.

2 *Reaction function.* The second set of regressions seeks to measure more explicitly the link between changes in interest rates and movements in the monetary aggregates relative to their target. Here we regressed the absolute change in the interest rate on the series for percentage point deviations of each monetary aggregate from its target. The assumption is made here that, in the short run at least, market rates can be influenced by official policy. (Clearly this may overstate the effect of official intervention if market forces affect interest rates in the same direction in response to monetary developments.) In this exercise the lag on the monetary series was constrained to two months only, on the assumption that policy was not responsive to deviations in the aggregates from further back. The results are summarised in Table G.

These equations seem to confirm the impression created by the first exercise. Indeed the *F*-statistic suggests that only in the USA and the UK was there any significant relationship between changes in interest rates and (prior) developments in the deviation of the monetary target from its planned path.

Conclusions

The conclusions from this exercise are subject to many caveats. In particular, it may be argued that a country which operates an effective monetary targetry may, perhaps, be able to achieve stable monetary growth while at the same time avoiding sharp fluctuations in interest rates. This may be the case in West Germany. However, the purpose of this appendix was primarily to examine whether in the UK there appeared to be a relative unwillingness to allow interest rates to vary to any large extent. Much depends upon the quantification of *sufficient* variability. Nevertheless this exercise does seem to show that the relative responsiveness of interest rates to monetary deviations is greatest in the UK, and hence the problems of monetary management lie in the inelastic response of components of the aggregate to interest-rate changes, rather than in the lack of interest-rate responsiveness *per se*.

TABLE F

Interest-rate determination

The table below provides coefficient estimates and summary statistics from regressing the interest rate on three-month Treasury bills against the percentage change in the relevant monetary aggregate (seasonally adjusted) with five lags and two leads, the lagged dependent variable, TB_{t-1}, and a constant: t-statistics are in parentheses; ρ is the Cochrane–Orcutt transformation. Estimation period June 1974–January 1979.

	% change in the monetary aggregate (seasonally adjusted)											
	$t-5$	$t-4$	$t-3$	$t-2$	$t-1$	t	$t+1$	$t+2$	**TB_{t-1}**	**Constant**	ρ	R^2
West Germany	0.16 (1.31)	−0.23 (1.88)	−0.03 (0.27)	−0.09 (0.78)	0.0 (0.02)	−0.02 (0.14)	−0.08 (0.75)	0.07 (0.67)	0.76 (5.07)	1.17 (1.19)	0.58 (2.48)	0.97
USA	0.10 (0.82)	0.08 (0.60)	0.22 (1.72)	0.13 (1.00)	0.46 (3.48)	0.03 (0.24)	−0.18 (1.47)	−0.13 (1.09)	0.98 (13.07)	−0.20 (0.35)	0.34 (2.20)	0.94
Canada	0.06 (1.77)	0.07 (2.10)	0.07 (1.83)	0.01 (0.24)	0.06 (1.32)	0.01 (0.30)	−0.02 (0.51)	0.01 (0.40)	1.01 (10.79)	−0.20 (0.23)	0.41 (2.23)	0.93
UK	−0.19 (1.31)	0.05 (0.33)	0.28 (1.97)	0.50 (3.29)	0.22 (1.48)	0.08 (0.50)	0.14 (0.86)	0.31 (1.84)	1.02 (10.56)	−1.24 (1.58)	0.29 (1.01)	0.89

TABLE G

The table below provides coefficient estimates and summary statistics from regressing the interest rate on three-month Treasury bills against the percentage deviation from the monetary target in each country, with two lags and leads, the lagged dependent variable, with two lags, and a constant: *t*-statistics are in parentheses. Estimation period August 1975–January 1979.

	Deviation from monetary target					Treasury Bill rate		Constant	F[a]	R^2
	$t-2$	$t-1$	t	$t+1$	$t+2$	$t-2$	$t-1$			
West Germany	−0.04 (0.60)	0.08 (1.09)	−0.05 (0.64)	0.05 (0.74)	−0.02 (0.31)	0.04 (0.27)	0.23 (1.32)	−0.00 (0.10)	0.63	−0.07
USA	0.02 (0.16)	0.38 (3.16)	0.16 (1.48)	−0.24 (2.15)	−0.09 (0.82)	0.30 (1.99)	0.16 (0.99)	0.02 (0.56)	4.5	0.34
Canada	−0.14 (0.39)	0.01 (0.24)	0.04 (0.95)	−0.04 (1.19)	−0.03 (0.08)	0.13 (0.70)	0.39 (2.14)	0.02 (0.58)	1.59	0.10
UK	0.38 (2.27)	0.20 (1.21)	0.11 (0.60)	−0.15 (0.83)	0.25 (1.48)	−0.18 (1.15)	0.41 (2.58)	0.15 (1.10)	3.33	0.30

[a] The F test is designed to test whether the deviations from the monetary targets, taken as a whole, had a significant effect on Treasury bill rates. A value greater than 2.3 implies significance at the 1% level.

Appendix 2: The Forecasting and Control of Bank Lending

Introduction

This note seeks to assess the econometric evidence on the controllability of bank lending to the non-bank private sector. If varying the cost of credit (i.e. interest rates) should be the main instrument for regulating the rate of growth of bank lending, the authorities' ability to control that aggregate will depend upon:

(a) the authorities' ability to forecast future movements in bank lending due to movements in variables other than interest rates.
(b) the size and speed with which the demand for credit responds to changes in interest rates.

If bank lending only responds to changes in interest rates after a number of quarters, the authorities will only be able to offset any undesirable movements in bank lending if they are able to forecast these movements a number of quarters in advance and vary interest rates accordingly.

A number of attempts have been made to model bank lending, and these can be used to assess the controllability of that aggregate. An indication of the responsiveness of bank lending to interest-rate changes can be gained by calculating:

(a) the *impact elasticity* of bank lending with respect to interest rates (the percentage change in bank lending which occurs in the same period as a result of a permanent 1 per cent change in interest rates, other things being equal)
(b) the *long-run elasticity* of bank lending with respect to interest rates (the percentage change in bank lending after an infinite number of quarters as a result of a permanent 1 per cent change in interest rates, other things being equal)
(c) the *median lag* (the number of quarters after a step-wise change in interest rates by which time half the long-run change in bank lending has occurred) or the *mean lag* (the weighted average of the lags where the weights used are the ratios of the estimated coefficient on each lag to the sum of the coefficients).

The impact elasticity gives some indication of the immediate effect of a change in interest rates. The long-run elasticity is a measure of the eventual size of the change in bank lending resulting from an interest-rate change. The median and mean lags are summary statistics which indicate the speed with which bank lending responds to interest-rate changes.

The forecasting accuracy of the models can be assessed by using the estimated equations to make out-of-sample forecasts of bank lending and comparing these forecasts with the out-turns. The various models were estimated over differing periods, and therefore the out-of-sample forecasts had to be made for different components of bank lending, some of which are expressed in nominal terms, while others are deflated by an assortment of price deflators. Nevertheless the root mean square percentage error (RMS%E) of the *ex post* forecast levels is independent of the level of bank lending and the number of forecast periods and therefore may be a reasonable comparable measure of forecasting performance.

Results

Six models of bank lending in the UK were considered: Artis[**1**], Norton[**2**], Moore and Threadgold[**3**], Savage[**4**], Spencer and Mowl[**5**] and Coghlan[**6**].[1] The elasticities,

[1] References can be found on page 145.

median and mean lags were calculated from the estimated coefficients of the models and are given in Table H. All the models surveyed were in linear form and therefore the elasticities depend upon the level of lending and interest rates. By convention, the elasticity was calculated for the mean interest rate and mean value of the dependent variable over the estimation period. However, there is no reason to expect the mean interest rate to be associated with the mean value of the dependent variable, and the current elasticity at any time may be markedly different from the 'mean' elasticity. In the Moore – Threadgold and Savage models, the dependent variable is expressed as a first difference, whereas the own interest rate is a level. In order to calculate a comparable impact elasticity, a levels series for the dependent variable has to be calculated for the estimation period. The Moore – Threadgold model does not have sensible long-run properties; a step-wise rise in interest rates results in a continuing fall in the level of bank lending, and therefore the long-run elasticity is infinite. However, the impact elasticity of the Moore – Threadgold model is plausible, being similar to that of other models, and the short-term out-of-sample forecasting performance of the model appears to be satisfactory.

The RMS%Es of the various models are given in Table I. The level of bank lending is not the dependent variable in either the Coghlan or the Moore – Threadgold models, but the implicit forecast of the level of bank lending was calculated in order to make the results comparable with the other models. In the Artis model there is a lagged dependent variable, and therefore the RMS%Es of both the static and dynamic forecasts are given. In the former the out-turn value is used for the lagged dependent variable, and in the latter the predicted value of the previous period is used.

The RMS%Es of the out-of-sample forecasts may provide a better indication of the forecasting performance of the equation than any measures of within-sample fit (coefficient of determination, standard error of equation) since equations which explain a high proportion of the variance of the dependent variable may still have unstable parameters resulting in forecast errors. Nevertheless, the reported RMS%Es can only give an indication of the forecasting accuracy of bank lending contingent upon forecasts of the explanatory variables. However, even if accurate forecasts of the explanatory variables could be made, it is doubtful whether any of the existing econometric models could forecast bank lending with sufficient accuracy so that bank lending could be kept on target in the short run.

Moreover, the RMS%E statistic can only give an indication of the problems of forecasting bank lending. In practice it may be more important to avoid large errors in the forecasts up to four quarters ahead, whereas errors in forecasts of more than four quarters ahead may be less serious. The RMS%E summary statistic gives equal 'weight' to each forecast error, rather than giving greater weight to earlier forecast errors. However, a partial solution to this limitation of the RMS%E statistic is to compute the RMS%E over a year as well as over two years. Ideally, successive out-of-sample forecasts ought to be made, each time re-estimating the equations with an additional quarter's data. The recursive estimation of the equations would provide statistically meaningful implications for the forecasting performance of the equations. However, this exercise was not attempted, since the specification of the reported equations tends to be specific to the data period for which they were estimated.

Some of the equations for the components of bank lending, particularly lending to industrial and commercial companies, achieved better results. Although fluctuations in lending to industrial and commercial companies are an important part of fluctuations in total lending, errors in the forecasts of lending to the personal sector and lending to other financial intermediaries are likely to raise the percentage errors of the forecast of lending as a whole. The errors in the components of lending are unlikely to offset one another and, in fact, the case for estimating forecasting equations for disaggregated bank lending depends on the cross-elasticities between each component being low.

Interpretation of results

The estimated elasticities vary depending upon the category of bank lending being predicted, the interest rate used and the other variables included in the specification of the equation. However, it is fairly clear that the impact elasticity of actual bank lending is very low – below 0.1. The long-run responsiveness of bank lending to interest changes is unclear, ranging from zero in the Coghlan model to over 2.0 in one of the Artis equations. The estimated median and mean lags appear to vary depending on the specification of the equation and the data period over which the equation is estimated. In fact, much of the variation in the estimated median or mean lags may be due to dynamic mis-specification of the equations, in particular overly restrictive lag structures. The use of seasonally adjusted series, which have been adjusted with different filters, together with unadjusted series in the same regression equation, may cause the estimated distributed lag structure, and therefore the mean and median lags, to be biased. However, when the mean or median lag is low, the estimated long-run responsiveness of bank lending tends to be low, so that the effect over six months is small in all the equations for realised bank lending.

However, irrespective of the particular explanatory variables used in the models, there are a number of problems which may render interpretation of the results difficult. Most of the recent demand for bank lending equations use real bank lending as the dependent variable and relate this to real economic activity and other explanatory variables. This effectively imposes the restriction that the nominal demand for credit is homogeneous of degree one in the price level and that the nominal demand for bank credit responds instantaneously to changes in the price level. While price homogeneity may be a reasonable long-run property, instantaneous price response is extremely unlikely. However, attempts to estimate an equation for the demand for nominal bank lending, with a price deflator and real economic activity as explanatory variables, yields unrealistic long-run price and real income elasticities. More plausible real income elasticities can be achieved if the equation is estimated with real bank lending as the dependent variable, but the invalid imposition of the homogeneity postulate may reduce the reliability of the estimated interest elasticities.

In all but the Spencer – Mowl model, the effect of official 'requests' on bank lending has been represented by dummy variables in the demand for credit equations. If requests induce non-price rationing, it is common in applied work to represent this by a shift in the notional demand for credit schedule. However, non-price rationing may occur for other reasons, and therefore, if the demand for credit is to be properly identified, it may be better to model non-price rationing and other supply-side factors explicitly. The Spencer – Mowl model for lending to the personal sector is the only set of equations considered which attempts to estimate the supply of and demand for bank lending. The requests and Competition and Credit Control dummies are included in the supply, rather than the demand equation, and non-price rationing depends upon the excess demand for credit. The own interest elasticities appear to be much higher than the other equations' elasticities, but non-price rationing may reduce the responsiveness of actual bank lending to persons. The Spencer – Mowl personal-sector demand for credit equation also includes a parallel money market rate with a positive sign. Thus, if base rates move roughly in line with parallel money market rates, movements in short-term interest rates will tend to have a relatively small effect on bank lending to persons.

TABLE H

Responsiveness of demand for bank credit to changes in interest rates on bank lending[e]

Model	Estimation period	Dependent variable	Own interest rate	Mean impact elasticity	Mean long-run elasticity	Mean lag (quarters)	Median lag (quarters)	Lag structure
Artis[a]	(a) 1956III to 1971III	London clearing bank	Bank Rate	−0.007	−0.363	49.00	34.31	Single lagged
	(b)	advances excluding		−0.063	−2.116	32.22	22.76	dependent
	(c)	nationalised industries at current prices		−0.003	−0.018	4.55	3.49	variable
Norton[b]	(a) 1955III to 1966II	LCB advances exclud-	Bank Rate	−0.030	−0.028		0.29	Single lagged
	(b)	ing nationalised indus-		−0.063	−0.058		0.29	dependent
	(c)	tries at current prices		−0.031	−0.028		0.27	variable
Moore and Threadgold[c]	(a) 1965III to 1978II	Sterling bank lending to	Base Rate +2%	−0.026				
	(b) 1965IV to 1978II	industrial and commer-	Base Rate +2%	−0.003				
	(c) 1965IV to 1978II	cial companies at cur-		−0.003				Almon lags
	(d) 1965III to 1978II	rent prices	*less* expected	−0.003				
	(e) 1967I to 1978II		inflation rate	−0.0005				

Savage	1965I to 1977III	Bank lending to personal sector for non-house purchase at 1970 consumer expenditure prices	Base Rate plus mark-up	−0.041				
Spencer and Mowl[d]	(a) 1964IV to 1974IV	Sterling bank lending to industrial and commercial companies at 1975 total final expenditure prices	Base Rate + 1%	−0.075	−0.246	2.12	0.69	Almon lags
	(b) 1964IV to 1979I			−0.009	−0.153	4.01	3.77	Almon lags
	(c) 1965I to 1977IV	Notional demand for sterling bank lending to persons at 1970 prices	Base Rate plus 3.75%	−0.865	−7.034	7.13	5.281	Single lagged dependent variable

[a] Artis equations (a), (b) and (c) correspond to equations (1), (2) and (5) in table 6.2 [**1,** p. 262]. Equations (3) and (4) have been omitted because Bank Rate was excluded from these equations. Artis did not list the coefficients of the seasonal dummies, and therefore seasonally adjusted bank lending was forecast. This was compared with unadjusted out-turns, and as a result the RMS%E statistics may indicate a poorer forecasting performance than was in fact the case.

[b] Norton equations (a), (b) and (c) correspond to equations (3.1), (3.2) and (3.3) of table 3 in [**2,** p. 487].

[c] Moore–Threadgold equations (b), (c), (d) and (e) correspond to the real interest-rate equations in table 6 of [**3**].

[d] Equations (a) and (b) of Spencer–Mowl are re-estimated using 1975-based data. Equations (a) and (b) have the same specification, but are estimated over different periods. Equation (c) is the notional demand for bank credit by the personal sector. Actual lending may be less because of non-price rationing and therefore actual lending may be less responsive to interest-rate changes.

[e] The Coghlan model is omitted because there is no own interest rate on bank lending.

TABLE I

Out-of-sample forecasting performance of demand for bank lending equations

Model	Estimation period	Out-of-sample forecast period	Static/ dynamic forecast	Root mean square percentage error
Artis[a] (London clearing bank advances)	1956III to 1971III	1971IV to 1972IV	Static	11.746
			Dynamic	23.553
		1971IV to 1972III	Static	19.282
			Dynamic	21.385
Threadgold–Moore[b] (sterling lending to industrial and commercial companies	1964IV to 1976IV	1977I to 1978IV	n.a.	2.79
		1977I to 1977IV	n.a.	0.787
Coghlan (sterling bank lending to the private sector)	1952 to 1975	1977 and 1978	n.a.	6.312
		1977	n.a.	3.707
Spencer–Mowl (lending to industrial and commercial companies: 1975 base)	1964IV to 1976IV	1977I to 1977IV	n.a.	7.520
		1971I to 1977IV	n.a.	7.517
		1977I to 1978IV	n.a.	6.729

[a] The out-of-sample forecast of the Artis model is given for one year and for the maximum period over which the out-of-sample forecast can be made. The clearing bank lending series used ceased to be reported after 1972IV.

[b] Out-of-sample forecasts of one and two years are given for the Moore–Threadgold, Coghlan and Spencer–Mowl models. The Coghlan model used annual data.

Proper identification of the demand for credit may also require the inclusion of a government reaction function in a simultaneous model of credit and money creation. If the authorities respond to a rise in bank lending by raising interest rates, in order to meet their monetary target, there is effectively a behavioural relationship in which a rise in bank lending results in a rise in interest rates. A rise in interest rates may eventually choke off the increased demand for credit, but attempts to estimate this relationship in isolation from the government's role in influencing interest rates may produce misleading results.

All but the Moore – Threadgold models use nominal interest rates, though real interest rates may be more appropriate. Rises in nominal interest rates, when real interest rates are constant, may still reduce the demand for credit because of historic-cost pricing by companies and companies' wishes to maintain an acceptable gearing ratio, though the immediate effect of nominal interest rate rises may be to raise lending because of increased interest charges. However, the effect of these factors on bank lending would really have to be modelled explicitly rather than by simply including a nominal interest rate.

Finally, the growth of disintermediated forms of lending during periods of direct controls, a recent example of which was the resale of bank-accepted commercial bills to the non-bank private sector, may cause misleading results if the uncontrolled forms of lending are not included in the definition of the dependent variable. As a result, the efficacy of direct controls on the clearers between 1965 and 1971, and the corset, while it has been in operation since 1973, may be overestimated. Conversely, the efficacy of interest rates may be underestimated.

Conclusion

The evidence on the controllability of bank lending is extremely difficult to interpret. The results of the existing equations, however, indicate that it is doubtful whether bank lending can be controlled over a period of less than six months, if not a year. Since bank lending takes a number of quarters to respond to interest-rate changes, short-run control of that aggregate would require relatively accurate forecasts over a period of at least four quarters ahead – a forecasting performance that cannot be achieved at present.

References

1 Artis, M. J., 'Monetary policy, part 2', in F. T. Blackaby (ed.), *British Economic Policy 1960–74*, NIESR, 1978.

2 Norton, W. E., 'Debt management and monetary policy in the United Kingdom', *Economic Journal*, vol. 79, no. 315, September 1969. Republished in H. G. Johnson (ed.), *Readings in British Monetary Economics*, Oxford, Clarendon Press, 1972.

3 Moore, B. J. and Threadgold, A. R., *Bank Lending and the Money Supply*, Bank of England Discussion Paper No. 10, 1980.

4 Savage, D., *The Monetary Sector of the NIESR Model: Preliminary Results*, NIESR Discussion Paper No. 21, 1978.

5 Spencer, P. and Mowl, C., *The Model of the Domestic Monetary System in a Financial Sector for the Treasury Model*, Treasury Working Paper No. 8, 1978.

6 Coghlan, R. T., *A Small Monetary Model of the UK Economy*, Bank of England Discussion Paper No. 3, 1979.

V

Structural Changes in the Banking System and the Determination of the Stock of Money

1. Introduction

The pace of structural change

The structure of the banking system is in the midst of profound change. Some aspects of this have already been largely completed, for example the banks' switch to liability management; some are still in progress, for example the continuing shift to variable rate lending, away from fixed rate lending – though this shift reflected worsening inflation, and could cease, or even reverse, were inflation conquered; others are still in the pipeline – their outline may already be discernible, but they have not yet fully taken effect; these last include prospective changes in the structure of retail deposit business and the form of payments technologies. In this chapter I shall consider these changes and explore their implications for monetary control, notably for the achievement of target rates of growth for certain specified monetary aggregates.

There is clearly now in process a set of structural and technological changes which appear likely to change the form of banking and financial intermediation. Structural changes of this magnitude within the banking industry seem to come in waves: for example, there was a wave of such development during the course of the nineteenth century, when there was a major extension of payment services from currency alone to chequeable deposits with the banking system. During the course of the nineteenth century banks developed from a rudimentary state at the beginning of the century to a stage by its end which in form, structure and basic technology remained broadly constant through the rest of the twentieth century until the 1960s. Whereas an economist surveying monetary and banking developments through the nineteenth century would have had to have concentrated on structural changes, describing and accounting for the historical evolution of financial institutions and discussing the changing conceptual form of money itself, it is possible for economists studying money and banking from the end of the nineteenth century up until about 1970 to treat structural changes as of relatively minor significance, occurring sufficiently slowly and gently over time not to become a central element in the main analytical record. Consider, for example, Friedman and Schwartz's *Monetary Trends in the United States and United Kingdom*[**3**];[1] in this book the authors are aware of the importance of structural changes during the century (1870–1970), but they argue: 'However, many elements in the financial structure remain the same throughout the period and have been common to both countries.'

Indeed, at the end of the 1970s, the structure and form of *retail* financial services was still looking much the same as it had done by about the beginning of the twentieth century, at least in English-speaking countries, with the branch banking system, the cheque book, the system of cheque clearing, the provision of mortgages through specialised housing institutions (the building societies in the UK), the provision of insurance services by insurance companies, etc., which had been in place at the end of the nineteenth century, largely unchanged. It is the thesis here, however, that we have once more entered a period of more rapid structural change, so that analysis of financial development will once again have to pay serious attention both to structural changes and also to consequential conceptual reconsiderations, rather than undertaking analytical studies on the basis of an assumption of a largely unchanged monetary system.

The causes of structural change

These current structural changes are mainly caused by three interrelated factors: high, variable and unpredictable inflation, leading to high and variable nominal interest rates; the existence (in some countries) of restrictive and burdensome regulations discriminating against certain forms of financial (banking) intermediation; and finally the rapid development of technology, speeding up and cheapening the flow, retrieval and analysis of information. These factors interact. For example, the high and variable inflation brings high and variable interest rates, which in turn make certain of the restrictions on banking intermediation, for example in the form of non-interest-bearing reserve requirements and limits on interest payments, more burdensome, while the development of information flows, via the new technology, allows financial flows to be shifted more easily into channels where such regulations have less effect.

The pace of structural change has therefore tended to be greatest in those countries where inflation, and thus also interest rates, have been quite high (though this is not by itself sufficient to generate structural change, i.e. one can point to several high-inflation countries where it has not taken place), where discrimination against certain forms of financial intermediation has been burdensome (but where there has been freedom for entrepreneurs to

---

[1] References can be found on page 181.

shift to other forms of financial intermediation without general constraint and intervention from the state), and where progress in information technology has been greatest. It is therefore no surprise to find such change has probably been greatest in the USA. In the UK the rate of inflation and its variability have been more extreme than in the USA, but the constraints imposed by the authorities on banking intermediation were considerably eased in 1971 (and again in 1980 with the abandonment of the 'corset'), and the pace of structural change has been somewhat slower than in the USA. Structural changes of a broadly similar kind are also proceeding at quite a rapid rate in other English-speaking countries – e.g. Australia in the aftermath of the 1981 Campbell Report, and in Canada and South Africa.

In Continental Europe, however, the pace of such structural change to date appears to have been somewhat slower than in the English-speaking countries. There are differing reasons for this. In certain countries, such as Greece, and to a somewhat lesser extent in France and Italy, the scope of regulation has been so pervasive that the possibility of shifting the flow of financial intermediation to avoid the burden of regulation hardly becomes possible. Thus one factor encouraging structural change tends to be absent.[1]

In certain other European countries, for example West Germany and Switzerland, the average rate and variability of inflation, one of the other elements forcing the pace of structural change, has been less virulent, thus reducing the incentive towards structural change within the financial system.[2] Of course, the institutional forms and legal arrangements under which banking and deposit taking operates have a generalised effect on the evolution of each individual country's banking system.

The forms of structural change

The first major changes to the *domestic* banking system began in the late 1960s, in the USA, with the switch from *asset management* to *liability management.*[3] This occurred before the onset of rising and variable inflation,

---

[1] An alternative to those financial channels subject to internal domestic constraints has always been to shift financial flows abroad, to the international Euro-markets. The continuation of comprehensive constraint over domestic financial intermediation therefore requires reinforcement with extensive external exchange controls. Should such exchange controls be abandoned, for example in pursuit of the ideal of free movement of capital over national boundaries, then it would follow that much of the domestic framework of financial control within these countries would rapidly unravel.

[2] Even so, there have been important structural changes in German banking. There has been increasing competition to attract small-scale deposits, both transactions and savings deposits. And with relatively low inflation not sufficing to prevent sharply varying nominal interest rates, often for external reasons, and high real interest rates, the banks have reacted by shortening the average maturity of their loan books. What is less clear is how far they are also switching their lending on to a variable rate basis, or are restricted from doing so by the authorities.

[3] This switch towards liability management via wholesale markets first occurred in fact in the *international* Euro-dollar market. Thus the first of the wholesale markets to emerge, at the end of the 1950s, was the Euro-currency market, initially mainly centred on London. The first statistics

and was initially mainly adopted as a means of avoiding the constraints on growth and on the expansion of bank balance-sheets caused by the exhaustion of 'surplus' public-sector debt on the asset side, and by the restrictions on the rate of interest that could be offered on retail-type deposits on the liability side (Regulation Q). This development, in part following the example of the already rapidly growing Euro-markets, was induced not only by the desire to avoid the constraints of regulation, but was also encouraged and facilitated by the development of computers and other developments in information technology, and proved highly efficient; it soon spread to other countries' domestic money markets. These developments and their consequent implications for monetary control are described relatively shortly (because they are already well known and appreciated) in the immediately succeeding section.

The next set of structural changes, considered here, mainly represents a response to the rising, high and variable rates of inflation that developed during the 1970s. The main feature of these changes involves the shift by both borrowers and (bank) lenders to *variable* rate lending, away from *fixed* rate lending. As will be described, once such a shift towards variable rate lending has taken place, then the contemporary *level* of interest rates comes to have a less direct influence both on the demand of borrowers for funds and on the supply of funds by (bank) lenders; this is obviously so because the initial rate of interest no longer holds throughout the period of the loan, but can be expected to vary, generally in line with variations in inflation, at shorter, prearranged rollover dates throughout the life of the loan. Even so, the contemporary level of interest rates will continue to have a (lesser) effect on credit markets both indirectly through its generalised effect on demand and activity (perhaps especially through its effects on exchange rates), i.e. through changing macroeconomic conditions, and also through some residual effect on the demand for individual channels of credit. Nevertheless, an increasingly important influence on the demand for, and the supply of, bank credit under these conditions becomes (not so much the general level of interest rates but) the spread charged by the bank, i.e. the margin between the going market rate for (wholesale) deposit funds and the market rate for loans, for example as expressed by the margin over LIBOR (London Inter-Bank Offer Rate) in the Euro-markets.

The final set of structural changes considered here involves innovations in the forms of retail banking and payments services. The application of improved technology is bringing cash-management techniques that were initially only available to wholesale banking customers now increasingly into

on the operation of the Euro-currency market date back to 1962, when the Bank of England began to collect data on the external liabilities and claims of banks in the UK. This was followed in the 1960s by the development of a market for wholesale funds within the USA. Since the main interest here is with the implications of structural changes for domestic monetary control within a single country, our main focus of interest will be on domestic wholesale markets, not on the Euro-currency market.

the area of retail deposit banking. This could have the effect of further blurring the already fuzzy distinction between transactions and savings balances, with perhaps the bulk of transactions balances, other than cash, bearing market-related interest rates. There may, perhaps, come to be a still wider range of differing forms of liquid asset holdings available for retail depositors, encompassing differing combinations of payments services and interest rates. The effect of technology in cheapening transmission mechanisms may encourage and facilitate a wider range of competition in retail banking activities. Again, technological developments, by cheapening certain forms of transmission mechanisms, should lead to a faster rate of growth in these rather than others. For example, it is possible that a much larger proportion of payment transactions will be made through the means of plastic or other cards, and be met initially out of credit facilities, rather than from low or zero interest-yielding transactions balances. So the immediate buffer of funds available to families in order to undertake immediate transactions may well come to reside in a pool of credit facilities, carried on behalf of the individual transactor by the institutions looking after individuals' cash management, rather than in deposit balances as in the past.

The final section deals with the implications for financial control and monetary targeting of these latter two forms of structural change.

2. Liability Management

Historical development

At the end of the Second World War, banks in certain major countries, notably the USA and the UK, emerged with swollen holdings of public-sector debt, proportionately much larger than they had normally held in their balance-sheets, and equivalently much lower holdings of loans to the private sector; this was a result of the pattern of financing during the war. The data for the proportionate holdings of public- and private-sector debt in banks' assets for the UK are shown in Table A.

These 'excess' holdings of public-sector debt provided the banks with a cushion with which to absorb the growing demands of private-sector borrowers, and were a source of flexibility, enabling banks to adjust to the changing demands of borrowers, while at the same time continuing to respond passively to inflows of deposits obtained at interest rates constrained either by regulations, such as Regulation Q, or by oligopolistic arrangements (as in the cartel in the UK until 1971, and in Canada until 1967). In short, banks adjusted to cash-flow pressures primarily by asset management, particularly by varying their holdings of public-sector debt, while rates on their deposit liabilities were constrained *not* to react fully to variations in market rates. In such a constrained system, control over the total size of bank deposit

TABLE A

Proportion of UK and US banks' assets held in public- and private-sector debt

	UK–LCBs		US commercial banks	
	Public[a]	Private[a]	Public[b]	Private
At end-December				
1939	31.7	44.9	30.2	32.2
1946	60.0	19.0	53.4	23.5
1950	49.1	27.7	42.0	33.8
1955	47.1	28.9	35.3	41.1
1960	26.7	44.5	30.5	46.9
1965	17.6	53.2	26.0	54.5
1970[c]	12.1	61.0	22.8	54.4

[a] Public-sector debt comprises British government securities, and Treasury bills and Treasury deposit receipts. Available sources included local authority debt as private-sector debt. Certain items, notably cash, special deposits, money at call and short notice, premises and other fixed and working capital, etc., are excluded from this table, so the figures do not add to 100 per cent.

[b] Public-sector debt comprises US government securities and state and local government securities.

[c] Average of mid-December 1970 and mid-January 1971.

Sources: D. K. Sheppard, *The Growth and Role of UK Financial Institutions 1880–1962*, London, Methuen, 1971; *Bank of England Quarterly Bulletin*; *Federal Reserve Bulletin*.

liabilities (though *not* over the growth of bank lending to the private sector – which was in some cases subject to additional direct controls, i.e. ceilings on advances, and direct requests) was relatively easy. Open-market sales by the authorities, when they wished to be restrictive, would squeeze the cash base of the banks and encourage them to sell off their holdings of public-sector debt. The direct, and indirect, effect of such open-market operations (the indirect effect being the subsequent induced sales by the banks) would lead to a rise in the yields on longer-dated public-sector assets, and to yields on marketable securities rising generally relative to deposit rates.[1] Moreover, because a rise in market rates, engineered by the authorities in the pursuit of monetary control, would cause such rates to rise relative both to non-interest-

[1] Even then, there were some limitations to the authorities' willingness to control the rate of growth of the monetary aggregates by this means, because of their fears of the consequences of having to make sufficiently large changes in yields on public-sector debt. Aggressive steps to raise rates of interest, particularly if this was to be in the form of direct action to reduce bond prices, were, for a time at least after the second World War, in both the UK and the USA, considered dangerous, and bond market conditions were felt to require sensitive handling. In part, this sensitivity was the result of the very high ratios of public-sector debt to nominal incomes in the post-war period. Not only did this entail relatively large interest payments as a proportion of public expenditure, but also very large proportionate maturities in relation to the need for new public-sector debt. Any development which might weaken confidence in the market for this swollen volume of public-sector debt was felt to be inherently dangerous.

bearing and also to interest-bearing deposits, owing to the limited flexibility of the latter, the growth rates of both narrow and broad money tended to be strongly positively correlated, though their respective demand-for-money functions tended to have differing interest-elasticities. So movements over quarters and over years of broad and narrow money were relatively similar, and their relationships with movements of nominal incomes, their velocities and demand-for-money functions, tended to exhibit somewhat similar features during these early post-war years, from 1945 until the mid-1960s.

This extra cushion of flexibility, provided by public-sector debt holdings, was largely exhausted, as can be seen by Table A, by the mid-1960s. In the USA the banks then developed the ability to borrow very large sums of money on marketable instruments, e.g. CDs, on market-related terms.[1] The resulting growth of such wholesale funds was extremely rapid and spread quickly to other countries, such as Canada and the UK (see Figure A); in the UK this occurred most strongly after the direct constraints on bank lending had been removed in 1971 as part of the shift to the new system of Competition and Credit Control.

Monetary control

The advent of such liability management in wholesale money markets drastically affected the authorities' ability to control the total size of banks' books. Previously, with banks engaging in asset management, while generally accepting external constraints on interest rates on deposits, the authorities were in a position to enforce shifts in *relative* interest rates by varying the *general* level of market rates. Thus when they wished to be restrictive and increased the general level of interest rates, market rates generally would rise relative to bank deposit rates, because the latter were more or less constrained, thus inducing an outflow of funds from bank deposits to other assets, and so forcing banks to sell their surplus reserve assets, in this case generally their 'excess' holdings of public-sector debt. But once the banks shifted to liability management, it became very much more difficult for the authorities to shift relative interest rates unfavourably against *all* bank deposit rates[2]

---

[1] Large negotiable CDs, in their present form, have been used as a source of funds since 1961, and those issued by large commercial banks reached a volume of around $20 billion by 1966. Because of the growing sophistication of corporate treasurers, the banks were faced, in the mid-1950s, with a reduction in the rate of growth of corporate deposits, as funds were diversified into short-term interest-bearing investments such as Treasury bills. Negotiable CDs, with their extensive secondary market, enabled the banks to offer a more competitive interest rate on a highly liquid asset. The rate of interest offered on the CDs was not, however, always market-related because, until 1973, Regulation Q interest-rate ceilings applied to negotiable CDs. Two sharp reductions in market volume, in 1966 and 1969, were caused by market interest rates exceeding the ceilings. In 1973 Regulation Q ceilings were lifted for CDs of over $100,000.

[2] In so far as certain deposit rates, e.g. on demand deposits or retail deposits, remained constrained, it continued to be the case that the authorities' control over the general level of interest rates also ensured their control over the relative pattern between such market rates and the *constrained* deposit rates.

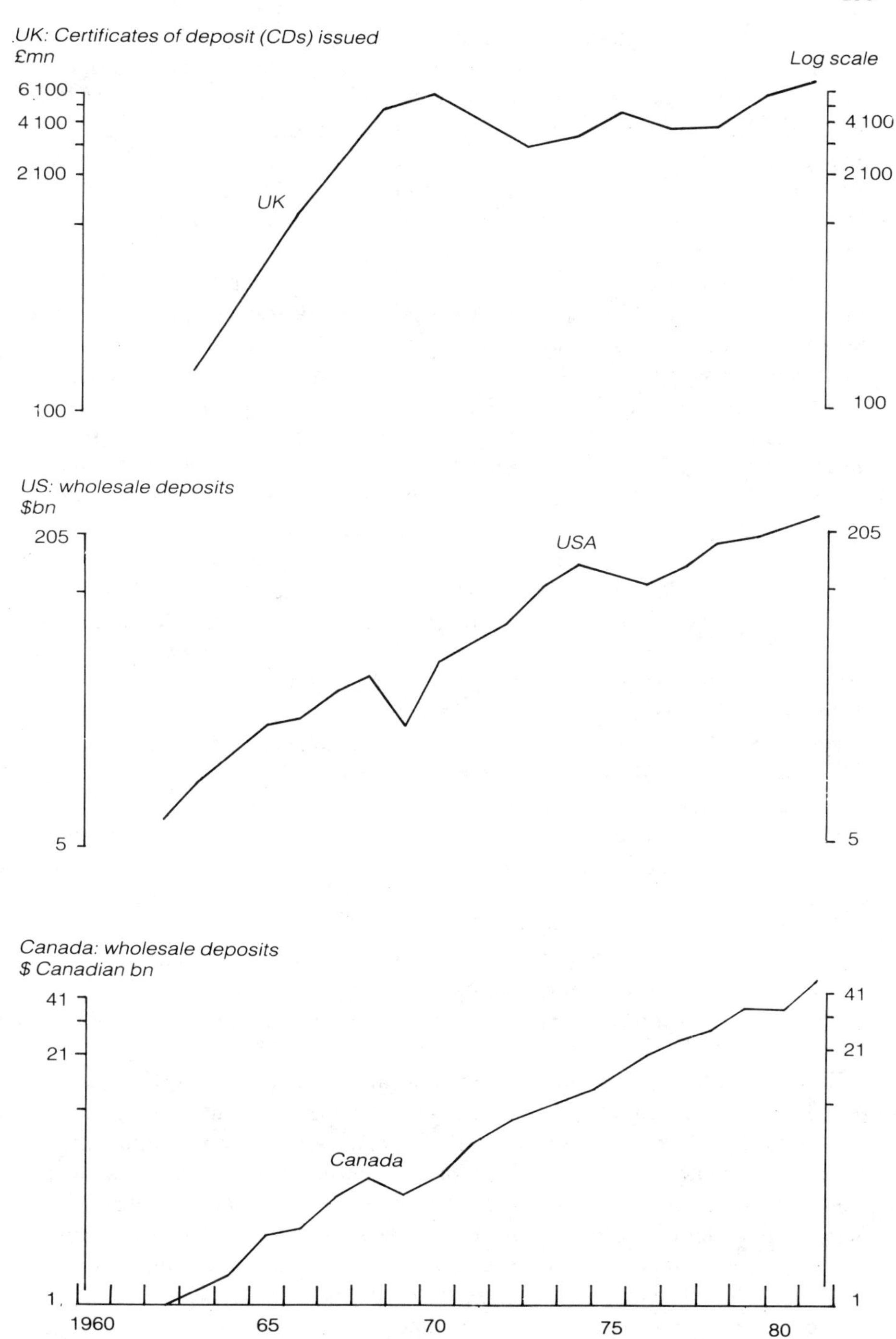

FIG. A *Growth of wholesale deposits in the UK, USA and Canada*

when they raised the general level of market rates. Once the banks turned to liability management, however, a cash outflow (whether because of an increase in the demand for bank loans, or as a result of a fall in retail deposits, with the latter perhaps caused by the authorities raising interest rates in pursuit of a more restrictive policy) could be met by the banks by compensatory increases in interest rates on wholesale deposits in order to obtain the required funds to meet the demand for additional loans, or to replace a deposit drain.

So, while retaining control over the general level of interest rates, the authorities now found it much harder to maintain control over the relativities between market rates and those deposit rates for wholesale funds which the banks were using aggressively in order to fund their books. So long as banks could find profitable lending outlets for funds, they would bid for deposits in wholesale markets in order to provide the finance for such lending. For the individual bank access to such markets appeared to provide it with a much more elastic and flexible source of funds than had previously been available. Even for the banking system as a whole, particularly in open economies without exchange controls on international capital movements, the development of such markets will presumably have raised the elasticity of shifts of funds in response to *relative* interest differentials. Consequently the supply of funds to banks could be adjusted to meet demand, so control over the total size of banks' books came to depend increasingly on the interest-elasticity of demand for bank lending, an interest-elasticity which was always somewhat uncertain and low in the short term. Moreover, assessment and analysis of such interest-elasticity of demand for bank borrowing was distorted by the authorities' own use of credit controls (and of various forms of moral and other suasion on banks) to restrain bank lending at particular times, and indeed by the possible application of various forms of non-price limitation on credit availability by the banks themselves. So there were probably periods when the market for bank credit did not clear. Accordingly, attempts to estimate demand and supply functions for bank loans, particularly their interest-elasticity, were complicated. Moreover, as will be described in section 3, this elasticity was further affected by the switch from fixed-rate loans to variable rate lending.

Previously under asset management, the interest-elasticity of demand for broad money depended on the authorities' ability to vary the *relativity* between bank deposit rates and market rates, as they – the authorities – operated to control the general level of short-term market rates. Now, with liability management, the effective interest-elasticity on broad money came to depend much more on the interest-elasticity of the demand for bank loans, i.e. the major element in the asset books of banks. Consequently the elasticity of demand for broad money, in response to general changes in market interest rates, fell sharply. It was not that the responsiveness of banks, or bank customers, to interest rates declined; indeed, their general reaction to relative rate differentials, if anything, became even more sensitive. Rather, the authorities' ability to vary the general *level* of interest rates had signficantly less impact on the relevant *differentials* once liability management came into play. As a result, the response of the overall balance-sheets of banks, i.e. the variation of their total loans and deposits, to changes in interest rates became less elastic and also less predictable, since it would depend largely on how banks themselves would react to the authorities' pressures. (By the same token, the reactions of the system in response to changes in the level of base money, in the form of changes in interest rates as well as quantitative changes, became somewhat more volatile and less predictable.) The *LM* curve (from standard Keynesian analysis), with money broadly defined, became more vertical, but also more subject to unpredictable supply-side shifts.

This led to a change in the previous relationship between narrow money, normally termed M_1, and broader monetary definitions, with the latter including large elements of wholesale deposits, bearing market-related interest rates. Whereas the advent of liability management changed the relationship between movements in the general level of interest rates and broad money, the relationship between narrow money, M_1, and incomes and interest rates remained largely unchanged, since at this time (i.e. the 1960s and 1970s) the determination of interest rates on the various components of M_1 remained largely constrained by regulation or convention. Under liability management, a rise in the demand for credit would tend to raise the general level of interest rates, but the banks would then raise rates on wholesale deposits even further in order to provide funds to meet that rise in credit demand: so, under these circumstances, the total of interest-bearing deposits would rise, and often the total of broad money would increase, while M_1 would unambiguously fall. With asset management prior to the end of the 1960s there was a generally positive correlation between narrow and broad money, but after the advent of liability management through the course of the 1970s there was often either no correlation between narrow and broad money, or even in some cases signs of a negative correlation. While this generalisation holds for the Anglo – Saxon countries, i.e. USA, UK, Canada, and also for Switzerland, it does not do so in the case of France, Japan and West Germany, as shown below. It may be that in France and Japan the continuation of credit ceilings (*encadrement du crédit* and *window guidance* respectively) constrained the development of liability management. I cannot explain the German result, except in so far as the risks of extending loans on a fixed rate term led German banks to ration credit availability as interest rates rose. These shifts in the relationship between the quarterly and annual percentage changes of movements in narrow and broad money between the 1960s generally and the 1970s are shown in Table B.

This structural change made control over the growth of broad money more difficult, and caused problems in some of the countries that focused on such

TABLE B

(a) Correlation between annual percentage changes in broad and narrow money[a]

	Correlation coefficient	
	1960s[b]	1970s[b]
Canada	0.60	−0.13
Switzerland	0.45	−0.54
UK (using £M_3)	0.95	−0.39
(using M_3)	0.97	−0.45
USA	0.64	0.26
West Germany	0.79	0.82
France	0.92	0.86
Japan	0.87	0.97

(b) Correlation between quarterly percentage changes in broad and narrow money[a]

	Correlation coefficient	
	1960s[b]	1970s[b]
Canada	0.71	0.30
Switzerland	0.91	0.65
UK (using £M_3)	0.91	0.55
(using M_3)	0.92	0.46
USA	0.93	0.85
West Germany	0.94	0.82
France	0.90	0.93
Japan	0.52	0.93

[a] For UK, M_1 and £M_3 or M_3 as shown. For other countries figures are taken from *International Financial Statistics*, published by the IMF, for money and quasi-money: i.e. narrow money = currency outside banks and private-sector demand deposits; broad money = narrow money plus residents' time, savings and foreign currency deposits.

[b] Because of data problems periods used are in some cases slightly different.

wider monetary aggregates. There was, however, no effect (of this change in banks' behaviour) on the determinants of narrow money, so in those countries in which the authorities were targeting mainly, or exclusively, on narrow money, this had little or no effect on their ability to achieve their chosen monetary targets. In the countries, however, that adopted broad money targets, notably the UK, there were varying responses to the declining ability of the authorities to control their chosen broad monetary aggregates through the use of their main instrument, i.e. the control over the general level of interest rates. In some cases, as in Italy,[1] the authorities reverted to

[1] The Italian target has been 'total domestic credit expansion' rather than broad money. There is, however, a considerable overlap between these two aggregates.

direct controls over bank lending. In other cases the authorities tried to restrain, or rescind, the freedom of the banks to bid freely for wholesale deposits. An example of this latter was the Winnipeg agreement in Canada of 1972. Perhaps the most sophisticated attempts to apply direct controls to the rate of growth of total bank lending and total bank deposits are to be found in France, with penalties on marginal bank lending,[1] the *encadrement du crédit*, and in the UK with the supplementary special deposits scheme, the 'corset', which penalised the marginal rate of growth of interest-bearing deposits above some allowable trend.

With the growth of bank lending to the private sector often representing a reasonable proxy for the growth of total bank credit, with the growth of deposits of domestic non-bank residents representing a reasonable proxy for the growth of total bank liabilities, and with total bank liabilities equal to total bank assets (as an identity), there can at times be room for confusion in countries with broad monetary targets whether their main concern was with credit expansion or monetary expansion. An example of this occurred in the UK during the course of 1981. An overshoot in the £M_3 target was tolerated in part on the grounds that this resulted from a switch in the provision of mortgage lending from building societies to banks. However, if the focus of the target was on the monetary liability side, then it should have made no difference what changes in credit markets may have formed the counterpart to the increase in monetary liabilities. Alternatively, it could be argued that bank deposit liabilities were such close substitutes with building society deposits that a switch of funds between such holdings would be largely immaterial. But if so, the appropriate target should not be £M_3, but a wider aggregate encompassing both sets of liquid assets. The adoption of a target for PSL2, (an abbreviation for Private Sector Liquidity, Second Definition), which is such a wider aggregate – in addition to £M_3 – in 1982 supports the second interpretation.

In most countries with broad monetary targets, the weight of opinion has been that the main focus should be on the liability, monetary side, rather than on the credit market side.[2] In such cases one response to liability management, in conditions of sizeable and unpredictable shifts in the demand for bank lending, has been to devise, to encourage and to maintain conditions in which increases in bank lending to the private sector, relative to the target rate of growth, could be financed through banks, but in what could be described as 'non-monetary' ways. For example, in both Holland and West Germany sizeable proportions of bank liabilities are held in forms which are considered to be of sufficiently long maturity, with sufficient constraints on early withdrawal, to be described as non-monetary in form. Thus in Holland,

[1] Similar schemes of lending ceilings and penalties have also been applied in Italy and Ireland.

[2] In those countries with narrow monetary targets, such as Switzerland and Canada, massive variations in bank lending, and in the total size of banks' books, are frequently accommodated and coexist with maintained control of, even very slow growth in, the narrow monetary elements.

when there was such a large demand for bank credit as to threaten the monetary target, the authorities have on occasion brought into play a form of credit ceiling, which directly limits neither the banks' ability to issue additional loans, nor the size of the banks' balance-sheets in total; instead, it limits the extent to which the banks can fund the additional lending by monetary liabilities and therefore requires them to raise the yield on 'non-monetary' liabilities, and thus attract the additional funds into such 'non-monetary' form. In France the rules governing restricted lending allow the proceeds of bond issues (and equity issues) by banks to be on-lent without restriction; and banks take full advantage of this when market conditions are favourable. As in Holland, this gives the larger banks with easier access to the bond market a competitive advantage. Demand for such bonds increased in 1981 when the authorities restricted the rate of interest that could be offered on certain domestic deposits. Similarly, in West Germany the system works in such a way that shifts in the demand for bank credit are frequently met through non-monetary financing.

In the UK, however, there has been much less development by the banks, or bank customers, of holdings of longer-term savings deposits with the banking system.[1] No such development occurred in the UK even when there was a clear advantage to the banks in attracting such longer-term deposits under the 'corset' system, an advantage because deposits with a maturity over two years would not have been caught by the corset. It is not clear why such a market for longer-term savings deposits with banks has not grown up in the UK; one factor may possibly be because the building societies had already established a sizeable market in such deposits; another factor may be the wider range of government savings instruments available for personal investors in the UK, as compared with most other countries in Europe.

In so far as shifts over the boundary from assets designated as 'monetary' into those designated as 'non-monetary' leaves the economic position and opportunities of deposit holders largely unchanged (and the above qualification should be emphasised), it could then be argued that 'control' established in this way, by encouraging possibly quite small shifts in the maturity holdings of bank deposits, is somewhat cosmetic in its overall economic effect. Admittedly, shifting the public's asset holdings outwards along the maturity spectrum must always be regarded as restrictive;[2] nevertheless the extent of such real shift may not be measured well by concentrating on any one, or even a few, aggregates; on the other hand, trying to assess 'liquidity' as a whole, *à la* Radcliffe, leads into a conceptual and statistical quagmire. It can, however,

[1] The definition of the target aggregate, £M_3, however, encompasses all deposit holdings by UK residents, including the relatively small amounts of savings-type deposits of longer maturities.

[2] For example, in Italy the banks are constrained by credit ceilings and other regulations on interest rates, so the authorities have been able to induce a shift of funds out of bank deposits into Treasury bills.

be argued that the continuing stability and satisfactory performance of demand-for-money functions of the different Ms, and the stability and predictability of the velocity of these Ms, such as they may be, represents an econometric test of how far such shifts in asset holdings involve real changes in economic behaviour, or are largely cosmetic.

Playing the yield curve

On occasion it has been suggested that, if the authorities' ability to control the broad monetary aggregates through varying the general level of market rates has become impaired – as a result of liability management (or in terms of monetary base control, if the variability and uncertainty of changes in interest rates in response to changes in the base have become greater) – then the authorities could restore some of their ability to control the broad monetary aggregates by altering the shape of the yield curve, rather than by trying to vary just the general level of rates. Unfortunately what is gained on the one hand in terms of making deposits less attractive to deposit holders when long yields are raised relative to short yields tends by the same token to induce borrowers to shift short, borrowing more from banks and less from capital markets. When faced with an excess demand for funds by borrowers and an insufficiency of deposits, banks will respond by raising deposit rates, thereby offsetting the shift in the yield curve set in motion, in so far as they can, by the authorities.

Per contra, some observers in the UK have suggested that the appropriate response for the authorities when they try to be restrictive is to raise short yields relative to long ones, in order to persuade borrowers to shift from banks back into capital markets, but such a tilt in the yield curve would (perversely) attract asset holders short, e.g. by selling (or not buying) long-dated (government) bonds, in order to add to their bank deposits. Again, with an excess of deposit funds, and an insufficiency of demand from borrowers, banks would tend to lower their general level of rates, again tending to offset the tilt in the yield curve which the authorities might try to establish. Although there may be occasional market opportunities[1] for operating in such a way as to encourage *both* borrowers and depositors to shift longer by appropriate market tactics, the exercise does not seem to me easy, obvious, or probably long sustainable.

[1] For example, if the assets available to savers are mainly in fixed-interest form, whereas borrowers predominantly borrow from financial intermediaries on a variable-rate basis, then expectations of falling interest rates may lead depositors to want to shift into longer-dated assets without provoking a countervailing shift shorter by borrowers.

3. Inflation, Variable-rate Lending and the Importance of the Spread

Maturity transformation and interest-rate risk

One of the main functions of financial intermediaries is to hold liabilities to the account of depositors and claims on borrowers in the maturities preferred by their customers. In general, the preferred maturity of depositors and borrowers do not match, so the maturities of liabilities and assets on the books of financial intermediaries differ, i.e. financial intermediaries undertake maturity transformation. In some specialised cases, where the financial intermediaries are acting as long-term savings institutions, concentrating on the provision of life insurance or pensions, the liabilities held by such intermediaries may on average be longer than their assets. More generally, and particularly in the case of monetary institutions, the usual preference of depositors is for the holding of short-term claims, or deposits, on the (banking) institutions, while borrowers have a preference for loans on more extended terms. In some cases the extent of maturity transformation is restricted by legislation, as in Italy, where the 1936 Banking Law broadly restricts lending by banks to a maximum term of eighteen months. In the UK a large proportion of bank lending is undertaken in overdraft form, which is nominally repayable on call by the banks, but in practice is outstanding for an indefinite period.

Thus banks, and other non-bank financial intermediaries (NBFIs), engage in maturity transformation. This involves the intermediaries in various kinds of risk, particularly interest-rate risk, if the interest rates on their assets/liabilities are fixed for the duration of the maturity. This risk arises because, with their liabilities generally on a shorter-term basis than their assets, a rise in the general level of interest rates would force them to refinance lending, undertaken earlier at lower (fixed) rates, on the basis of funds obtained later at higher interest, thus enforcing a running loss. With assets longer than liabilities, and both undertaken on a fixed-rate basis, any unforeseen rise in nominal interest rates would bring about an unexpected loss to the banks, while any unforeseen fall in interest rates would lead to a windfall gain. More generally, interest risk arises whenever there is a mismatch in the periodicity over which interest rates on assets and liabilities are fixed; this can occur even when there is no *maturity* transformation, i.e. if the maturity of the assets and liabilities is the same, but there is some resetting of interest rates on one side of the balance-sheet which is not similarly matched on the other. This interest-rate risk is obviously greater when nominal interest rates become more variable and unpredictable. The variability of nominal interest rates will tend to rise with an increased variability in the rate of inflation. (Such variability may also, at least in the short run, be greater if the authorities are trying to maintain continuous control over the path of monetary growth, rather than allowing monetary variations to respond in an accommodating manner to short-term fluctuations in money market conditions.) Over the last decade, and more particularly in the last few years, the variability of nominal interest rates has increased, and this has had serious effects on those institutions sticking to fixed-rate financing; the plight of the S&Ls, Savings and Loans companies, in the USA is a prime example of the dangers of continuing with fixed-rate financing in a conjuncture subject to sizeable and unforeseen fluctuations in the level of nominal interest rates.

It is possible to obtain protection from interest-rate risks of this kind by the adoption of some form of variable-rate lending in which lending rates are not fixed but change over time in response to changes in market conditions.[1] There are various ways in which interest rates on longer-term loans can be varied over time in response to such changing conditions. The rate can be varied administratively by the lending institutions, as in the case of building societies in the UK; but leaving rates to be varied at the administrative fiat of the lending institution may in normal circumstances be regarded as leaving the borrower potentially subject to exploitation. However, the particular institutional position and historical traditions of building societies (as mutual funds) enabled the administrative variation of their lending rate to be generally acceptable in the UK. Alternatively, interest rates could be related to the current rate of inflation, plus a margin to provide a real rate of return; and indeed indexation of this kind, often described as 'monetary correction', has been adopted in several countries with especially high and variable inflation rates, for example Brazil and other countries in South America. Nevertheless, indexation has not been widely adopted, despite the onset of higher and variable inflation rates, in major industrial countries.[2] The more usual relationship between a variable lending rate and market conditions is to have the lending rate tied to the going market rate for large wholesale funds, with the rate varied at prearranged adjustment dates, so that a two-year loan, for example, would represent in effect a series of, say, three-month loans at the going wholesale three-month deposit rate, plus negotiated spread. Such floating rate loans originally emerged in the Euro-markets.[3]

This latter step greatly reduces the interest-rate risk, notably to the lender, but also, in general, to the borrower, if his/her loan would otherwise have been on a fixed term without break clauses. For the lending intermediary, it reduces the risks of undertaking maturity transformation. With the norm

[1] The protection will be greater, the closer the periodicity of the adjustment of lending rates to the adjustment of borrowing rates.

[2] In some cases the reasons why indexation has not been adopted are clear, e.g. official hostility to it, or fiscal arrangements which make it disadvantageous. But there are instances where there appear to be no barriers to its introduction, e.g. in the USA, and the reasons for the failure of indexation arrangements to emerge there are not fully understood.

[3] The reasons are straightforward: (i) volatile deposit source and an almost exclusive dependence on the wholesale and inter-bank market when funding loans; (ii) a large number of market participants, of different nationalities, makes it impossible to agree lending conventions – a market rate is an impersonal measure, whereas even agreeing on an appropriate inflation rate on which to base short-term interest rates could raise problems.

being for their financial claims to have a longer maturity than liabilities, the usual historical tendency has been for the profits of financial intermediaries to be squeezed as interest rates rise. This has been dramatically demonstrated with the S&Ls in the USA, and still occurs in countries largely persisting with fixed-rate lending, for example West Germany. Many German banks have still not fully recovered from losses made from long-term fixed-rate lending in 1978, and subsequently financed by increasingly expensive deposits. Also, in Switzerland rates on such lending tend to be sticky, with changes largely administratively determined. So the banks can lose out severely in times of rising interest rates, while not necessarily gaining equivalently in the converse situation if administered rates were lowered more rapidly.

In countries, though, which have historically worked on a variable-rate basis, or have come increasingly to use this technique,[1] a reverse effect on profitability may now hold. With a proportion of deposits continuing to bear a fixed rate of interest (notably sight or demand deposits, the majority of which in the UK and most other countries still have a zero interest rate), more assets than deposit liabilities may now be on a variable rate basis. In this case, then, profits tend to rise as interest rates rise, since the interest rate on a larger proportion of deposit liabilities maintains a fixed rate. This has become known in the UK as the *endowment effect*;[2] thus banks, essentially the clearing banks, having a sizeable proportion of zero interest-rate demand deposits, receive larger 'endowment' profit as interest rates rise. This effect is, however, subject to erosion over time, as funds are switched from non-interest-bearing deposits to higher yieiding assets. (The implications of this for monetary control are discussed further in section 4.)

The switch to variable-rate lending is as important to the borrower as it is to the banks. The borrower will benefit most when the (unpredictable) developments causing changes in the variable rate are closely correlated with changes in the borrowers' cash flow. If there is a likelihood that fluctuations in the borrower's cash flow and in variable rates might be negatively correlated, then the adoption of variable rate financing could well *increase* borrowers'

---

[1] Both these conditions would apply to the UK; thus historically mortgage lending in the UK by the building societies has been on a variable-rate basis; more recently the banks have been moving towards the provision of large volumes of medium-term lending which again are now increasingly, possibly almost entirely, on a variable-rate basis.

[2] This endowment effect is, however, considerably reduced if banking profits and accounts are calculated on an inflation-adjusted basis rather than on a historic-cost basis. Bank liabilities include capital as well as deposit liabilities, so with total assets equal to total liabilities, banks hold monetary claims on other sectors which exceed their monetary liabilities, i.e. they hold *net monetary assets*. As the rate of inflation rises, these net monetary assets depreciate, and the fall in real profits is especially marked if real interest rates happen to be low as inflation rises. With inflationary expectations apparently lagging beind the reality during the course of the 1970s, this was frequently the case, so that, despite the high nominal profits induced by the endowment effect, the real profitability of the banking system, particularly on a post-tax basis, was much less. Of course, the same inflation effect on banking profitability also impinges on those financial intermediaries which have continued to maintain fixed-rate lending, so in their case true profitability is doubly affected by the interest-rate risk at a time of inflation upsurge.

risks. It was the rise in Euro-dollar interest rates at a time when export earnings came under severe pressure that has now highlighted this latter possibility internationally. Recent experience of cash-flow pressures on companies at a time of high nominal interest rates reiterates the same lesson domestically.

Nevertheless the conjunction of variable inflation and variable interest rates has led a sizeable proportion of borrowers to prefer to switch on to a variable-rate basis. In practice, the 1970s were a decade when it would, with the benefit of hindsight, have been highly profitable for most companies to have borrowed on a fixed-rate basis. Yet it was just in this period when, in the UK at least, virtually none did, and the long-term debenture market in the UK became moribund. In some part this was, perhaps, because company treasurers as a group 'got it wrong', believing that the current level of medium and long-term interest rates was unnaturally high, just at a time when it was, in reality, due to rise yet higher. Yet even those who may have realised that there was a good chance that interest rates would rise further felt themselves unable to borrow at such high rates, because of the risk that rates might come down, and they would become landed with unacceptably high fixed-rate borrowing, particularly with the outlook for profits, even in nominal terms, becoming more uncertain; moreover, the risk appeared the greater, in so far as their colleagues elsewhere were not themselves borrowing. To stick one's neck out in a risky venture by oneself is much more dangerous than it is to stick one's head out as a member of a large group. So the rising rate of inflation, and with that the rising medium- and long-term interest rates, led to the virtual demise of the debenture market for companies in the UK.

There is, however, now some question whether companies (except perhaps really large companies) would go back to raising long-term fixed-rate debt on the capital market, even if inflation and nominal interest rates should come back down. With the demise of the debenture market, companies turned increasingly to the banks for their medium-term finance.[1] There is a possibility that the banks have now developed a superior product to the capital market. The costs of capital transactions on the debenture market are high (especially in view of the fixed costs involved in new issues for medium and smaller companies). When there is a need to deal with many small purchasers there is a concomitant requirement to provide them with sufficient information and sufficient protection. Thus there is a need in the capital market for an expensive prospectus, and the whole process of financing a large new debenture issue with underwriting and sub-underwriting is expensive. Dealing with banks in the provision of medium-term funds, even with a banking syndicate when there is a lead bank, may be considerably cheaper and easier than facing the transactions costs of the debenture market. So, even if inflation and nominal interest rates should now fall appreciably, there is still

[1] And this was facilitated in the UK by the removal of direct controls on bank lending.

some likelihood that the banks will continue to take a larger share of such medium-term lending than was the case in the 1960s. With lower inflation and lower nominal interest rates, the form of such medium-term lending by banks could revert to being at fixed rather than at variable rates, perhaps thereby also inducing UK banks to seek, rather more keenly than in the past, for medium-term fixed-rate deposits. The extent of continued involvement by the banks in this area will, however, in part depend on how spreads (and fiscal conditions) develop. During periods of low interest rates, endowment profits are low, and spreads tend to be higher, forcing borrowers into the capital market. The reverse was true during the 1970s.

The effects of the switch to variable-rate lending

The change from fixed-rate lending to variable-rate lending will have reduced the interest-sensitivity of borrowers to variations in the level of nominal interest rates.[1] Unless the expected duration of the borrowing is rather short, the shift to variable-rate lending means that the timing of the borrowing no longer matters greatly. With fixed-rate lending, it is obviously of crucial importance to seek to arrange the borrowing when the interest rate is relatively, or believed to be, low, because that low rate will pertain throughout the life of the borrowing. Equally there will be a considerable advantage in avoiding borrowing at times when the rate, persisting throughout the life of the loan, is thought to be temporarily high. With variable-rate lending, it no longer will matter to the borrower whether the rate is thought to be temporarily high or temporarily low. If a loan is expected to be of a duration as long as an expected cycle of interest rates, then the borrower will even out the swings and the roundabouts in that cycle. So the current,

[1] This assertion can be challenged on theoretical grounds. The most abstract argument is that, even if only fixed-rate lending is available, a borrower could in theory operate in futures markets so as effectively to transform the fixed-rate contract on to a variable-rate basis. In practice, at least in the past, the absence of a full set of futures markets and transactions costs in the existing markets restricted such opportunities. Additionally, so long as lenders' and borrowers' expectations were symmetrical, it could be argued that both fixed-rate yields and the average of expected variable rates over the relevant period should adjust equally in response to (policy-induced) changes in short rates, and in the associated shape of the yield curve, so that the mean expected yield on both would always remain in equilibrium. Such symmetrical response is uncertain. Banks may tie fixed-rate medium-term lending to current prime, or base rates, while borrowers may have more regressive expectations about future rates. Probably more important, even if the *mean* expected yield would be the same in either case, the risk of having borrowed on fixed terms at temporarily unpropitious times will weigh more heavily (than in the case of variable-rate borrowing). Experience in other capital markets, e.g. with new issues in equity and debenture markets, suggests that the elasticity of borrowing to such risk considerations and/or to asymmetric expectations of borrowers and lenders may well be considerable, i.e. that new issues are more sensitive to the current level of equity and debenture prices than might have been expected on the basis of rational, symmetric expectations.

momentary, *level* of market interest rates no longer matters as greatly to a medium-term borrower.[1]

Instead, what now matters much more to the borrower is the spread that he is charged above the general market level of rates. Indeed, the spread between the variable rate charged on loans and the rate paid on short-term deposits represents, in an important sense, the cost of intermediation. The cheaper the cost of intermediation, the larger the volume will be. In the USA, of course, large customers can directly enter the commercial paper market, as borrowers or lenders, if the cost of bank intermediation becomes too large. Large companies, especially multinationals, can generally turn to the Euro-markets, if domestic intermediation costs rise too far.

The cost of bank intermediation for large customers has come down over the course of recent years so far that many, indeed most, large customers, who can enter wholesale markets, probably now have both debit and asset positions outstanding at the same time with the banking system. It is no longer the case that all banking customers, with outstanding debts to the banks, will seek to run these down as far as they can, so long as they have spare assets available. This is, perhaps, most obvious in the case of sovereign borrowers, who will continue to wish to maintain gross positive reserve positions, often in the form of holdings in the Euro-dollar markets, and yet who will also wish to borrow for general development when the terms are attractive.

The same is increasingly true now for corporate clients, who may be running gross asset and debit positions considerably in excess of their net position, whichever sign that may be, with the banking system. During the course of the last few years in which the company sector in the UK has been under severe cash-flow pressure, it has still built up its gross liquidity ratio. The lower the spread, the more attractive it will be for such customers to maintain liquidity, on the basis of borrowed funds, and to meet their

[1] Furthermore, the development of a broad market in financial futures should allow risk-averse borrowers and lenders to shift such interest-rate risks to speculators. In so far as the (perceived) variability of interest rates increases as the level of nominal interest rates (and inflation) rises, this capacity to shift risk via the futures market might facilitate the continuation of more bank intermediation in the face of high and rising nominal interest rates and inflation, and thus further reduce the interest-elasticity of the provision of bank loans.

The abolition of legal or administrative ceilings on interest rates on lending, e.g. owing to usury laws, will also allow bank lending to continue more strongly as nominal interest rates rise.

The main influence on the demand for borrowing is, presumably, the post-tax real cost. In most countries the tax system is only partially, if at all, inflation-adjusted. So long as the borrower has profits, or income, available against which nominal interest can be offset, an equal rise in inflation and nominal interest rates actually *reduces* post-tax real rates of interest. While the level of nominal interest rates has some independent effect, e.g. via front-end loading of real interest payments and income gearing, the unadjusted form of the tax system in most countries must have further reduced the responsiveness of the demand for bank borrowing to variations in the level of nominal interest rates, when these have accompanied variations in the (perceived) rate of inflation.

additional financial requirements by borrowing, rather than by running down their existing deposit holdings. Indeed at the limit, if the spread is zero, given that liquidity has some utility, the demand for both bank lending and deposits would theoretically be infinite. Owing to the existence of rigidities and distortions in certain interest rates, there have even occasionally been times in the UK when the interest rate on bank borrowing has actually fallen temporarily below an interest rate on deposits of a similar maturity, so that there was even a turn to be made by borrowing in order to redeposit; this has been termed 'round-tripping'.

So, one of the increasingly important determinants of the volume of both bank borrowing and bank deposits, given the widespread adoption of variable-rate lending, is the spread required by banks. The importance of the spread as a determinant of the rate of increase of intermediation has been clearly recognised in the case of the Euro-markets.[1] The importance of the spread as a determinant of the volume of bank borrowing and deposits is, however, rather less clear, as yet, in most domestic money markets, but some research has been done in the Bank of England on the determinants both of the rate of growth of broad money (£M_3) and also on the demand for loans which suggests that variations in the spread may have a significant effect. The effect of the spread on the total of loans and deposits is, however, difficult to quantify, in part because it depends on reactions to relatively small variations in the differential between two highly correlated variables, and also because adequate data on actual rates at which transactions, borrowing and depositing, are undertaken are frequently not available, or sufficiently accurate, for the purpose of econometric testing.

A reduction in spreads will tend to raise the rate of growth of the banks, which are, in effect, thereby pricing their products more competitively; but by the same token a reduction in spreads reduces profit margins, and therefore erodes capital ratios, the ratio of the capital stock to the volume of business being undertaken. An increase in competition, a desire for growth for its own sake, and confidence in the soundness of the business being undertaken (a belief that risk of bad debts are low) will all tend to squeeze the size of

[1] The evidence shows that the volume of newly announced syndicated medium-term Euro-credits expanded very rapidly at the same time as spreads were falling (see Johnston[**4**]). But, arguably, the supply of intermediation services by banks should be a positive function of the spread, *ceteris paribus*. Having allowed for credit risks, etc., the residual trend of spreads was still downwards in the 1970s, which can be explained by increasing international banking competition. This trend may continue as marginal banks continue to enter the market; but the supply function *should* slope upwards after some 'equilibrium' has been reached. On the side of borrowers, the econometric evidence shows that the demand for syndicated medium-term Euro-credit is quite spread-sensitive – and much more so than with respect to the level of short-term interest rates (LIBOR).

One complication is that, in addition to the spread, the charge for financial intermediation is taken in the form of various fees and initial charges. Indeed, in some cases, because the spread is seen as a public indication of a relative credit standing, some borrowers in the Euro-markets have a preference for a package with higher fees and a lower published spread.

spreads. A natural danger for the banking industry is that a successful run of years of financial operations will encourage an erosion of capital/asset ratios to a stage at which a deterioration in economic conditions generally, leading to an increase in bad debts, could cause difficulties for the banking system. One could therefore envisage a cycle, with misplaced confidence eroding capital adequacy, and then being found to have been excessively optimistic, so that the capital position is impaired yet further by bad debts. The resulting shock to confidence would induce a subsequent recovery in spreads and profit margins, which would have the effect of bringing about a (sudden) slowdown in the rate of expansion of financial intermediation, or even some decline.[1]

Capital and reserve ratios and the size of banks

In the above analysis the overall size of banks' books is seen as depending on the volume of capital resources that the banks are able to attract, and on the ratio of total assets/liabilities to such capital that they seek to maintain. The size of the banking business, as with other financial intermediaries, is viewed as being determined essentially in the same way as the size of any other business, depending on the volume of basic resources, essentially capital, that it can employ, and the opportunities available to the industry for the employment of such resources. These opportunities exhibit themselves for financial intermediaries in the form of the interest rates available, and the lending and deposit business that they can undertake in financial markets. Shifts in the extent of competition, and therefore in spreads, i.e. the cost of intermediation, may encourage bank customers to increase both their holdings of claims on the banks and their liabilities to the banks, and may therefore alter the velocity of (at any rate) the broader monetary aggregates. So, increasing competition could raise the ratio of broad money to nominal incomes, subject to such constraints as the maintenance of capital adequacy places on such a trend. To some extent, changes in velocity may be a function of changing conditions within the banking business, rather than necessarily having any wider economic significance, though concern may remain that the apparent shift in the liquidity of the private sector's asset portfolio could affect future economic developments and hamper the authorities' ability to control such developments. Shifts in velocity for broad money that are accompanied by changes in banks' capital adequacy ratios may also provide some indication of changing financial risks, and the ebb and flow of competitive pressures, and perhaps of financial strength (or fragility). While it is difficult to establish any strong case for a particular ratio of capital to risk assets to be an optimum, an equilibrium, or a desideratum, nevertheless it is

[1] In the Euro-market, spreads rose very sharply following the banking crises in the summer of 1974, to reach historically high levels in 1975 and 1976. At the same time, despite the massive increase in global payments imbalances, there was a fall in the rate of expansion of syndicated medium-term Euro-currency loans.

possible to chart whether the financial exposure of the banking system is becoming greater or less.

It may be argued that the market will act to deter excessive financial risk-taking by the banking system, by reducing the equity value of those banks which the market feels have been taking an excessively risky position. It is difficult, however, to feel confident that the market will be able to, or will generally, act in this way. Assessment of the trade-off between higher earnings and greater risk is not easy for the general public to make. The market lacks detailed information about the nature of the particular business of individual banks;[1] and the banks, for reasons of competitive secrecy, are unlikely to be prepared to give such information publicly and openly. In addition, there are many who believe that the market's time horizon is relatively short, that it suffers from myopia, and that it is too prone to extrapolate short-term developments, frequently forgetting longer-term traditional norms of safety in the pursuit of a 'quick buck'. On such grounds, there is, of course, an argument for prudential controls in order to restrain the degree of fragility and risk adopted by the banking system and to ensure the sufficiency of capital adequacy, and the maintenance of sufficiently large spreads in the business. With the move of wholesale banking business into the international arena, with easy substitution into financial channels abroad (in place of domestic banking), there is, moreover, good reason in theory for some international harmonisation of prudential controls over capital adequacy, even though this is difficult in practice. Otherwise, those countries which allow their banks to maintain the lowest ratios of capital will also enable them to offer the lowest spreads, to become 'unfairly' competitive and to grow in size relative to the banks in those countries undertaking a more prudent position. If, however, banks in the countries allowing a riskier position were then to get into trouble, the resulting effects on the banking business, and on the world economy generally, could spill over, e.g. into those countries where the banks had maintained a more prudent position.

If the size of banks' books is therefore determined by their access to capital resources and their capital/deposit ratios, what role is left for the monetary base as a determinant of the overall size of bank deposits? Of course, in many countries, banks are only required to hold reserves against a section, or proportion, of their deposits, notably their demand deposits, or transactions balances; so it could already be said, perhaps, that banks' access to reserves does not determine the *overall* size of their books. But even in the case of countries where reserves are required against total deposit liabilities, how does this requirement affect the overall size of their business? First, any countries undertaking monetary base control would observe a rise, possibly a

[1] For example, 'hidden reserves', varying provisions (general and specific) for bad debts, deferred taxation provisions, problems of inflation adjustment, etc., can make outside assessment of the conditions of individual banks from their published accounts a difficult exercise.

sharp rise, in interest rates as the 'reservable' deposits rise, above their target rate of growth (though such a rise in interest rates – not perhaps of the same speed or magnitude – would also generally occur even with a more discretionary reaction to monetary growth greater than the target). This would affect, and depress, the general level of activity in the economy in the normal way. This reduction in economic activity, combined with some residual direct effect of interest rates on the demand for bank borrowing, would have the effect of reducing the growth and size of banks' business.

Perhaps more importantly, required reserves, if they do not bear a market interest rate, represent a form of tax on banking business. The higher interest rates go, the higher is the burden of this tax on banking. So relatively high required reserves, bearing low or zero interest rates, will directly act to reinforce the restrictive effect of rising interest rates: for this 'tax' on banking intermediation will vary both with the size of the required reserves and with the general level of market interest rates. Indeed, it has been argued by some, for example Davis and Lewis[**2**] in Australia, that, following the abolition of administratively fixed interest rates, the authorities need the support of a variable tax on banking intermediation (in conditions of liability management, variable-rate lending, and market-related interest rates) in order to maintain sufficient control over monetary growth. While one can see the advantages of having such a tax, the impact of which would vary with the level of interest rates, it would also have the disadvantages common to all such taxes of giving rise to reallocations of resources and avoidance. In particular, there would be a tendency, when such tax appeared particularly onerous, for intermediation to be shifted into other channels. Accordingly, if the burden of such tax tended to be high for more than short periods, there would be an increasing tendency for financial intermediation to be shifted abroad, or through other non-banking routes, which in turn would affect the velocity of the controlled banking sector, and the proportion of financial intermediation done by it. Over time this would weaken and lessen the effect of the control itself.

4. Technology and the Retail Depositor

Electronic banking?

We appear to be on the verge of several new applications of electronic and computer technology to banking practices, especially to retail banking processes. There has recently been a veritable flood of articles, not only in the specialised banking journals, but also in the press more widely, for example in the *Financial Times*, recording the technical possibilities and increasingly the commercial application of these new developments. A whole new glossary of technical terms (and of acronyms) is having to be learned by those interested in the banking industry, e.g. EFT (electronic funds transfer). Perhaps the most visible innovation has been the recent surge in the use of ATMs (automated teller machines), notably – but not only – in the USA, where they are evolving from their earlier humble guise as simple cash dispensers into a more advanced form of machines that can carry out a wider range of operations, broadly replacing the function of the human bank clerk, or teller; such operations include the receipt of cash and cheques, the provision of statements, the provision of travellers' cheques, and the automatic processing of standard loan applications.

A more advanced concept, though its use is only just beginning, is that of home banking, whereby individual depositors, or families of depositors, can access – through a machine attached to their television set – their own banks' computers. This enables them to communicate with the computer, to receive information and send instructions.[1] Other developments are extending the use of the plastic card, which had its origin as a source of credit, now also as a debit card in ATM and point-of-sale (POS) machines (communicating directly with bank computers), and by coding additional information on to the card itself, e.g. the card contains on itself data on the remaining available funds in machine-readable form; this latter technique is being used in telephone kiosks by British Telecom and, more ambitiously, as a general payment card in some regional experiments in France. Another set of developments involves accelerating, cheapening and simplifying the transfer of information, e.g. notably of payments instructions, between banks. There are several examples of this kind of development. In the USA settlement systems are provided by the Federal Reserve (Fed Wire) and by the private sector: Bank Wire (for domestic payment) and CHIPS (for payments between New York banks). In Japan the Zenyin system provides an inter-bank transfer service and there is a similar system in France. The UK banks will shortly be launching CHAPS, a highly sophisticated inter-bank payment service. Internationally, SWIFT, jointly owned by banks in many countries, provides financial message services (but without settlement facilities).

These innovations carry an aura of technological glamour, and have an excitement in their own right. What is, perhaps, less easy to assess is exactly how these developments are likely to change the behavioural patterns of bank customers and users of financial intermediary services; and what consequential implications these changes may therefore have for those involved with monetary control. For the purpose of this latter type of analysis it may, perhaps, be desirable to try to classify and characterise the effects of these changes in an economic and analytical framework. For this purpose I shall use

[1] The home screen obviously cannot dispense cash. Cash could be sent by post instead, but in so far as this latter is slow and/or unreliable the home screen needs to be complemented by ATMs.

the simplest of economic classifications, i.e. the division into the effects on supply and on demand, in order to consider how these changes may affect the supply of financial intermediary services, and subsequently the demand by bank customers for such services.

Structural changes in the supply of financial services

In the same manner as technological changes improve productivity in other industries, technological changes in the provision of intermediary services should raise productivity here, thereby reducing costs and the requirement for both labour and capital, in a system 'drowning in a sea of paper'. In so far as input factor costs go down, the cost of intermediation, i.e. the spread, can be reduced without imperilling profit margins, thereby encouraging some further extension of the volume of intermediation. This development is likely, however, to be gradual, and perhaps not do much more than act as a counterweight to the otherwise rising labour costs of processing the rising flood of paper transactions. Considerably more important for the developing shape of the financial system will be the likelihood that the technological changes may drastically alter the relative cost structure of providing transmission services (and other elements of retail banking) for differing potential suppliers of such services.

Previously the provision of retail financial services required the physical presence of custom-built branches, combining bricks and mortar, office equipment (e.g. processing machines of varying degrees of sophistication) and human operators. The provision of such a branch network was extremely expensive. This gave an advantage to those institutions with an established branch network, such as the banks and also the Post Office. It would require a vast outlay of capital in order to establish from scratch a branch system sufficiently widespread to provide effective competition. So, once established, the main systems offering retail financial services tended towards oligopoly, protected from competition by economies of scale and the high costs of entry. There is, however, an exception to this, but an exception which was brought into being artificially by government intervention and legislation. This is to be found in the USA, where the McFadden Act prevented inter-State branching, and where limitations on branching, both Federal and within certain States, has resulted in a fragmented banking system.

Now, however, these retail financial transmission services *may* be capable of being provided more cheaply, without such a massive initial outlay of capital and with far less labour input. ATMs can be set up in place of branches. The transmission network, in the form of electronic equipment, can also be linked in with other, already existing non-financial activities, e.g. a chain of department stores, or even a large chain of garages. At the extreme, home banking, as exemplified by the Verbraucher Bank in West Germany, would allow all users of the network, wherever situated in the country, to be linked electronically to a single financial and computer centre; in a sense each home becomes its own personalised branch of the single bank.

The implication of this is that setting up a large-scale network to transfer payment instructions over that net could now become cheaper. Even so, the installation of a new network, *de novo*, would remain exceedingly expensive, and it would be extremely risky for a newcomer to seek to challenge those already established in the provision of retail payments services. In the USA these developments may at the outset have the effect of binding the artificially segmented banking system into larger effective groupings. This could occur because ATMs, not counting legally as separate branches, can be set up across State borders.[1] There is therefore some pressure on banks in adjoining States to co-ordinate in order to set up ATMs which can be accessed by users of banks within that group in many States. This could have the effect of bringing about some common operations of banks joining in the single ATM franchise. It may also allow other (non-banking) institutions to enter the industry and to compete more effectively and directly with the established providers of retail banking services. Merrill Lynch and Sears Roebuck are examples in the USA. In the UK, building societies, such as the Abbey National and the Leicester Building Society, have taken some initial steps in the provision of payment services, though at the moment they are using the banks' transmission systems; and other building societies are considering possible future developments in that direction. In some cases the services provided by building societies may be offered in conjunction with a bank; and the possibility of cheaper entry into the provision of retail services in the UK may encourage certain banks, e.g. US banks, which have not previously sought to enter into this part of the banking industry, to do so.[2]

In so far as new competitors enter into the provision of retail banking, especially if these new competitors come from outside the banking system, as presently designated, this development will, of course, bring into (further) question the present statistical boundaries between the differing financial institutions, and more fundamentally the adequacy of the present definitions of banks and deposit-takers. All this may allow a rather wider range of (currently differing) institutions to become general providers of retail financial services. In addition, though, to such providers of general retail financial services, there is likely to remain a continuing sizeable penumbra of more specialised, and generally wholesale, financial institutions, concentrating, for example, on wholesale banking, or on operations in futures markets or on money market brokerage, or perhaps specialised in the provision of mortgage

[1] ATMs cannot, however, take deposits across State lines.

[2] Whereas the introduction of ATMs seems likely to reduce the cost of entry into the retail financial market, it can be argued that other technological innovations, e.g. home banking, POS, may increase the competitive dominance of existing large banks, because of the high initial costs and the large banks' competitive ability to induce large retail outlets to join their payments networks.

finance; also there would be continuing room for providers of financial services for special groups, etc.

The above outline of possible future developments is based on the expectation that technology will in due course cheapen information flows over a single widespread network. It is difficult, however, now to see just how far, or how fast, such developments may alter the shape and form of the supply of retail financial intermediary services. There are obstacles on the way. One of these is that the technological changes cheapen information flows over a *single* network, but the use to the customer of any one individual network also depends crucially on the ability to transfer information and instructions between the one single electronic network and other related networks. For example, the use of an existing retail financial system, such as Lloyds Bank in the UK, would be far less effective and serviceable for the retail depositor if he could not receive payments from customers of other banks, or again make payments to customers of other banks, or only do so at an exorbitant cost. In the UK the main retail clearing banks have joined together, through the cheque-clearing system, to provide one single, overall, transmission network; although, at its initiation, there had been some thought that the development of the Giro through the Post Office system might provide a separate financial network, in practice the Giro has not been able to attract a sufficiently large number of customers to form a wholly separate network, and has now joined the main clearing system. In many other European countries, however, there are two completely separate networks, with the Giro network on the one hand and the banking clearing system on the other. In the UK, because of historical experience, we tend to think of one single clearing network as the norm. In fact, however, this need not be so, and there could be a multiplicity of separate networks with, or without, effective and efficient links between them.

So the question arises, if a new competitor wanted to set up a new individual network, whether it could join the existing clearing system, or whether it would have to seek to develop an entirely separate clearing system. The position in differing countries on this issue depends on their particular historical and institutional situation. Thus, for example, in the USA, the banking system is so fragmented that the new large competitors in the provision of financial intermediary services, such as Merrill Lynch, can frequently find a relatively small bank within the clearing system that is prepared to act as their point of access into the existing clearing network. The situation in several other countries with a more concentrated retail banking system, where the clearing system is dominated by large oligopolistic retail banks (e.g. in the UK, Canada, Australia), is *potentially* different. In these cases the existing retail banks *might* be in a position to raise the cost of entry into the clearing system of a new competitor, subject, however, to legal and other factors preventing restrictive trade practices.

In so far as the main retail banks sought to restrict the advent of competitors into the existing clearing network, then they could in theory be able to restrain competition and/or require the duplication of main clearing systems, with resulting important implications for efficiency, the allocation of resources, etc. It is on this latter question, the ability of newcomers, new competitors, to link into the existing clearing systems that important issues for the regulatory authorities in many countries are quite likely to arise. The pressure of competition, however, between existing retail banks may well be such that newcomers will be able to find an existing bank which is willing to sponsor them.

The effect on the demand for financial services

Besides customers benefiting generally from improving productivity and a cheapening of the provision of financial services, these technological innovations should provide specific advantages to customers for retail financial services in the form of easier access to cash, to credit, and to information on the depositor's cash-flow position. There will be easier access to cash through the medium of ATMs, especially those that are available 'through the wall', and therefore open at all times even when the institutions themselves are shut. In so far as it becomes easier, and less costly in time and effort, to replenish cash holdings, so that the costs of running out of cash are less, because there are more available sources to provide additional cash funds, then the expectation is presumably that average personal holdings of cash will be less, and the frequency with which cash is replenished will be somewhat greater, even though easier access to cash may slow the trend towards making payments for goods in other non-cash media. Moreover, the existence of cash dispensers, and even more so of ATMs offering wider services, in places of work, e.g. large factories and office blocks, is likely to be a factor in shifting the habits of the work-force away from wage payments in cash into wage payments in paper, or, perhaps, increasingly in forms of electronic direct transfer. Besides making the banking habit more widespread, this tendency is likely to bring about some further reduction in the usage of cash. In addition, the larger proportion of purchases which in future may be paid for through the medium of the plastic card should also tend to reduce cash usage. In the UK at any rate over the period 1980–2 the usage of cash has fallen quite sharply below that which would have been predicted on the basis of earlier, well-fitting, econometric equations. Our present view is that this shortfall (compared with forecast) in currency holdings has arisen because of the accelerating trend towards wage payment in other than cash form and, perhaps, to some growing usage of plastic cards for making transactions.

Although the means of making payments may come increasingly to depend on the plastic card, it is currently starting from a low base.[1] Initially such

[1] In the Monopolies Commission Report of September 1980 in the UK on *Credit Card Franchise Services*[**6**], it was stated that in 1976 credit cards accounted for only 0.3 per cent of all

plastic cards primarily provided the user with a form of short-term credit on an interest-free basis until the first payment date, and thereafter in the form of a consumer loan at relatively high interest rates. But in future the increasing development of card-operated payments (e.g. POS) may more frequently involve these card-operated transactions instigating adjustments in the depositors' current accounts with banks. In those countries which have a tradition of extending overdrafts, such card-initiated payments may be honoured so long as the overdraft does not run above a certain, probably prespecified, borrowing limit. The usage of plastic cards, whether they are formally credit or debit cards, may have the effect of further increasing access to automatic credit for most depositors and card-users. In so far as such a credit line is effectively automatic, and is known to be so by the customer, his/her access to immediately available funds clearly includes the extent of that credit line.

So the 'true' money stock, as Keynes noted long ago, should in theory include such unused credit lines. The adjustment, therefore, to unforeseen cash flows may be buffered in the short run as much by shifts in customers' debit positions (their overdrafts) with banks as in variations in their credit, deposit, balances. Already in the case of large customers, it is arguable that it is changes in their *net* position with banks that better represent the changes in their overall liquidity position. The further development of plastic cards could imply that short-term variations in individuals' cash-flow positions will as easily be met by variations in their borrowing from banks as in variations in their deposit balances. It could be the net position of the customer with the bank that would absorb these shocks, rather than just changes in the deposit balance; so it may become increasingly misleading to focus on variations on the deposit side of the banking system alone as an indication of the financial position of bank customers. Moreover, in so far as the 'true' money stock is effectively increased by any addition to such credit facilities, the lower may be the average balance that depositors will still need to feel that they should hold in their deposit accounts. So easier access to credit facilities, via plastic cards or otherwise, may tend to reduce the ratio of demand (sight) deposits to incomes and expenditures.

Easier, quicker and cheaper access to information for the individual on his/her cash flow will also presumably allow depositors to economise on lower-yielding transactions balances, by facilitating and expediting shifts

payments (by adults) over 50p, 1.5 per cent for payments of £5 and over, and 2.1 per cent for payments of £25 and over (para. 2.22, p. 21). The amounts of such credit outstanding at end-years 1976–9 were also shown (Table 2.1, p. 11); during this period credit cards grew proportionately more strongly than other forms of consumer lending, rising from 5.5 per cent of all such lending at end-1976 to 9.7 per cent at end-1979. Subsequent data are not available, because of disclosure problems, but it may be that increased nominal interest rates since 1979 may have retarded the faster rate of growth of this relatively expensive form of borrowing.

In the USA, moreover, the proportion of transactions effected by money and credit varied only slightly during the 1970s; the share of purchases using currency and demand deposits remained about 70 per cent over the decade.

between higher-yielding savings balances and transactions balances. However, the main, and more important, change in this respect is that a combination of competition, technological change and in some cases de-regulation (as in the USA) is likely to induce financial intermediaries to offer more competitive interest rates, with these varying more closely in line with market rates, on balances that remain usable for transactions. A whole new range of techniques having this effect has become available in the USA. These include negotiable orders of withdrawal (NOW) and automated transfer from savings (ATS) accounts, money market mutual funds (MMMFs), cash-management accounts, as run by Merrill Lynch, and bank offerings of short-term repurchase agreements (RPs), whereby banks invest any surplus balances in transactions accounts in interest-bearing, very short-term overnight funds, and then make these balances available for transactions on the next day, and sweep accounts, which have the same general effect. These latter, RPs and sweep accounts, have been offered for some time to larger, corporate, customers, but the further development of technology and competition could increasingly induce banks to offer these services to smaller and smaller customers, though their popularity to these will depend on the continuation of high nominal interest rates. These varying developments have differing distorting effects on the data. NOW and ATS accounts are included in M_1; the rate at which depositors transfer savings into these accounts will distort the historical comparability of the M_1 series, and this has indeed been acknowledged by the Federal Reserve in its interpretation of the data for the purposes of monetary policy. The funds 'deposited' in MMMFs are generally included in M_2. However, the funds which have been shifted into cash-management accounts are not included in the narrower or wider monetary aggregates, while the funds which are shifted into RPs are included in M_2 only if they are overnight RPs issued by banks.

Such developments are also beginning to appear in the UK. Two of the main clearing banks, Midland and Lloyds, are test marketing special arrangements whereby depositors can obtain interest on balances, which they can transfer into cash, e.g. through a cash dispenser, but which cannot be used for the whole range of transmission services, e.g. in the form of writing cheques on these. A much smaller bank, a subsidiary of the Co-op Bank, is providing interest on transactions balances, at nearly the market rate, which balances can, however, still be used for the whole range of transactions services. As already noted, the building societies are also dipping a toe into this area of providing payment transmission services. The likelihood must be that this trend will continue further, since a combination of competitive forces and available technology, as well as the example from the USA, and possibly other countries, will further ecnourage it. On the other hand, a fall in nominal interest rates – as inflation fell – would reduce the pressure for change.

This trend (towards the payment of a market-related interest rate on transactions balances) is, however, restrained and moderated in the UK by the present nature of the tax regime. The provision of transmission services, e.g. in clearing cheque payments, is extremely costly.[1] Most depositors, however, do not bear these costs themselves, and are generally unaware of the extent, or even perhaps the existence, of such costs. This occurs because the transactions costs are offset under UK arrangements against *notional* interest payments on non-interest-bearing demand deposits. This provides an advantage to many depositors, since if both the interest payments and the transactions costs were specifically and separately charged, under present fiscal arrangements, there would be tax to pay on the interest on demand deposits, but the transactions costs would not be allowable against tax. The Inland Revenue will not allow the individual transactions costs generated by the individual depositor to be offset against his/her specific interest receipts on his personal deposit. Accordingly, in the schemes that have been devised so far to offer interest payments on bank current accounts, the interest is paid only after debiting for an *average* charge, averaged over all customers, or alternatively, as with the Midland, the interest is only offered on such forms of deposit which are restricted in the nature of the payments which they can be used for, and therefore in the transactions costs generated.

Although the extent, and speed, of the spreading of the payment of market-related interest rates on transactions balances will depend both on the continuation of high and variable inflation and interest rates,[2] and also on the particular institutional and fiscal arrangements in each country, nevertheless the interaction of competitive pressures and the developing technological capacity are likely to make this a continuing trend. What are the implications?

First, during the period in which these innovations are being introduced, some instability in the functional relationships between the monetary aggregates affected and general economic developments is to be expected. Holdings of 'traditional' transactions balances, both cash (see p. 174) and ordinary zero-yielding sight balances, will probably grow slower – relatively to nominal incomes, while holdings of these newer forms of interest-bearing balances, capable of being used for making payments, will grow fast initially, drawing funds both out of 'traditional' transactions balances and from

---

[1] In 1977 the Prices Commission[7] found, in *Banks: Charges for Money Transmission Services*, that the costs of these [money transmission] services were amply covered by imputed income from deposits, [when LIBOR (London Inter-Bank Offered Rate), which provides a measure of the general level of market interest rates, was high]. At the time of writing, with LIBOR around 6¾ per cent the result for the banks cannot be better than neutral' (ch. 11, para. 11.4, p. 49).

Subsequently in 1981, David Lomax[5] claimed that the cost of providing such services had increased yet further: 'because the workload has increased while the balances have declined in real terms, the up-to-date figure [for the equivalent cost of providing money transmission services] is about 9 per cent' (p. 5). Subsequently, even a higher figure of 11 per cent has been mentioned publicly.

[2] The payment of interest at such market-related rates has been generally available for some time in Italy, but has not yet been introduced in most other European countries. In several other countries, e.g. Belgium, Switzerland and Holland, a very low and sticky interest rate is available on current accounts, but it is not a market-related rate. German banks, like British banks, pay nothing.

'traditional' savings deposits. The rapidity of this growth, and the extent that such balances may be drawn from 'traditional' transactions or from savings deposits, will not be easily predictable; and the apparent growth rates of the narrow aggregates may come to depend crucially on the precise statistical definition adopted in each case, with markedly differing growth rates for the differing definitions, e.g. non-interest-bearing MI (nibMI) and M_1 in the UK and, in some earlier years, MIA and MIB in the USA.

Second, with transactions balances coming to bear a more market-related interest rate, such balances will also become less responsive to variations in the general level of interest rates, because an increase in the *general* level will tend to have less of an effect on interest-rate *differentials*, i.e. those between the interest rates on transactions balances and on other forms of assets. This does *not* mean that the depositor in the future will become any less sensitive to the pattern of *relative* interest rates; indeed, with easier access to information, e.g. in the form of home banking, the depositor of the future is likely to become *more* sensitive to minor variations in relative interest rates between differing assets and liabilities. As a result, there is almost bound to be some increasing volatility of flows of funds between channels and between assets, which the authorities cannot easily control since these will depend on shifts in interest differentials, where the shifts will depend crucially on the reactions and responses of the various financial intermediaries to the varying pressures on them, whereas the authorities can only so act as to adjust the general overall level of interest rates and cash pressures. What this represents is simply an extension of liability management, as previously described, from wholesale banking increasingly into retail banking. Just as the extension of liability management to wholesale banking impaired the authorities' ability to control the overall size of banks' books, so also this further development will impair the authorities' ability to control the narrow monetary aggregates as well.[1]

All this will also have major implications for financial intermediaries, particularly for banks. As these developments occur, which may, or may not, take place gradually, the banks will lose their ability to rely on large solid blocks of low-cost retail deposits, whose variation is subject to the law of large numbers and is largely predictable. So long as this block of low-cost retail deposits exists, it offers endowment profits as interest rates rise, as earlier noted, offsetting the greater risks and bad debts that also increase in periods of high and rising interest rates. So the existence of such low-yielding current accounts provided a counterweight to the fluctuations in the variability of banking risk and profitability over the course of the interest-rate cycle. With the (gradual) erosion of such low-cost retail deposits, therefore, banking

[1] Moreover, the multifarious forms in which transactions/savings balances can be packaged and offered by varying institutions, some of them outside the monetary sector, some of them even perhaps physically abroad, could make reserve requirements and monetary base control virtually impossible to operate.

business will become riskier, as already noted in the USA, reinforcing the need to pay more attention to prudential control and capital adequacy.

On the other hand, the endowment effect encouraged banks to expand loans as interest rates rose. In so far as the objective of policy was to control the broader monetary aggregates, this made control more difficult, since banks tended to become more expansionary/aggressive just when the authorities wished for greater restraint, and vice versa. But it might also be argued that such bank behaviour had some counter-cyclical advantages, in so far as rising interest rates squeezed company profits and made them more dependent on external funds.

While it is the thesis of this section that a combination of technological development, high and variable inflation and interest rates and competition between financial intermediaries makes the introduction of new forms of interest-bearing transactions balances inevitable, there remains a question of the time scale involved. There are reasons for believing that the time scale could be protracted. So long as the bank customer in the UK is receiving 'free banking' – with charges for transmission services offset against notional interest payments – he/she is likely to be somewhat apathetic about learning/adopting new payments methods (e.g. POS) whose benefits in cost reduction may accrue mostly to banking profitability. There remain, in the UK at least, legal difficulties to be resolved relating to the use of electronic funds transfer (EFT). Thus there is established case law and statute in relation to cheques and bills of exchange, but there is no equivalent law in regard to the use of a personal identification number (PIN) in conjunction with a plastic card, nor indeed with respect to electronic transfers more generally. Moreover, the adoption of new payments mechanisms and systems will generally require a large initial investment – though not one comparable with the cost of setting up a full set of branches – and will require some large flow of transactions to be profitable. The expense and uncertainties involved may act as some deterrent. On the other hand, the successful introduction of such new methods in one country will encourage its spread in other countries; and these new methods are now being introduced, if still mainly experimentally, in various countries, primarily in the USA. Even there, however, the process is retarded by technical and social frictions, and by the costs of offering all customers a market rate on their balances. The man/woman in the street may have a NOW account (paying 5¼ per cent), but overnight 'SWEEP'ing to money market investments will probably continue to operate initially only with a high minimum balance, while the minimum value for cheques drawn on MMMFs may well remain over $200.

To the extent that the spread of these innovations is slow and steady, it may be possible to make some allowance for the likely shifts in the relationships between the monetary aggregates and economic developments. This is the hope of those who wish to continue to base monetary policy upon the adoption of quantitative targets (see on this Axilrod[**1**], pp. 17–18). Whether or not that will be the case, time will tell. In the meantime, however, the possibility that a swing in monetary growth may reflect a shift in the pace of monetary innovation rather than a 'real' development will have some influence on the authorities' reactions to such developments. The present changes imply that monetary aggregates should be interpreted and analysed with scrupulous care – on a judgemental, institutional and empirical basis, rather than just mechanically extrapolated from previously fitted equations.

5. What can the Central Bank Control?

So long as the central bank continues to have a monopoly of the supply of legal tender currency in the economy, and so long as there remains a demand for such legal tender currency, the central bank will be able to control and determine the general level of money market interest rates. If people wish to hold the legal tender currency of the central bank, either in order to make certain payments in currency form, or as a result of some continuing residual suspicion of the safety of banks and other NBFIs', then banks will in their turn need to ensure the convertibility of their deposits (and also their non-legal tender notes outstanding) into legal tender currency. They, too, will therefore need to hold currency in their tills and hold balances with the central bank. The central bank can therefore continue to operate to affect this cash base in order to influence the general level of short-term interest rates. This has always been the main central bank instrument. This instrument, and this form of control, is not impaired in the slightest by any of the technological, or other, banking developments described earlier; the only requirement for such control is a continuing demand to hold the (zero-yielding) notes issued by the central bank.

What, however, is more likely to be impaired is the central bank's ability to use either variations in the general level of interest rates, or changes in the level of the monetary base, in order to bring about pre-planned changes in the rates of growth of the various monetary aggregates. In the past, when the central bank altered the general level of interest rates, by the same token it shifted the relative pattern of interest rates in such a way as to make holding deposits with the banking system more or less attractive. Although this coherence between the general level of interest rates, and the relativity between rates on non-monetary assets and on bank deposits, is now increasingly being broken, the central bank can still have a strong impact on the growth of the monetary aggregates; but in future this impact is as likely to be *indirect*, with the changes in interest rates affecting primarily levels of incomes, expenditures and exchange rates, and with these general macroeconomic effects feeding back into the demand for bank lending and the money stock–as contrasted with a direct form of effect with changes in interest rates (and/or the monetary base) having an immediate impact on the monetary aggregates (via shifts in interest differentials), which in turn subsequently feed through various transmission routes into an effect on the level of incomes and expenditures. Moreover, shifts in the various monetary aggregates will increasingly become a function of changing competitive pressures, and therefore changing relative yields, in a world where technological changes *may* cause these to vary quite sharply. Increasingly the definition of the banking system, the proper definition of money, and the sense of concentrating mainly on the deposit liabilities of the banking system (rather than customers' net positions), will come into question.

References

1 Axilrod, S. H., 'Monetary policy, money supply, and the Federal Reserve's operating procedures', *Federal Reserve Bulletin*, January 1982, pp. 13–24.
2 Davis, K. T. and Lewis, M. K., 'Can monetary policy work in a deregulated capital market?', in the Campbell Inquiry Symposium, *Australian Economic Review*, 1st quarter 1982, pp. 9–21.
3 Friedman, M. and Schwartz, A. J., *Monetary Trends in the United States and the United Kingdom*, A National Bureau of Economic Research Monograph, University of Chicago Press, 1982.
4 Johnston, R. B., *Banks' International Lending Decisions and the Determination of Spreads on Syndicated Medium-term Euro-credits*, Bank of England Discussion Paper No. 12, September 1980.
5 Lomax, D. F., 'The case against the banking levy', mimeo, Banking Information Service, London, 1981.
6 Monopolies and Mergers Commission, *Credit Card Franchise Services*, Cmnd 8034, HMSO, 1980.
7 Prices Commission, *Banks: Charges for Money Transmission Services*, HMSO, 1978.
8 Sheppard, D. K., *The Growth and Role of UK Financial Institutions 1880–1962*, Methuen, 1971.

VI

Analysis of the Determination of the Stock of Money[1]

1. Introduction

It is generally the case that macroeconomic models are constructed around a framework of accounting identities. For example, Keynesian models are based on the national income accounts. In monetary theory the identity $MV=Py$ plays a central role. There is nothing reprehensible about constructing a model around a solid framework of identities. Indeed, the process of distinguishing key identities, whose existence or importance had not been previously recognised, has played a major role in the development of theory; for example, a relatively minor extension of the Keynesian identities led to the formulation of Kaldor's theory of distribution[**15**].[2]

It is therefore not in the least pejorative to state that modern analysis of the determination of the money stock, at least as commonly taught in most universities, is firmly based on an identity. In this analysis the money stock (M) is defined as comprising two main components, being respectively currency (C) and bank deposits (D) held by the general public.[3] It is therefore, possible to set down the identity

$$M = D + C \tag{1}$$

which must hold exactly by definition. Similarly it is possible to define the sum of currency held by the general public (C) and the cash reserves of the banking sector (R) as 'high-powered money' (H). If the currency in the hands of the public was transferred by them to the banks in exchange for bank deposits, the banks' cash reserves would rise equivalently. High-powered money can therefore be regarded as the total of existing assets which either are, or potentially could be, used as cash reserves by the banking sector. The term 'high-powered' reflects the fact that bank deposits are some multiple of the banks' cash reserves, so that – assuming the banks maintain fairly stable

---

[1] I am very grateful to my colleagues in the Economic Section of the Bank, especially Miss Margaret Mayne, for their help, criticism and support. More generally, the development of my views on this subject has been much influenced by my reading of the works of Professor Tobin.

[2] References can be found on pages 200–1.

[3] For a detailed note on various possible alternative definitions of the stock of money in the UK, see [**2**].

reserve ratios – one would see a multiple increase in bank deposits accompanying an increase in the banks' cash reserves. The additional identity

$$H = R + C \tag{2}$$

(where H is high-powered money, R is banks' cash reserves) can thus also be set down, which again must hold by definition.

By algebraic manipulation of these two identities it is possible to arrive at a third identity

$$M = H \frac{(1 + C/D)}{(R/D + C/D)} \tag{3}$$

describing the money stock in terms of the level of high-powered money and two ratios, R/D, the banks' reserve/deposit ratio, and C/D, the general public's currency/deposit ratio.[1] Since this relationship is also an identity it always holds true by definition; changes in the money stock can therefore be expressed in terms of these three variables alone.

To be able to express changes in the money stock in terms of only three variables has considerable advantages of brevity and simplicity, though even these advantages may be lost in those circumstances where there is a plethora of differing kinds of banks and deposits, each involving separate reserve ratios. Nevertheless the use of such an identity does not in any sense provide a behavioural theory of the determination of the stock of money,[2] though it is not entirely unknown in the literature for economists to regress changes in the money supply on changes in H, R/D and C/D and claim that the resulting excellent fit provides support for the money multiplier theory (see, for example,[**7, 8**]).

To provide a behavioural theory from the underlying structure of identities requires further steps. First it is necessary to examine the behavioural relationships which determine the desired levels of the variables in the system. The next stage is to explore the dynamic process which ensues when some shock causes the desired value of one, or more, of the variables in the identity to diverge from its actual value.

2. Deficiencies of the Usual Approach

The main theme here will be that these subsequent steps, necessary to move on from a *description* of the movements in the money stock in terms of

[1] An array of slightly differing identities can be obtained from algebraic manipulation of the two basic identities. The differences between them have no analytical significance. See [**11**, esp. app. B] and [**4**, esp. chs 1 and 2].

[2] Money supply multipliers can, however, also be derived as a reduced-form solution of a somewhat larger system containing parameters determining aspects of the portfolio allocation of the public and of the banks; cf. the excellent paper by Jaffee [**13**, pp. 6–8]. If the parameters in this system are taken as constant, however, then this alternative approach also contains virtually no behavioural content.

accounting identities[1] to a *theory* of its determination, have not, broadly speaking, been taken far enough. A common disadvantage of using identities, which show the definitional or accounting relationship that must hold between assets as the basis for analysis is that they tend to obscure the key role played by relative price (yield) movements in the adjustment process; indeed, the adjustment process is often described, in the case (for example) of both the consumption and money multipliers, as a purely mechanical process in which relative price (yield) movements do not enter at all. The potential defect in this approach to the analysis of the determination of the stock of money is made far more serious by a general failure to probe the behavioural factors determining the level of, and changes in, the high-powered money base. Whereas most studies (for example, [**3**, esp. pp. 242–56]) in this field in recent years have taken into consideration the effect of relative price (yield) movements on the desired values of R/D and C/D, there still seems little or no awareness that taking the level of H as exogenously given pushes out of sight the most important parts of the adjustment process.[2] All too often in the literature this total is taken as given, as exogenous, as fixed by the authorities, and no further steps are taken to examine the factors determining its level. A number of arguments may be deployed against this common practice.

As a start, ask the question why should the authorities seek to set the level of high-powered money at any particular value? The answer which is usually supplied is that they do so in order to achieve some desired level of the money stock, not out of concern for the level of H *per se*. But if the authorities are trying to fix the level of the money stock, then they presumably attempt to alter H in a way which would offset variations in the two other elements in the basic multiplier identity. To the extent that they can do so, it is misleading to ascribe causal significance to a description of changes in the money stock in terms of variations in the three separate elements of the identity. It is the money stock that should in this case be treated as the exogenous element in the system, while H is not independent, but instead is endogenous. Only if variations in the other two elements in the identity cannot be predicted by the authorities would it be proper to regard H as exogenous.

[1] Indeed we have several of these descriptive accounting identities, since it is perfectly possible to describe the change in the money stock in terms of alternative identities, relying, for example, on banking balance-sheet identities to work from bank assets to bank liabilities. This is, in broad terms, the approach used in the description of domestic credit expansion and movements in the money stock in official statistical publications (see [**1a**] and [**5**]).

[2] Even in Jaffee's paper [**13**], which compares, and to some extent reconciles, the 'old' [money multiplier] and the 'new' [Tobin] view of the determination of the stock of money, his simplified model takes high-powered money as given. In this respect his analysis also precludes a proper examination of major parts of the complete portfolio adjustment process of the banks and the public.

In a number of models, the ability of the banks to borrow from the central bank, as lender of last resort, is explicitly treated by taking borrowed reserves as endogenous, a behavioural function of relative interest rates and other factors. It makes, however, no significant difference to the arguments here whether it is the level of H, of unborrowed reserves, of free reserves, or some other variant of the monetary base which is treated as exogenous.

Of course, it may be argued that the authorities are not in a position to observe and to offset variations in the banks' reserve ratio or the public's currency/deposit ratio perfectly. It is even possible to undertake statistical tests to see how far the authorities have undertaken such offsetting action.[1] To that extent, there may be some useful behavioural information to be obtained by examining the variations in the three elements of the basic identity separately. But if that is the case presented, one can ask why it is not taken further. Several of the monetary flows which bring about changes in the total of high-powered money are no more under the direct control of the central bank than are the changes in the banks' reserve ratios, for example foreign exchange inflows under a regime of fixed exchange rates,[2] encashment of national savings, etc. If it is recognised that the authorities may find it difficult to offset completely all variations in, say, the banks' reserve ratios, then will they not have just as much, or even more, difficulty in offsetting monetary flows, not under their direct control, causing variations in H?

The only distinction which may be prayed in aid of the practice of taking the level of high-powered money, but not the level of the money stock as exogenously given, is that data on the total outstanding volume of high-powered money are, in principle at least, continuously available to the authorities, while banking statistics are gathered only at intervals. The information, potentially available, might therefore enable the authorities to control H with a greater precision than M. This argument has some, but not much, validity. Banking data are generally collected sufficiently frequently to prevent unforeseen systematic variations in reserve or currency-deposit ratios developing far enough to distort the authorities' aim. The main complications for the authorities do not come in *observing* the fluctuations in those elements in H or M not under their direct control but rather lie in the technical task of *offsetting* them. In this respect fluctuations in certain elements which affect the level of H, for example foreign exchange inflows, government budget deficits, have in the UK during recent years at least posed a far more difficult problem for the monetary authorities in trying to achieve their objectives than have the variations in the reserve ratios or the currency/deposit ratios.

It would therefore seem difficult to sustain the argument that the degree of control which the authorities can maintain over H is qualitatively different from their ability to control M. If so, this implies that it is wrong to take the level of H as exogenously given. Either the authorities can and do want to offset autonomous variations in all these other monetary flows, so that on these two strong assumptions the money stock itself is the proper variable to

[1] For example, Courchene and Kelly[**6**] examine how far the Bank of Canada offsets changes in currency holdings outside banks.

[2] Economists working at the IMF under the guidance of Polak and Argy have taken the lead in the analysis of the interrelationship between domestic credit expansion, external currency flows and changes in the domestic money stock. Recent issues of IMF Staff Papers include several articles on this subject.

take as exogenous, rather than H. Or alternatively if one wishes to probe further into the *process* of the determination of the money stock, it is necessary to examine more closely the determinants of changes in the level of high-powered money itself rather than treat these as given.

The second reason why it is wrong to take H, or M for that matter, as given exogenously is that these variables would be policy targets, not exogenous variables, in those circumstances when the authorities are trying to fix their level. There is an important methodological difference between these two. Exogenous variables are those whose values are determined outside the system under consideration. Policy targets are control variables whose value the authorities at the very centre of the system attempt to set. To treat policy targets as exogenous variables implies that the authorities do not alter their control variables in response to the developments of the system.

It is perhaps true that the response of the authorities to economic developments is more fitful, wayward and unpredictable than the response of the mass of consumers. Apart from abrupt changes in direction caused by political events, the authorities are, possibly, more liable to be influenced by the changing fashions of economic theory. Even so, the presumption that the reactions of the authorities are less predictable than those of consumers, or trade-union leaders for that matter, is doubtful. The authorities do react, and often in a highly predictable fashion,[1] to changes in past, current and predicted developments in the economy. For example, in the UK it has usually been possible to predict a good deal about changes in certain policy instruments by looking at only two variables, the level of unemployment and the level of foreign exchange reserves.[2]

It is therefore mistaken to take a policy target as given independently of the previous history of the development of the economy. If an economist wants to study the past, to understand what happened, he has to regard such policy targets as more akin to endogenous variables than to exogenous variables. Rather than taking H or M as exogenous, the economist should construct a reaction function. Of course, it remains true that the change of policy will continue to have an independent effect, whether or not the change is some predictable function of other economic developments – in just the same way as a fluctuation in consumption has an independent effect on the economy, whether or not it is a predictable function of other economic developments. But it does mean that the statistical techniques required to evaluate the effect of past changes in policy need to be considerably more subtle and complex than would be the case if policy was indeed arbitrarily selected.

Taking H, or M, as given, whether treated as a policy target or exogenous variable, would appear to require the prior assumption, even if not made

---

[1] One of the best papers on this subject is by Wood[**24**]. One of the few empirical studies on the authorities' reactions in the UK is provided by Fisher[**9**].

[2] Fisher[**9**, pp. 821–31]; see also Goodhart[**12**].

explicitly, that the authorities' intentions – whether or not they are entirely successful – are to control these monetary aggregates. If the authorities have other targets, for example to control the level of interest rates, then they may not also be able – as in the case of the above example – to control the level of *H* or *M* independently. To take another example, in a relatively small, open country in circumstances conducive to a large interest-elasticity of international capital flows, the authorities may choose to maintain fixed exchange rates. If so, they can act to control domestic credit and foreign exchange flows, but their power to alter either *H*, *M* or the level of domestic interest rates is strictly limited.

To treat *H*, or *M*, as an exogenous variable, or a policy target, therefore involves a strong, positive assumption about the authorities' behaviour. It may be possible to decide on logical grounds how the authorities ought to behave, but the treatment of *H*, or *M*, as exogenous or a policy target in any exercise to explain past events implies a positive claim about how they have behaved. This is an empirical matter. Those who have seriously studied the behaviour of the monetary authorities in those countries with whose monetary history I am familiar have usually come to the conclusion that with the exception, to a greater or lesser extent, of the most recent years the monetary authorities have not treated the rate of change of monetary aggregates as target variables. Instead they have usually sought to control interest rates.[1]

The third reason, therefore, why it is wrong to treat *H*, or *M*, as exogenously given, or as a policy target, is that it is based on an implicit positive assumption about the behaviour of the authorities which has in the past been generally invalid. It is curious that certain economists who are most vocal in their criticisms of central banks for failing to adopt control of the monetary aggregates as their target nevertheless base their policy prescriptions on the behaviour of a model which incorporates the assumption that the monetary aggregates have in fact been exogenously determined.

This approach to the determination of the money stock, relating *M* to an exogenously determined level of *H* via the basic identity, has been criticised thus far on the grounds that it involves implicit assumptions about the actions of the authorities which are invalid. The final and more serious argument for abandoning this analytical approach, or rather for developing and extending it along different lines, is that it leads to an erroneous appreciation of the underlying dynamic process whereby a change over time in the stock of money occurs, and in particular frequently causes a complete failure to comprehend the proper role of the banks and the public in the process.

---

[1] 'Whereas everyone agrees that the monetary authority is capable of determining the money stock, we must nevertheless recognise that we live in the real world where there are lags and where the monetary authority apparently has never sought to control the absolute level of the nominal stock of money, opting instead to affect "credit conditions" ' (Klein[**16**]).

'However, concern over market interest rate movements has been a major factor influencing Federal Reserve acquisition of Government debt over the last two decades' (Stewart[**21**]).

See also Thygesen[**23**, esp. ch. 5].

At the most simplified level, this approach often leads pedagogues to explain changes in the quantity of money in terms of a mechanical multiplier, in which high-powered money gets passed from hand to hand like a hot potato. The portfolio adjustments of the banks in this description apparently play no role in the process, except in so far as they may seek to alter their reserve ratios. The public's asset preferences are seemingly irrelevant to the determination of the stock of money except in so far as they seek to alter their cash/deposit ratios. Such teaching, and I can (alas) find quotations from a number of textbooks along these lines,[1] is such an incomplete way of describing the process of the determination of the stock of money that it amounts to misinstruction.

At a more advanced level, however, the 'money multiplier' can be regarded as a quasi-reduced form of a larger system of structural equations describing aspects of the portfolio allocation of the banks and the public in response to changes in some relative prices (cf. [**13**]). But even in such expositions the level of H, high-powered money, is taken as given. The effect of this assumption is to abstract from many of the more important facets of the process of portfolio adjustment. As one probes deeper to examine the determinants of H itself, so the process whereby the stock of money changes as a result of an interplay of portfolio adjustments by banks and the general public in response to relative price (interest-rate) changes will come more clearly and more completely into view.

3. The Determination of the Monetary Base

The first step in arriving at a more satisfactory theory of the determination of the money stock is to abandon the assumption of a given stock of high-powered money, and to proceed to an examination of the factors which determine this total. This can be done without prejudice to the subsequent empirical issue of what the authorities may be seeking to achieve. In order to do this it is possible to turn to yet another accounting identity, taken from the accounts of the flow of funds (see for example, [**1**]), which describes how the financial deficit (or surplus) of each sector is financed by flows of funds through the various financial markets. In order that this accounting identity may be satisfied, it is necessary that a public-sector deficit, after taking account of certain financial transfers, e.g. import deposits, local authority loans for housebuilding, etc., must be financed by borrowing from other sectors, by issuing additional debt to them or by running down claims upon them, e.g. foreign exchange reserves which represent claims on the overseas sector.

[1] For examples of the kind of analysis attacked, see Fisher[**10**, chs 4 and 5], and Jordan[**14**]. It is, however, unfair to single out particular individuals in this fashion, since this approach is so commonly utilised.

The provision of finance to the public sector occurs in a variety of ways [1b]. For the purpose of this analysis such borrowing may be grouped into three components: finance which directly brings about an increase in high-powered money, ΔH; finance raised by other domestic borrowing; finance raised by receiving the sterling counterpart of accommodating a currency outflow. It may be useful to subdivide this second item, the finance obtained by other domestic borrowing, into three separate components: the use of funds to repay maturing debt, transactions (borrowing or repaying) in non-marketable debt, e.g. premium savings bonds, national saving certificates, etc., and operations in marketable debt. This accounting identity can then be expressed algebraically as

$$PSD = OMO + NMD - MAT + ECF + \Delta H \qquad (4)$$

where *PSD* is the public-sector deficit after taking account of various financial transfers such as import deposits, *OMO* represents the outcome of the authorities' operations in marketable debt, *NMD* represents the outcome of transactions in non-marketable debt, *MAT* shows the required use of funds to pay off maturing debt, *ECF* gives the total finance obtained from, or required for, accommodating external currency flows and ΔH represents the increase in the public sector's monetary liabilities, high-powered money.[1]

This accounting identity can equally well be reversed, to show the various financial flows accompanying any change in high powered money, as follows:

$$\Delta H = PSD - OMO - NMD + MAT - ECF \qquad (5)$$

This identity at least points the analysis towards explicit consideration of those elements in the financial system which have traditionally been the main concern of the authorities, the size of the public-sector deficit, operations in public-sector marketable debt, the relative attractions of public-sector non-marketable debt, the weight of maturities to be financed, the impact on the foreign exchange market – and on the reserve position – of a balance-of-payments deficit (or surplus).

Certain of these financial flows in equation (5) are, largely or entirely, outside the control of the monetary authorities. For example, the volume of maturities to be refinanced in any one year is ineluctably determined by prior contractual arrangements. The problem of refinancing maturities can be exaggerated, however, since holders, such as financial institutions, who are attempting to maintain a balanced portfolio can usually be tempted to switch regularly towards slightly longer-dated debt to maintain the desired balance of their portfolios. Even so, the occasion of a maturity reduces the transaction cost to holders of moving out of public-sector debt, and causes such holders,

[1] Including for this purpose the increase in bankers' balances with the Bank of England Department (counterbalanced by holdings of public-sector debt by the Department).

of necessity, to reconsider their investment plans. For such reasons maturities of debt issues of a kind bought previously in large quantities by less active portfolio managers, especially in the personal sector, can be expected to cause more serious refinancing problems to the authorities.

Although the monetary implications of any proposed fiscal change may be given considerable weight in the determination of fiscal policy, many other considerations of very different kinds, however, also enter, and may well sway the judgement about the proper balance between expenditures and revenue of the public sector. To this extent short-term variations in the size of the deficit must also be regarded as outside the control of the monetary authorities. Indeed, variations in the size of the public-sector deficit may on occasions even hinder the intended thrust of monetary policy.[1]

Moreover, it is difficult to devise fiscal measures that can be frequently altered without involving considerable disturbance of one kind or another. It is therefore usual to alter tax rates and forward expenditure plans only once a year in the annual budget. Even then, lags intervene between the policy change and the resulting effect on monetary flows, so that the public-sector deficit in any given year may be conditioned as much by the previous budget as by current fiscal changes. For all these reasons the monetary authorities cannot hope to vary the size of the public-sector deficit in the short run as a flexible instrument for the purpose of achieving some desired rate of growth in the monetary aggregates. This problem is seen in even more extreme forms in other countries where the executive faces difficulties on occasions in obtaining legislative agreement to its fiscal proposals.

In principle it would be possible to envisage the authorities frequently varying the rates of interest offered on non-marketable debt for the purpose of inducing some desired level of flows into these instruments. In practice, however, for reasons that are not germane to this discussion, rates on some of these instruments have been notable rather for their constancy.[2] Thus in periods of monetary squeeze rates offered on non-marketable securities have generally tended to become less competitive. The result has been that flows of funds into national savings have tended to move inversely with fluctuations in market interest rates. Evidence of this can be obtained from some simple regressions, as shown below:

$$NMD_t = 18.98 - \underset{(18.70)}{47.98}\ dC_{t-1} - \underset{(22.54)}{31.54}\ dC_{t-3} + \underset{(0.14)}{0.594}\ NMD_{t-1}$$

$$\bar{R}^2 = 0.56$$

[1] Professor Tew[**22**] has termed the financing requirement which arises from the public-sector deficit and debt maturities 'the flood'. In order to check the growth of the monetary aggregates, the authorities have to undertake the often extremely difficult task of damming this flood.

[2] For example, the rate of interest on Post Office Savings Bank ordinary accounts, retitled National Savings Bank ordinary accounts in 1969, remained constant at 2½ per cent from the foundation of POSB in 1861 by Gladstone until 1970, when Jenkins took steps to raise the rate offered.

$$NMD_t = 18.58 - \underset{(22.19)}{65.09}\ dBS_t - \underset{(23.74)}{34.63}\ dBS_{t-1} + \underset{(0.12)}{0.594}\ NMD_{t-1}$$

$$\bar{R}^2 = 0.61$$

where NMD represents inflow into non-marketable debt in £ million (seasonally adjusted), dC is the change in Consol rates and dBS the change in building society deposit rates, observed quarterly over the period 1963III to 1970IV.

It therefore appears that three of the monetary flows (maturities, public-sector deficit, non-marketable debt) out of the set of flows, which must by accounting identity equal the change in the monetary liabilities of the public sector (ΔH), are not generally subject to the immediate or precise control of the monetary authorities. If these three flows should require a very large amount of financing, then any attempt to restrict the rate of growth of the monetary aggregates would impose a considerable pressure upon a central bank's operations in marketable debt.

The likelihood of capital inflows from abroad as domestic interest rates rise, thus altering the external currency flow to be financed (ECF), forms an apparent obstacle to the successful achievement of market operations intended to squeeze domestic liquidity. If such capital flows respond very sensitively, and in relatively large volume, to variations in financial conditions in any country, then under a regime of fixed exchange rates the autonomy of that country to undertake an independent financial policy is limited.[1] On the other hand, in such conditions it becomes easier to achieve a desired level of international reserves by inducing large-scale capital movements. It is important to ascertain how far domestic monetary policy is, both in theory and in practice, constrained by international financial conditions.

Thus two of the monetary flows affecting the level of H(PSD and MAT) are to some considerable extent outside the control of the authorities, while another two (NMD and ECF) tend to respond perversely to interest-rate changes, in that an increase in domestic interest rates will tend to lead to flows from these sources causing increases in the high-powered money base. In addition, in some circumstances there could be expected to be some decline in the banks' desired reserve ratios as interest rates on earning assets rise relative to rates on reserves.

In order to achieve a desired level of H, or more usefully of M, the authorities have to try to offset movements, which may on occasions be very

[1] It is occasionally argued that, if the interest elasticity of international capital movements is relatively large, it would be possible to lower the stock money by lowering interest rates, an apparently perverse response. In reality, so long as the money stock is defined to include only resident monetary balances, i.e. to exclude non-resident balances, and so long as the banking system is not directly constrained by direct controls or interest-rate ceilings, etc., such perverse reactions will not take place. The apparent plausibility of such perverse responses comes from the use of misleading partial-equilibrium analysis rather than a complete general-equilibrium model.

large, in all these other flows by inducing people to purchase, or if needs be to sell, marketable government debt.[1] These operations of the authorities are done in the open market, and the implication of this is that the authorities must accept a price at which the other party to the transaction will deal voluntarily, in order to induce a flow into, or out of, marketable securities.

The question whether it is preferable to view the authorities as operating primarily on quantities or on prices in this market, or set of markets, is entirely without prejudice to the separate empirical issue of which variables form the targets for policy (e.g. monetary aggregates or interest rates). The authorities may operate on quantities in debt markets in such a way as to influence interest rates, or on rates in an attempt to obtain certain quantitative effects. Indeed, the form of these operations may vary from market to market.

Nevertheless there is a distinction of some importance, relating to the practical characteristics of markets, between market interventions which take the form of quantitative offers and those which are expressed in price terms. Owing largely to the existence of costs of adjustment, it is not the case that markets are always able to clear instantaneously after some new development. If conditions change very markedly, so that the previous state of information on which market operators were basing their investment policies becomes clearly in need of major revision, a common reaction is to cease trading altogether, until a new considered basis for trading can be re-established. If the possibility of no trading, or even of no complete clearing, can exist, there will be circumstances in which the authorities cannot operate on quantities, but it will remain possible for them to operate on posted prices, even if no trades take place at such prices.

A related practical issue is that in those markets where the authorities might wish to operate primarily through quantities, they would not do so generally in a simple 'take it or leave it' fashion. Instead, the markets would usually be carefully prepared in advance for the quantitative offer. Tenders would be underwritten, prices discussed with key people in the market, repurchase clauses arranged, 'even-keeling' undertaken, etc. It is not proper to disregard the circumscribed nature of the authorities' quantitative operations. It is, at any rate in the UK, probably generally preferable to view the authorities as operating through prices rather than quantities in debt markets. Otherwise, far more attention would need to be given to the constraints on the authorities in their quantitative operations.

---

[1] There is, however, some tendency towards negative covariation in these flows, i.e. they seem to interact in a way that produces some partial compensation, which alleviates certain of the difficulties facing the authorities. A large foreign exchange inflow usually encourages sales of gilts and also reduces company demand for bank credit. A big public-sector borrowing requirement implies a large private-sector surplus, which may induce large private-sector purchases of public-sector debt and, perhaps, lead to some reduction in the demand for advances. Moreover, a large public-sector borrowing requirement is more likely to coincide with an exchange outflow than with an inflow.

It may be helpful to recapitulate and to summarise the propositions made. The authorities do not fix the level of high-powered money; instead, their main policy instruments involve the fiscal arm of altering the public-sector deficit and the debt-management arm of intervening in debt markets. The latter intervention may take the form of changing quantities or prices, but it is, probably, somewhat more in accord with market realities, at least in the UK, to envisage this as occurring through price changes. These interventions, whether initially in quantitative or price form, alter relative prices and so induce portfolio readjustments. These readjustments then bring about changes in H, as well as in M.

Simplifying considerably (by setting NMD, MAT and the current-account balance all equal to zero), these definitional relationships may be set out algebraically, as follows:

$$M_t = D_t + C_t \tag{1}$$

$$H_t = C_t + R_t \tag{2}$$

$$H_t - H_{t-1} = PSD_t - OMO_t - ECF_t \tag{5}$$

$$OMO_t = \frac{1}{r_{Bt}} B_t - \frac{1}{r_{Bt}} B_{t-1} \qquad (6)^1$$

Therefore,

$$r_{Bt}\, OMO_t = B_t - B_{t-1}$$

$$ECF_t = F_t - F_{t-1} \tag{7}$$

where

B_t = the number of nominal bonds outstanding (taken as Consols with a coupon of £1 per annum)
r_{Bt} = the yield on Consols
F_t = the net stock of foreign assets held by the UK public, the rate of interest on which is taken as exogenous.[2]

4. The Response of the Private Sector

In order to explore the ensuing process of the determination of the money stock, it is necessary to examine the response of the private sector to market interventions undertaken by the authorities. For this purpose it may be helpful to sketch out a greatly simplified, heuristic model of portfolio

[1] Readers will of course recognise that this is a discrete approximation to the real-world condition of continuously changing interest rates.

[2] This ignores also purchases of UK assets by non-residents.

adjustment in the private sector, distinguishing between the banking sector and the non-bank general public. The general public is at any moment of time confronted with a set of market prices and has some overall stock of wealth, which it distributes between the varying available assets, and liabilities, in proportions that depend, *inter alia*, on the relative yields on these assets. Subject to the important qualification that observable yields on variable price assets may not be good proxies for expected holding-period yields, one can express the posited behaviour of the non-bank public in terms of a set of behavioural equations, expressing the desired distribution of assets as a function of the existing vector of interest rates, subject to its balance-sheet constraint.

In this simplified model the public is taken to hold four assets, bank deposits (D),[1] currency (C), foreign assets (F), and bonds (B_t), and one liability, advances (A). Currency has a zero yield. Interest is paid on the other assets, and charged on advances. The foreign asset has a fixed capital value. We ignore the public's holdings of equity in the banking system. The current account of the balance of payments is taken to be zero. The balance-sheet constraint (W represents wealth) can therefore be treated either as

$$W_t = PSD_t + D_{t-1} + C_{t-1} + F_{t-1} - A_{t-1} + \frac{1}{r_{Bt}} B_{p(t-1)} \tag{8}$$

or

$$W_t = D_t + C_t + F_t - A_t + \frac{1}{r_{Bt}} B_{pt} \tag{8a}$$

The behavioural equations, showing the proportions in which the assets will be held, can all be written in the general form:

$$\frac{X_i}{W} = \int(r_B, r_F, r_D, r_A, W, Z) \tag{9}$$

where X_i is the ith asset, r_B, r_F, r_D, r_A the yields on the respective assets, and Z is a vector of other independent variables.

The behaviour of the banks is somewhat more complex, even in this greatly simplified model. (For a more detailed analysis, see [**18**].) The general public, for the purpose of this exposition, could be treated as distributing a given wealth between assets in response to changes in interest rates, which rates they have to accept as price-takers. The banks, however, in several important instances do not act as price-takers. The provision of advances by banks is not undertaken in an open market, unlike (for example) government bonds,

[1] For simplicity we have not distinguished current and deposit accounts separately. In any extension of the model this could, of course, be done, though it would be rather hard to provide any operational index of the yield on current accounts.

which are traded on an open market. Instead, advances are usually arranged on an individual basis between client and banker. In such circumstances banks set the rates on advances, adjusted for risk and any other special considerations, and accommodate the demand for loans forthcoming at these selected rates, even in circumstances where there is considerable competition between banks.[1] Similarly, banks set the rates which they offer on deposits and accept all money placed with them at these rates. There are therefore two sets of behavioural equations for the banks, one determining these desired rates, and the other desired quantities in those instances where they do act as price-takers, in addition to the familiar balance-sheet identity that liabilities must equal assets, as set out below:

$$D_t + K_t = R_t + \frac{1}{r_B} B_{bt} + A_t \tag{10}$$

where D represents deposits, K non-deposit liabilities (largely capital and reserves),[2] R cash reserve items, B_b bonds held by the banks[3] and A advances.

The rate offered by banks on deposits is likely to be a function of the rates available on earning assets[4] and the liquidity of the banks' portfolio, as represented by the reserve ratio (R/D) and, perhaps, also by the investment ratio (B_b/D). The rate to be charged on advances will reflect the rate available on alternative assets, and the liquidity of the portfolio.[5]

---

[1] Indeed, it is rather when banks are constrained, say by rate ceilings or cartel agreements, from varying advances rates freely that they tend to revert to the attempt to offer a larger or smaller quantity of advances to borrowers – for example, by varying risk categories – at the constrained rate. The system of credit control, introduced in the UK in September 1971, has relaxed the constraints on the banks' ability to vary advances rates autonomously, and so gives greater verisimilitude to the simplified model outlined above. See also [**25**].

[2] A further definitional equation gives

$$K_t = K_{t-1} + \frac{1}{r_{bt}} B_{b(t-1)} - \frac{1}{r_{b(t-1)}} B_{b(t-1)}$$

[3] There is, of course, another identity that $B = B_p + B_b$

[4] As Jaffee points out [**13,** pp. 12 and 19–20], the extent of competition will influence the spread between the rates charged on loans and offered on deposits.

[5] Monti points out [**18,** p. 179] that 'Under all the objective functions considered, the optimal asset selection rule is to equate the marginal revenues from loans and from bonds (and also from reserves). Given the assumption of a perfectly competitive bond market, this means that the marginal revenue from loans must be made equal to the rate of return on bonds... Neither the deposit interest rate, nor the parameters of the deposit demand function have any influence on it.' Unlike Monti, however, we allow for uncertainty, approximately, by including ratios reflecting the liquidity of the portfolio as arguments in the equation determining advances rates. This provides an indirect link between deposit and advances rates. Consider the case in which deposit rates are so low relative to advances rates that banks' portfolios are tending to become less liquid. This will push up actual rates on advances (and the implicit certainty-equivalent yields on reserves and bonds), and thus encourage upwards pressure on deposit rates. The upwards movements in both advances and deposit rates will reduce advances and increase deposits, thus leading to a restoration of desired liquidity.

$$r_D = f\left(r_A, r_B, \frac{R}{D}, \frac{B_b}{D}\right) \quad (11)$$

and

$$r_A = f\left(r_B, \frac{R}{D}, \frac{B_b}{D}\right) \quad (12)$$

The banks, however, act as price-takers in deciding on their desired holdings of reserve assets and bonds. Since r_D and r_A are given by the above equations, the volume of liquid assets (including both bonds and reserves) available to the banks at any time is determined and their only remaining choice is the distribution in which these are held. The relative yield on reserve assets, as compared with bonds, depends on the yield on bonds, r_B, since the yield on reserve assets is assumed to be fixed at zero, and on the level of deposits, which is taken as a proxy for the requirement for reserves to meet possible cash drains. Thus the demand for reserve assets becomes

$$R = f(r_B, D, D - A) \quad (13)$$

where the first two arguments in the function represent factors determining the relative yield of bonds and reserves, and the final term represents the available liquid asset constraint. In practice, however, once D enters as an argument in this equation, it is far from clear how, if at all, the division of the counterpart bank assets between bonds and advances affects the demand for reserves.[1] Given the total of liquid assets, and the demand for reserves, the demand by banks for bonds emerges as a residual.

The authorities may also intervene to affect the demand for reserves by requiring adherence to some minimum reserve ratio, X,[2] in which case the equation would become, after dropping the term $D - A$:

$$R = f(r_B, X, D) \quad (13a)$$

Setting such a required ratio tends to reduce the amplitude of variation in the desired ratio, and thus tends to increase the predictability and, perhaps, also the speed of the adjustment of the system to changes in the authorities' policy instruments.

General-equilibrium systems of this kind can be estimated empirically, if the necessary data are available. A number of general-equilibrium models of the UK financial system have been constructed and estimated, for example by

---

[1] Indeed, it may even be more likely that, for a given level of D, a larger holding of advances, fewer bonds, would raise the demand for reserves.

[2] Since the imposition of a required reserve ratio affects the liquidity of the balance-sheet, X will also enter as an argument in equations (11) and (12).

Norton[**19, 20**], Wymer[**26**] and Miller[**17**]. Of these the model constructed by Miller is closest in sympathy to the simplified model outlined here.

[*Author's note*: At the time when this paper was first presented in 1972 it was accompanied by an appendix setting out the model in greater detail, and providing a simulated solution to the system, which appendix was largely the work of Miss M. Mayne. This is not reproduced here. Moreover, I also then hazarded the prediction that, despite numerous problems, the Bank of England would soon be developing a general-equilibrium stock-adjustment model of the financial system. This forecast turned out to be too optimistic. At the time, as reported below, I was mainly conscious of certain technical problems of constructing such a model. In the event the essential difficulty was that the financial system has been innovating and evolving rather rapidly during the last decade, so that neither the structure of the system as a whole nor of key structural equations within it, for example the demand for bonds and the demand for bank lending, has appeared sufficiently stable to model successfully.]

Because we think this approach is better than any other, a model of this kind often lies in our minds, even if we do not yet have accurate empirical estimates of the coefficients involved. For one thing the necessary time-series data giving the market value of assets held by the various sectors are only just beginning to become available in the UK. The technical econometric problems of estimating portfolio stock adjustment processes are complex. The size of any model that would represent a sufficiently close approximation to the real world to avoid the need for patently unrealistic assumptions would probably be so large that it would be difficult to manage. Nevertheless it is worth while trying to explore the workings of such a system, even if this has to be done in somewhat qualitative terms.

For example, consider the effect of a change in the price of government debt brought about by the authorities. It is, perhaps, worth repeating that treating the authorities' intervention in this market in price rather than quantitative terms is without prejudice to the choice of intermediate targets and accords more closely with institutional realities. The first issue of importance is how this change in price will affect the expected holding period yield on government debt. If the authorities' actions can trigger off unforeseen changes in expectations, then the effect of their intervention on the desired holdings of government debt will be to that extent unpredictable.

The second main issue is how far a shift into public-sector bonds, induced by raising the holding-period yield on such assets, will be financed by reducing net holdings of foreign assets[1] or by running down domestic monetary assets. To the extent that there was a much larger elasticity of substitution between UK public-sector bonds and foreign assets than between UK public-sector

[1] For this purpose a purchase of UK public-sector debt by non-residents, either directly or via bank intermediation, may be treated as a reduction of UK net holdings of foreign assets.

bonds and domestic monetary assets, the impact of open-market operations would fall mainly on international capital flows and fluctuations in foreign exchange reserves rather than upon the domestic money stock.

Nevertheless an improvement in the relative attraction of bond yields should cause the public to wish to transfer some of its assets from deposits to bonds, thus putting pressure on the banks' reserves, since the transfer reduces bank cash reserves and deposits equally. In part this pressure may be absorbed by a reduction in the desired reserve ratio as the yield on bonds rises, but in a system in which limits are set by the imposition of a required reserve ratio this source of flexibility is likely to be limited. Instead the main response of banks is likely to be – given the behavioural equations (11) – (13) – to seek to regain equilibrium either by bidding for funds (raising r_D) and/or by selling bonds. Both these reactions in turn will lead to upwards pressure on advances rates (r_A).

Assuming for the purpose of this exposition that the authorities were content to allow the effect of the banks' sales of debt to be fully reflected in further price changes in bonds, then relative yields – abstracting from expectational complications – would move further in favour of bonds. The public would continue to move out of deposits into bonds. The banks' reserve position would only be assuaged through such sales by the reduction in deposits or as a result of rising capital inflows from abroad.

The banks will, however, to an extent depending on the relative cost of the alternatives as they appear to each individual bank, also respond to pressure by bidding more for deposits. This reaction is likely to have a stronger restorative impact on the banking system's reserve ratio, since it will shift relative yields in favour of deposits and against both public-sector bonds and foreign assets.

So any attempt by the authorities to squeeze the banking system and to reduce deposits may be countered by the banks raising the stakes by bidding more for deposits. The question, then, is what determines how far the banks will and can go in matching the upwards pressure on rates.[1] Assuming that there are no direct constraints on rate movements, this largely depends on the interest-elasticity of the public's demand for advances. If the demand for advances is interest-inelastic, the banks will be able to match upwards pressure on rates, lifting both deposit and advances rates, so that the authorities will have to press market intervention that much further to achieve a given reduction in deposits and advances.

To recapitulate the main argument up to this point, in the light of the somewhat sketchy general-equilibrium model outlined, there would seem to

[1] This might be taken as a rationale for the imposition of a Regulation Q. I would not accept this, however, on the grounds that movements in the money stock may, when unconstrained, represent a reasonably good indicator of the effects of policy, but do not have a direct causal impact on expenditures. Thus distortion of the monetary aggregates by direct controls prevents their use as a reliable indicator, without, very likely, having much effect upon total expenditures.

be four main critical issues influencing the determination of the stock of money. These are (i) the size of the public-sector deficit, (ii) market reactions to the authorities' open-market operations, (iii) the elasticity of substitution between foreign and domestic assets, and (iv) the interest-elasticity of demand for advances.

Consequently the most useful statistical approach to the presentation of monetary data, for purposes of interpretation and analysis, is that which highlights these critical factors. Accordingly official monetary statistics, in the *Bank of England Quarterly Bulletin* and the CSO's *Financial Statistics*, contain tables (e.g. [**1**a, **5**]) of that accounting identity in which changes in the money stock are expressed in terms of the following components: the public-sector deficit, sales of public-sector debt to the non-bank public, bank advances to the private sector and external financing of the public sector. As is obvious, this accounting identity does not of itself provide any theoretical explanation of the process of the determination of the money stock. But it should lead the user of the statistics to go further to enquire the reasons for the fluctuations in debt sales, in international capital flows, etc. One cannot display the complete working of the monetary system in a single table, but one can at least encourage users to ask the right kind of question about the more important behavioural relationships by one's choice of accounting identities.

5. Conclusion

None of these four critical issues which affect the determination of the stock of money appear in the money multiplier analysis. This is simply because virtually all the critical behavioural responses, and the great bulk of the basic process of portfolio stock adjustment in response to relative price changes, is subsumed – simply pushed out of sight – by the simple expedient of treating the high-powered money base as given. The use of the money multiplier identity obscures, rather than illuminates, the fundamental nature of the process of the determination of the money stock.

The theory of the determination of the money stock ought to be treated as one branch of the more general theory of portfolio adjustment in response to relative price changes. Instead, the use of the money multiplier identity shortcircuits this approach – basically by taking H as given. And at its absolute worst, which is what is often taught to first-year undergraduates, the money multiplier analysis does not explicitly involve or appear to require any interest-rate changes at all. The process appears to be mechanical. There seems to be no need for the public or the banks to desire to hold voluntarily the volume of deposits established by the process. Instead, they apparently cannot avoid treading the circular multiplier around and around (e.g. in period 1 the banks obtain ten in extra reserves and lend out nine, in order to restore their desired reserve ratio, then in period 2 they get back seven in cash from the public who have a currency/deposit ratio of 2/9, and of this the banks lend out... etc.). The only facets of their portfolio distribution choices which seem to affect the results at all are the public's desired cash/deposit ratio and the bank's desired reserve ratio.

All that is, to be blunt, absolute baloney. The determination of the money stock involves a process of general portfolio adjustment in response to relative interest-rate changes. The time path of the process depends on the various speeds of adjustment of the various sectors to relative price changes. It is simply not true that the only way in which the banks and the public affect the process of the determination of the money stock is when they alter their reserve ratio and their cash/deposit ratio respectively. The process is not mechanical, and does not proceed in those awful circular series summing in the limit to the value of the multiplier.

The reason why this error of interpretation can continue to be perpetrated is that the assumption that H is fixed implies that the authorities can, and do, perfectly and instantaneously offset all the other behavioural responses of the banks and public, in order to maintain H at its desired level. As was pointed out earlier, in section 2, if you are prepared to swallow this, why not engorge the whole hog and assume that the authorities can also offset all variations in R/D and C/D in order to keep M at its desired level. Indeed, it may be, in some circumstances, a fair approximation to the truth to argue that the monetary authorities are controlling the level of M. Nevertheless, taking H, or M, as given obscures the underlying process of monetary determination, and entirely abstracts from the problems that a central bank may face in trying to achieve such control.

References

1 Bank of England, *Quarterly Bulletin*, 'Analysis of financial statistics' published in each issue. (a) in vol. 11, no. 4 (December 1971), table J, pp. 468–9; (b) in ibid, table L, cols. 1–3, p. 472, and table D, p. 460.

2 Bank of England, *Quarterly Bulletin*, vol. 10, no. 3, 1970, pp. 320–6.

3 Brunner, K. and Meltzer, A. H., 'Some further investigations of demand and supply functions for money', *Journal of Finance*, vol. 19, no. 2, pt 1, 1964, pp. 240–83.

4 Cagan, P., *Determinants and Effects of Changes in the Stock of Money, 1875–1960*, Columbia University Press for NBER, 1965.

5 Central Statistical Office, *Financial Statistics*, no. 115 (November 1971), pp. 68–70, tables 56–8.

6 Courchene, T. J. and Kelly, A. K., 'Money supply and money demand: An econometric analysis for Canada', *Journal of Money, Credit and Banking*, vol. 3, no. 2, pt. 1, 1971, pp. 230–1.

7 Crouch, R. L., 'A model of the UK's monetary sector', *Econometrica*, July–October, 1967, pp. 392–418.

8 Crouch, R. L., 'The genesis of bank deposits: New English version', *Bulletin of the Oxford University Institute of Statistics and Economics*, vol. 27, no. 3, 1965, pp. 185–99.
9 Fisher, D., 'The objectives of British monetary policy, 1951–1964', *Journal of Finance*, December 1968, pp. 821–31.
10 Fisher, D., *Money and Banking*, Irwin, 1971.
11 Friedman, M. and Schwartz, A. J., *A Monetary History of the United States, 1867–1960*, Princeton University Press for NBER, 1963.
12 Goodhart, C., 'British monetary policy, 1957–67', in *Monetary Policy in the Atlantic Community*, ed. K. Holbik, Federal Reserve Bank of Boston, 1973.
13 Jaffee, D. M., 'The structure of models of financial intermediation', mimeo, Univeristy of Essex, Discussion Paper No. 36, October 1971.
14 Jordan, J. L., 'Elements of money stock determination', *Federal Reserve Bank of St Louis Review*, vol. 51, no. 10, 1969, pp. 10–19.
15 Kaldor, N., 'Alternative theories of distribution', *Review of Economic Studies*, 1955, pp. 83–100.
16 Klein, J. J., Discussion on D. Fand, 'A monetarist model of the monetary process', *Journal of Finance*, May 1970, p. 322.
17 Miller, M. H., 'An empirical analysis of monetary policy in the United Kingdom from 1954–1965', unpublished PhD thesis, Yale University, 1971.
18 Monti, M., 'A theoretical model of bank behaviour and its implications for monetary policy', *L'Industria Revista di Economia Politica*, no. 2, 1971, pp. 165–91.
19 Norton, W. E., 'An econometric study of the United Kingdom monetary sector, 1955–1966', unpublished PhD thesis, University of Manchester, 1967.
20 Norton, W. E., 'Debt management and monetary policy in the United Kingdom', *Economic Journal*, vol. 79, September 1969, pp. 475–94.
21 Stewart, K., 'Government debt, money and economic activity', *Federal Reserve Bank of St Louis Review*, vol. 54, no. 1, 1972.
22 Tew, B., 'The implications of Milton Friedman for Britain', *The Banker*, vol. 119, no. 522, 1969, pp. 757–71.
23 Thygesen, N., *The Sources and the Impact of Monetary Changes: An Empirical Study of Danish Experiences, 1951–68*, Copenhagen University Economic Institute, Study No. 17, 1971.
24 Wood, J. H., 'A model of Federal Reserve behaviour', in *Monetary Process and Policy*, ed. G. Horwich, Irwin, 1967.
25 Wood, J. H., 'A model of commercial bank loan and investment behaviour', paper presented at the Money Study Group Conference, Bournemouth, February 1972.
26 Wymer, C. mimeographed papers, London School of Economics, 1970.

VII
Monetary Base Control

1. Introduction

This article considers whether monetary base control should be the means by which the authorities control the monetary aggregates. We have approached this subject as economists rather than as representatives of the Bank of England, and we seek to contribute to what has hitherto in the UK been only a limited discussion. Many of the subjects raised in the discussion are candidates for detailed consideration on both a theoretical and a practical level. Moreover, the various proponents of monetary base control often have widely differing proposals in mind, a fact which significantly increases the scope of the analysis required. What follows here, therefore, is not intended to be an exhaustive treatment of the subject. In particular, it concentrates on the more theoretical, economic issues and only raises in passing some of the implications of the various proposals for the structure of existing financial markets and for the authorities' present methods of operation.

To this end, a brief background for the subject is provided in section 2. The monetary base is then defined (section 3), its historical relevance in the UK noted (section 4), and its possible theoretical relevance briefly set out (section 5). The various possible forms of control, as we understand them, are then considered; the implications of strict forms of control are outlined in sections 6–8, and more relaxed versions are discussed in section 9. A brief summary of our views is provided right at the end.

2. The Background

In a number of countries, there are now formal monetary targets. Even where there are not, it is probably much more widely recognised than was the case, say, ten years ago that movements in the stock of money have considerable economic relevance, though the form and extent of this relevance are hotly debated.

Among those who believe that 'money matters', there is a group which considers that an appropriate degree of control over the rate of monetary growth can only be obtained by operating primarily to control the rate of growth of the monetary base.[1] To some in this group, current attempts in the

---

[1] There are also those who consider the relevance of the monetary base to be its value as a leading indicator rather than its potential as a control device. This view is considered further on p. 215.

UK to control sterling M_3 are wrongly directed, because the authorities are said to lack the means at present to achieve an adequate degree of short-term control over sterling M_3. The alternative proposed is that the authorities should seek to ensure the desired growth of whichever monetary aggregate they consider most appropriate by operating on the monetary base. Others in the group would go further and suggest that the monetary base – as well as being the means of control – could also be the appropriate target rather than (as in the UK, France or West Germany) a broad monetary aggregate such as sterling M_3 or (as in Canada) a narrower monetary aggregate, M_1.

3. What is the Monetary Base?

In current economic literature, there is a generally accepted concept of 'high-powered money', which is thought of as the sum of the balance-sheet liabilities of the central bank (strictly speaking, the monetary authorities)[1] to the private sector. Thus anything which leads the central bank to have reduced liabilities to the private sector (for example – and assuming that the government banks with the central bank, as it does in the UK – an excess of tax receipts over expenditure, or net sales of government debt) acts to reduce the volume of high-powered money. The phrases 'high-powered money' and 'monetary base' are often used interchangeably. Here, however, we should like to adopt a more precise terminology and use the phrase 'monetary base' to describe that set of the liabilities of the monetary authorities which they may seek particularly to control.

Exactly which liabilities should go into this set is no easy problem. In essence, the issue boils down to asking which set of their liabilities the monetary authorities think that they should control. Among the candidates for inclusion are:

(a) notes and coin in circulation with the public
(b) notes and coin held by banks (vault cash)
(c) bankers' balances at the Bank of England;[2]
(d) potential liabilities of the Bank of England, i.e. liabilities incurred as the counterpart to the assets that the Bank may have to assume because of commitments previously given or because of 'automatic' borrowing rights of others (in particular, the lender of last resort facilities to the discount market).

The definitions actually adopted by those countries where the base is considered relevant vary quite widely. Here, we prefer to begin with a definition that covers just (b) and (c) of the above list, on the view that this

---

[1] For example, in the UK, the Bank of England issues notes, but coin is issued by a quite separate body (the Royal Mint).

[2] We have deliberately ignored the comparatively small balances held at the Bank of England by the non-bank sector.

pair – or alternatively (c) by itself[1] – might be operationally most relevant in the UK and also with the hope that this will make the subsequent discussion easier to handle without losing its general relcvance. Thus, for example, the size of the base would be greatly increased by the inclusion of (a), notes and coin with the public. But the amount of currency so held is hardly a variable over which the authorities would (or could) seek control. In any case, if the aim is to influence some monetary aggregate consisting primarily of bank deposits, the relevant variable would seem to be that definition of the base – (b) and (c) or (c) alone – directly related to the assets of the banks. Otherwise variations in the non-bank private sector's demand for currency could lead to undesirable fluctuations in the growth of monetary aggregates.

The argument over whether (d) should be included is rather different. Under strict forms of base control, such facilities would not exist and therefore the problem would not arise. However, where such facilities did exist, their inclusion would imply a relationship between the base and the *potential* rather than the actual stock of money. In general, proponents of base control have argued against a definition of this type and, although it has been adopted in certain countries at certain times, it is not considered further here.

4. The Historical Relevance of the Monetary Base in the UK

A banking system as we know it could not have developed had banks not learned how to make loans without collapsing, through want of liquidity, if some depositors wanted their money back. The first line of defence for any bank against such illiquidity was traditionally provided by holding a stock of generally acceptable assets – coin or notes 'behind the counter'. The second consisted of balances with other banks that could be used to obtain additional generally acceptable notes. As the Bank of England became increasingly important as a note issuer and as a 'central bank', it became increasingly convenient to hold Bank of England notes and balances at the Bank.

Over time, the liquidity of the banking system came to be increasingly assured by the Bank's extension of lender of last resort facilities to the discount houses (for then banks could safely make secured short-term deposits with the houses and have no doubts about the liquidity of these

---

[1] The question of whether or not to include banks' holdings of vault cash in the definition of the monetary base raises a number of difficult questions. Since banks with differing kinds of business have differing operational needs to hold vault cash in the normal course of business, the issue of equity as between banks arises. If vault cash were to be excluded from the defined monetary base, however, banks could seek to adjust to their required cash ratio by making otherwise unnecessary transfers between vault cash and bankers' balances at the Bank. Such unnecessary transfers would have implications both for the Bank's ability to control the monetary base tightly and for costs.

funds) and also by the extension of markets in liquid financial assets, notably Treasury bills. Thus, when we now think of the liquidity of a single bank, we consider the liquidity provided by the existence of markets on which it can quickly raise new debt or sell existing assets and not just of the level of its holdings of cash and balances at the Bank of England. Similarly, for the liquidity of the banking system as a whole, the relevant point is the preparedness of the central bank to provide unlimited support to the system in times of crisis, not banks' aggregate holdings of cash and bankers' balances.

Thus, when it became accepted practice after the Second World War for the London clearing banks to keep a minimum ratio of 8 per cent of cash to deposits,[1] no operational relevance (in the sense of using the Bank's potential control over the supply of cash to restrict the level of bank deposits) was attributed to the ratio; in so far as the requirement had justification, it was prudential. Instead, the authorities were primarily concerned with the level and structure of interest rates, and they were consequently willing to ensure that the clearing banks did not go short of cash.[2] As a result, the clearing banks did not need to hold sizeable excess cash reserves, and the recorded ratio was generally very close to 8 per cent.

After 1971, even the 8 per cent cash ratio was abolished, but the London clearing banks instead agreed to keep an average of 1½ per cent of their eligible liabilities[3] in the form of non-interest-bearing balances at the Bank.[4] Even more obviously than with the 8 per cent cash ratio, there has been no attempt to use this ratio as a device for imposing a ceiling on the stock of eligible liabilities. [*Author's note:* This latter arrangement was superseded in turn in 1981. Since then there has been no required cash ratio. For details of the arrangements introduced in 1981 see the *Bank of England Quarterly Bulletin*, vol. 21, September 1981.] As before, the Bank of England has chosen – through its open-market operations and lender of last resort facilities – to concentrate on influencing short-term interest rates, being prepared always to provide funds requested by the banking system but on interest-rate terms of its own choosing.

---

[1] See paragraph 351 of the *Report of the Committee on the Working of the Monetary System* (the Radcliffe Committee). Cmnd 827, HMSO, 1959. The ratio could be met by any combination of vault cash and balances at the Bank.

[2] See 'The management of money day by day' in the *Bank of England Quarterly Bulletin*, March 1963, p. 15.

[3] Broadly, for any bank, these equal sterling deposits excluding those with an original maturity of over two years, plus sterling resources obtained by switching foreign currency into sterling, less the bank's net holdings of claims on the rest of the banking system.

[4] The commitment by the clearing banks in banking month t relates to the level of their eligible liabilities on the make-up day in banking month t_{-1}. There is no requirement that the ratio be maintained strictly on a day-to-day basis; daily deviations from the 1½ per cent ratio can be averaged over the banking month and shortfalls or excesses carried forward.

5. Why the Monetary Base may be Relevant

If banks have to maintain a minimum ratio of cash to deposits and if the central bank exercises sufficiently vigorously its undoubted potential power as 'the' source of cash, then clearly the size of the high-powered money base imposes a ceiling on the level of bank deposits and thus, indirectly, on the stock of money, however defined.

More formally and at its simplest, we can write

$$M \equiv C + D \tag{1}$$

where

M = the stock of money
C = notes and coin in circulation with the non-bank private sector
D = the deposit liabilities of the banks

and

$$H \equiv R + C \tag{2}$$

where

H = the high-powered money base
R = the banks' reserves (say, vault cash plus balances at the Bank of England)

Both (1) and (2) are identities, not behavioural equations, and by simple manipulation they can be made to yield a third identity.

$$M = H\frac{(1 + C/D)}{(R/D + C/D)} \tag{3}$$

In other words, *if* the authorities act so as to fix H[1] at some predetermined level, *if* the ratio of currency to deposits is constant and *if* the ratio of banks'

[1] Earlier, it was argued that the authorities should take as their monetary base all or some of the reserves available to the banking system, i.e. R, rather than the total of high-powered money which also includes currency in the hands of the non-bank public, C. The above identity, of course, holds irrespective of how the authorities operate, but focus on the banks' reserve base, R, would reduce the effect on the money stock of fluctuations in the non-bank public's desired cash holdings (the C/D ratio in the above identitty).

reserves to deposits is constant, then the size of M is determined by H. For example, let us assume that:

(a) all banks always maintain 4 per cent of deposits as vault cash to meet immediate operating needs and 1½ per cent in balances at the Bank of England
(b) this 5½ per cent of deposits constitutes the monetary base and that the banks begin with no excess reserves
(c) notes and coin in circulation with the public always amount to 15 per cent of deposits
(d) the balance-sheets of the Exchange Equalisation Account (EEA) and the overseas sector have been omitted and those of the Issue and Banking Departments of the Bank of England consolidated.

Let us suppose, then, that, in a given period, the public sector is a net recipient of one unit from the non-bank private sector (because, say, tax receipts have exceeded government disbursements). The resulting changes in the equilibrium positions of the Bank of England, the banking system and the non-bank private sector are shown in the two halves of Table A.

Before the change, the base stood at 5.5 (vault cash 4, bankers' balances 1.5), permitting banks to take deposits of 100. In the final equilibrium position, the base stands at 5.13 (vault cash 3.73, bankers' balances 1.4), again exactly 5.5 per cent of total deposits (93.3). The payment of 1 by the non-bank private sector has actually been accomplished by a fall of 0.9 in the notes they hold, plus a 0.1 reduction in bankers' balances at the Bank; the corresponding gain of course accrues to the public sector, whose deposits at the Bank rise from 5 to 6.

For the banking system, however, the process has been altogether more significant, because the decline of 0.37 in the base has necessitated a multiple contraction of deposits of 6.7 (i.e. $0.37 \times 100/5.5$). Nothing so far has, however, shown how this contraction occurs, and this major question is considered in the next section.

The presentation of the determination of the money stock in this fashion has a distinguished academic pedigree, which includes contributions from Phillips, Keynes and Meade.[1] As we have seen, the authorities have not, however, attempted to control H or R. Nor is it the case that the ratio of currency in circulation to deposits necessarily stays constant over time. Obviously this ratio may be affected by technological change (for example, the development of credit cards), but also, from a theoretical point of view, there is no obvious reason why the ratio of currency to bank deposits should stay constant over time, at least when the latter are defined broadly to include

[1] C. A. Phillips, *Bank Credit*, New York, Macmillan, 1920; J. M. Keynes, *A Treatise on Money*, London, Macmillan, 1930; J. E. Meade, 'The amount of money and the banking system', *Economic Journal*, vol. XLIV, 1934, pp. 77–83.

TABLE A

	Bank of England			Banking sector			Non-bank private sector	
	Liabilities	Assets		Liabilities	Assets		Liabilities	Assets
Position before the change								
Bankers' balances	1.5		Deposits of non-bank private sector	100.0		Deposits with banking sector		100.0
Vault cash in commercial banks	4.0		Capital of banks	10.0		Equity holdings in banks		10.0
Notes in circulation with non-bank private sector	15.0		Bankers' balances		1.5	Notes		15.0
Public-sector deposits at Bank of England	5.0		Vault cash		4.0			
			Liquid assets and advances		104.5			
	25.5	25.5		110.0	110.0		125.0	125.0
Position after the change								
Bankers' balances	1.4		Deposits of non-bank private sector	93.3		Deposits with banking sector		93.3
Vault cash in commercial banks	3.73		Capital of banks	10.0		Equity holdings in banks		10.0
Notes in circulation with non-bank private sector	14.1		Bankers' balances		1.40	Notes		14.1
Public sector deposits at Bank of England	6.0		Vault cash		3.73			
			Liquid assets and advances		98.17			
	25.23	25.23		103.3	103.3		117.4	117.4

both transactions *and* savings balances. Finally, there is no reason under the present arrangements why banks' reserves of cash and bankers' balances should show a stable relation to any particular monetary aggregate. Only the clearing banks maintain the 1½ per cent ratio, and even that requirement is over a period of time rather than for any particular day and is related to eligible liabilities rather than directly to deposits as recorded in the monetary aggregates.

It follows, not surprisingly, that, given present arrangements, there is no close relationship in the UK between changes in the monetary base and those in any other monetary aggregate. Indeed, to the extent that there has been any causal relationship, it could reasonably be argued that it has run *from* money to the base, rather than the other way round, a causality exemplified by the fact that the 1½ per cent ratio relates to the previous month's eligible liabilities and that the authorities have always chosen to provide, at a price, the base money required. Nor has there been any close relationship between movements in the base and in nominal incomes. Indeed with high-powered money (H) largely consisting of currency in the hands of the public (C), and the latter being demand-determined, (according to our econometric estimates largely in response to current and past changes in consumers' expenditure) the direction of causation runs clearly from nominal income to notes and coin in circulation (C) and high-powered money (H).

The relevant question, however, is what would happen if present attitudes and institutional features were changed and the authorities sought to use the base rather than interest rates as a means of controlling the rate of growth of the monetary aggregates. Unfortunately, as noted in the introduction, the answer is related to the form, in particular the time horizon, of the monetary base regime in question. Further complications are added by the existence of a number of other issues that are not of major theoretical relevance in their own right but which represent awkward technical problems to be tackled before at least some forms of base control could be considered in practice.

6. A Strict Control of Money

First we examine the implications of seeking to control the money stock strictly on a short-term basis. Even if it were universally accepted that strict short-term control of the monetary aggregates was undesirable, if not impractical, it would still be useful to consider the implications of strict control as an expositional device in order to clarify the issues. Moreover, there are a number of proponents of strict short-term control of the monetary aggregates, and of these some advocate the use of monetary base control to achieve this end. Of course, it is possible to envisage ways in which banks' deposit liabilities might be subject to strict short-term control other than through regulation of the base. Bank deposits could be forced to grow at a predetermined rate by government fiat, or by the imposition of some form of permanent supplementary special deposits scheme, with penalties on those banks whose deposit liabilities grew too slowly as well as on those whose liabilities grew too fast.

Returning to control via the monetary base, the most extreme form of regulation imaginable is one where the operations of the central bank were such as to predetermine the monetary base (for some of the problems involved see pages 214–15) and where the banks were required to achieve their reserve ratio requirement exactly on a daily basis. If short-term control of the monetary base were to be translated into equivalent short-term control of the monetary aggregates, the ability of the banks to vary their actual (free) reserve holdings relative to their required level would have to be limited, for example by penalties applying to both excess and deficient reserves. Examination rapidly suggests that the idea of such tight management is impracticable but, as it throws up a number of points of general relevance to any attempt to control the base over any period, the arguments are worth considering.

The most appropriate starting-point is perhaps the mechanism by which banks are supposed to adjust to, say, a shortfall of reserves (i.e. the base provided does not permit them to meet their reserve requirements on their existing level of deposits). When considered at all, the mechanism is usually held to be that the banks cut back on lending or sell off marketable assets. However, while this may improve the relative position of one bank, such action only eases the reserve position of the banking system as a whole fractionally, with that fraction depending on the required reserve ratio. Thus *unless the authorities relent and choose to provide more base money*, the only ways that the banks as a whole can overcome their reserve asset shortage are:

(a) to reduce their assets and liabilities by a multiple of the initial shortage of base money
(b) to attract notes and coin from the public (which would be difficult to do, unless banks were to offer a variable premium for currency, thereby breaking convertibility between currency and deposits)
(c) if there were lower reserve requirements on time than on sight deposits (as in the USA), to induce customers – by adjusting relative yields – to switch funds from sight to time deposits.

To illustrate this essential point, suppose that a bank sells off its Treasury bill holdings. Its balances with the Bank of England will rise, i.e. it will receive more reserve assets; the banks of those who buy the bills will lose an equal amount.[1] Only if the Bank of England steps into the market to buy the bills will the base be increased.

[1] Provided the non-bank private sector does not purchase Treasury bills with notes and coin, the bank will receive net claims on other banks; its balances at the Bank of England will thus rise and those of other banks fall correspondingly.

A similar conclusion follows with regard to the effect of foreign exchange transactions on the monetary base. As the banks try to improve their individual position by selling assets, they will force up interest rates. Other things being equal, this will increase the demand for sterling by foreigners who now wish to obtain sterling assets, the rate of interest on which has become more attractive. However, the stock of the monetary base will remain unaffected and under the control of the authorities if either the exchange rate is allowed to appreciate freely, or, if this is unacceptable, the inflow of capital is sterilised. A rise in the exchange rate might be forestalled without increasing the monetary base if, when the authorities purchase foreign currencies with sterling and accumulate international reserves in the EEA, they then finance these purchases by the sale of Treasury bills or some other debt instrument which is not included in the definition of the monetary base. Nevertheless, the sale of these debt instruments may raise interest rates further and also maintain monetary tightness, thereby attracting continuing inflows from abroad. This could lead to an unstable situation with persistently rising reserves together with rising domestic interest rates.

The same conclusion follows if the banks make what is now the more likely response to reserve pressure of bidding for funds (so-called liability management) by, for example, issuing certificates of deposit. Again, the effect will be to push up interest rates without increasing the base (except in so far as (b) or (c) on p. 210 apply). But this time there could be an additional difficulty if the authorities have a broad money aggregate in mind as an intermediate target, in that liability management can have a perverse effect on the adjustment process of the banking system as a whole, since it tends to raise the yield offered on bank deposits relative to the yields on other liquid assets. This could accelerate the interest-rate spiral likely to develop as banks come under reserve pressure and, if rates of interest on bank lending do not keep pace with the rise in market interest rates, actually increase the demand for credit by making it attractive to borrow funds to on-lend in the wholesale money markets.

These problems might be mitigated if the reserve requirements on time deposits were lower than those on sight deposits. Then, as interest rates rose – increasing the opportunity cost of holding sight deposits[1] – holders would, over a period of time, switch their funds from sight to time accounts, progressively reducing the banks' overall need for reserves. However, the authorities would presumably only seek to control the monetary aggregates with a differential reserve requirement, in which sight deposits were given a higher weighting than time deposits, if they attached greater importance to the rate of growth of sight deposits than to that of time deposits. In the extreme case where the authorities attached no weight to the rate of growth of time deposits, they could set an M_1 target and only impose reserve require-

[1] This assumes that the implicit or explicit return on sight deposits is either constant or at least not quickly responsive to changes in market interest rates.

ments on sight deposits. Nevertheless, even with an M_1 target, the speed of adjustment of the non-bank private sector's asset portfolio in response to changes in the differential between sight and time deposit rates might not be fast enough for the banks to be able to meet their reserve requirements at all quickly. As a result, an interest-rate spiral might still emerge.

The conclusion of this line of argument is that strict control of the base (which would, of course, imply an end to all the present lender of last resort facilities) would continually threaten frequent and potentially massive movements in interest rates, if not complete instability. Changes in the base would inevitably carry implications for interest rates, and the greater the emphasis on control of the base, the less the possibility that the central bank could intervene to ameliorate any interest-rate fluctuations. In the strictest form of control (the day-to-day regulation noted earlier), the problem would, of course, be at its most acute as no adjustment time (e.g. for the banks to curtail their loans to the non-bank public) would be available. Indeed, it is highly dubious whether such a system could possibly work, mainly because of the time it would take for markets to adjust to the interest-rate changes induced by the banks in their attempts to meet their reserve requirements. But even for control over longer periods of time, strict control of the base would throw on to financial markets the whole burden of adjustment at present 'shared' by the Bank of England's lender of last resort facilities, its open-market operations, its foreign exchange intervention, and the permitted short-term variability in the level of balances held by the clearing banks at the Bank of England.

7. Structural Adjustments in Response to Strict Control

In extreme form, then, base control could imply enormous potential pressure on financial markets. It is a moot point as to how far they would develop to meet the burden. Other reactions would also be likely.[1] We now explore some of these on the assumption that the transitional problems of adjusting to the new system had been overcome.

One development might well be the sharp curtailment or disappearance of the overdraft system, indeed the curtailment or disappearance of any exposure, whether by formal or informal commitment, to an obligation to extend loans at some future time. At present, banks extend facilities to customers that in aggregate are roughly only half-used at any time. This is an element of flexibility provided by the banking system which most observers would regard as highly desirable. Even under the present supplementary special deposits scheme, the existence of these facilities may be an embarrassment to a bank, particularly as most empirical work on the demand for bank

[1] They would indeed follow from *any* short-term strict control over the money stock.

credit in the UK suggests that a bank's major defence in such circumstances – to raise the cost of borrowing – may not have a large (and certainly does not have a rapid) effect on the demand for credit.[1] It follows that the stricter the control of money (whatever the form of that control), the more risky it would be for banks to provide overdraft facilities in their present form.

A related development likely to occur would be that the banks would come to hold a larger proportion of their portfolio in easily saleable assets, or, in so far as this was allowed, in excess reserves, correspondingly reducing relatively illiquid lending to the private sector. Similarly, the non-bank private sector, being less able to obtain bank facilities, might also seek to hold larger amounts of liquid assets.

Such conclusions follow from the fact that the more tightly controlled the banking system, the greater the short-term risk of illiquidity for all concerned. In the longer term, when such a system was fully established, it would seem to exhibit a certain inefficiency – with more risk than strictly necessary, balanced by larger liquidity holdings – but otherwise it could conceivably be workable. Such an approach would, however, appear to carry a higher risk of disturbances to the banking system reminiscent in some respects of those in the UK in the nineteenth century and in the USA before the establishment of the Federal Reserve System. Even under a monetary base control regime, the Bank of England would have to retain the right to use lender of last resort facilities to forestall a banking crisis, and assistance might have to be extended to individual banks more frequently than in the past. In the short run, any sudden change to the new system, with a possibly large but unpredictable increase in the demand for liquid assets in response to the increased risk perceived, would make assessment and management of the overall economic situation more difficult.

A third likely development would be the growth of holders of liquid assets not subject to cash ratio requirements who would arbitrage between short-term liquid assets (such as Treasury bills) and bank deposits,[2] thereby reducing the extent of interest-rate fluctuation. Similarly, the banks might be able, at times of their own choosing, to rearrange some of their on-balance-sheet advances as off-balance-sheet acceptances, so that although they would resell some of their holdings of commercial bills to the non-bank private sector, they would guarantee the ultimate holders of these commercial bills against default by the original issuers. The rapid increase in acceptances almost immediately after the reimposition of the supplementary special

[1] Peter Spencer and Colin Mowl, 'The model of the domestic monetary system' part 1 of *A Financial Sector for the Treasury Model*, Government Economic Service Working Paper No. 17 (Treasury Working Paper No. 8), December 1978.

[2] One requirement for such arbitrage to occur is that liability management of the kind described on p. 211 did not prevent Treasury bill yields from rising faster in response to reserve asset pressure than the deposit rates offered by banks.

deposits scheme in June 1978 suggests that the banks are able to rearrange their portfolios to some extent in this way.

Equally, however, such structural developments, resulting in an expansion of near-money liquid assets and an increased elasticity of response in velocity to changes in interest rates, would reduce the significance of a tight control over the money stock and also the monetary base. The financial system evolves continuously to meet the needs of the economy and will, in time, find ways round artificial road blocks.

All these developments would be likely to follow from any strict form of base control, though the 'adjustment problem' in each case would be worse, and the speed of the developments faster, the shorter the time horizon over which control was attempted.

8. Some Technical and Operational Changes Required

As noted above, day-to-day control of the base is very difficult to envisage. Under present institutional arrangements, there are unforeseen swings into and out of central government balances of up to several hundred million pounds a day, and the first requirement for day-to-day control would be either that the government moved its business to the commercial banks or that the banking system moved to a next day settlement basis for all transactions. The logic of the first change is that unexpected flows – say from the non-bank private sector to the government – would then leave bankers' balances at the Bank of England unaffected; at present, as noted earlier, the result of such flows is to alter these balances. The logic of the second change, which in administrative terms at least would constitute a retrograde step, is that the authorities would then have one day's notice of unexpected movements of funds.

Even then, however, the authorities would not have any advance warning of shifts in the public's demand for currency, which even on a daily basis can be large. The Bank of England already forecasts the demand for currency on a daily basis, as part of its projection of key factors affecting money markets, and, on occasion, errors here have been of the order of £100 million and are frequently £25–30 million.

Furthermore, whatever the length of period over which control of the base is desired, the authorities' predetermined path would have to be set in non-seasonally adjusted form. As presumably their objective would be to obtain a smooth seasonally adjusted growth in the base or in some monetary aggregate, they would need to work from a seasonally adjusted to an unadjusted projection of the base. Given the complexities and uncertainties of the seasonal-adjustment process for financial series, such a procedure could be sensible for, say, quarterly projections, but daily forecasts on such a basis would be subject to very large margins of error. Any attempt to control the banking system strictly on a very short-term basis would therefore result in unintended gyrations in the level of deposits.

A final difficulty with any form of very short-term control arises out of the question of the appropriate accounting basis for the banks. A lagged accounting basis is used for the purpose of calculating required reserves in virtually all countries, and is indeed suitable when the purpose of the reserve ratios is to provide a fulcrum for money market operations to control interest rates. Virtually by definition, however, when the total of required reserves is related to the past level of deposits and where there are no excess reserves at the outset in the system, changes in deposits must cause the authorities to allow changes in bank reserves, and not vice versa, so that monetary base movements can hardly either control, cause or even indicate future movements in bank deposits.

One possibility would be to move on to a current accounting basis, with required reserves related to current liabilities. Even in this case, delays in obtaining current information on movements in liabilities (and, depending on the form of the required reserve base, delays also in information on movements of vault cash held at branches) would tend to mean that the banks would simply not be in a position to know what adjustments would be necessary during the course of the day to try to meet their required ratios.

It would be more in the spirit of monetary base control, though we do not know of any case where this has been applied, for the reserve ratio to be put on a lead accounting basis, that is to say that the liabilities of a bank at some future time, $t + n$, should be related through a required ratio to its current reserve base at time t. The strictness of the monetary base control regime would then relate to the adjustment time allowed, the averaging procedures adopted and the penalties imposed for non-compliance.

9. More Relaxed Versions of Monetary Base Control

A number of the operational changes described above could be avoided and the problems of adjustment substantially mitigated with a more relaxed form of base control. Thus the authorities could perhaps have a desired level for the base over, say, a six-month period but not insist that the base average out exactly at that level and not withdraw the lender of last resort and other facilities which at present avoid sharp short-term instability in financial markets.

Indeed, at the limit, i.e. with no penalties for failing to meet a particular ratio, in effect with no *required* reserve ratio at all, movements in the monetary base could be regarded primarily as another monetary aggregate, possibly a leading indicator, movements in which could convey information on future developments. (Under present institutional arrangements, as explained earlier, the monetary base in the UK does *not* act as a useful leading indicator.) However, even with a long run of data, the monetary base series might not come to be a satisfactory leading indicator. Banks might wish to hold additional excess reserves, perhaps as a counterpart to a decline in the demand for bank credit, or an increase in their demand for liquidity. Accordingly, the rate of growth of banks' reserve holdings might not provide a good index of how expansionary the monetary stance was at the time. It has been argued, not least by monetarists, that the attention paid, for example, in the late 1930s by the Federal Reserve Board in the USA to the banking system's excess reserves was misdirected.

If the nature of the monetary base series were changed, say with banks required to hold a uniform reserve ratio[1] and a current or lead accounting basis, then it is possible, subject to the comment above, that the series could come to convey more useful information. After such a structural change, however, it would be several years before enough experience, e.g. of seasonal fluctuations, was amassed to enable such movements to be interpreted adequately. Thus under the changed system banks would most likely have a greater incentive to hold excess cash reserves, depending on the costs involved in holding such excess reserves as against the costs and risks to each bank of finding itself short of cash reserves. It would be some time before any regular pattern of behaviour would be established and discernible.

Moreover, the Bank of England already obtains weekly monetary data from a sample of banks. While this experience is revealing only too clearly the difficulties of interpreting movements in a new series, such weekly data may in time come to provide the authorities with prompt information on monetary developments. Only if the movements in the monetary base should provide a reliable *leading* indicator of monetary developments would the series help the authorities to assess developments.

In practice, the phrase 'monetary base control' is not tightly defined; it can range from an attempt to control certain monetary aggregates on a tight day-to-day basis through to a generalised concern with the series as a potentially useful leading indicator, possibly among others, of future monetary developments. Between these two polar positions exists a relatively unexplored territory of gradations from tighter to easier control.

The purpose of sections 6–8 was to show that an attempt to use monetary base control rigorously over short periods would be neither desirable nor feasible. The same objections do not hold, at least not to anything like the same extent, to proposals for considerably more relaxed versions of this approach, in which proper and sufficient adjustment time is given to the banking system. Indeed, because it is the role of the banking system to absorb and to meet shocks occurring in the demand for or supply of money and credit

[1] As already noted in footnote 1 on p. 204, the fact that banks do differing kinds of business and have differing balance-sheet structures makes any approach to 'uniformity' rather difficult in practice.

within the economy, the search for tight short-term control of the money stock, for example on a week-by-week basis, would seem to be misguided. This is *not*, however, to deny the possibility of improving control techniques for influencing monetary developments over a longer horizon measured, say, in terms of four to six months.

In this respect there are perhaps two main ways in which the adoption of a 'relaxed' monetary base system which did *not* aim to force the banking system into unduly rapid adjustment by imposing penalties on short-term divergences from a required ratio (for example, such relaxation could be obtained by some combination of generous averaging procedures, gentle initial penalties or even an absence of a *required* cash ratio) might improve the authorities' control over the system.

First, if movements in the monetary base did prove to be an informative leading indicator of future developments, it would provide the authorities with information with which to respond more quickly and firmly to diverging monetary trends than they are now able to do. Indeed, with such a monetary base approach – assuming that it did prove to be a reliable leading indicator – there would perhaps be some presumption that firmer action might be taken more quickly, as the authorities reacted to movements in the monetary base. Nevertheless, against such putative longer-term benefits would have to be set the costs of structural changes involving disturbances and dislocations to well-established arrangements. Moreover, for several years while the system was adjusting to the structural change, it would be virtually impossible for the authorities to glean any worthwhile information from the new series. Furthermore, it must be emphasised that the use of the monetary base as an adjunct for improving control over monetary developments is *not* an alternative to varying interest rates for that purpose, but indeed a means of trying to ensure that interest rates vary sufficiently quickly and widely to achieve such greater control.

The second possible source of benefit from the adoption of monetary base control might occur if such a system entailed or encouraged a change in the structure of financial markets which allowed the authorities to control the volume of debt sales to the non-bank public more closely and effectively: for control of the broad monetary aggregates, e.g. sterling M_3, whether with monetary base control or not, must involve sales of sufficient debt by the authorities to offset other factors (for example, the budget deficit) tending to augment monetary growth. Indeed, some proponents of monetary base may see the main advantage of a move in this direction, not in any way as providing any mechanical or 'multiplier' method of monetary control, but rather as a means of forcing or stimulating the growth and development of debt markets, particularly short-term debt markets in a way that might give the authorities greater control over the total debt sold to the non-bank public in any period. This would, however, be a very roundabout way of trying to achieve changes in the structure and nature of such markets, for such changes do not logically require the adoption of a move to monetary base control and could be considered directly on their own merits.

10. Summary

To summarise: the critics of the authorities' approach to monetary management often contrast this with what might be obtained if the authorities were instead to adopt monetary base control. We have shown that there are several variants of monetary base control (an imprecise term) and have indicated reasons why *rigid* monetary base control would be unacceptable. More relaxed versions of such a control system might be accompanied by changes in the functioning of certain debt markets, though any such changes should perhaps be considered on their own merits quite separately, and might provide the authorities with additional information to allow prompter and firmer countervailing action. Any such putative benefits would, however, have to be weighed against the costs of making major structural changes in the system.

VIII
Money in an Open Economy

1. Introduction

The most notable difference between the US and the UK economies is that the latter is an open economy – indeed its history and circumstances have made the UK more open to external influences than most other countries of a similar size, whereas the USA approximates almost to a figurative closed economy. The interrelationship between domestic monetary developments and the balance of external payments has been close, important and involved in the UK. Moreover, the nature of this relationship has varied, particularly in response to changes in the exchange-rate regime in existence. The change from a regime of pegged, but adjustable, exchange rates – the Bretton Woods system – to a regime of more flexible, but still managed, exchange rates, a change which dates from June 1972 in the UK case, has caused modellers some (continuing) difficulty in adjusting their models to the new system.

This interrelationship of domestic and international monetary flows within the UK institutional framework is the main subject here. The basic statistical identities relating such monetary flows are set out in the following section. Then, various approaches to modelling these interrelationships for the UK in the period of pegged exchange rates (prior to 1972) are considered. Three such approaches are reviewed: standard Keynesian, monetarist and supply disturbance.

One of the main difficulties of modelling this part of the economic system – the domestic – international monetary flow nexus – from 1972 onwards is that the present exchange-rate system (if it can indeed be dignified by the term 'system') has not approximated closely either of the heuristic paradigms whose properties have been academically studied, a fixed exchange rate or a freely flexible exchange rate.

However complicated and untidy this experience may have been, the economic modellers are still obliged to capture as much of the essence of the workings of the present system as possible. The final section therefore reviews the various attempts of modellers in the UK to do so. It would probably be widely accepted that such modelling is a difficult task; indeed, I would doubt whether any modeller in the UK would claim now to have specified the present interrelationships with any certainty or exactitude. There is much room in this field for further improvement and reassessment.

2. Statistical Identities

Many, perhaps most, analytical studies of the nexus of domestic – international monetary flows start from the basis of the broad accounting relationships set out below.[1]

Balance of Payments						:	*Domestic Monetary Determination*				
Current account	*plus*	capital account	=	reserve flows		:	reserve flows	*plus*	domestic credit expansion	=	money supply change

This accounting relationship illustrates the way in which domestic monetary developments and the balance of payments are linked through reserve flows; it reveals nothing, of course, of the direction of causation, for example whether reserve flows are effectively determined by domestic monetary developments (given the exchange-rate regime in existence) with elements of the balance-of-payments accounts adjusting to that, or *vice versa*.

The question of appropriately modelling the direction of causation will be considered in subsequent sections. The purpose of the remainder of this section is to note that the accounting relationship set down above to describe domestic monetary determination is inexact. This inexactitude can lead to errors. For example, it is commonly believed that in those circumstances when official financing of the balance of payments is zero, which is one possible definition of free floating, the effect of the flows of external payments on the domestic money stock would also be zero; this is not the case.

It may be helpful at this stage to set down the basic accounts of the UK banking sector's position in sterling (£). This is as follows:

UK Banks' Sterling Balance-Sheet

Assets	*Liabilities*
Lending to UK public sector	UK residents' deposits
UK private sector	Non-resident deposits
Overseas	Non-deposit liabilities
	Switched-in position

[1] In countries other than the UK this accounting relationship between external and domestic monetary flows is perhaps more commonly constructed in terms of the respective effects of external and domestic influences on the monetary base, with the money stock related to the base through a multiplier. While such an accounting relationship, as an identity, could be statistically constructed for the UK, institutional and operational practice has been to influence the elements of domestic credit expansion, such as the public-sector borrowing requirement and bank lending to the private sector, directly, and not to work through a form of monetary base control.

There has been a debate recently whether this conceptual framework has any relevance for the

The monetary aggregate now used as the target variable for policy purposes is sterling M_3, which comprises all UK resident sterling deposits with the UK banking sector plus notes and coin. A slightly broader definition, M_3, also includes UK residents' holdings of foreign currency deposits (for example, dollar deposits) with UK banks. The latter measure is now given less emphasis for policy purposes for several reasons. These include the ease of substitution of dollar deposits held by UK residents between banks situated in the UK (included in M_3) and abroad (excluded) and also that an internal, unpublished study in the Bank of England suggested that holdings of such foreign currency balances related mainly to UK residents' investment activity abroad and had little behavioural relationship with developments in the UK economy. [*Author's note*: The above comments related to the situation existing while exchange control was still in force. Now that exchange control has been removed, in October 1979, some of the considerations may change.]

Be that as it may, the money stock (sterling M_3) will be affected, for example by external flows, if and only if the transaction(s) leads to a change in UK residents' sterling deposits with UK banks (or their holdings of notes and coins). Domestic credit expansion, as its name indicates, relates to the *asset*, or lending side, of the banks' balance-sheet. Thus DCE is defined in the UK as the increase in banks' sterling loans to the UK private sector and to overseas borrowers, together with such amounts of the public-sector borrowing requirement as are financed by the banks and the overseas sector (that is to say, PSBR less debt sales to UK non-bank residents).

Set out in accounting terms we have:[1]

Part of DCE *Adds to M_3*

PBSR	−	debt sales to UK non-bank residents	−	borrowing[2] from overseas	+	increase[2] in foreign exchange reserves	=	additional bank loans to UK public sector	+	additional holdings of notes and coins

This statistical framework provides a basis for qualifying the original simplified accounting relationship that

$$\text{reserve flows} + \text{DCE} = \text{money supply change}$$

USA, which provides the main reserve currency for the international monetary system: see, for example, Balbach[3] and Kubarych[**14**]. It is not necessary for the purposes of discussion of modelling monetary interrelations in the UK to enter this particular argument. (The references are to be found on pages 239–40.)

[1] There are, of course, problems in dealing with valuation changes – when the exchange rate alters, for example.

[2] The PSBR can be financed equivalently by borrowing foreign currency and selling such funds for sterling or by a decline in the foreign currency reserves which produces sterling.

Obviously public-sector borrowing from (repayments to) abroad financed by an equal change in the reserves affects neither DCE nor sterling M_3. This is widely understood about large official transactions (for example, with the IMF), but exactly the same holds true for overseas investment in UK public-sector debt, for example gilts and Treasury bills. If a US resident purchases sterling from the authorities and uses that to buy UK gilts from the authorities (or from the banking system), official liabilities to, and assets on, overseas residents rise by an equal amount with no resultant change in DCE or M_3.

Turning to the liabilities side of the accounts, as set out before – if an increase in, say, bank lending to the public sector, which may in turn be associated with an increase in DCE or an inflow of reserves over the exchanges, is financed by an increase in non-residents' deposits, non-deposit liabilities or the switched-in-position of banks, there is then no change in UK resident deposits, and the money supply, as defined, would be unaltered, at least initially.[1] Non-resident sterling deposits were excluded from the definition of the UK money stock mainly because they were thought to consist largely of speculative investment balances whose ebb and flow would bear little relationship to the development of the UK economy. Non-deposit liabilities include the banks' own sterling funds, both capital and reserves. The switched position reflects the banks' use of funds placed in foreign currency liabilities with them to buy sterling to lend on in sterling terms (or vice versa when switching out, though exchange control regulations limit the ability of the banks to extend their switched-out position).

So, *given DCE*, there are several flows besides the reserve flow influencing sterling M_3. Set out formally:

$$\begin{aligned}\text{sterling } M_3 = {} & \text{DCE} + \text{change in reserves} \\ & - \Delta\,(\text{government borrowing from overseas}) \\ & - \Delta\,(\text{non-resident deposits}) \\ & - \Delta\,(\text{switched position}) \\ & - \Delta\,(\text{non-deposit liabilities})\end{aligned}$$

The growth of non-deposit liabilities is quite stable over time, though erratic on a month-by-month basis; it picks up any errors in the accounting system. However, when sterling is strong, and funds are flowing in across the foreign exchanges, quite a sizeable proportion of that will generally be reflected in non-residents' acquisitions of UK public-sector debt and in non-residents' UK

[1] The accompanying change in the asset structure of the banks, including possibly a change in their reserve asset ratio, could, however, lead the banks to take subsequent action, for example by expanding bank lending to the private sector, that might lead to a secondary increase in UK residents' deposits.

TABLE A

DCE and sterling M_3, 1976 and 1977

	1976		1977	
DCE	7,438		1,184	
Net external flows	−2,906		3,580	
of which:				
Official financing		−3,629		+7,361
Other public-sector external financing		+ 626		−1,881
Overseas sterling deposits (−indicates increase)		− 141		−1,632
Banks' foreign currency deposits net of f.c. assets (− indicates increase)		+ 238		− 268
Non-deposit liabilities	− 967		− 665	
Increase in sterling M_3	3,565		4,099	

bank deposits, and the banks are likely to move to a switched-in position. Accordingly the size of reserve flows – of official financing of the balance of payments – is likely to be considerably greater than that of net external influences on the money stock. This is illustrated by the statistics for 1976 (when sterling was weak) and for 1977 (when sterling was strong) in Table A.

This analysis, as set out in tabular form, also shows that holding official intervention in the exchange market at zero would *not* cause net external flows influencing the money stock to be zero. If, for example, the UK private sector had a current plus capital account surplus which was financed by non-residents drawing on their existing sterling deposits, then sterling M_3 would rise despite there being no change in DCE or in reserve flows. Put another, and perhaps simpler, way the UK private sector gets its hands on additional money by running a surplus in its transactions, on both current and capital account, with the overseas sector. Such a private sector surplus on current and capital account *will* raise sterling M_3 (*given DCE*) whether that surplus is financed by the public sector (for example, increasing reserves or repaying external debt), or by non-resident capital flows or by banks' switching operations. It is *not* the cessation of intervention by the authorities in the foreign exchange market *per se* that will shut off the effect of net external flows on the money stock, though it will greatly help to do so, but rather the effect of that cessation in driving exchange rates to a level where the net surplus (deficit) on current account plus private-sector capital account becomes virtually zero.

It is worthwhile emphasising that thus far the discussion has concerned purely accounting relationships without causal implications. In the last few paragraphs an implicit causality has crept in, because the assumption that DCE is a given, fixed total allows one to claim immediately that any further increase in sterling M_3 must be causally associated with a net external inflow.

Of course, the extent to which DCE has remained independent of external flows is a subject of considerable analytic dispute. It is to such disputes about causality and the analysis of the behaviour of domestic – international monetary flows that we next turn.

3. Monetary Flows under Pegged Exchange Rates

The standard Keynesian model

Ever since the latter part of the nineteenth century the Bank of England has been concerned with maintaining its ability to determine the level of short-term interest rates. During this period, until 1972, the key short-term rate, Bank Rate, was administratively fixed; other short-term market rates had only a limited room to vary relative to Bank Rate. In general it appeared that external pressures, namely a weakening balance of payments, were the main influence on the monetary authorities that caused them to raise interest rates, in defence of the pegged exchange rate: if external conditions allowed, a weakening domestic economy and in particular rising unemployment made the authorities keener to lower interest rates. Only temporarily towards the end of this period, in 1969–70, under the influence of the IMF did the authorities seek to operate the instruments of monetary policy (interest rates, lending ceilings, etc.) to achieve any intermediate quantitative target for a monetary aggregate; in this particular instance the target was expressed in terms of DCE.

Although the balance of the authorities' objectives no doubt shifted over time, there was sufficient continuity in the broad aims of monetary policy, within the context of the Bretton Woods exchange-rate regime, to allow the authorities' response to events to be modelled in terms of a reaction function. This was done on numerous occasions by academics (for example, Fisher[**6**], Goodhart[**8**] and Nobay[**18**]), usually finding external influences, such as changes in the level of foreign exchange reserves and variations in US interest rates, to be highly significant, and domestic cyclical indicators, such as unemployment, to be quite significant, but generally finding no significant relationship between Bank Rate and inflation.

Although a reaction function could have been used, it was more common in the models actually used, certainly in Treasury – Bank forecasts, to treat Bank Rate as an exogenous variable. In practice, however, it was set by an implicit reaction function. A forecast would be made of US interest rates; given the initial expectations of the development of the current account and of the cyclical state of the economy, a 'plausible' path for Bank Rate would then be adopted, which could, at least in principle, be reconsidered and altered in subsequent iterative stages of the forecast.

With the path of short-term rates thus set in the forecast, it would then have become possible to estimate long-term fixed interest rates, using a term structure equation, and equity yields, along the lines followed by Ando and Modigliani in the (Fed, MIT, Penn) FMP model in the USA. In practice these relationships were rarely modelled as formally as this in UK forecasting models. The difficulty of modelling equity price movements soon becomes clear to any aspiring model-builder. There was, and remains, an assortment of differing ways of estimating shifts in the yield curve, but in general it has not been possible to improve much on the precept that long rates move synchronously with short rates, but by a lesser extent.

In the standard Keynesian models monetary factors affected the real economy through the influence of interest rates on expenditures. Such influence was, however, generally found to be slight in the UK (for a survey see Savage[**22**]) – and, until fairly recently, thought to be non-existent in terms of the influence of wealth/equity values on consumption, a key route in the FMP model in the USA. This was one reason why empirical study of linkages between yields on alternative financial assets was not pursued more assiduously.

The institutional framework of the UK financial system is such that the demand for credit in some cases, particularly credit flows to persons, can be limited by direct rationing as well as by price. This is, perhaps, most important in the case of mortgage lending by building societies. The societies for various reasons (nicely modelled by Hendry and Anderson[**10**]) are slow to adjust their own rates (on both liabilities and assets) to movements in competing market rates. So, when market rates rise relative to building society rates, their inflow falls off and they ration mortgages at the pegged (cartelised) rate. Such rationing has had a marked effect on the housing market, stronger than the effect of changing mortgage *rates*. Most models have incorporated a building society sub-sector. Another example of possible significant rationing effects was to be found in the often significant influence of bank lending to persons for consumption. Direct official ceilings on bank lending, particularly aimed at personal lending, in force for much of the period before 1972, provided an economic rationale for this variable but at the same time made it extremely hard to model.

With interest rates thus determined, effectively independently of domestic monetary and financial flows, the standard Keynesian model of the UK did not require *any* monetary or financial sector (except for a building society sub-sector) for completeness. Even where a companion monetary – financial flow of funds forecast was completed, as was done by the Treasury together with the Bank, this was done quite largely out of interest for monitoring financial developments for their own sake, *not* because such developments fed back into the main model of the UK, at least in any formal explicit manner.[1] Indeed, once interest rates were determined (as described) and

[1] On occasions large movements in companies' financial position, for example, would cause the financial forecasters to suggest that the national income forecasters should adjust the residuals on company expenditure equations.

instances of rationing credit to the private sector explored, the remainder of such studies of monetary-financial flows as were undertaken (and which were usually judgemental rather than econometric) were little more than a vestigial appendix to the main, 'real', forecast.

Meanwhile the balance of payments was being forecast as a part of the main forecast. There is no need here to describe the current-account forecast. Forecasting the capital account generally posed severe problems, because it was both erratic and susceptible to so many special influences, such as exchange controls, factors affecting sterling balances, etc. Apart from these special factors, attempts were regularly made to model such flows in terms of variables expected to influence speculation about future exchange-rate movements, usually proxied by past and current movements in the current account and trade balance, and in terms of an interest rate differential. The effect of the latter, though quite often significant, was usually weak, (but not always; unpublished work by Minford and Beenstock in the Treasury appeared at one time to find a large effect on capital flows of the differential between *long-term* rates).[1] The developments of monetary aggregates were *at that time* generally not regarded as determinants of capital flows, in relation either to exchange-rate expectations or to their influence on current relative monetary conditions.[2] With the current and capital account thus estimated, the forecast for reserve flows therefore followed as the end-product of the balance-of-payments forecast.

An economic aphorism is that no market operator can simultaneously determine both the price and the quantity sold in any free market (without rationing). With the level of interest rates determined as described above, the authorities could not also determine the quantity of money. Accordingly, *demand-for-money* functions – functions of the level of real output, prices and (largely policy-determined) interest rates – were estimated by several economists towards the end of the 1960s, and were then considered to be quite stable (see Artis and Lewis[**1**], Hacche[**9**], Johnson[**11**, ch. 2] and Price[**21**]). So far as models included econometrically estimated monetary sectors at all,

---

[1] Findings of a lack of sensitivity in response to interest-rate differentials may largely have reflected the problems of dealing satisfactorily with simultaneous determination.

[2] In more recent years, of course, many modellers, including those in the Bank, have introduced the development of monetary variables, such as DCE, as influences on exchange-rate expectations. While the above seemed to be the state of the art among model-builders, at least in the 1960s, their view was not shared by the monetary authorities in a more practical, policy-oriented context. The rationale for introducing bank lending ceilings (and import deposits) included a belief that squeezing the financial position of UK companies would limit capital outflows, especially in the forms of leads and lags. Moreover, the exchange market operators often were concerned about 'money sloshing around'. However, partly because of exchange control regulations, which constrain personal-sector transfers of funds most tightly, concern about the general effect of financial ease or tightness on capital flows tended to concentrate on the company-sector financial position, and was not, to the best of my recollection, ever formulated in terms of the monetary aggregates as a whole (at least before 1968/9, when the IMF introduced the UK monetary authorities to the concept of DCE).

such functions generally played a major role in that sector during the early 1970s. However, following the introduction of Competition and Credit Control in 1971, the previous apparent stability of the demand-for-money function (at least for sterling M_3) broke down, and this has led, as discussed later, to changes in methods of modelling the monetary sector.

None the less, with both the money stock and reserve flows thus independently estimated, DCE became by definition a residual variable. Within DCE, the PSBR was of course determined by the interplay of fiscal policy and economic developments. Attempts have been made by various model-builders in the UK to model the determinants of bank lending to the private sector (for an early attempt to do so, see Norton[**19**]). Perhaps partly because of the proclivity of the authorities to constrain such lending by various forms of direct controls, of varying coverage and efficacy, the attempt to forecast bank lending – whether econometrically or judgementally – has, however, been only fairly successful. Such equations often find significant and correctly signed interest-rate effects but the lags appear to be surprisingly long. Moreover, the extent of explanation of past variations is quite weak; the 'fit' is relatively poor, and the forecasting ability of such equations has been limited.

This left public-sector debt sales to the non-bank public, the largest part of which is normally represented by gilt sales, or a combination of gilt sales and bank lending to the private sector, as the usual residual (implicitly or explicitly) which varied to satisfy the balance-sheet 'adding-up' constraints. Gilt sales were in many ways a suitable residual, being large, very variable, erratic and extremely difficult to model with any success, though attempts continue to be made.

The implication of this approach, however, was that a shift in the other counterparts to monetary growth, for example a reserve flow or a change in the PSBR, would, *given the determinants of the demand for money* (nominal incomes and interest rates), be matched one for one by an offsetting change in gilt sales (and/or bank lending). This inference was, however, found more worrying – by most UK economists – with respect to the PSBR than to reserve flows. If a rising PSBR should coincide with an unchanged level of nominal incomes (say, because other autonomous expenditures fall) and of interest rates, would gilt sales really rise (bank lending fall) at those unchanged interest rates to allow an unchanged monetary growth? Would not the balance between bonds and money holdings be changing, and would that not require a shift in interest rates? If interest rates then rose, in response to a changing bond/money ratio, would a higher PSBR (given unchanged incomes) really lead to a falling money supply?

In contrast, the implication that a rise in the reserves of £*X* million would be, more or less automatically, accompanied by higher gilt sales (lower bank lending) of the same order was regarded as a near enough approximation to the truth by those close to the workings of those markets. Bank spokesmen always stressed how closely the gilt and foreign exchange markets watched each other. Any new information of a kind likely to change sentiment markedly on the foreign exchange market would affect confidence in the same way in the gilts market (not least because the authorities were expected to vary administered short-term interest rates in response to external developments). Moreover, it was widely believed that, whenever expectations of any likely change in the exchange rate took hold, companies would seek to defend their position by leading and lagging payments over the exchanges, and that the resulting financial disequilibria would be more usually financed by a changing usage of bank borrowing than by companies varying their holdings of transactions sterling deposit balances. In short, the implication of this approach, that reserve flows would be offset in these circumstances virtually one for one by changes in gilt sales and bank lending (and thus in DCE) seemed – at least to Treasury – Bank financial forecasters – reasonably in line with reality.

Monetarist models of the fixed exchange-rate regime

Before the 1970s standard Keynesian models predominated; there were no monetarist forecasting models. Since that time a number of empirically estimated, fully articulated, monetarist models of the UK have been developed (Laidler[**15**], Minford[**17**], Smith[**23**]). Some of these have been estimated over longer time periods (annual data since 1880 – Smith), others refer primarily to the period since 1972 (Minford). None of these has yet been regularly used for forecasting. [*Author's note*: This is no longer true. Minford's model has now been regularly used for forecasting since 1979.] The London Business School model, which is of course used for forecasting purposes, has moved in some respects towards a more monetarist stance but this shift of approach has only occurred since the change to a managed float.

Be that as it may, perhaps the most interesting comparison of monetarist and standard Keynesian analysis within the UK context (for the fixed exchange-rate period prior to 1972) can be found in the presentation of Laidler's model, alongside more standard Keynesian models such as that of the National Institute, at the National Institute Conference (December 1977), as recorded in Posner[**20**]. There are, of course, a number of important differences both in causal analysis and in model methodology (for example, the use of small models) between monetarist and standard Keynesian approaches. The crucial difference for analysis of the nexus of domestic – international monetary flows, however, lies in the assumption made by Laidler that DCE is 'exogenously' determined. This assumption is now commonly made in 'international monetarist' analyses (see Frenkel and Johnson[**7**] and Whitman[**24**]) of open economies under fixed exchange rates. Laidler does not discuss or seek to justify it (Laidler and O'Shea[**15**, p. 2]). The status of this assumption is not clear to me; in particular whether it implies a belief that (i) the authorities have actually sought and been able to control DCE exactly; (ii) the authorities have sought to control DCE with an outcome diverging from their intention that was random or unrelated to other economic developments; (iii) the authorities *could* have controlled DCE, so, whether or not they did, it is right to assume that it was independently determined; or (iv) some other unstated rationale.

If the justification is (iii), this seems to me to be an invalid approach. There are many variables that could in principle under certain hypothetical circumstances (for example, after a change to a more socialist economy) be policy-determined. If in the actual economy being modelled, however, such variables are endogenously determined, that is how they should be modelled, whether or not they could in principle be policy-determined. How can one tell whether, or not, a particular variable has been policy-determined? I find it difficult to comprehend how any variable could be described as policy-determined, unless the authorities themselves were consciously trying to determine it. In this period until 1972, apart from the 1969–70 episode, the authorities did not attempt to control DCE.

There are those, moreover, who query whether, even in those episodes, 1969/70, 1977/78, when the authorities *were* trying to limit the growth of DCE, they had sufficient control of the system to do so effectively. It may be noted that the London Business School regards control over the size of the PSBR as the only really effective way for the authorities to control DCE. Certainly in 1969/70 and in 1976/77 changes in fiscal policy appeared to be an essential ingredient in controlling monetary developments. Apart from such crisis periods, however, fiscal policy has usually been determined mostly by 'real' macroeconomic considerations without much direct concern for its monetary implications.

With the PSBR determined by such 'real' considerations, control of DCE would then have depended on monetary means. These inevitably involve either controlling the volume of credit flows by price, through interest-rate adjustments, or by rationing. The authorities in the UK have frequently felt forced to resort to some form of quantitative control, bank lending ceilings prior to 1971, the 'corset' on occasions since then. The disadvantages of such rationing devices are, however, considerable, and monetarists tend to be particularly sceptical of the efficacy of direct controls.

Apart from such direct controls, monetary measures to influence DCE, particularly to influence bank lending and public-sector debt sales, work through changes in interest rates. As noted earlier when discussing equations for modelling bank lending and gilt sales, movements in interest rates have not had any very clear, quick or predictable effect on these financial flows. There are a number of economists and outside observers who believe that changes in the institutional structure, for example moving to an auction system for gilt sales or control of the monetary base, would allow much greater control over the monetary aggregates, possibly without much offsetting loss (if any) in greater instability in interest rates. It is not the purpose here to analyse such arguments. But, even were it true in principle that the monetary authorities might have changed the system to exert more grip on DCE, the crucial point remains that we must model the system as it has actually been, *not* as it hypothetically might be.

On the other hand, for the purpose of modelling the nexus of domestic – international monetary flows, it may not matter (to an international monetarist) exactly how DCE is determined, so long as its determination is independent of reserve flows. If DCE, however caused, should be independent of reserve flows, then given the demand-for-money function, the interplay of the (otherwise given) DCE and the demand-determined money stock[1] *must* cause reserve flows, which thus become determined entirely within the monetary field.

Unfortunately for the simpler international monetarist models, this independence does not exist. It may be reasonable to posit that there is unlikely to be much short-term feedback from reserve flows to the government's fiscal position, for example the CGBR and PSBR. Accordingly a finding of some correlation between short-term (monthly) movements in the CGBR and external flows (as has appeared in some Bank of England studies) might be interpreted in terms of one-way causation. For the other elements of DCE, for example gilt sales and bank lending, I have already outlined why officials in the Bank believe in the existence of strong two-directional causality.[2] Such two-directional causality would result in reserve outflows causing DCE to rise, as well as 'autonomous' increases in DCE causing reserve outflows. If uni-directional causality is assumed, then the resulting bias will lead the apparent statistical relationship to appear exaggeratedly strong.

Once, however, one assumes that causality is one-way, from DCE to reserve flows, reserve flows must by definition be determined entirely within the monetary field. International monetarists have, however, on several occasions (Bean[**4**] and Zecher[**25**]) sought to establish the point empirically in the following manner. Given a demand-for-money function of the form, $M_D = f(Y,i)$, and identities (subject to the qualifications in section 2) R +

[1] In some international monetarist models an increase in DCE is offset one for one by a decline in international reserves. Apart from depending on the stability of the demand-for-money function, this latter conclusion would also seem to require that a change in DCE would not of itself bring about a change in the arguments in the demand-for-money function. Of course, by definition (remembering the appropriate qualifications from section 2) $R = \Delta M - DCE$. But unless ΔM is fixed independently of DCE, it will not be true that $dR/dDCE = -1$. I am indebted to R. N. Brown for spelling this out for me.

[2] B. Hilliard of the Economic Intelligence Department of the Bank has been studying daily data of foreign exchange and gilt markets over the period March 1976–March 1977 to see if more frequent observations can throw any light on the direction of causality. His results suggest that, during this period, there was no causal relationship between exchange flows and gilt market interest rates, but that there was bi-directional causality between exchange flows and official gilt sales with a somewhat stronger link from exchange flows to gilt sales then vice versa.

$DCE = \Delta M_s$ and $M_s = M_D$, it is a simple matter of substitution and linearisation to construct the equation

$$R = b_1\Delta Y + b_2\Delta i - b_3\ DCE$$

where $b_1>0$, $b_2<0$ and $b_3 = 1$. Such an equation is then run, and if the values of the coefficients are as stated above, and its various statistical characteristics successful, then the international monetarist theory is said to be confirmed. In fact, nothing of the sort is confirmed. What the equation actually represents is no more and no less than a roundabout method of testing the stability of the demand for money, the only behavioural function involved. Meanwhile the crucial issue for international monetarism is whether DCE can be assumed to be fixed *independently* of external flows, and what is really required to be proved is instead assumed at the outset.

With reserve flows given by monetary developments, the remainder of the balance of payments must dance to the monetary tune. Subject perhaps to the general proviso that monetarists, being market optimists, tend to expect higher (long-run) price elasticities than do Keynesians, monetarist equations for the current account, in so far as such an equation is included at all, might be roughly similar to Keynesian equations. Let us anyhow for the moment take the estimated current account (*CA*) as given. Then in turn we can construct an international monetarist equation (see, for example, Kouri and Porter[**13**]) for the capital account (*KF*), as follows:

$$KF = b_1\Delta Y + b_2\Delta i -_3 DCE - b_4 CA$$

where b_1, b_2, b_3 take on exactly the same values as in the equation determining reserve flows, and $b_4 = 1$.

On this basis, therefore, we appear to be asked to believe that capital inflows into a country are reduced by rising interest rates and an improved current account (one for one with respect to the latter) and raised by higher domestic nominal incomes. Although it is quite plausible to expect rising interest rates and capital outflows to be synchronously related (causality goes in both directions, and 'bad' news will induce both capital outflows and higher interest rates), the causal process implied by the above equation seems to me totally counter-intuitive.

In another respect, however, 'international monetarists' agree closely with standard Keynesians that the money stock is demand-determined under a fixed exchange-rate regime. Not only are interest rates set by the authorities (or by the level of world interest rates) but also the exchange rate is pegged. International monetarists give particular emphasis to the elasticity of substitution between domestic and foreign (financial) assets, so that the money stock is (assumed to be) always brought back very rapidly into equilibrium with the quantity demanded by such external flows.

Supply disturbances

There is no doubt that there can be shocks and disturbances to various elements (for example, credit markets) affecting DCE and reserve flows, on the supply side of the monetary system.[1] The standard Keynesian analysis, usually assuming that the demand-for-money function is always exactly satisfied, implies that the monetary effects of such supply-side disturbances are (virtually immediately) dissipated by shifts between any excess (shortfall) of money resulting from the disturbance and public-sector financial assets (bonds). This can be viewed as the natural consequence of a standard Keynesian assumption of a close substitution between money and (short-dated) bonds and bills. The international monetarists, as noted above, emphasise instead the substitutability between domestic and external financial assets.

Several economists in the UK, and more particularly in Australia, have queried this assumption of quick adjustment, whether or not interest rates and exchange rates are fixed. They argue that a supply-side disturbance, such as, for example, a sizeable increase in net public expenditures or in bank lending, will initially put money balances into recipients' hands in excess of the amount that they would want to keep in relation to their incomes and the going level of interest rates. Only in some instances will the recipients want to use such excess balances directly to buy public-sector debt or foreign assets at their pegged rates. Accordingly these economists (Jonson, Moses and Wymer[**12**] and Coghlan[**5**]) see a disequilibrium between the supply of money and the demand for money as one of the main short-term factors driving nominal expenditures (incomes) in the economy, irrespective of the nature of the exchange regime.[2]

This approach has so far only been incorporated into one fully fledged forecasting model, that for the Australian economy by the Reserve Bank of Australia, 1976 (Jonson *et al.* [**12**]). Certain aspects of this model have been applied empirically to the UK (Atkinson and Blundell-Wignall[**2**]), but no

[1] Economists brought up in other institutional systems may think instead of disturbances affecting either the high-powered monetary base or the banking multiplier.

[2] During the course of the 1970s movements of M_3 in the UK became more volatile and virtually all previous forecasting equations for M_3 'broke down'. Accordingly many forecasters in the UK, such as the London Business School, built up their predictions of M_3 from the supply side, i.e. DCE plus net external flows. The set of resulting supply-side equations could be regarded as providing an implicit demand-for-money function, by means of the accounting identity. This implicit equation was, however, rarely examined and made explicit. The resulting predictions for M_3 may have been in some cases checked for plausibility against subjective ideas of demand-for-money functions. However, in general, the demand for money in these forecasts was treated as a slack residual, because it was so difficult to predict. This approach, in which the demand for money was treated as a residual, has to be carefully distinguished from the Australian (Reserve Bank of Australia, 1976 – see Jonson *et al.*[**12**]) approach, in which the disequilibrium between supply and demand (separately estimated) enters as an argument into expenditure and other functions in the model.

complete forecasting model in either the USA or the UK had, up till 1979 to my knowledge, tried to utilise a similar disequilibrium analysis.

This analysis has considerable intuitive attraction, particularly so after a period in which, and in a country where, there do seem to have been sizeable monetary disturbances occurring from supply-side shocks, for example the dramatic surge in bank lending after 1971 and the large – and often unforeseen – variations in the PSBR. Nevertheless there are difficult analytical, technical and econometric problems in modelling such disequilibrium processes which make such an approach hard to adopt. For example, although there are no doubt autonomous supply-side shocks, equally it is the case that certain flows within DCE, for example the public's purchases of public-sector debt, will react endogenously to pressures within the system within a very short time. As was emphasised earlier, when discussing international monetarism, it is wrong to treat DCE as a completely exogenous variable over any feasible time horizon (*even including daily data*). The counter-argument, of course, is that it is also wrong to treat supply-side factors in aggregate (DCE plus net external flows) as entirely endogenous, particularly over relatively short time horizons, *even when the authorities are pegging certain asset prices.*

Return for a moment to the earlier example, in which there is a rise in the PSBR, but the level of incomes remains initially constant, say because a rise in public expenditures just offsets a fall in personal consumption (a higher savings ratio). If interest rates remain constant (because pegged by the authorities), standard Keynesian analysis would predict no change in the money supply.[1] Those concerned with supply disturbances would, instead, expect a rise in DCE and the money stock (taking it above the desired level), with the latter offset by some external outflows, and that the monetary disequilibrium would then have a separate, subsequent effect on money incomes, additional to and independent of the standard Keynesian multiplier.[2]

Nevertheless, such disequilibrium processes are almost by definition of relatively short-term importance. In a fixed exchange-rate regime, feasible rates of price inflation and of nominal interest rates will in the medium term be determined internationally. If the underlying rate of growth of productive potential is fixed (by other 'real' factors, such as education), then the maximum level of nominal incomes would also be determined in the longer term independently of monetary (or other demand-management) policy. If the economy should tend to return towards this maximum feasible level,

---

[1] If the exchange rate were fixed, international monetarists would, I think, predict the same. However, they might expect a transitory rise in DCE and outflow of reserves if the larger PSBR had a particularly expansionary impact on the (high-powered) reserve base of the monetary system.

[2] The rise in the savings ratio, and fall in consumption, would lead to some decline in bank lending, offsetting the PSBR increase, but this would only be a partial offset.

whether through natural market adjustments (monetarists) or through the skilful use of demand-management policy (Keynesian), then all that is left for monetary policy in this regime is to determine the division of the supply side of the monetary system into claims on the domestic system (domestic credit) and claims on foreigners, or to minimise short-run instability.

4. Modelling Domestic–External Monetary Flows under the Present Exchange-rate Regime

In June 1972, however, the UK authorities ceased defending a pegged exchange rate. The problem of modelling the external position in the subsequent period has been compounded by the spasmodic and indistinct nature of the present system. For certain periods of time it has approximated to a fixed rate system; though even during those periods there was generally no officially announced commitment to the 'cap' or 'peg' inserted, and a general understanding that such 'cap' or 'peg' could be withdrawn by the authorities at any moment. At other times the rate has been allowed to float relatively freely, though even during those periods the authorities more often than not intervened to prevent 'excessive' rate movements on 'narrow' markets, and there was a general understanding that the authorities might intervene again on a large scale if the rate movements were felt to imperil other objectives, such as competitiveness or control of inflation. The problem of modelling the past, moreover, is always far easier than the task of predicting the future, and the exercise of trying to specify how the authorities might respond to future events, when they themselves are feeling their way uncertainly forward, is not easy or straightforward.

Although the present exchange-rate regime does not conform closely to the paradigm of either a fixed, or a freely floating, system, these are the two (limiting) cases whose analytical properties have been most closely studied. Accordingly the initial, and most common, response of model-builders to the 1972 change in the external position was to treat the UK economy as if it were in one or other of the two paradigmatic exchange regimes.

Prior to 1972 the exchange rate entered most models as a policy-determined, 'exogenous', variable. It was still possible to treat the exchange rate in the same way after 1972. Simply because the exchange rate is assumed to be 'policy-determined', it need not also be held at a fixed rate.[1] One approach to modelling the UK system, post-1972, has been to make some opening assumption about a 'plausible' path of exchange rates, for example that these should be such as to maintain competitiveness, or kept constant in effective terms, or whatever other assumption seems both possible and

[1] In the same way Bank Rate until 1972, and MLR thereafter, is usually seen as policy-determined. That does *not* imply that it should be modelled as if it were fixed.

interesting at the time. Then this assumed path of exchange rates is treated as an exogenous datum, and calculations of reserve flows and the balance of payments can be carried out, exactly in the same model context as before 1972. In principle this approach could be adopted just as easily by monetarists as by Keynesians. In practice, however, monetarists tend to have an inherent sympathy for flexible price systems, and Keynesians relatively more sympathy for fixed price systems; so it has been usually the more Keynesian models that have followed the approach of modelling the system as if it were a fixed-rate system.

There are a number of difficulties with this approach, though some are not serious. Starting with the least pressing problems, it is perfectly possible that, having started with some assumed exchange-rate path, it could appear from the model that there will be a (residual) inflow of reserves at a time when the assumed exchange-rate path is going down, or vice versa. Not only is it difficult to envisage how this might occur in markets, but it would seem to cause international problems; for example, it would run counter to IMF guidelines on exchange-rate management. The modellers could, however, respond that this would in itself be a useful indication to them, and to policy-makers, of likely pressures on the exchange rate, which could be taken into consideration in further adjustments to the assumed exchange-rate path and subsequent iterative forecasts.

Indeed, even if the authorities should be thought to have zero net intervention in exchange rates as an objective, it is in principle possible to model that by starting with an assumption for an exchange-rate path and iterating until the sum of the capital and current accounts comes 'reasonably' close to zero. Technically, of course, such iteration is a bore. More importantly, some of the Keynesian models, including that in the Bank, indicated that the whole system might be unstable, or only barely stable, if official intervention was to be stopped and the exchange rate allowed to find its own level. If there is a *J* curve in the current-account equation, and if the capital-account equation reacts strongly to recent changes in the current account and extrapolatively to exchange-rate changes and weakly to relative interest rates, then the exchange rate and the balance of payments can shoot off on a dynamically unstable path[1] unless and until sharply changing rates of inflation and rates of interest have a major impact on domestic expenditures. This, again, the modeller might respond, is not a fault of the model but an important lesson (if true) about the nature of the world.

The real weakness of this approach lies rather in the fact that it is a mis-specification of the actual system. For example, most assumed paths of

[1] If, in addition, many elements of the capital account are treated as exogenous, and the interest-rate path is also treated as fixed (by policy determination), then the tendency for models to exhibit dynamically unstable exchange-rate behaviour is obviously exacerbated. Factors such as these, together with the difficulty of modelling the determinants of the market's expectations, make most existing capital-account models inadequate for the task of simulating floating.

exchange-rate adjustment tend to be smooth and gentle. In practice exchange-rate changes have tended to be larger and more volatile. This may result partly from the authorities' penchant for trying to filter out 'small' deviations around the trend while not resisting major changes of trend and partly from the aims of market operators to drive any currency exchange to a level where the next short-term direction of movement is as likely to be up as down. Be that as it may, the gentle, smooth paths of exchange-rate adjustment frequently assumed are just as frequently out of date within a week or two of the forecast being made.

As indicated above, market operators know that they are in a system which does *not* approximate to a fixed-rate regime. Accordingly capital flows (and even possibly current-account flows) are influenced by expectations of future movements of exchange rates. Since these expectations are presumably based on a view of the system in which the exchange rate cannot be treated as if purely policy-determined, there would seem to be an in-built inconsistency between appropriate modelling of capital flows and the assumption of quasi-fixed exchange rates.

The chief alternative has usually been to model the system as if it were operating under a freely flexible exchange-rate regime. The usual tendency in this case has been to model movements in the exchange rate directly, and to bypass more detailed, disaggregated studies of how such rate changes bring the components of the balance of payments, the current and capital account, to sum to zero by treating the capital account as a residual, or 'slack' variable. Once again, in principle this approach could be adopted equally as easily by Keynesian as by monetarist forecasters. Thus Keynesians could model exchange-rate movements, and expectations thereof, on the basis of any set of variables they might prefer, which could if they wished include variables such as unit labour costs and exclude monetary variables. In practice, however, for the reasons discussed earlier, monetarists have been keener to adopt this approach than Keynesians.

Generally monetarist forecasters have sought to relate exchange-rate movements to relative monetary growth. This raises several questions, for example the growth of *which* monetary aggregates, *relative to what* in each case. In West Germany the authorities concentrate on *central bank money* (CBM), which can be regarded as a weighted average of currency, demand deposits and time and savings deposits; in the USA the authorities concentrate mainly on M_1; and in the UK on sterling M_3. So emphasis is placed on different aggregates in different countries. Moreover, the various monetary aggregates do *not* all move closely together in every country; the correlation between the movement of M_1 and sterling M_3 in the UK since 1972 has been notably low, at about +0.1. In practice most such models in this country have been based on the comparative growth of broader monetary series (M_2 or sterling M_3), but that may be due to little more than our own (UK) emphasis on such broader series.

A more difficult question is to what other variable(s) should monetary growth in each country be related? If the underlying rate of growth of productive potential in country *A* is much larger than in country *B*, then monetary growth in *A* would have to be larger than monetary growth in *B* in order to maintain a stable exchange rate and constant competitiveness in exportables. Accordingly relative monetary growth in the two countries has to be 'adjusted' to take account of their differing conditions in order to assess the likely effect of relative monetary growth on the exchange rate. But which conditions need to be taken into account: the trend developments of productive potential, the immediate cyclical state of the economy, financial market conditions including interest rates? The answer(s) to this question is by no means clear. The London Business School approach appears to be to adjust monetary growth for differing trends in both productive potential and possible divergences in prices in tradeables compared with non-tradeables. Since their approach depends on adjustment for longer-term trends, it is not clear whether it can properly be used for short-term forecasting or policy advice, or indeed over what time horizon it might be best employed.

That there is a relationship between relative monetary growth and exchange-rate development is an idea whose time has indeed become ripe, both in markets and among academics. Nevertheless both the analytical and empirical work necessary to model this relationship is in its infancy. Indeed, the empirical results of the present models, as unpublished work done in the Bank shows, are patchy. Nevertheless, at least in the case of the sterling – dollar exchange rate, relative monetary growth does seem to provide a better predictor of exchange-rate movements than movements in the real or nominal trade balance, which generally appeared statistically insignificant (even when allowance for the market's appreciation of the *J* curve was made) – again this statement reflects unpublished Bank work. Moreover, given the erratic nature of exchange rate movements, even patchy econometric results may seem at this relatively early stage in this work to be quite encouraging.

There are, however, certain additional problems involved in adopting this approach of trying to model exchange-rate movements directly from a quasi-reduced-form equation (based normally on relative monetary growth). As noted earlier when considering international monetarism in a fixed exchange-rate regime, the implicit equation for capital flows seems counter-intuitive. For example, *ceteris paribus*, a rise in the UK's current-account surplus would on this kind of analysis lead to an equal and opposite worsening of the capital account.

Perhaps more important, the approach appears mis-specified in that the authorities have *not* been maintaining a freely floating exchange-rate system. Instead they have continued to intervene, on occasions massively; this has led to often large divergences between DCE and sterling M_3 (M_2 in other countries). On one view it then becomes DCE, rather than sterling M_3 (M_2), which reflects the domestic monetary impulse[1] in each country, an impulse

[1] Always, however, remembering the qualification that DCE is normally endogenous, not exogenous.

whose effect is partly taken up in changes in reserves and partly in exchange-rate changes, depending on the authorities' policy response.[1] It is, however, possible to try to model this response also, in reaction function form. Such a reaction function can then be combined with the exchange-rate equation in order to try to model 'managed floating'. Some work of this kind has been done by the IMF and in the Bank, but is as yet in a very early stage.

There are therefore certain disadvantages and difficulties about the two sets of approaches discussed so far, based respectively on treating the system 'as if' it were either a fixed or freely floating rate. Analytically both seem flawed, because the heuristic 'as if' assumption is incorrect in either case. Methodologically both are unsatisfactory because neither integrates a complete forecast of the balance of payments with an econometric explanation of exchange rate determination.

Treasury economists recently have been developing an alternative approach in this area which does seem more promising. Essentially it starts with an equation to estimate expectations of the 'equilibrium' exchange rate, e^*; this can be based on whatever variables are thought, or found to be, relevant. Since many market operators seem to have become monetarist in outlook, even confirmed Keynesians tend to accept that monetary variables may (albeit perhaps 'irrationally') affect expectations. The key step is then to include the divergence between the actual exchange rate and the expected equilibrium exchange rate as an argument in the equation determining (a subset of) capital flows. This provides a link between the balance-of-payments forecasts and the exchange rate forecast. It indicates, *ceteris paribus*, the trade-off between intervention and exchange-rate adjustment, and also the interrelationship (supposing that monetary growth is a major variable affecting exchange-rate expectations) between monetary growth and exchange-rate

[1] An alternative view adopted by some monetarists (for example, Meltzer [**16**]) is that intervention to buy or sell domestic for foreign currency is primarily an open-market operation, with an effect on fundamental economic conditions virtually identical to any other open-market operation, for example bond markets. 'Once the growth rate of money is chosen, it matters little whether the growth rate is achieved by purchasing or selling foreign or domestic assets' (Meltzer[**16**, p. 12]). On this approach it would remain correct to give prime attention to the growth of the money stock, rather than to DCE, *even* when the authorities are intervening on a very large scale.

Two arguments can be advanced for concentrating on monetary growth, rather than DCE, despite large-scale intervention. First, as far as key expectational variables, such as expectations of future inflation rates and exchange rates, depend primarily on aggregate monetary growth, then the division between DCE and external flows becomes less important. Second, the greater the degree of substitutability between domestic and foreign financial assets, the less will it matter whether the open-market operations of the authorities are carried out in one or the other market. These arguments have some force, but neither seems compelling, especially the latter since exchange-rate uncertainty and exchange controls would tend to reduce substitutability between domestic and foreign assets. To take an example, the UK authorities capped the exchange rate against upward pressures between January and October 1977 and took in $11b of net reserve inflows. Would the basic economic situation, future expectations, etc., have really been the same on 31 October 1977 if the UK authorities had floated freely, but had undertaken an equivalently smaller volume of bond sales, leaving the growth of sterling M_3 unchanged?

movements. This latter relationship is, however, essentially expectational, rather than direct, in its supposed transmission mechanism; monetarists may object to that. The equation also allows a forecast of the exchange rate, if the authorities are not intervening, to be easily obtained, simply by setting capital flows to equal the current account and, given e^*, working out the implied level of e.

The work in this area in the UK is, however, still in an early, tentative and experimental state. It will remain an important and keenly researched subject over future years.

References

1 Artis, M. J. and Lewis, M. K., 'The demand for money in the United Kingdom', *Manchester School*, vol. 44, no. 2, June 1976, pp. 147–81.

2 Atkinson, P. and Blundell-Wignall, A., 'Independent monetary policy and the monetary approach to the balance of payments: a model of the monetary sector of the United Kingdom', mimeo, paper presented at a Money Study Group seminar, 1978.

3 Balbach, A. B., 'The mechanics of intervention in the exchange markets', *Federal Reserve Bank of St Louis Review*, vol. 60, no. 2, February 1978, pp. 2–7.

4 Bean, D. L., 'International reserve flows and money market equilibrium: the Japanese case', Frenkel and Johnson (eds), *The Monetary Approach to the Balance of Payments*, pp. 326–37.

5 Coghlan, R. T., 'A new view of money', *Lloyds Bank Review*, no. 129, July 1973, pp. 12–27.

6 Fisher, D., 'The instruments of monetary policy and the generalised trade-off function of Britain, 1955–68', *Manchester School*, vol. 38, no. 3, September 1970, pp. 209–22.

7 Frenkel, J. A. and Johnson, H. G. (eds), *The Monetary Approach to the Balance of Payments*, Allen & Unwin, 1976.

8 Goodhart, C. A. E., 'Monetary policy in the United Kingdom', in K. Holbik (ed.), *Monetary Policy in Twelve Industrial Countries*, Federal Reserve Bank of Boston, 1973, pp. 465–524.

9 Hacche, G., 'A review of demand for money relationships', *Bank of England Quarterly Bulletin*, vol. 14, no. 3, September 1974, pp. 284–305.

10 Hendry, D. F. and Anderson, G. J., 'Testing dynamic specification in small simultaneous systems: an application to a model of building society behaviour in the United Kingdom', Cowles Foundation Discussion Paper No. 398, 1975.

11 Johnson, H. G. (ed.), *Readings in British Monetary Economics*, Oxford University Press, 1972.

12 Jonson, P. D., Moses, E. R. and Wymer, C. R., 'A minimal model of the Australian economy', Reserve Bank of Australia, Research Discussion Paper No. 7601, November 1976.

13 Kouri, P. J. K. and Porter, M. G., 'International capital flows and portfolio equilibrium', *Journal of Political Economy*, vol. 82, pp. 443–67.

14 Kubarych, R. M., 'Monetary effects of federal reserve swaps', *Federal Reserve Bank of New York Quarterly Review*, vol. 2, no. 4, Winter 1977–8.

15 Laidler, D. E. W. and O'Shea, P., 'An empirical macro model of an open economy under fixed exchange rates: the United Kingdom 1954–70', Research Report 7810, Department of Economics, University of Western Ontario, April 1978.

16 Meltzer, A. H., 'The conduct of monetary policy and current monetary arrangements', mimeo, revised draft, January 1978.
17 Minford, P., Brech, M. and Matthews, K., 'Speculation and portfolio balance–a model of the UK under floating exchange rates', University of Liverpool, paper presented at the Konstanz Seminar on Monetary Theory and Policy, 1978.
18 Nobay, A. R., 'A model of the United Kingdom monetary authorities' behaviour 1959–1969', in H. G. Johnson and A. R. Nobay (eds), *Issues in Monetary Economics*, Oxford University Press, 1974, pp. 290–322.
19 Norton, W. E., 'Debt management and monetary policy in the United Kingdom', *Economic Journal*, vol. LXXIX, no. 315, September 1969, pp. 475–94.
20 Posner, M. V. (ed.), *Demand Management*, Heinemann, 1978.
21 Price, L. D. D., 'The demand for money in the United Kingdom: a further investigation', *Bank of England Quarterly Bulletin*, vol. 12, no. 1, March 1972, pp. 43–52.
22 Savage, D., 'The channels of monetary influence: a survey of the empirical evidence', *National Institute Economic Review*, no. 83, February 1978, pp. 73–89.
23 Smith, D., 'A monetary model of the British economy, 1880–1975', *National Westminster Bank Quarterly Review*, February 1977, pp. 18–32.
24 Whitman, M. von N., 'Global monetarism and the monetary approach to the balance of payments', *Brookings Papers on Economic Activity*, 3: 1975, pp. 491–551.
25 Zecher, J. R., 'Monetary equilibrium and international reserve flows in Australia', in Frenkel and Johnson (eds), *The Monetary Approach to the Balance of Payments*, pp. 287–97.

IX
The Measurement of Monetary Policy

1. Deterministic Models

Economists have generally tried to represent the complex real world by models that are implictly assumed to capture its underlying structure perfectly. In other words, no uncertainty is formally attached to the coefficients in the behavioural equations (most of which are assumed to be zero); uncertainty enters explicitly only through an additive error term. Moreover, the expectation of that error is zero, so that for forecasting and simulation purposes most models become deterministic in form. Careful economists will, of course, be aware of the unreality of the implicit claim to perfect knowledge of the structure of the system; nevertheless most forecasting takes place in the context of such deterministic models. We shall begin by discussing the measurement of monetary policy in such a context, then move on to take specific account of additive stochastic error, and end by considering the implications of uncertainty about the form (the coefficients) of the models themselves.

In a deterministic model there are, of course, no problems in measuring the effects of changing any policy instrument, *ceteris paribus*. The effects of some policy instruments may be small or even nil; readers will no doubt be able to think up examples for themselves. It is also possible that two nominally separate policy instruments may have virtually identical effects on the system, e.g. various forms of personal tax relief. Again, the exercise of one variable as an instrument may require a given path for another variable, and vice versa. For example, for any given path of a monetary aggregate there may be a unique consistent path for an interest rate, and vice versa; it makes no difference in such deterministic conditions whether one expresses monetary policy in terms of monetary growth or interest-rate movements.

Because they can in principle solve their system of equations to read off the effects of a change in any policy instrument, *ceteris paribus*, model-builders in general and forecasters in particular do not have much need of portmanteau measures of the thrust of policy. Of course, such measured effects will vary from model to model. In some post-Keynesian models, monetary variables (whether movements in quantities, monetary aggregates, or in prices, i.e.

[1] The references are to be found on pages 252–3.

interest rates) have little effect. In other models, for example in the kind of rational expectations model analysed by Sargent and Wallace[**11**][**12**], output (employment) will vary from its 'natural' level only if decision-makers are misguided by insufficient (incorrect) information: in this system the only policy open to the authorities, in anything but the very short term, is to inform the public about the rule of monetary growth that they *will* follow, which will then determine the rate of inflation. The differences between these supposed effects of monetary actions depend then on differences between the models themselves: that is, they are an aspect of model uncertainty – within each model measurement is conceptually simple.

Even so, there are some issues concerning measurement worth discussing in this context. These for the most part concern the balance between the various instruments, which I shall discuss mainly against the background of the extended neo-Keynesian models in common use. Among other things held constant within a deterministic model in order to measure the effect of any instrument change are the other possible instruments of policy. However, such instruments interact. Thus the choice, say, of a target monetary growth rate will have different effects on the economy depending on whether the PSBR is larger or smaller. Equally the effect of any fiscal stance will depend on the setting of the other instruments of policy. Accordingly, even in a deterministic model, one cannot measure the thrust or stance of any one instrument in isolation without specifying the state of the other instruments and the initial conditions in the system.

The balance between the various instruments may matter considerably. For example, consider combinations of easier monetary/more restrictive fiscal policies compared with tighter monetary/easier fiscal policy packages having the same deterministic impact on output/employment. The first package would probably have in many models lower interest rates, a higher output of tradeables, a lower output of non-tradeables, a higher rate of inflation, less consumption, more investment, a stronger current account and a weaker capital account. Of course, this is not to say that one or other package should be preferred on the basis of such model simulations alone. Lots of other factors should enter the judgement, including such considerations as the degree of model uncertainty attached to various policies (e.g. people may feel more confident about the value of the coefficients in the equations involving fiscal variables than they do about monetary effects), or the effects of the policies on income distribution, or the long-term stability of the various strategies, etc. Nevertheless, the point remains that in most models (though not, for example, in Sargent – Wallace type, rational-expectations models) one cannot measure the thrust of any single instrument in isolation.

So far it has been implicitly assumed that the authorities *can* undertake monetary policies of the traditional kind, i.e. can control monetary aggregates or interest rates. It is well known, however, that a small country that has an exchange-rate objective (usually to peg it against another currency) can affect neither the level of its monetary aggregates nor its interest rates. Various frictions, including induced obstacles such as exchange controls, lessen the validity of this conclusion, and in any case medium-sized countries, such as the UK, may have a small influence on world monetary growth and world interest rates even in a fixed-rate system.

Moreover, the balance of payments in the UK has often tended to weaken (strengthen) when the economy is cyclically strong (depressed), and this has tended to mean that the general direction of (monetary) policy for domestic purposes has normally accorded reasonably well with the needs of exchange-rate policy. In so far as this was true, it would have allowed domestic monetary policy-makers an illusion of autonomy, in that they were able to feel that they were choosing to slow down the growth of the monetary aggregates or to raise interest rates in order to restrain an over-active economy just at the time when pursuit of an exchange-rate policy would have had to involve a combination of policy changes and market reactions that would have led inevitably to just those monetary changes.

At the extreme, for a small open economy with a fixed exchange rate, monetary policy is limited to attempts to influence domestic credit expansion (DCE) and the level of reserves. There have been occasions when, owing to lack of reserves to sustain an exchange-rate policy, this has approximately been the situation in the UK. More generally, even with a given exchange-rate policy, there has been some latitude for autonomous policy actions. Of course, much the same considerations apply for fiscal policy. This raises the question of how far it is sensible or helpful to seek to measure the thrust or stance of either monetary or fiscal policies if both are constrained by a prior commitment to an exchange-rate policy.

If, instead of an exchange-rate policy, the authorities pursue a foreign exchange market intervention policy (which may be zero intervention – free-floating – but can also encompass non-zero intervention, for example to pay off public-sector debt), then both monetary and fiscal policies are free of that immediate constraint. In view of the interaction between exchange-rate movements and inflation, and the continuing objective of restraining inflation, it is now much less clear than it once seemed whether moving from an exchange-rate policy to an intervention policy would necessarily provide the authorities in an open economy with a useful degree of extra autonomy to direct and control the thrust of domestic policies.

Not only are there several policy instruments, but there is also a range of objectives, in general more objectives than instruments. Although it may therefore be easy enough, within the context of a deterministic model, to *measure* the effects of changes in different instruments on the various objectives, e.g. employment, price stability, growth, the composition of output (investment and consumption), etc., it will not in general be possible to state normative preferences for using one instrument (or one package) rather than another without introducing implicitly or explicitly some preference function applying relative weights to the various objectives, and indeed within a dynamic system a function that can give relative weights to their respective achievement over time.

This problem of evaluating trade-offs arises less acutely in some models. For example, monetarists tend to argue that employment and growth will be determined by natural forces, so that all that the authorities can do is to control the rate of inflation by monetary measures. Some post-Keynesian economists believe that domestic labour costs are determined by non-economic factors, so that, apart from concern about the inflationary impact of changing terms of trade, the authorities can affect output through demand management without affecting the rate of inflation. In so far as trade-offs or potential conflicts between objectives *do* remain, it is not helpful to concentrate entirely on the interrelationship between one variable and one objective, whether that be monetary growth and inflation or fiscal policy and employment.

2. Additive Stochastic Uncertainty

With the expected value of the error term being zero, it is possible to use models consisting of systems of behavioural equations as if they were deterministic in form for forecasting and simulation purposes. *Inter alia*, this can mean that, for a given path of one variable (say, a monetary aggregate), there may be a uniquely determined path for another variable (say, an interest rate), and vice versa, so that policy could be expressed just as well in either form. If this relationship is behavioural in form (i.e. involves a behavioural equation, not just identities), such correspondence will cease when the error term takes on non-zero values. Although the mean expectation of error may be zero, the likelihood of the error term actually taking on a zero value is also infinitesimal.

Once allowance has to be made for unforeseen shocks, there ceases to be an exact correspondence between monetary movements and interest rates; a choice has to be made whether to express policy in terms of interest rates or monetary growth. The standard analysis of this question was developed by Poole[**9**] based on a simple *IS*/*LM* model, assuming price constancy. He showed that the choice depended on the relative variance of the error term (the size of the disturbances to be expected) in the market for goods (the *IS* function) as compared with that in the market for money (the *LM* function). If the goods market was relatively unstable, holding the money stock constant caused interest rates to vary in such a way as to act as an automatic stabiliser. If the demand for money function was unstable, holding interest rates constant would sterilise the goods market against such financial disturbances.

A considerable part of the day-to-day debate on monetary policy is cast in these general terms, though rarely as elegantly as Poole put it. For example, when monetary growth diverges from its planned path, there will be those who will suggest that this is due to shifts in liquidity preference, to some change in the demand for money, at any rate to a disturbance originating purely within the financial system. Against this, others will point to comparisons of the relative stability of the relationship between money and incomes in the longer run, as compared with the relationship, say, between 'autonomous' and 'induced' expenditures (for example, in the famous *American Economic Review* debate in 1965 between Friedman – Meiselman[**8**] and Ando – Modigliani[**1**] and others).

That debate continues. However, the original Poole analysis was seriously deficient in that it assumed constant prices. Introducing an inflationary process into the standard *IS/LM* model significantly shifts the likely balance of advantage towards fixing monetary policy in terms of the growth of the monetary aggregates. The reason for this can be illustrated in the simple model below.

$$O_t = f(r_t - \dot{p}_{et}, z_t, O_{t-1}) + e_1$$

$$\dot{p}_t = f(O_t - \bar{O}, \dot{p}_{et}) + e_2$$

$$\dot{p}_{et} = f(\dot{p}_t - \dot{p}_{et-1}) + e_3$$

$$M_t = p_t f(O_t, r_t) + e_4$$

where O is real output, $\bar{O}$ the natural (or full-employment) level of output, r nominal interest rates, $\dot{p}_e$ the expected rate of inflation, z autonomous expenditures, p the price level, $\dot{p}$ the actual rate of inflation, and M the money stock. If the authorities try to peg r, the nominal interest rate, the system will be generally unstable. If they put r too low, O_t will rise relative to $\bar{O}_t$, raising p, and thereby feeding through to an upwards shift in inflationary expectations and a further fall in real interest rates. If the authorities instead peg M, the system will be stable. If nominal monetary growth is initially set too low to maintain the feasible level of real output, the fall in real output will depress inflation (and inflationary expectations), thereby allowing the rate of growth of real money balances and the economy to recover (though this recovery may for a time be hampered by the effect of expectations of lower rates of price increases on expenditures).

It may be suggested that the authorities could seek not to control nominal interest rates, but to control real interest rates instead (thereby largely restoring the choice between monetary control and real interest-rate control to the same factors set out in Poole's original analysis – the relative variance of e_1 and e_4). The difficulty of this is mainly that price expectations cannot easily be discerned or measured and are not homogeneous. Furthermore, price expectations are very volatile. Accordingly, the authorities could not easily measure the movements in real interest rates.

Indeed, as inflation becomes both higher and more volatile, the ability to judge whether any level of interest rates is likely to prove attractive or discouraging to potential borrowers becomes harder. Even if we could measure price expectations adequately (and if these were homogeneous), the abstract concept of the real interest rate will probably not provide an adequate or sufficient indicator of conditions in financial markets. The concept leaves out such factors as the changing riskiness of borrowing, shifts in income gearing and debt gearing, liquidity problems, etc., whereas the growth of the monetary agregates does reflect how much the public and private sectors *have* chosen to borrow from the banking system. For all these reasons it is perhaps natural that the sharply worsening inflationary experience of the 1970s has led to a wide-spread move among monetary economists and central banks towards placing more emphasis on monitoring the growth of the monetary aggregates and less on trying to select an appropriate path for interest rates.

Most central banks try to hold the rate of growth of the monetary aggregates to their intended path by varying interest rates to that end – this was, for example, prior to October 1979, the case in the USA where the Federal Reserve Board adjusted the federal funds rate for the purpose of controlling the growth of M_1. A forecast was made of the likely growth of the economy over the next few months and the federal funds rate was then set so that the money supply should grow at the intended rate given the perceived growth in the economy. If, then, given this chosen federal funds rate, M_1 grew faster than expected, this could only be due either to nominal incomes having grown faster than forecast or to an erratic error in the demand-for-money function. [*Author's note*: The Fed became dissatisfied with this procedure, because the resulting adjustments in interest rates appeared too little and too late to prevent systematic divergences of M_1 from the desired target path. So they changed, in October 1979, to a *modus operandi* of seeking to control the non-borrowed reserve base. Most other central banks, however, continued to vary interest rates for the purpose of controlling their monetary target.]

Thus, it has been argued, monetary developments, which are generally reported relatively quickly and accurately, might provide early useful information on developments in the real economy. In so far as unexpected variations in monetary growth reflected unexpected variations in the growth of nominal incomes, there would be a case for stabilising the growth of the money stock and thereby also hoping to stabilise the growth of nominal incomes along its planned path. B. Friedman[7] has analysed the case for the adoption of intermediate monetary targets on exactly this basis, that they provide additional early information on the development of nominal incomes.

This argument does not, I would contend, apply in the case of the UK. With weekly monetary data still in their running-in period, partly to allow estimates to be made of seasonal intra-monthly variations, we still have to depend for the time being on once-monthly snapshots of monetary conditions. The erratic, stochastic error in these single snapshots is relatively large. The process of collection, compilation and checking the data takes several weeks. It therefore takes several months before any trend divergence of monetary growth from its planned path can be clearly identified. By that time a range of more direct statistical indicators on the state of the economy, for example industrial output, retail sales, retail prices, car sales, trade balance, etc., will have become available.

In any case, in the short run, over a few months, movements in the monetary aggregates are likely to be influenced largely by the ebb and flow of sentiment in financial markets, e.g. temporary shifts in the pattern of investing the funds accruing to the contractual savings institutions. This is, perhaps, just another way of stating that in the short run – periods measured in terms of months rather than years – the extent of uncertainty and random variation in the money market is considerable.

Returning to Poole's original analysis, this would suggest that it would be wrong to place great weight and emphasis on *short-term* movements in the monetary aggregates. This point has indeed been emphasised by many monetary authorities. I shall suggest, however, in the next section that in the *longer term* the relationship between monetary developments and the growth of nominal incomes, especially of price inflation, is closer and more reliable. The long run is, however, no more than the summation of short runs. Although it will *not* generally be possible to state at any point of time that a current divergence of monetary growth from its planned path probably reflects a current divergence in the economy from its path, which might need correcting, none the less, a long continued undesired trend in monetary growth is – I would suggest – likely to be accompanied by an undesirable trend in the real economy.

This dichotomy between a looser short-term and a stronger longer-term relationship between money and incomes of course makes it tactically more difficult to know how soon and how strongly to alter course in response to any immediate monetary divergence. In some large part we try to obtain extra information to enable us to resolve this question. This information consists mainly of an analysis of the movements of the credit counterparts to monetary developments, i.e. the public-sector borrowing requirement(PSBR), debt sales to the non-bank public, bank advances (which together form DCE) and external flows. These data enable a story to be constructed that can help to indicate why M_3 departed from its planned course, and permit a more informed assessment to be made of whether this is likely to be a temporary blip or a more prolonged and serious trend.

In this section I have sought to review how the presence of additive stochastic errors affects the choice between monetary aggregates and interest rates as the main index of monetary policy, and also whether unforeseen developments in monetary growth could serve to provide early additional information on developments in the real economy. It is, possibly, worth ending with a slight *obiter dicta* by noting that the path of single aggregative indices of fiscal balance provides even less information on current economic developments. The divergence of the PSBR, for example, from its expected path during the course of the year provides by itself virtually no indication whatsoever of the concurrent path of the economy. The PSBR may be lower than expected because the economy is stronger than thought and tax revenues are higher, or because government expenditures (and thence the economy) are below their planned path. At least, with monetary variables there is some expectation that short-term divergences (of *M* and *Y*) will have the same sign; with aggregate fiscal variables there is no such expectation. In this latter case, for purposes of assessing current developments, it is essential to disaggregate, to review the separate developments of the various elements of expenditures and revenues. Indeed, for those watching the ongoing development of the economic system, the regular monthly data on the outcomes for the PSBR and CGBR are regarded as more important for their implications for financial markets and monetary developments than for any light that they might cast in themselves on 'real' economic developments.

3. Model Uncertainty

Most economists appear to believe, more or less, in the model which they construct. Indeed, the present fashion in model-building is to incorporate expectation-generating functions into each model whereby the modelled actors (e.g. labour, business) are put as believing that that particular model is correct. Blessed with knowledge of the true model of the economy, there is (as was noted in section 1) no difficulty in measuring the effects of any policy instrument (which may be zero) on the ultimate economic objectives. However, the presence of additive stochastic errors, erratic disturbances, may (as was noted in section 2) cause the economist to counsel greater (or less) reliance on one, or other, policy measure depending on the nature of the expected disturbances and the availability of information on their occurrence.

Unfortunately, there are many alternative models of the economy, and some of these – as has already been indicated – are contradictory rather than complementary; there is, for example, little in common between the Cambridge Economic Policy Group (CEPG) model (see **[5]** and **[6]**) and rational-expectations models (see **[11]** and **[2]**). In the real world the authorities have to steer a course amid conflicting advice and differing perceptions of how the economic system works. There is currently a greater diversity of viewpoint – indeed, turmoil of ideas, theories and judgements – than at any time since the 1930s. In both these periods severe problems of economic management appeared (massive unemployment in the 1930s, recession with galloping inflation in the 1970s) which the authorities found it hard to remedy; in both periods the economics profession has been in, often unhappy, ferment with differing ideas and theories.

In this difficult context the authorities look for some reassurance that they are moving in the right general direction, and they also want to be able to communicate that reassurance to the general public, whose members will generally find it difficult to form a coherent picture of the economic system for themselves, the more so when the experts offer conflicting stories. In a sense the authorities have to apply weights to the various models/theories/perceptions offered to review which relationships are really trustworthy and over what time horizon, and then seek to try to communicate their control over such trustworthy relationships to the general public. Such a weighting system is inherently subjective. A proposition that might, however, receive fairly general assent is that the effects of monetary policy instruments are least certain (relative, for example, to fiscal measures) the shorter the time period considered, but become more reliable and better understood over longer time horizons.

In recent years, for example (that is, in the 1970s though not in the previous decade), alternative definitions of the money stock, in particular M_1 and M_3, have had plainly disparate short-term fluctuations. The movements of M_1 can be reasonably well explained by variations in incomes and interest rates (see [**4**]). The movements of M_3 have been subject to a more complex range of influences, including financial 'distortions' resulting from changing patterns of interest relativities, especially those in wholesale money markets and, perhaps at times – especially in 1972–3 – supply-side disturbances. Although the problems of interpreting the movements in M_3 are perhaps more severe, there is more supporting information wherewith to analyse and assess its developments (in particular, the credit counterparts) and an instrument at hand (the 'corset' or supplementary special deposits scheme) to restrain untoward distortions resulting from perverse interest-rate relativities. There is some additional information, in particular on financial conditions, to be gained by looking at the widest possible range of financial series, prices as well as quantities. It would, in my view, be wrong to infer that the authorities' actions in specifying a preferred (target) rate of growth for a single monetary aggregate implied that they thought that this would provide a wholly comprehensive and individually sufficient indicator of the stance of monetary policy whatever the latter might be taken to mean.

Furthermore, the links between changes in monetary conditions and in the real economy in the short run remain relatively poorly defined, though perhaps less so than in the 1960s. In recent years, following the shift towards greater exchange-rate flexibility, the interrelationship between domestic monetary policies and exchange-rate movements has become apparent – and one could argue that in the fixed exchange-rate period there was no such thing as an autonomous monetary policy to measure anyhow. There has also been increasing attention paid to the effect of asset holdings on consumption. Even so, the estimation of the effects of monetary changes on the economy in the shorter run remains relatively uncertain, in particular perhaps the division of such effects into output and price responses.

In contrast, the short-run impact and multiplier effects of fiscal policies remain relatively clear cut, though uncertainties about likely developments (and reasons for these) in savings and import propensities have increased. Possibly more importantly, however, such fiscal actions may also generate market and confidence reactions in the economy more broadly, which could affect the overall outcome. In part such reactions can be ascribed to an earlier market response to the possible longer-term implications of various fiscal strategies. These longer-term implications are more difficult to disentangle, but generally suggest that the short-term effects of fiscal actions may be eroded or even possibly reversed in the longer term. Thus fiscal action, leading to a changed borrowing requirement, must affect the rate of acquisition and the balance of portfolios of financial assets by the private and overseas sectors. Increasingly over time, the initial once-for-all Keynesian-type impact will become overlaid by the longer continuing financial consequences. In particular, if monetary growth is held unchanged, the longer-term financial/wealth consequences of fiscal actions could lead to instability (see, for example, Christ[**3**]). The longer-term consequences of changing fiscal actions while holding to a given monetary policy are, to say the least, uncertain.

Against this, one could well argue that it should be a strategic purpose to maintain co-ordination between fiscal and monetary policy, so that a changed fiscal policy *should* involve a changed monetary policy. However in the long run, many would contend, the economic system does move towards a closer approximation to a monetarist model in which output, productivity, growth, work and leisure are determined by real, or natural, forces, and in which the rate of growth of prices depends on the rate of growth of the monetary aggregates (and on this time scale it again should not matter greatly which monetary aggregate is taken as the index). This is not to say that over this time horizon fiscal policies will not matter; indeed, they would do so greatly, but rather for their structural and microeconomic effects on efficiency, risk-taking, the return to capital, etc. Thus in the long run the main direction of fiscal policies should be towards structural improvement, while monetary policies maintain macroeconomic stability, in particular price stability.

Even if this long-run position were agreed in theory – and many would not accept it – its practical importance depends on how long this long run may be. Perhaps the long run is becoming telescoped in time, as individuals and markets perceiving the longer-term implications (as they see them) of fiscal and monetary actions seek to anticipate them by their short-term response. Thus an expansionary fiscal action, accommodated by a more expansionary policy for monetary growth, could lead to a quick fall in the exchange rate and rise in inflation sufficient to negate much of that expansion – whereas an expansionary fiscal policy, unsupported by any change in monetary growth, might be largely crowded out.

The longer the time period under consideration, the relatively more clearly understood the macroeconomic effects of monetary policies, measured in terms of the growth of one or other definition of the monetary aggregates, become (relative to fiscal policies; indeed, the longer the time period, the more important become the microeconomic and structural implications of fiscal policies relative to their macroeconomic implications). The schema outlined here is one in which fiscal actions have clear and strong short-term, but uncertain long-term, macroeconomic consequences, while monetary policies have uncertain short-term but relatively clear long-term consequences. Faced with a largely similar conclusion at the Brown Conference on Monetarism[**13**], Cagan noted that the Federal Reserve Board could act quickly, but was less deliberative and less subject to democratic pressures than was Congress; accordingly, he suggested (not entirely seriously) that the proper attribution of responsibility was for the Fed to control fiscal policy and Congress to determine monetary policy – an *obiter dicta* that he, alas, cut out of his published note as discussant to the paper by Tobin and Buiter.

The gist of the above is that monetary policy, and in particular trends in monetary growth, should be viewed in a medium/long-term context (whereas fiscal changes have a more immediate impact effect). Such considerations, if they were accepted, should presumably influence the way in which the regular statistics are assessed and interpreted. The authorities have certainly tried to focus attention on longer-term monetary trends, rather than on the erratic month-to-month variations, and have had some limited success with this. Certainly it has been easy (possibly too easy, for there is a danger of oversimplification) to communicate to the public the general nature and importance of monetary targets. The problem has been rather to discourage excessive attention to short-run movements of little significance.

The response to this accusation (of excessive concern with short-term monetary movements) from outsiders has often been that they, and their colleagues, are perfectly aware of the slight importance of individual monetary observations. What they doubt – they add – is at times the willingness of the authorities to take the necessary actions to restore monetary growth to its preferred longer-term trend rate of growth and/or their ability to do so without inducing a major change in market conditions. Accordingly, any sign of a trend developing which is pushing growth above the upper limit may be taken by them as a sign of potentially serious market disturbances ahead.

It does seem somewhat easier to express and communicate monetary developments to the general public than to do this for fiscal policy. Although monetary developments are the counterpart of many influences, e.g. fiscal policy through the PSBR, debt management, bank lending, external flows, etc., the aggregate, compiled monetary series is simple, direct and easily understood. The articulation of the two parts of fiscal policy – tax changes and public expenditure changes – seems less well understood and indeed is less frequently discussed both in Parliament and elsewhere; as is well known, the problem with simply comparing revenue with expenditures and treating changes in the difference of these two main components – that is, in the public-sector deficit – as a measure of the change in fiscal policy is that the latter is itself influenced by movements in both real incomes and prices. Trying to deal with this latter problem by estimating some 'full-employment budget balance' has not been entirely successful; the resulting numbers are a complicated artificial construct, which vary depending on the intricacies of the calculation, and which are based on counterfactual assumptions. In addition, the result depends on the nature of the aggregate tax function, yet it is not clear that the *slope* of the function (which depends of course on the types of tax that happen to be levied) is necessarily relevant to assessing the overall fiscal stance at a particular time. In this respect monetary indicators have considerable relative advantages.

To conclude, it is often asked whether there are 'measures of monetary policy' comparable with those (e.g. the full-employment budget deficit) available for fiscal policy and if not, why not?' I have, however, increasingly come to wonder whether this is a sensible question. In section 1 I argued that it is not possible to measure the effects of any policy change without taking into account the state of other instruments of policy and initial conditions in the economy; moreover, even then, it would not be possible to make normative statements about alternative policy settings without being explicit about (subjective) preference functions. In section 2 it was suggested that the weight to be attached to any potential instrument should depend both on the nature of the economic disturbances foreseen and the availability of information on these. In section 3 it has been argued that uncertainty about the nature and workings of the economic system is such that the authorities have to base their actions on judgement about which relationships are likely to prove most reliable and trustworthy. Against this kind of background, the concept that there is some satisfactory single measuring-rod of the stance of policy, whether for monetary or fiscal policies, seems unrealistic. This is not to say that it may not be sensible for certain purposes to adjust the budget deficit for cyclical factors (on to a full-employment basis) to remove certain feedback effects (a possible distorting influence from which monetary aggregate series appear relatively immune). To suggest, however, that such artificial, and counterfactual, adjustments thereby provide a better measure, whether for positive or normative purposes, of the stance of fiscal policy than is available for monetary policies seems to me difficult to sustain.

References

1 Ando, A. and Modigliani, F., 'The relative stability of monetary velocity and the investment multiplier', *American Economic Review*, vol. 55, September 1965.
2 Barro, R. J., 'Rational expectations and the role of monetary policy', *Journal of Monetary Economics*, vol. 2, 1976.

3 Christ, C. F., 'Some dynamic theory of macroeconomic policy effects on income and prices under the government budget restraint', *Journal of Monetary Economics*, vol. 4, 1978.

4 Coghlan, R. T., 'A transactions demand for money', *Bank of England Quarterly Bulletin*, vol. 18, March 1978.

5 Coutts, K. J., Cripps, T. F. and Anyadike-Danes, M., *The CEPG Model of the UK Economy: Technical Manual, 7th Edition*, pamphlet, Department of Applied Economics, Cambridge Economic Policy Group, 1981.

6 Fetherston, M. J., *Technical Manual on the CEPG Model*, pamphlet, Department of Applied Economics, Cambridge Economic Policy Group, 1976.

7 Friedman, B. M., 'The inefficiency of short-run monetary targets for monetary policy', *Brookings Papers on Economic Activity*, no. 2, 1977.

8 Friedman, M. and Meiselman, D., 'Reply to Ando and Modigliani and to DePrano and Mayer', *American Economic Review*, vol. 55, September 1965.

9 Poole, W., 'Optimal choice of monetary policy instruments in a simple stochastic macro model', *Quarterly Journal of Economics*, vol. 84, May 1970.

10 Sargent, T. J., 'A classical macroeconomic model for the United States', *Journal of Political Economy*, vol. 84, April 1976.

11 Sargent, T. J. and Wallace, N., ' "Rational" expectations, the optimal monetary instrument and the optimal money supply rule', *Journal of Political Economy*, vol. 83, April 1975.

12 Sargent, T. J. and Wallace, N., 'Rational expectations and the theory of economic policy', *Journal of Monetary Economics*, vol. 2, 1976.

13 Stein, J. L. (ed.), *Monetarism*, North-Holland, 1976.

X

Disequilibrium Money – A Note[1]

1. Introduction

In recent years there has been a growing application of the concept of 'disequilibrium' between the demand for and supply of money, both as a means of elucidating certain monetary developments, i.e. to help explain movements in the observed monetary aggregates [**5, 6, 11, 13, 31, 33, 34, 38**],[2] and, more comprehensively, to treat such disequilibria as one of the major forces driving economic developments in economic models of certain countries, e.g., UK, Australia, USA [**15, 16, 20, 31, 32, 41**]. However, the basic concept of 'disequilibrium money' is contentious (see in particular White [**57**]), the empirical basis for adopting the approach is debatable, and its application in economic analysis still in a fledgeling stage. It is the aim of this note to explore these issues. The next section discusses some general theoretical and/or partly semantic questions concerning the nature of this disequilibrium. The subsequent section describes evidence from the UK which appears consistent with the existence of disequilibrium money holdings, and difficult to explain in other ways. The final main section considers briefly how adoption of this approach may influence the modelling of the structural form of relationships between monetary developments and the economy more widely.

This approach has several points in common with the unanticipated/anticipated money division developed by Barro [**7, 8**], for example the division of monetary changes into two parts which then affect subsequent economic activity differently; and there is likely to be some considerable empirical overlap between estimated time series for 'disequilibrium' and 'unanticipated' money. Nevertheless, as will become clearer in the following, the genesis of 'disequilibrium' money is quite different from that of 'unanticipated' money. There is also a discussion of the differences in the supposed impacts on the economy of disequilibrium/equilibrium money on the one hand and unanticipated/anticipated money on the other in the final main section.

---

[1] In the search to clear my own mind on the question of 'disequilibrium money' I have been much helped by colleagues in the Bank and by James Davidson, Laurence Harris and David Laidler. They are not, however, responsible for such confusion and error as may have remained.

[2] The references can be found on pages 274–6.

2. The Concept of 'Disequilibrium'

The term 'disequilibrium' in this context is perhaps unfortunate, since it raises unnecessary hackles among several schools of economic thought. Among the Chicago School (for example, see Reder [**51**]), it is often argued that each individual would rationally so arrange his/her affairs as to maximise his/her utility in the context of perceptions about the conditions and options available. Thus for an individual money holder, or an aggregate of such holders, to be said to be in disequilibrium would be contrary to basic economic principles, and *a priori* implausible. Keynesians, on the other hand, object that, since money is the most liquid of all assets, it is the one most easily adjusted, so that the money market is perhaps the market least likely to be in 'disequilibrium': recall, for example the Radcliffe Report [**49**, paras 387–92]).

Part of the problem in this respect is undoubtedly semantic, and the term 'disequilibrium' is perhaps loosely used. It is, however, by now probably too late to establish any different nomenclature, other than 'disequilibrium money', to describe the approach adopted by its adherents, of whom perhaps Laidler [**38, 39, 41**] is the most persuasive and influential. So the purpose of the rest of this section is to describe more precisely what is (really) meant by this term.

The essence of this approach is to regard money holdings as in some large part being used as a buffer stock. The analysis and rationale of buffer stocks is reasonably well understood, notably in the case of analysis of the role of inventories. Decision-making is costly in itself; the decision to change plans, e.g. of price levels, production processes, durable expenditures, itself involves various costs, and may be quasi-fixed in the sense that they would be expensive to reverse (for example, the resale value of a durable asset is usually well below its purchase price); the organisational effort involved in restructuring inputs in a productive process is considerable. Moreover, there is difficulty in interpreting signals about changing economic conditions and options, e.g. the distinction between transitory and permanent changes. So economic agents may rationally and optimally decide to respond to the continuing stream of developments, 'news' and 'shocks', *not* by a thoroughgoing, continuous reconsideration of their full economic dispositions, but allowing such shocks to impinge[1] initially upon certain assets/liabilities whose characteristics make them suitable to act as buffers. Once the holdings in these buffer stocks pass a pre-set limit, or a major (permanent) shock is perceived, then the agents will proceed to reconsider their economic dispositions. This seems rational behaviour and accords with considerable practical evidence.

---

[1] Indeed, the existence of such buffer stocks may enable agents to economise on the time and trouble involved in obtaining fuller information on the nature of these shocks, a point which Laidler has made.

The next stage in the argument is to claim that money holdings are pre-eminently suitable to be used by agents as buffer stocks. Shocks in other markets involving unforeseen changes in the price, or volume, of transactions must involve counterpart changes in cash flows. So shocks in *all* other markets[1] will tend to have a counterpart effect on cash flows. For example, if goods are rationed and subject to price control, as has occurred during wartime and in socialist economies, the initial effect of that is likely to find a reflection in holdings of money. For most agents fluctuations in cash flows are settled through variations in monetary balances, so money holdings become the focus through which shocks elsewhere in the system are initially absorbed. This is not universally so, however; in some cases such shocks may be met in large part by changes in outstanding credit positions (e.g. trade credit), especially in the case of companies. The interrelationship between credit markets and money markets is a crucial, but complicated, part of this story which is considered further later. Despite this important qualification, the function of money as a means of payment does tend to cause shocks in other markets to have a counterpart focus, initially at least, on money holdings.

Furthermore, there is relatively little cost to the money holder in allowing money holdings to vary up and down in response to such shocks. Compared with the cost of altering labour programmes, durable asset purchases, price/wage levels, or even inventories of consumer/producer goods, the cost of allowing money holdings to vary, within limits, is slight. The main cost that has been identified is forgone interest, and the main short-term alternative to money holding is generally seen as some other financial asset. Meanwhile competitive pressures and technological developments have been making it increasingly easy for funds to be switched quasi-automatically out of zero-, or low-, yielding deposits into interest-bearing deposits. Although the treatment of money holdings as flexible inventories was initially developed by economists such as Baumol [**10**], Tobin [**53**], Miller and Orr [**43, 47**] and Akerlof [**1, 2**] primarily in relation to sight (demand) deposits, there must now be a more general (institutional and empirical) question whether a wider set of monetary (liquid) assets now plays the main role of short-term buffer.

If, then, money holdings are to be seen in some large part as fulfilling a buffer-stock role, one has to review the question of how the individual agent and/or the system as a whole responds to changes in the supply of money. Consider a case in which the authorities expand the monetary base and encourage the extension of bank loans and some reduction in interest rates. Not only may the initial borrower of the loan be for a time willing to hold (part of) the extra funds from that loan in money balances, while in the

[1] It is sometimes argued by Keynesians that these fluctuations in cash flow, causing shocks to money holdings, are only the monetary reflections of income shocks. It is generally true that income/expenditure shocks will have such monetary reflections in individuals' money holdings (see, for example, Darby[**19**]), but shocks to monetary holdings can also come from other markets, credit markets, asset markets more generally.

process of disbursing the funds, but also the recipient of the resulting additional expenditures will hold the higher balances for some period of time – depending on his/her initial balance, his/her preferred limits, and the frequency of inspecting his/her balances/making decisions, etc.

Thus an initial shock to the supply of money is likely to be buffered, in the short run, both by a larger proportion of agents moving towards the top end of their acceptable inventory of holdings and by the delays between holdings going beyond such notional limits and decisions being taken and made effective to return money holdings to their preferred starting-point, e.g. by expenditures on other assets, or by changing work/leisure programmes. Even when the tolerance, the range between the limits, is quite small and the speed of individual agents' reactions to shocks is fast, the overall lag in adjustment for the system *as a whole* in response to a supply shock, particularly if that shock is concentrated narrowly in the system rather than widespread, can be lengthy, because of the resulting long-lasting interaction between the atomistic agents within the system.[1]

I would contend that throughout this process each individual agent is behaving rationally and achieving his optimal position, given external conditions. Yet there will be a time lag between the supply shock and the system as a whole adjusting to that.[2] In that sense aggregate demand and aggregate supply are not in full equilibrium.

It is desirable at this stage to try to differentiate the above kind of lagged adjustment – in response to supply-side shocks with no change in the underlying demand for money, in the sense that the pre-set limits and the preferred return point (S, s, z in the notation of Miller and Orr) are unchanged – from those lags arising from the slow adjustment of individuals' *demand for money*[3] in response to changes in the arguments in the demand function. Thus in most studies of the demand for money this is found to respond relatively slowly to shifts in the arguments that influence such demand, e.g. changes in real expenditures and receipts, in prices and in interest rates [**24, 26, 37**]. The analytical basis for such long-lagged responses is not, however, particularly persuasive, and the case for including such lags is generally empirical and positive; they appear to exist in econometric studies.

---

[1] For a study of the lags involved in adjustment within an atomistic banking system, see Hester and Pierce[**28,** esp. ch. 12]).

[2] Laidler would describe this as the distinction between the 'individual experiment' and the 'market experiment': 'Money is very easy for the individual agent to get rid of, but very difficult for the economy as a whole to get rid of, if it is being pumped in through credit creation', (personal correspondence).

[3] Once money is regarded, in large part, as serving as a buffer stock, there ceases to be, for any individual agent, a single valued demand for money. Instead, money holdings vary within limits; even so, there remain determinate parameters affecting such money holdings: the upper and lower limits themselves, Ss, and the preferred return point, z, using the Miller – Orr notation, and these parameters in turn will be structurally determined by economic variables, such as the scale and variability of cash flows, relative interest rates, etc.

Some of the reasons, however, that can be advanced for believing that money can be regarded as a buffer stock, so that shocks are absorbed in such holdings, have also been advanced to justify and to explain the posited slow adjustment in the demand for money. The combination of an assumption that money supply always equals money demand, and slow adjustment of the latter, implies that the various shocks in the economy are *not* absorbed in money holdings but somewhere else within the system – a 'somewhere else' automatically unspecified in single-equation, partial-adjustment, studies. Among the reasons advanced for slow adjustment in the demand for money are that this relates to permanent, rather than transitory, shifts in the explanatory variables (but, if so, exactly where are transitory changes in income/wealth absorbed in the asset portfolio?); generalised adjustment costs (but then, which other asset can be varied at lower cost to absorb shocks?); and failure to appreciate that levels of real expenditure, prices and interest rates have actually changed (this latter suggestion, in view of the length of lag, and implied discrepancy between actual levels of the variables and the implicit supposed 'perceived' level, sometimes appears to involve a degree of irrationality, error and illusion that would seem entirely out of keeping with rational and efficient economic agents).

Essentially the problem is that, if some forms of economic behaviour respond slowly to shocks, others have to respond the more violently, since the shocks have to be absorbed somewhere within the system.[1] Most models of the determination of the money stock imply that desired money holdings respond instantaneously to money supply shocks and relatively slowly to changes in the explanatory variables, e.g. incomes, prices, interest rates. Thus:

$$M_{Dt} = M_{st} \tag{1}$$

and

$$M_{Dt} = f(Y_t, Y_{t-1}, \ldots, Y_{t-n}, P_t, P_{t-1}, \ldots, P_{t-n}, i_t, i_{t-1}, \ldots, i_{t-n}, M_{t-1}, \ldots, M_{t-n}) \tag{2}$$

Usually in this system, especially with quarterly or higher frequency data, the coefficients on Y_t, P_t and i_t are quite low, often lower than the coefficients on Y_{t-1}, P_{t-1}, i_{t-1}, while the coefficient on M_{t-1} is generally the largest in the whole equation; and the lagged M coefficients dominate the dynamic relationships. What this must imply is that a supply-side monetary shock is transmitted with enhanced force on to the real economy, a form of financial

[1] This is, of course, the basis for the overshooting hypothesis in international monetary economics (see, for example, Dornbusch[**21**]). Since prices adjust – by assumption – slowly, other 'jump variables' e.g. asset prices, including exchange rates, have to vary by more in the short run than long-term equilibrium would require.

overshooting. Since a (short-term) change in the money supply *has to be* fully absorbed into desired money holdings, and since these latter only respond very slightly in response to short-run changes in prices, incomes and interest rates,[1] then these latter have to adjust violently in the short run. This is the basic source of Holbrook's instrument instability [**29**]; indeed, this particular problem, of overshooting in response to monetary shocks was clearly perceived by several monetary economists many years ago [**52, 55, 56**].
In particular, accepting the normal assumption that real incomes and prices are subject to considerable inertia, the lengthy lags in the demand-for-money function should have the consequence that money supply shocks would cause extreme fluctuations in interest rates.[2] Yet when interest rates are themselves regressed on movements in the money stock, incomes, prices, etc., there is rarely any trace of such apparent overshooting.[3]

Despite this latter finding, there may well be considerable validity in the view that supply-side shocks emanating in money and credit markets could cause considerable instability, overshooting, in asset prices, unless accommodated. Indeed, it is the practical experience of the instability that can ensue, primarily in other financial markets, that has made central banks so wary of trying to force short-term monetary growth into a straitjacket. If there should be an autonomous shift in the supply function, e.g. caused by a change in bank behaviour, which is not accommodated by the central bank, but instead the Bank tries to maintain M_s on the same steady path, then the result could be short-term instability and overshooting in 'jump variables', asset values in other financial markets (see Radecki [**50**]).

---

[1] White[**57**, pp. 551–5]) presents a (complicated) argument that the speed of adjustment of *desired* money holdings to short-run variations in prices, incomes and interest rates, especially the latter, will be higher when these variations are themselves triggered by money supply shocks. On the assumption that lags in the demand function are caused by transactions/stock-adjustment costs, this follows because the change in interest rates/prices (following the expenditure of part of the unexpectedly raised money supply) then validates some of the extra money balances without requiring any further adjustment; ergo, the full long-run elasticity should apply. There are several doubts about this analysis. First, if the supposed lags in the demand-for-money function are due to reasons other than the costs of stock adjustment, then this argument does not apply. Second, this argument would suggest that one should observe much shorter lags between movements in money and incomes/interest rates, when the main cause of variation is shocks to the money supply function. Even admitting the possibility/likelihood that the dynamic response of the system may shift depending on whether the shocks came (primarily) from the supply or the demand side, this argument would suggest that the observed relationship between monetary changes and income/interest-rate changes either results primarily from demand-side shocks, and/or hides even longer lags, lower short-run elasticities, in response to pure demand-side shocks.

[2] Having run a standard demand-for-money function (both £M_3 and M_1), we used it to examine how much (long-term) interest rates would have to jump in the same quarter in order to equilibrate a 1 per cent change in the money stock, on the assumption that real incomes and prices remained unchanged. The answer (for both £M_3 and M_1) was about 3 per cent (300 basis points).

[3] Similarly, we regressed the (long-term) interest rate against the money stock, real incomes and prices. Again we used the results to examine the supposed effect of a 1 per cent change in the money stock, real incomes and prices remaining constant, on interest rates in the same quarter. The answer (for both £M_3 and M_1) was about 0.05 per cent.

Even though there may be *some* practical rationale for the view that money demand responds instantaneously to shocks to the money supply, but only after a long lag to shocks to arguments in the demand equation, it is questionable whether this extreme view of the relative speeds of adjustment is the whole truth. If the money stock does act in some large part as a buffer stock for individual economic agents, then can one continue to require, at the aggregate level, that $M_S = M_D$, that equation (1) holds? If, instead, we should call the individual agent's demand for money the level of his/her preferred return point (z), when re-adjusting after hitting a limit, then clearly it is *not* necessary either for individuals or for an aggregate of agents in any short period to be in a condition where $M_S = M_D$. In the next section I shall outline various reasons, largely based on historical developments in the UK during the 1970s, that have led me to believe that $M_S \# M_D$ at any individual observation.

3. UK Monetary Experience and 'Disequilibrium'

Historical experience, 1971–81

During the course of the 1970s and early 1980s the UK monetary system experienced a number of changes in its regulatory and structural framework, accompanied by both consequential and autonomous changes in bank behaviour, that could be described as inducing a series of 'supply-side shocks'.

At the outset in the autumn of 1971 direct quantitative controls over bank lending, which had been in force on the main clearing banks continuously since 1964 and had been applied for most of the post-war period, were removed. A combination of this easing of credit restrictions, the advent of liability management, increased competition from foreign and 'fringe' banks, a boom atmosphere in 1972–3 with strongly rising asset prices, etc., led to a dramatic expansion in banking growth, bank lending and interest-bearing (largely wholesale) liabilities.

The pressures that this monetary expansion generated, both on inflationary developments, such as the asset price surge, notably in housing and land prices, and on official policies, notably on the level of nominal interest rates, led to the introduction of a new form of direct control, the supplementary special deposits scheme, or 'corset', at the end of 1973, which imposed increasing penalties on marginal extensions of interest-bearing eligible liabilities beyond a certain rate of growth; this had the effect of constraining liability management (see Hotson [**30**]). A combination of this, a downturn in the economy following the first oil shock, falling asset prices, and a shift in banking attitudes back towards prudence, higher margins and caution in the aftermath of the secondary banking crisis and the 'lifeboat', Herstatt, etc., led to a period of several years (1974–7) during which monetary and credit growth was comparatively quite subdued, at least in relation to the concurrent rate of inflation and growth of nominal incomes.

With the economy beginning to recover in 1977–8, partly on the basis of an unsustainable fall in short-term interest rates,[1] and with the traumas of financial fragility of 1974–5 fading slightly into the background, monetary expansion started to gather strength again. For a time the renewed expansion was held in check by the reimposition of the 'corset' in June 1978. But particularly after the abolition of exchange controls in October 1979 it became apparent that much of the effect of the corset was largely cosmetic, diverting financial flows into other channels rather than blocking them. Nevertheless, when the 'corset' was abolished in June 1980, the resulting reintermediation and jump in the monetary data was stronger than had been expected.

Despite high interest rates, again largely established in order to restrain monetary growth (and despite the partly resulting fall in output, inflation and rate of growth of nominal incomes), bank lending, and to a lesser extent £M_3, continued to grow at a very rapid pace throughout 1979–82. Moreover, at a time when there was some temporary decline in the pace of bank lending to industry in 1981, the clearing banks embarked on an aggressive entry into the housing mortgage market, which, apart from an earlier spree in 1973, they had previously left to building societies. In addition, during 1981, there were further disturbances to financial markets resulting from the civil service strike; since the strike largely took the form of refusing to process tax receipts, this resulted in vast cash outflows from the public sector during and immediately after the strike (as rebates were cleared before arrears were called), followed by almost equally massive cash inflows in the latter half of 1981/82.

The paths of bank lending to the private sector and of the broad monetary aggregate, £M_3, over the period 1970–82 are shown in Figure A. This brief historical account above has set out grounds for believing that the main fluctuations in these time series were significantly influenced by supply-side shocks.

Be that as it may, studies of the demand for money in the UK at the beginning of the 1970s, **[22, 26, 40]** had suggested that the demand for £M_3 was reasonably well behaved, and about as stable and good-fitting as the demand for M_1.

During the course of the 1970s that finding, of the stability of the demand for £M_3, collapsed. In general, subsequent findings from empirical studies have shown that the value of the lagged dependent variable tended to rise to or above unity, so that no long-term 'equilibrium' values could be ascer-

[1] This occurred over the period January–October 1977, during which time the authorities struggled to hold down the level of sterling, which appeared obviously undervalued, by a combination of interest-rate reductions and exchange-market intervention, with the latter largely sterilised by gilt sales.

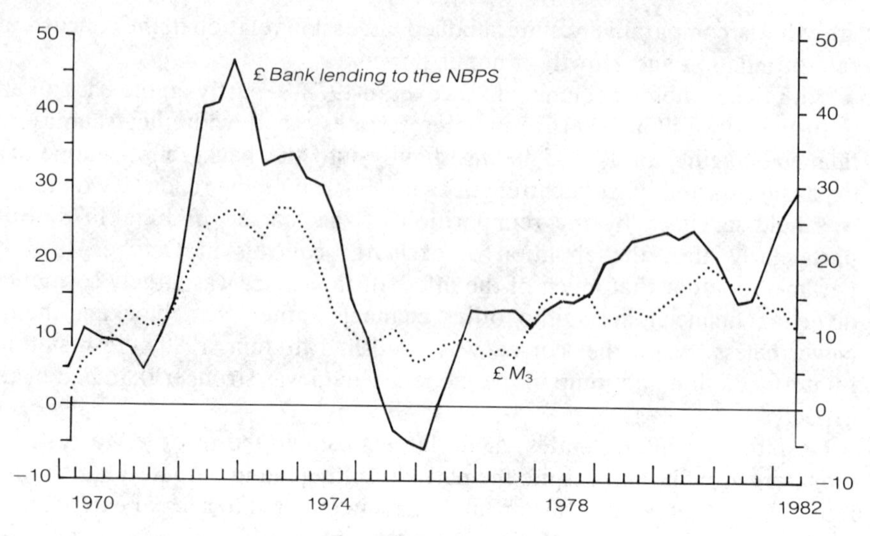

FIG. A *Bank lending and money supply: % rate of growth over previous year (seasonally adjusted)*

tained; the effect of interest rates often ceased to be significant; the coefficient on output and prices varied, often unstably, in differing periods.[1]

Although less research and econometric effort was expended in the late 1960s and early 1970s to estimate bank lending equations, early studies [**4, 46**] also held out hopes that reasonably stable demand-for-bank borrowing functions could be found. The breakdown in the demand-for-money (£M_3) function in the 1970s was accompanied by the collapse of bank lending equations. These proved virtually totally incapable of forecasting the main fluctuations in such lending during the course of the decade, despite repeated attempts (for a recent review see [**18**]).[2]

Adjustment to shocks in credit or debit balances?

As indicated in Figure A, spells of rapid expansion in the broad monetary aggregate, £M_3, during this period were generally associated with rapid expansion in bank lending to the private sector. Indeed, with such bank lending representing about two-thirds (66–70 per cent) of total sterling bank assets during these years, such an association is only to be expected. The

[1] 'In fact to this day no demand for money function for M_3 or sterling M_3 has been traced that exhibits even "sensible" let alone "stable" responses and which may therefore be said to provide a "reliable foundation for policy design"' (Courakis[**17**, p. 309]).

[2] 'If control of a wide monetary aggregate is to be maintained the demand for bank loans must be brought under control. Such control requires a stable and predictable demand for loans function. Our empirical results suggest that we are some way from this ideal state' (Cuthbertson and Foster[**18**, p. 72]).

simple correlation between annual (and quarterly) percentage first differences of the two series were +0.85 and +0.42 respectively. Indeed, I would argue that, with the adoption of liability management, the growth of bank lending is the major driving-force in the expansion of the banking system, since the banks will both seek and be able to attract the necessary funds to meet the demands of borrowers, by adjusting the rates which they offer for wholesale money relative to the general (or administered) rates elsewhere. But if that is the case, then in turn it may be argued that, while there may have been occasional supply-side shocks in *credit* markets, e.g. as restraints on bank lending were eased or tightened, the funds largely supporting such loans will have come largely from liability management, persuading wealth-holders, by variations in relative interest rates, voluntarily to shift additional funds into (wholesale) interest-bearing deposits. This, it may be argued, might be a supply-side shock in *credit* markets, but should not necessarily represent a *monetary* disequilibrium.

A practical, empirical difficulty with this latter analysis is that we have tried to quantify this effect, of liability management, in Bank of England studies of the demand for broad money, and have not been successful in modelling liability management in such a way as to re-establish a stable demand function for broad money. Thus in empirical work, from that of Hacche [**27**] onwards, we have tried variables, notably the differential between CD rate and the (sometimes administered) rate on bank loans (Bank Rate, MLR, banks' base rates), to proxy the relative incentive obtaining in money markets for making wholesale deposits. The empirical results frequently indicate that this (kind of) variable is significant, but generally it does *not* add enough to the explanation of money demand to obtain a stable, well-fitting, or adequate predictive equation. It may well be, of course, that we have used the wrong variable(s) as a measure of the incentive to place wholesale deposits with banks, or that this variable is itself poorly measured. One can never be sure that future research will not suggest that, properly analysed, the demand for money (£M_3) remained stable throughout the 1970s.

In any case the fact that banks now have the ability to manage their wholesale liabilities does not mean that this has necessarily become the main means whereby fluctuations (shocks) in bank lending to the private sector are funded. To the extent that the counterpart of extra bank lending is held, at least temporarily, in higher buffer-stock deposits, the less need will there be for aggressive liability management (on this point, see Coats [**13,** pp. 225–6]).

For whatever reason, in our research to date,[1] we have not been able to find a demand function for £M_3 that adequately models the actual path of the

[1] However, Johnston[**31**], using a demand-for-money function that incorporates both equilibrium and 'disequilibrium' components, following Chow[**12**], Darby[**19**] and Carr and Darby[**11**], claims to have re-established a more satisfactory equation for £M_3. So many refurbishments of this equation have been tried in the last few years in the UK, and subsequently failed, that most observers have grown sceptical of new, 'improved' relationships.

observed money stock during the last decade. Instead, there have been fluctuations in the path of the money stock which are relatively easily explicable in terms of supply-side shocks, particularly those affecting the path of bank lending, but which cannot be adequately explained in terms of the current and previous values of the arguments in the demand-for-money functions that have been tested. Moreover, if money holders had been trying to rearrange their portfolios in order to remain quarter by quarter on a stable demand function (of the kind with rather long lags in the demand function established by earlier empirical research), then one might have expected some dramatic short-term overshooting, notably in interest rates, in response to the various supply shocks, e.g. during the civil service strike in 1981. That did not occur, so far as could be ascertained.

In all this the interrelationships between the market for credit (i.e. bank lending) and the money market (i.e. the growth of bank deposits) appear both crucial and complicated. In the earlier description it was largely shocks emanating from changing bank lending behaviour that provided the supply shock, which at times in the last decade appeared to drive the supply of money away from the demand for money. Yet at the same time it is the relatively easy access of bank customers to credit facilities that is seen by some of the main critics of 'disequilibrium' money as a main, perhaps the main, reason for doubting its very existence (see [**35, 57**]).[1] In effect they argue that financial shocks will be as, or more, largely met by individual agents by buffering adjustments in their debit balances (overdrawn accounts) with banks, as by adjustments in their credit balances. Assume, for example, that a company or individual faces an unexpected drain of funds; cannot this be met as easily, if not more easily, by increasing borrowing as by running down deposits, at least in the institutional conditions pertaining in the UK, with access to overdrafts, credit cards, etc.? But if a monetary supply-side shock, say an increase in public-sector cash payments or more aggressive bank lending, is met elsewhere within the system by an offsetting reduction in borrowing, then there is no resultant unexpected, or 'disequilibrium', money injected into the system.

There is, again, considerable truth in the claim that a sizeable proportion of supply-side shocks are offset elsewhere within the credit counterparts. It was, perhaps, most obvious in the example of the 1981 civil service strike. The massive distortions in the monthly flow of cash between the public and private sectors were quite largely offset by opposite fluctuations in bank borrowing by the private sector, primarily by companies (see Figure B). In this case the

[1] 'If, as a result of such [bank] borrowing, more money comes into existence than the public at the given level of incomes (or expenditures) wish to hold, the excess gets directly or indirectly repaid to the banks and in this way the "excess money" is extinguished. In the case of credit-money therefore in contrast to commodity-money, it is *never* true to say that the level of expenditure on goods and services rises in *consequence* of an increase in the amount of bank-money held by the public' (Kaldor[**35**, para 55]; see also White[**57**, pp. 548–9]).

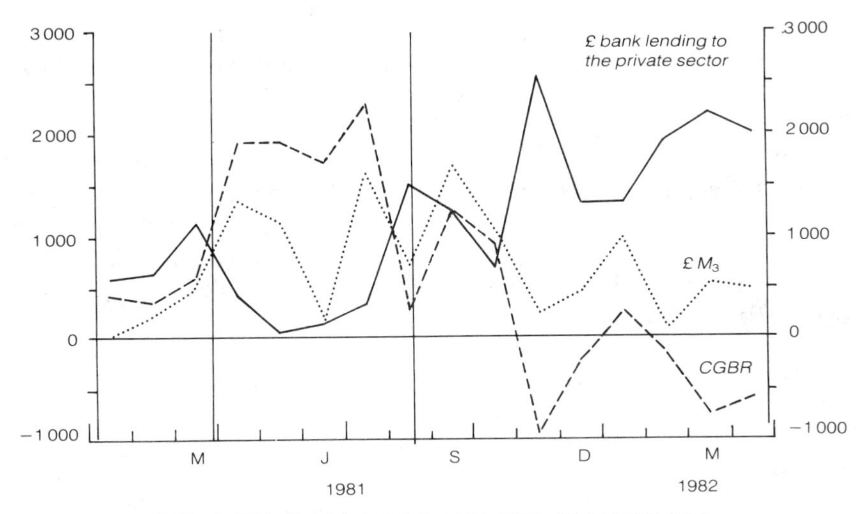

FIG. B *Seasonally adjusted banking months, flows, £mn*

offset in bank borrowing to fluctuations in the PSBR may have been as high as about 60 per cent. The 'normal' extent of such offsets is, however, difficult to measure empirically,[1] though some initial attempts have been made to do so in the Bank. Certainly, however, such resulting adjustments in bank borrowing do not eliminate altogether the effects of supply-side shocks; the offset is not 100 per cent.

The offset is probably greatest when the financial shock falls mainly on the company sector. Indeed, for large companies, and perhaps even for the company sector as a whole, the ease of access to borrowing facilities is such, and the cost of simultaneously maintaining both outstanding bank borrowing and also bank deposits (a cost dependent on the size of the 'spread') sufficiently slight, to regard their *net* position with the banking system, i.e. netting off debits against credits, as the crucial variable responding to cash-flow shocks rather than paying special attention to gross monetary assets or liabilities.[2] For large sections of the population, however, particularly persons, but also perhaps small, unincorporated companies, access to credit facilities, though improving, is still limited and expensive.[3] In these cases unexpected flows of funds would presumably continue to be buffered by changes in money holdings rather than in bank borrowing.

---

[1] Largely because causation is multi-directional, with resulting problems of simultaneous-equation bias.

[2] As is also the case with sovereign borrowers.

[3] Indeed in the personal sector money is often the only financial asset held (more so if one adds in building society deposits and national savings), and for such groups the interest-elasticity even in the long run must be near zero. All adjustment in this case is via expenditures, and hence presumably slow. I am indebted to James Davidson for this point.

This suggests that different agents, facing different (financial) opportunities, for example large companies on the one hand and persons on the other, may use different sets of financial assets/liabilities as their preferred financial buffer stock. This must be a possibility. If there are such differences among agents, it would imply that aggregated models would be subject to error. The only way to test whether different economic agents used (different) sets of financial assets/liabilities as buffer stocks would be empirical. In principle the study of portfolio-adjustment models for each of the various identified groups of agents might throw light on this, but in practice so far the results of those econometric exercises has seemed somewhat disappointing.

Disequilibrium in broad or narrow monetary aggregates?

So far in this account the monetary aggregate in the UK whose course has been described as in some considerable part occasioned by supply-side shocks has been the broad definition, £M_3. Not much mention has yet been made of narrower definitions, e.g. M_1, that probably approximate more closely to the concept of transactions balances. On the face of it, associating disequilibrium money balances with a broad monetary definition rather than a narrower, transactions balance, definition might seem odd. The theoretical/analytical studies of money as a buffer stock/inventory have generally related to a narrower, transactions balances definition.[1] Since payments out, and receipts in, are made on the basis of cheques drawn on transactions balances (when they are not drawn on unused credit facilities), the 'natural' reservoir for fluctuating inventories of immediately available funds would seem to be holdings of M_1 transactions balances.

There are, perhaps, two main reasons why studies of disequilibrium money in the UK have concentrated rather on broad money aggregates, e.g. £M_3. The first is purely empirical. With £M_3 being the main target monetary aggregate for much of the decade, the breakdown of the demand-for-money function in its case impelled immediate reassessment and alternative analysis of the factors determining its development. Not only was M_1 not so keenly a focus of attention, but more important its path over time continued to be modelled, tolerably well, by an apparently stable demand-for-money function (see, for example, Coghlan [**14**] and Trundle [**54**]). These equations, for M_1, did not fit closely, the standard error over a year being of the order of 5 per cent of the stock of M_1, and their predictive record has been patchy, but the equation has remained broadly stable over time, with 'sensible' significant coefficients whose value has remained reasonably constant in differing time periods. So there was not the same need in the case of M_1 to appeal to other

[1] Although, as noted earlier, the increasing facility with which transfers can be arranged into, and out of, interest-bearing deposits is blurring the distinction between transactions balances and other deposits.

factors, e.g. supply-side shocks, disequilibrium balances, to explain its historical course.

There is, however, perhaps another reason for relating disequilibrium to £M_3 rather than to M_1. Such disequilibria have been attributed in this note largely to supply-side shocks forcing M_S away from M_D. In the case of the broad monetary aggregates there is a clear and evident source of such shocks in the form of autonomous supply-side changes in the credit counterparts to the money stock. Changes in bank lending to the public and private sectors can derive from changes in bank behaviour – perhaps itself in reaction to regulatory changes – or from the position of the public sector, independently from changes in the private sector's money-holding preferences. Since total bank assets must equal total bank liabilities, these supply-side shocks must cause disturbances/adjustments in holdings of broad money balances. What is less clear is which *types* of deposit, on the liability side, react (most) to such credit market shocks. Empirically in the UK such shocks have appeared to affect £M_3 more than M_1, but Judd and Scadding argue that in the USA it may have been the case that M_1 was also affected by such credit shocks [**33, 34**], and in the very short run, i.e. one month or less, there is some evidence from preliminary work in the Bank of England that M_1 in the UK does respond to (erratic) fluctuations in (some of) the credit counterparts.

The phrase 'supply-side shock' has been used here to refer to shocks primarily in credit markets, in the credit counterparts. There are, however, other senses in which this same term, 'supply-side shock', may be used. One such meaning could relate to changes, innovations, in the way in which deposits are actually supplied by banks. In the 1960s and 1970s most of the main innovations, e.g. the adoption of CDs, the growth of liability management and wholesale deposits, primarily affected the broader monetary aggregates. The form in which chequeable sight deposits were supplied, at a fixed, zero, rate of interest, remained constant. In the last few years in the USA and prospectively in the UK, however, innovations in the form and nature of chequeable deposits appear increasingly prevalent.

There is a third possible meaning of the term 'supply-side shock'. Equations (identities in some cases) are frequently constructed relating the growth of the money stock to the monetary base and the money multiplier, for example

$$M = H\frac{(1 + C/D)}{(R/D + C/D)} \tag{3}$$

where M is the money stock, H total high-powered money, D bank deposits, R banks' cash reserves, and C currency in the hands of the public (and these are often described as supply-side equations). So a supply-side shock might be considered to arise from a change in the monetary base, or in the relevant money multiplier. While such equations may represent a reasonable *reduced-*

form approach for some purposes, it is dubious whether they can be properly described as a *supply* function for deposits, particularly in the case of demand deposits. In what manner do banks supply demand deposits? Prior to the innovations of the last few years, the banks have been entirely passive in the short run,[1] accepting all payments paid in to chequeable deposits at a fixed, zero rate of interest. Assume next that the authorities alter the availability of base reserves in the so-called supply function, say by open-market operations to reduce the reserve base. How can the banks react? They can try to adjust their asset portfolios, selling investments, charging higher loan rates, being more restrictive over loan conditions; they can enter money markets to seek to raise additional cash funds by bidding more aggressively for wholesale money; they can raise administered rates on smaller retail interest-bearing time deposits. One set of supply conditions which the banks have *not* sought to influence directly is that facing potential depositors of demand deposits, M_1 transactions balances. That may change in future, as competition and deregulation drive banks to offer chequeable deposits attracting market-related interest rates. Looking to the past, however, the banks have held the conditions under which they have supplied zero-interest demand deposits *constant* at all times, subject to the qualification in the previous footnote. Instead, changes in the monetary base affect demand deposits *indirectly*, via changes in interest rates and in wider financial and economic conditions, which is why equation (3) needs to be considered as a reduced-form equation, not a structural, behavioural equation.

Primarily, however, on the basis of empirical findings, it would appear that in the UK M_1 is predominantly demand-determined, responding to current and previous movements in incomes, prices and interest rates, while £M_3 is more influenced by supply-side shocks. As will be described further in the next section, this implies that fluctuations in £M_3 should feed through into *future* incomes, interest rates, etc., but the relationship between movements in £M_3 and current and past fluctuations in incomes, interest rates, etc., would be much weaker (than with M_1). Broadly speaking, this is the relative pattern of simple (bivariate) temporal relationships observed in practice in the UK (see Mills [**44**] and Batchelor *et al.* [**9**]). The contemporaneous relationships between M_1 and nominal incomes is stronger than in the case of £M_3; the relationships between M_1 and future values of nominal incomes weaken quickly; whereas the strongest relationship, though markedly less strong than the contemporaneous M_1/nominal incomes link, between £M_3 and nominal incomes appears to occur when £M_3 leads nominal incomes by about two years.

[1] In the longer run, fluctuations in the profitability of such business would lead to expansion/contractions of services offered jointly with the provision of transactions balances, e.g. the availability of branches and their hours open for business, crediting of notional interest against transactions charges, etc. But it is generally believed that these changes only occurred in a longer time horizon than that normally considered for monetary control purposes.

On such grounds most of the wider models which have been developed to incorporate the concept of disequilibrium money in Australia, the UK and the USA [**15, 16, 20, 31, 32, 41**] have based this on a broad money definition. In the USA, partly because of the focus on M_1, and concern about shifts in the stability of its demand-for-money function (the case of the missing money: see [**25**]), most of the empirical work on disequilibrium money has concentrated on M_1. But in this latter case, apart from Laidler's work[**38, 39, 41**], rather less has been done than in the UK or Australia to explore the wider implications of this concept, or to construct a model incorporating it. It is to this latter development that I now turn.

4. Modelling Disequilibrium Money in the Economy

The estimation of disequilibrium money

Although the genesis of 'disequilibrium money', as a form of financial buffer stock, is generally agreed among its adherents, there are differences in modelling it empirically. One group follows rather closely the approach adopted to modelling planned/unplanned inventories. Desired money balances (as with desired inventories) are related to long-term levels of output, prices and interest rates, while unplanned variations in money holdings are related to transitory movements in income/expenditures and also to monetary shocks directly, in so far as they can be modelled, plus an adjustment function. Models of this kind have been developed by Carr and Darby[**11**], Judd and Scadding[**33**] and Johnston[**31**].

For example, in the Carr – Darby model, with M_t being the logarithm of nominal money (M_1) in period t, P_t the logarithm of the price level, X_t a set of independent variables and $\bar{M}_t$ the logarithm of the anticipated nominal money supply, the following demand function[1] was constructed:

$$M_t - P_t = B\, X_t + a\,(M_t - \bar{M}_t) + U_t \tag{4}$$

In the Judd – Scadding model changes in bank loans were used to 'proxy for money supply shocks'[**33, 34**] in an otherwise standard demand function for demand deposits. Johnston[**31**], in part following Chow's[**12**] earlier study of the demand-for-money function, fitted an equation of the form:

$$M_t - P_t = a + b\,(Y_p, r) + c(Y/Y_p) + d\,(M-P)_{t-1} + U_t \tag{5}$$

where M_t is the logarithm of nominal money (£M_3), P_t the logarithm of the price level, Y_p the logarithm of 'permanent' income, r the comparative yield

[1] But also note the critique of this approach by MacKinnon and Milbourne[**42**].

on a substitute financial asset, and Y/Y_p the ratio of actual to 'permanent' income.

When monetary disequilibrium is considered to occur in a narrow definition of money, e.g. M_1, or in some sub-set of total bank deposits, such an approach seems the best possible. But in dealing with broader monetary aggregates, e.g. £M_3 in the UK, the approach, however, appears to overlook the historical appreciation that disequilibria in the broader aggregates have largely been occasioned by shocks, changed behaviour, in credit markets; the interaction between credit markets and monetary growth would, one might think, not be adequately captured by effectively reformulated, demand-for-money functions of the kinds developed by Carr and Darby and Johnston, though Judd and Scadding's approach is not so open to this criticism.

The alternative approach to modelling disequilibria in broad money, as adopted by Coghlan[**15, 16**], Jonson *et al.*[**32**] and Davidson and Keil[**20**], has been to assume that the money stock in the short run is *entirely* determined by the credit counterparts, by the use of the identity that bank assets equal bank liabilities. Thus the growth in total bank assets depends on bank lending to the public sector, which in turn is a function of the public-sector borrowing requirement (PSBR) less debt sales to the *non-bank* private sector (NBPS), plus bank lending to the private sector, plus certain external flows. This then leads to the (approximate) identity:

$$M_S = \text{PSBR} - \text{Debt sales to NBPS} + \text{Bank lending to private sector} + \text{external flows affecting money} \qquad (6)$$

Each of the elements on the right-hand side of this equation is then modelled separately.[1]

The difference between the money stock, thus determined in the short run by supply side considerations, and the 'underlying' demand for money then represents the disequilibrium. Simultaneity between conditions of excess/deficient money holdings and the credit counterparts is specifically modelled by allowing such conditions to influence the demand for bank lending and debt sales. Although this approach does make fuller use of information about credit markets, there are still a number of difficulties with it.

First, how is the 'underlying' demand for money to be modelled, when no single observation of the actual money stock may be a point of equilibrium between the monetary supply and the 'underlying' demand? In general, the answer has been to start with imposed, or broadly estimated coefficients that seem plausible on *a priori* grounds, and then search for values that improve the functioning of the model as a whole. This is, however, a point of weakness in these models.

There is a second point of weakness. This relates to the earlier discussion of

[1] In their model of the USA, Laidler and Bentley[**41**] more simply treat the supply of money as exogenously determined.

(some) agents' abilities to use debit balances with banks (borrowing from banks, e.g. on overdrafts) as buffers, as well as, or instead of, using their money balances for such a purpose. If this is a significant possibility, then there may be 'unplanned', 'excess' or 'disequilibrium' bank borrowings, as well as disequilibrium money holdings. It is germane to note that most equations for modelling bank lending have 'broken down' – i.e. failed to predict – at more or less the same time as the demand for money functions became unreliable (see [**18**]). Yet, apart from including a feedback term from disequilibrium money holdings, bank lending to the private sector has been modelled by the authors mentioned earlier in a standard fashion. But the implicit assumption that all buffering takes place within money holdings, and none within bank borrowing, seems unduly extreme. The construction, and estimation, of a model with a variety of (financial) buffers would, however, be a complicated exercise.

How disequilibrium money enters into economic models

By one or other route an estimate can be made of the time path of disequilibrium money. How, then, does it enter the other functional relationships in a more general economic model?

In an economy with a complete set of perfect markets, including markets in future contingencies, all possible developments, and shocks, can in principle be allowed for at the outset. In such an ideal system, the individual economic agent will be able to make his/her initial dispositions, taking account of all possible future states of the world, solely on the basis of the present value of wealth and of relative prices. Neither current income flows, nor current holdings of particular sets of monetary/liquid assets, would enter into expenditure functions when plans were initially made, nor subsequently. These ideal conditions do not, and cannot, of course, occur in reality. Information on future possibilities is scarce, unreliable and expensive to obtain. Problems of contract enforcement, moral hazard, etc., cause further imperfections in capital markets. So shocks can neither be fully foreseen nor completely hedged against in contingent markets.

In such real-world conditions agents will devise (second-best) methods of dealing with such shocks. A common reaction to such uncertainties is to use certain assets, both goods and financial assets, as buffers to absorb the initial impact of unforeseen, and possibly transitory, shocks. Only when the inventories of such buffer holdings rise/fall to some (pre-set) limit does a subsequent decision on economic dispositions become required.

So, for example, when such an inventory rises towards its upper limit, then there is greater probability that in the next time period the agent will hit the limit, and act to readjust his/her other economic dispositions, and to restore the inventory to its preferred starting level. Thus, if a company has an 'involuntary' accretion to stocks of final goods, there is a greater probability that in the next period it will readjust its factor inputs and production processes to run off such 'excess' stocks. For the company sector in aggregate, holdings of involuntary stocks, positive or negative, should enter directly into the companies' aggregate decision functions, e.g. on pricing policy, input usage, financial adjustment, etc.

In so far as money balances are similarly used as buffer stocks, shifts in such money balances–relative to the desired underlying level–should also enter directly into expenditure functions. This is the approach which has been adopted, with some empirical success in recent models[1] in Australia, the UK and the USA[**15, 16, 20, 31, 32, 41**], and some work has been currently continuing on this line in the Bank. No doubt the success or otherwise of this approach will depend largely on the positive results of such exercises, in comparison with other models. It is not, however, the intention here to restate the empirical results of these models. On the other hand, it may be useful to discuss how this approach may help to unify certain divergent trends in macroeconomics.

In so far as the complete market model represented an adequate representation of the real world, then monetary changes should only affect economic dispositions as a consequence of causing shifts in wealth or relative yields. With the effect of changes in nominal money supply on real wealth being limited,[2] this implied that changes in monetary conditions on economic dispositions should occur mainly through shifts in relative yields. But studies of the most obvious of such routes, e.g. the effect of interest rates on expenditures, generally turned up weak relationships. This was the basis for the earlier belief in the impotence of monetary policy.

This position has been challenged by the monetarists, notably Friedman, who have shown a strong relationship between monetary growth and nominal incomes (see, for example, Friedman and Meiselman[**23**] and Andersen and Jordan[**3**]). Pressed to explain the transmission mechanism involved, Friedman has appealed to myriad unobservable shifts in relative yields,[3] but since this process was so difficult to observe and/or to model directly, it could be, and has been, described as a 'black-box mechanism'.

The inventory, buffer-stock approach provides an alternative route/transmission mechanism whereby monetary fluctuations may reasonably enter

---

[1] Knoester[**36**] has been developing a model, on the basis of a similar approach, in the Netherlands.

[2] With rational expectations, expected monetary growth would be quickly absorbed in price inflation, so desired real balances and total financial wealth might decline, while unanticipated monetary growth could not, by definition, affect *ex ante* perceptions of wealth.

[3] 'The crucial issue that corresponds to the distinction between the "credit" [Keynesian] and "monetary" [monetarist] effects of monetary policy is not whether changes in the stock of money operate through interest rates but rather the range of interest rates considered. On the "credit" view, monetary policy impinges on a narrow and well-defined range of capital assets and a correspondingly narrow range of associated expenditures... On the "monetary" view, monetary policy impinges on a much broader range of capital assets and correspondingly broader range of associated expenditures'[**23**, p. 217]).

directly into expenditure functions, helping to explain the close relationship between changes in monetary growth and in nominal incomes without reference to unobservable shifts in relative prices. The approach borrows strands of analysis from both Keynesian and monetarist camps, without being clearly in either. Much of the inventory-theoretic approach to money holdings comes from neo-Keynesians (Tobin, Akerlof),[1] yet the result is to put monetary disturbances directly into expenditure functions. Whether the results of this approach are empirically successful is yet to be seen, but it does, perhaps, have the methodological advantage of building a bridge between differing schools of thought. (For a broadly similar view, see Pippenger[**48**]).

The approach also has much in common with that recently adopted by Barro, dividing monetary growth between unanticipated/anticipated components. In practice, it is quite likely that supply-side shocks would be a major cause of unanticipated monetary growth, as, I have argued, they are of disequilibrium money. Also, both disequilibrium and unanticipated money enter directly into expenditure functions and, by hypothesis, have a larger impact on expenditures than anticipated/equilibrium money holdings.

There are, however, significant differences between the two approaches. First the genesis, and rationale, of disequilibrium money is different from and–I would argue–richer than unanticipated money. Second, it is Barro's hypothesis that movements in anticipated money will pass through directly on to price inflation, with no effect on output. That is not the case with equilibrium money. The latter is by definition demand-determined, i.e. affected by current and past movements in incomes and interest rates. However, in the medium term (i.e. after the short-term effect of supply-side shocks has worked through the system) variations in velocity, the ratio of incomes to money holdings, can bring about shifts in relative prices, and yields, and these can have an effect on economic developments more generally. So findings, such as those by Mishkin[**45**], that variations in anticipated demand policy, dependent in some large part on observed past monetary growth, led to a systematic effect on real output would not discomfort an adherent of the disequilibrium money approach. (For a further discussion of the conceptual and empirical differences between the unanticipated and disequilibrium money approach, see Laidler and Bentley[**41**]).

Although this latter approach is, as yet, in a very early state of development, and still faces a number of conceptual and empirical difficulties, it has several advantages that suggest that perseverance would be desirable. It helps to explain historical monetary developments; it forces attention upon the relationships between credit and money markets; it might serve as a bridge between the methodologies of the Keynesian and monetarist camps.

[1] Coghlan in particular seeks to trace the disequilibrium approach back to Keynes.

References

1 Akerlof, G. A., 'Irving Fisher on his head: the consequences of constant threshold–target monitoring of money holdings', *Quarterly Journal of Economics*, vol. 93, no. 2, May 1979, pp. 169–87.

2 Akerlof, G. A. and Milbourne, R. D., 'The short run demand for money', *Economic Journal*, vol. 90, December 1980, pp. 885–900.

3 Andersen, L. and Jordan, J., 'Monetary and fiscal actions: a test of their relative importance in economic stabilization', *Federal Reserve Bank of St Louis Review*, vol. 50, no. 11, November 1968.

4 Artis, M. J., 'Monetary policy–part II', in *British Economic Policy 1960–1974*, ed. F. T. Blackaby, Cambridge University Press, 1978.

5 Artis, M. J. and Lewis, M. K., 'The demand for money in the United Kingdom, 1963–1973', *Manchester School*, vol. 44, June 1976, pp. 147–81.

6 Artis, M. J. and Lewis, M. K., *Monetary Control in the United Kingdom*, Philip Allan, 1981.

7 Barro, R. J., 'Unanticipated money growth and unemployment in the United States', *American Economic Review*, vol. 67, no. 2, March 1977, pp. 101–15.

8 Barro, R. J., 'Unanticipated money, output and the price level in the United States', *Journal of Political Economy*, vol. 86, August 1978, pp. 549–80.

9 Batchelor, R., Griffiths, B., Phylaktis, K. and Wood, G., 'How tight was monetary policy in 1980', The City University Centre for Banking and International Finance, Annual Monetary Review, Supplement, March 1981.

10 Baumol, W. J., 'The transactions demand for cash: an inventory theoretic approach', *Quarterly Journal of Economics*, vol. 66, November 1952.

11 Carr, J. and Darby, M. R., 'The role of money supply shocks in the short-run demand for money', *Journal of Monetary Economics*, vol. 8, no. 1, July 1981, pp. 183–99.

12 Chow, G. C., 'On the long-run and short-run demand for money', *Journal of Political Economy*, vol. 74, no. 2, April 1966.

13 Coats, W. L. Jr, 'Modeling the short-run demand for money with exogenous supply', *Economic Inquiry*, vol. 20, April 1982, pp. 222–39.

14 Coghlan, R. T., 'A transactions demand for money', *Bank of England Quarterly Bulletin*, vol. 18, no. 1, March 1978, pp. 48–60.

15 Coghlan, R. T., *A Small Monetary Model of the UK Economy*, Bank of England Discussion Paper No 3, May 1979.

16 Coghlan, R. T., *Money, Credit and the Economy*, Allen & Unwin, 1981.

17 Courakis, A. S., 'Monetary targets: conceptual antecedents and recent policies in the US, UK and West Germany', in *Inflation, Depression and Economic Policy in the West*, ed. A. S. Courakis, Mansell, 1981, pp. 259–357.

18 Cuthbertson, K. and Foster, N., 'Bank lending to industrial and commercial companies in three models of the UK economy', *National Institute Review*, no. 102, November 1982, pp. 63–77.

19 Darby, M. R., 'The allocation of transitory income among consumers' assets', *American Economic Review*, vol. 62, no. 5, December 1972, pp. 928–41.

20 Davidson, J. and Keil, M., *An econometric model of the money supply and balance of payments in the United Kingdom,* International Centre for Economics and Related Disciplines (ICERD), LSE, Econometrics Discussion Paper No. 27, July 1981.

21 Dornbusch, R., 'Expectations and exchange rate dynamics', *Journal of Political Economy*, vol. 84, no. 6, December 1976, pp. 1161–76.

22 Fisher, D., 'The demand for money in Britain: quarterly results 1951–1967', *Manchester School*, vol. 36, December 1968, pp. 329–44.

23 Friedman, M. and Meiselman, D., 'The relative stability of monetary velocity and the investment multiplier in the United States, 1897–1958', Research Study 2 in Stabilization Policies, prepared by E. Cary-Brown *et al.* for the Commission on Money and Credit, Prentice-Hall, 1964.
24 Goldfeld, S. M., 'The demand for money revisited', *Brookings Papers on Economic Activity*, no. 3, 1973, pp. 576–38.
25 Goldfeld, S. M., 'The case of the missing money', *Brookings Papers on Economic Activity*, no. 3, 1976, pp. 683–730.
26 Goodhart, C. A. E. and Crockett, A. D., 'The importance of money', *Bank of England Quarterly Bulletin*, vol. 10, no. 2, June 1970, pp. 159–98.
27 Hacche, G., 'The demand for money in the United Kingdom: experience since 1971', *Bank of England Quarterly Bulletin*, vol. 14, no. 3, September 1974, pp. 284–305.
28 Hester, D. D. and Pierce, J. L., *Bank Management and Portfolio Behaviour*, Cowles Foundation Monograph No. 25, Yale University Press, 1975.
29 Holbrook, R., 'Optimal economic policy and the problem of instrument instability', *American Economic Review*, vol. 12, no. 1, March 1972, pp. 57–65.
30 Hotson, A. C., 'The supplementary special deposits scheme', *Bank of England Quarterly Bulletin,* vol. 22, no. 1, March 1982, pp. 74–85.
31 Johnston, R. B. *A Disequilibrium Monetary Model of the UK Economy*, Bank of England Discussion Paper, Technical Series, forthcoming 1983.
32 Jonson, P.D., Moses, E. R. and Wymer, C. R., 'The RBA76 model of the Australian economy', in *Conference in Applied Economic Research*, Reserve Bank of Australia, December 1977.
33 Judd, J. and Scadding, J., 'Liability management, bank loans, and deposit "market" disequilibrium', *Federal Reserve Bank of San Francisco Review*, Summer 1981, pp. 21–44.
34 Judd, J. and Scadding, J., 'The search for a stable money demand function', *Journal of Economic Literature*, vol. 20, no. 3, September 1982, pp. 993–1023.
35 Kaldor, Lord N., 'Memorandum of Evidence on Monetary Policy to the Select Committee on the Treasury and Civil Service', *Treasury and Civil Service Committee, Session 1979–80, Memoranda on Monetary Policy*, HMSO, 1980, pp. 86–129.
36 Knoester, A., *Theoretical Principles of the Buffer Mechanism, Monetary Quasi-equilibrium and its Spillover Effects,* Institute for Economic Research, Discussion Paper Series (7908/G/M), Erasmus University, Rotterdam, 1979.
37 Laidler, D., *The Demand for Money: Theories and Evidence*, International Textbook Company, 1970.
38 Laidler, D., 'The demand for money in the United States yet again', in *The State of Macroeconomics: Carnegie–Rochester Conference Series,* ed. K. Brunner and A. H. Meltzer, vol. 12, North–Holland, 1980, pp. 219–71.
39 Laidler, D., *On the Short Run Demand for Money and the Real Balance Effect*, University of Western Ontario, Research Report No. 8105, 1981.
40 Laidler, D. and Parkin, J. M., 'The demand for money in the United Kingdom, 1955–1967: preliminary estimates', *Manchester School,* vol. 38, September 1970, pp. 187–208.
41 Laidler, D. and Bentley, B., 'A small macro-model of the post-war United States', mimeo, University of Western Ontario, July 1982.
42 MacKinnon, J. G. and Milbourne, R. D., *Monetary Anticipations and the Demand for Money,* Institute for Economic Research, Queen's University, Discussion Paper No. 435, Kingston, Ontario, July 1981.
43 Miller, M. E. and Orr, D., 'The demand for money by firms: extensions of analytic results', *Journal of Finance*, vol. 23, December 1968, pp. 735–59.

44 Mills, T. C., 'The information content of the UK monetary aggregates', Bank of England, mimeo, presented at AUTE Conference, University of Surrey, April 1982.
45 Mishkin, F. S., 'Does anticipated aggregate demand policy matter? Further econometric results', *American Economic Review*, vol. 72, no. 4, September 1982, pp. 788–802.
46 Norton, W. E., 'Debt management and monetary policy in the United Kingdom', *Economic Journal*, vol. 79, no. 315, September 1969.
47 Orr, D., *Cash Management and the Demand for Money*, Praeger, 1970.
48 Pippenger, J., 'Monetary policy, homeostasis, and the transmission mechanism', *American Economic Review*, vol. 72, no. 3, June 1982, pp. 545–54.
49 Radcliffe Report, *Report of the Committee on the Working of the Monetary System*, Cmnd 827, HMSO, 1959.
50 Radecki, L., 'Short-run monetary control: an analysis of some possible dangers', *Federal Reserve Bank of New York Quarterly Review*, Spring 1982, pp. 1–10.
51 Reder, M. W., 'Chicago economics: permanence and change', *Journal of Economic Literature*, vol. 20, no. 1, March 1982, pp. 1–38.
52 Starleaf, D. R., 'The specification of money demand supply models which involve the use of distributed lags', *Journal of Finance*, vol. 25, no. 4, September 1970, pp. 743–60.
53 Tobin, J., 'The interest elasticity of transactions demand for cash', *Review of Economics and Statistics*, vol. 38, August 1956.
54 Trundle, J. M., 'The demand for M_1 in the UK', Bank of England, mimeo, 1982.
55 Tucker, D. P., 'Macroeconomic models and the demand for money under market disequilibrium', *Journal of Money, Credit and Banking*, vol. 3, no. 1, February 1971, pp. 57–83.
56 Walters, A. A., 'Professor Friedman on the demand for money', *Journal of Political Economy*, vol. 73, no. 5, October 1965, pp. 545–61.
57 White, W. H., 'The case for and against "Disequilibrium" money', *IMF Staff Papers*, vol. 28, no. 3, September 1981, pp. 534–72.

Index